THE
COLONEL

THE
COLONEL

The Life and Wars of

Henry Stimson

1867–1950

Godfrey Hodgson

Alfred A. Knopf

New York

1990

Grateful acknowledgment is made to the following for:
"The Reminiscences of Harvey Bundy (1960), in the Oral History
Collection of Columbia University, hereafter Bundy, COHC."
Reprinted by permission of Columbia University, Oral History
Research Office.
Excerpts from an article by Henry L. Stimson and an article by
George F. Kennan, 1947. Copyright 1947 by the Council on
Foreign Relations, Inc. Reprinted by permission of *Foreign Affairs*.
*Excerpts from Turmoil and Tradition: A Study of the Life and Times
of Henry L. Stimson* by Elting E. Morison. Copyright © 1960 by
Elting E. Morison. Excerpts from *Shattered Peace* by Daniel Yergin.
Copyright © 1977 by Daniel H. Yergin. Excerpts from *The Life
of Roosevelt* by William Roscoe Thayer. Copyright 1919 by
William Roscoe Thayer. Reprinted by permission of Houghton
Mifflin Company.
Excerpt from an essay by David Watt, from *The Special Relationship*,
edited by Louis and Bull, Oxford University Press, 1986. Reprinted
by permission of Oxford University Press, Oxford, England.
Excerpts from *The Making of the Atomic Bomb* by Richard J. Rhodes.
Published by Simon & Schuster, Inc. in 1987. Reprinted by
permission of Simon & Schuster, Inc.
Two letters to Mrs. Stimson, January 31, 1918, and July 21, 1945,
and excerpts from diaries and papers of Henry L. Stimson, from
the Henry L. Stimson Papers, Manuscripts and Archives, Yale
University Library. Reprinted by permission.

Library of Congress Cataloging-in-Publication Data
Hodgson, Godfrey.
The colonel: the life and wars of Henry Stimson,
1867–1950 / Godfrey Hodgson.—1st ed.
p. cm.
Includes bibliographical references.
ISBN 0-394-57441-9
1. Stimson, Henry Lewis, 1867–1950. 2. Statesmen—United
States—Biography. 3. United States—Foreign relations—
20th century. 4. United States—Politics and
government—1901–1953. I. Title.
E748.S883H63 1990
973.91′092—dc20   73400
[B]   89-43474 CIP

Picture of Henry and Mabel Stimson and picture at end of insert
courtesy of Culver Pictures. All other pictures courtesy of Henry L.
Stimson Papers, Manuscripts and Archives, Yale University.

Uxori meae dilectissimae

Contents

Acknowledgments

It is impossible to thank all of those who have helped over the years that this book has been in the making. I owe special gratitude, however, to the staff of the Bodleian Library, Oxford; the Library of Congress, Washington, D.C.; Leicester University Library; the Yale University Library; and, most of all, to Alan Bell and the staff of the Rhodes House Library in Oxford.

Among many friends who are too numerous to thank individually, I cannot forbear to name McGeorge Bundy, for his generous help and acute reminiscence; his brother William P. Bundy, for his meticulous editing skills and for some remarkable insights; their niece Lowell Winkelmann, for her help in understanding her family history, so closely interlinked with Stimson's life; Peter Kaminer, for educating me in the lore and history of Stimson's law firm and for lending me his copy of *My Vacations;* the late Kingman Brewster, for an understanding of many things in Stimson's life; Lord Sherfield, who as Roger Makins saw the world Henry Stimson lived in from the Hoover, Roosevelt and Truman administrations and shared his recollections with me; Robin W. Winks, for his generous hospitality and for teaching me the history and spirit of Yale; Anthony Storr, for his insight into Stimson's personality; Professor David Adams; Professor Jack Pole, Dr. Peter Carey and Dr. Lawrence Whitehead, of Oxford University; and many others who contributed knowledge and ideas on which I have drawn.

Of all the hundreds of historians, biographers and other authors on whose work I have drawn, I must mention two in particular: Professor Elting Morison, without whose work my portrait of Stimson would have been in monochrome; and Richard Rhodes, who helped me to understand the full sweep of the decisions that went into *The Making of the Atom Bomb*.

I am equally in the debt of those friends who helped me with their unstinting hospitality during my research trips to the United States, in particular Harry and Trish McPherson; Philip Babbit; and John and Diana Zentay, who also showed me around Woodley.

I have dedicated this book to my wife, Hilary, but that does not excuse me from the duty of thanking her for her support when the going was rough. I also want to thank my friends, especially Nicholas Faith, for his patience and kindness; and my children, Pierre, Francis, Jessica and Laura, for restoring both spirits and perspective.

This book owes more than I can express to its chief begetter, my doughty agent and valued friend, Robert Ducas, and to all of those at Knopf who have driven me on and rewarded me with the quality of a beautifully produced book, especially Melvin Rosenthal, George Andreou and that incomparable taskmistress and inspiration, Elisabeth Sifton.

G.H.

THE
COLONEL

I

American Leadership

On Sunday, October 14, 1962, a U-2 reconnaissance aircraft piloted by Major Rudolph Anderson brought back aerial photographs of what analysts the next day rightly concluded were Soviet missile installations in a meadow near San Cristóbal, in western Cuba. The next day President Kennedy's special assistant for national security, McGeorge Bundy, was telephoned by Ray Cline, a deputy director of the Central Intelligence Agency. The pictures confirmed reports, Cline said, that the Soviet Union had sneaked missiles and aircraft into Cuba that were capable of delivering nuclear warheads to targets in a large part of the United States.

So began the most dangerous two weeks in more than forty years' confrontation between the United States and the Soviet Union. In the second week, the world knew how close it was to catastrophe. After

the President went on television on Monday, October 22, to disclose
the presence of the missiles and to announce that he had called for a
naval blockade of Cuba, people everywhere asked themselves how close
they were to nuclear war. Most people confronted that risk with stoic
dignity. A few in the Washington suburbs and elsewhere hoarded
canned food or tried to run away.

But in the first week, the burden of fear and decision had to be
shared in secret by no more than a few dozen people. Not all of them
were government officials. In this, his most dangerous crisis, President
Kennedy—conscious of his own youth and inexperience—also consulted elder statesmen who had been through earlier times of trouble
in World War II and the Cold War. So Dean Acheson, Secretary of
State under President Truman, was summoned in secret to the White
House. And so was Robert A. Lovett, who had been Assistant Secretary of War in charge of the Army Air Corps in World War II, had
served as Under Secretary of State and Secretary of Defense in the
Truman administration, and had been offered by President Kennedy
the choice of the three top jobs in his Cabinet: State, Defense or Treasury. Lovett was an American grandee, the son of a legal adviser and
close friend of the railroad magnate E. H. Harriman, and himself an
investment banker and one of the moving spirits of the famous house
of Brown Brothers Harriman.

Lovett, in other words, was neither new to the world of great
decisions nor hesitant by nature. When he arrived in Washington he
went to McGeorge Bundy's crowded office in the basement of the west
wing of the White House, and there on a side table he spotted a small
picture of Bundy's mentor, Henry L. Stimson. "All during the conversation," Lovett recalled later, "the old Colonel seemed to be staring me straight in the face."

Finally Lovett said to Kennedy's adviser, "Mac, I think the best
service we can perform for the President is to try to approach this as
Colonel Stimson would."*

W̲ho was Colonel Stimson, that at the height of the Cuban
missile crisis some of the sagest and most experienced of a young Pres-

---

*There is a vast literature, scholarly and journalistic, on the Cuban missile crisis. See, for ex-
ample, Elie Abel, *The Missile Crisis;* Graham T. Allison, *Essence of Decision: Explaining the Cuban
Missile Crisis;* James G. Blight and David A. Welch, *On the Brink,* which has very full source
notes. For Lovett's remark, see Walter Isaacson and Evan Thomas, *The Wise Men,* p. 624.

ident's advisers would turn to his shade for guidance? For in October 1962 Henry Lewis Stimson had been dead for twelve years.

For one thing, as Secretary of War in the wartime administration of Franklin D. Roosevelt, Stimson had been served both by Lovett and by Bundy's father, Harvey Bundy, who were assistant secretaries of war under him. With both men, indeed, as with half the men who had exerted influence over American foreign policy from Theodore Roosevelt's time to that of Franklin Roosevelt, Stimson had been connected by a web of shared beliefs and shared experiences, common interests and common friendships.

Many articles and several books have been written about what is called the American foreign-policy establishment, and one short answer to the question, Why did President Kennedy's advisers ask themselves, "What would Colonel Stimson have done?" might be: Because he was the founding father and patron saint of that establishment. Yet this answer, while true, is inadequate. Henry Stimson was that, but he was much else besides.

Few Americans in the twentieth century served so long in high public life or over so long a period; none spanned in a single career so drastic a transformation of the United States's position in the world. The emperor Augustus boasted that he found Rome a city of brick and left it a city of marble. Henry Stimson first came to Washington when it was a quaint little southern town, and left it as the unchallenged capital of the greatest power the world had ever seen. Stimson was born less than three years after Lincoln was assassinated, and survived FDR by five years. His personal experience of life stretched from the last Indian wars of the frontier to the partners' rooms of downtown New York law firms, from the chanceries of Western Europe to the sunbaked grandeur of the Spanish Viceroy's palace in Manila. Few men, after all, have had named for them both a peak they discovered in the Rockies and a great Wall Street law firm.

His experience of war, in particular, stretched from Indian battles to atomic attack. As a Yale undergraduate on vacation in Colorado in 1887, Stimson lived through a Ute Indian rising and spoke to men whose friends and relations had been tortured "by Indian methods"; he commanded an artillery battalion in France in World War I; and it fell to him to be responsible for the decisions to drop the only two atomic bombs thus far used on human targets.

His experience of diplomacy, if not quite so long, was arguably even greater than his experience of warfare. In the 1920s, as a private citizen, he helped to negotiate the settlement of the Tacna-Arica dispute between Chile and Bolivia, which had originated in 1883; and in 1945 he was present at Potsdam when Truman, Churchill and Stalin met to divide the legacy of Adolf Hitler, in the shadow of the bomb Stimson had helped to build.

Henry Stimson's life thus spanned the whole period of the rise of American power, from the beginning of American involvement in world affairs in the first Roosevelt's time, to the apex of American power under the second. For almost fifty years he was near the center of power, alternately wielding it himself or in the confidence of those who did. An intimate friend of the older President Roosevelt, he served in the Cabinet of the younger, and was the only Cabinet member with the standing and self-confidence to criticize FDR for deviousness to his face. He was Secretary of War in the Taft administration and Secretary of State under Hoover. On the day when he took the oath of office as Secretary of War in 1911, the army of the United States mustered 74,638 officers and men, virtually all of them dispersed in dusty camps across the West to keep an eye on the Indians, roughly one such camp to a state, to keep the senators and congressmen happy. On April 12, 1945, when it fell to Stimson, Secretary of War once again, to break to the freshly sworn-in President Truman the news that the United States would within weeks possess the atomic bomb,* there were more than fourteen million Americans under arms: an increase of roughly two-hundredfold. The growth in American power conferred by the bomb, which was built under Stimson's authority and dropped on Hiroshima and Nagasaki on his orders, was incalculably greater.

Having taken the responsibility for using atomic weapons for the first (and, one hopes, the last) time in history, Stimson was also the first responsible American leader to grasp the new dangers they threatened, and one of the first to grapple seriously with the intellectual and moral problems presented both by controlling the new weapons and by failing to do so. And his last act in public life was to propose that nuclear technology be internationalized in the hope of persuading the Soviet Union not to start an arms race.

"The chief lesson I have learned in a long life," he told President Truman, "is that the only way to make a man trustworthy is to trust

---

*President Truman had been sketchily informed already by his friend James F. Byrnes.

him.''* That was something he had learned in dealing with Filipino nationalists like Manuel Quezon. It may be doubted whether it was a wise principle for dealing with Josef Dzhugashvili Stalin. In the short run, Stimson's dreams of international control of atomic power were to be disappointed, though not before they had led to the Lilienthal-Acheson initiative and President Eisenhower's Atoms for Peace proposals. In a longer perspective, however, and in the context not just of nuclear warheads but of whole arsenals of delivery systems, including intercontinental ballistic missiles, Stimson's insistence that atomic weapons must be controlled, and controlled on an international basis, looks not naïve but prescient.

In January 1902, as a thirty-four-year-old lawyer, Stimson was in Washington with his wife, Mabel, to stay with his old friend Gifford Pinchot, chief forester of the United States and the moving spirit behind the national parks. The occasion was the annual dinner of that circle of well-bred big-game hunters, the Boone and Crockett Club. The afternoon before the dinner, he and a friend borrowed two of Pinchot's horses and went for a ride in Rock Creek Park, the splinter of the Appalachians which meanders so rurally through northwest Washington. It had been raining, and the creek was high.

Suddenly Stimson was hailed by name by four men walking through the woods on the other side of the creek. At first he was astonished, for he was a comparative stranger in Washington. Then he recognized the voice of President Theodore Roosevelt, laughingly asking him to swim the creek and join them. Then a voice even better known to him, that of the Secretary of War, his own former law partner Elihu Root, called out, "The President of the United States directs Sergeant Stimson of Squadron A to cross the creek and come to his assistance by order of the Secretary of War."

"That's an order, sure enough," cried Stimson to his companion and shouted back, "Very good, sir!" as he put Gifford Pinchot's old horse Jimmie at the creek.

*Memorandum for the President, September 11, 1945, quoted in Henry L. Stimson and McGeorge Bundy, *On Active Service in Peace and War*, pp. 642–46. The book was actually written by Bundy, son of one of Stimson's close associates, working with Stimson's diary and papers, and calling on his memory by means of many hours of conversation. Although written in the third person, the book, Bundy wrote, "has no other aim than to present the record of Mr. Stimson's public life as he himself sees it."

Jimmie, like his rider, did as he was ordered, and jumped in, at a place where the creek was revetted on both sides by a masonry wall. But the horse lost his footing in the spate and "began to roll and plunge downstream," as Stimson wrote in an autobiographical fragment seven years later, "a good deal of the time both of us being completely under water." Eventually Stimson was able, breast-high in the swift, cold water, to lead the horse downstream to a break in the wall, get him up on the bank, and ride him down to a bridge and over to where the President of the United States and the Secretary of War stood, looking "like two small boys who had been caught stealing apples." Roosevelt protested with some words about his not believing the order would be obeyed because Stimson could have seen that it was impossible. That gave Stimson his chance. "Mr. President," he said, "when a soldier hears an order like that, it isn't his business to see that it is impossible." Roosevelt laughed and said, "Well, it was very nice of you to do it; now hurry home and drink all the whisky you can." And that night at the dinner he hailed his impetuous admirer as "young Lochinvar."*

Plunging your horse into a torrent in obedience to a frivolous order was just the sort of reckless manliness Theodore Roosevelt and his circle admired. Certainly it can have done Henry Stimson no harm in the President's eyes, and may well have helped him to be chosen for his first federal job, as U.S. Attorney for the Southern District of New York, four years later. Although Stimson did not serve with Teddy Roosevelt's Rough Riders in Cuba in 1898, an omission he regretted ever afterward,† he imitated the older man's cult of physical toughness. Like Roosevelt, he hunted grizzly bears, mountain sheep, elk and moose in the West. For nine years he was a keen member of Squadron A of the New York National Guard, which taught him, he recalled later in life, camaraderie, expert horsemanship—and the usefulness of the flat of a cavalry sword for dispersing rioters.‡

As soon as the earnings from his law practice allowed him to,

*Stimson told the story, seven years after the event, in a *Memorandum of interesting (to me) occasions and events in my life during the past few years*, which he began on January 17, 1909, and which forms the opening passage of the first (of fifty-one) volumes of his diary.
†*On Active Service*, p. 92: "For nearly twenty years he had felt a certain regret that he had not been free to go to the Spanish-American war."
‡"I also learned that the sabre, while almost obsolete in war, might become a humane and effective method of dissolving a dangerous mob, when its flat side was used in connection with close charges of well trained cavalry." HLS, *My Vacations*, p. 117.

Stimson bought himself a home in Huntington Township, on the North Shore of Long Island, not far from his hero's Sagamore Hill; and there, like TR, he led the life of an American squire, shooting over his coverts and riding to foxhounds. Though Roosevelt privately held it against Stimson that he served in the administration of William Howard Taft, Stimson was for twenty years a member of Roosevelt's inner circle. He kept three letters from TR in his pocket throughout the time he was on active duty with the artillery in France in World War I, as well as—honesty requires it to be recorded—one from William H. Taft. Stimson visited Theodore Roosevelt in the hospital a few days before his death. "Thank Heaven," his old chief said characteristically, "I never spared myself for the sake of a problematical old age."

Stimson was to be the last survivor—in the days of the United Nations, the atomic bomb and the Cold War—of that influential coterie of unashamed nationalists which included, besides Theodore Roosevelt himself, Charles Francis Adams, General Leonard Wood and Admiral Alfred Thayer Mahan. At the very time when, as Secretary of War during World War II, he was pushing forward the Manhattan Project to build the atomic bomb as fast as possible, he was fighting a rear-guard action to preserve the United States cavalry, a job for which, he told his friends, he had more enthusiasm than for helping to devise the Sherman tank.*

Few Americans in public life, indeed, have matched Stimson's sheer intellectual and political versatility or continuity. He was asked to serve in Herbert Hoover's food administration in World War I. He declined because he felt he had played so prominent a part in encouraging young men to go and fight that he ought to fight himself. He survived a year in France as an artillery officer to serve as Hoover's Secretary of State; then joined Franklin Roosevelt's administration when it was time to persuade a new generation of Americans that there was another war to fight.

In the middle of May 1940 the Nazi panzers punched through the French armies and, pouring westward, encircled both British and French divisions and attacked them from the rear. By June 4, 338,000 British and French troops had been rescued from the trap on the French

*HLS, *My Vacations,* p. 116.

coast at Dunkerque. But, as Winston Churchill said at the time, wars are not won by evacuations. That night Churchill promised the House of Commons that, even though many old and famous states might fall under "the odious apparatus" of Nazi rule, Britain would fight on "until, in God's good time, the New World, with all its power and might, steps forth to the rescue and liberation of the Old." It was clear the French could not fight on. On June 12 Churchill, signing himself "Former Naval Person," made a personal appeal to President Roosevelt to intervene to save France, and on June 13 he went further. He set off on as desperate a venture as any British Prime Minister ever undertook. Flying in his light Flamingo aircraft to Tours, where the French government had halted in its flight from Paris to Bordeaux, he offered France all he had to give, "the indissoluble union of our two peoples."

In this desperate hour of Europe's agony, when streams of panic-stricken refugees clogged the roads of France and it looked as though nothing could prevent the triumph of barbarism, it was summer as usual in the United States. Roosevelt was maneuvering with the patience of an elephant and the cunning of a fox to teach the American people what was at stake. Public opinion was beginning to move. In that same month of June 1940, the proportion in the public-opinion polls favoring introduction of conscription moved from one-half to two-thirds. But Roosevelt's opportunity had not yet come. He believed that to advocate the draft openly at that juncture would lead to a "political disaster," and so it might have done, since at this very moment Republican professionals were advising Wendell Willkie that his only hope of beating Roosevelt in the forthcoming presidential campaign would be to scare the American people and denounce the President as a warmonger.

At this moment Henry Stimson left New York on a journey about as different from Winston Churchill's forlorn dash to Tours as could be imagined. Stimson had been educated at Phillips Academy at Andover, Massachusetts, and he was the most loyal alumnus of that august establishment. In 1940 he was due to give the commencement address at Andover, and the summer weather was delightful, New England a vision of peace that contrasted painfully with the martial alarums and the tragic columns of refugees on the other side of the Atlantic.

Stimson, however, was troubled, and not only by the fate of Europe or even by the isolationists in his own Republican Party. He was seventy-two years old and bothered by insomnia, indigestion and poor health generally. He had been involved for months in the biggest lawsuit of his career, indeed what was at the time the biggest case ever heard at common law, the Blaustein case, over the ownership of what was to become the Amoco oil company. He was exhausted by the work involved in preparing and trying the case, and he had allowed himself to be rattled by counsel for the defendants, who included another great Wall Street lawyer, John W. Davis, founder of the Davis, Polk law firm and candidate for the 1924 Democratic presidential nomination.

In these circumstances Stimson resolved to defy his party, and in his address at Andover on Friday, June 14, he put the case for conscription, national preparedness and, if need be, war. On Saturday, he wrote a second, more explicit speech in favor of conscription and compulsory military training, which he gave at the Yale University commencement on Monday. Then, after watching the Yale-Harvard baseball game, he sat down and prepared a radio talk which was broadcast the next evening, June 18.

That was also the day General Charles de Gaulle made his famous appeal to "Frenchmen and Frenchwomen" from a BBC studio in London. An argument can be made that Stimson's speech was the more important event. For if De Gaulle was making certain that France would emerge from her agony with at least some shreds of honor intact—at first only a relative handful of Frenchmen and Frenchwomen, both inside and outside France, responded to his appeal—Stimson, by emphasizing that it was not only Democrats who backed the President's call for preparedness, played a large part in enabling FDR to get at least the minimum he required from a recalcitrant Congress.

"The United States," Stimson began his address, "faces probably the greatest crisis in its history." A group of powerful governments had set out to reverse all the principles on which civilization had been developed. A victory for the totalitarians, he argued, was "an appalling prospect," and all that stood between the Nazis and the Americas was the British fleet. Only if Britain were supported by American production, American aid and American air power could the Nazis be held in check. And so Stimson made his recommendations: repeal the neutrality acts; supply Britain and—if she remained afloat—France with planes, munitions and every other kind of assistance; adopt at once a system of universal compulsory military training and conscription.

The next day, President Roosevelt called and offered Stimson the job of Secretary of War. He made it plain that another anti-isolationist Republican, Frank Knox, had been offered, and had accepted, the post of Secretary of the Navy. Stimson had heard that some of his friends* had put his name forward, but he was taken aback that FDR would have acted on their suggestion. He asked for time to consult two of his law partners and Mrs. Stimson. He sought to be reassured that the President would not be embarrassed by his radio speech. And then he accepted.

The Republicans were furious. The defection of so eminent and so respected a Republican expert on international affairs—Stimson had been, after all, the last Republican Secretary of State—sabotaged any hope of mounting a united campaign to portray FDR as a warmonger. Far more important, a decisive step had been taken to remove from the realm of politics the question whether the United States would, in God's good time, or at least in Franklin Roosevelt's, abandon neutrality.

The day after "V-E Day"—May 8, 1945, the formal end of the war in Europe—the Secretary of War received in his new office in the Pentagon a delegation of senators and congressmen led by Senator Alben Barkley of Kentucky. They had just returned from Europe, where they had visited the concentration camps at Bergen-Belsen, Dachau and Nordhausen. Several of them freely admitted that before the trip they had been skeptical of reports of German atrocities, dismissing them as exaggerated or even as projections of Allied propaganda. What they had seen changed their minds. "They were unanimously of the opinion," Stimson wrote in his diary, "that the so-called atrocities had represented a deliberate and concerted attempt by the government of Germany to eliminate by murder, starvation and other methods of death large numbers of Russians, Poles, Jews and other classes of people."†

That meeting began at eleven o'clock. An hour earlier there met in the same room for the first time the committee charged by the Secretary of War with deciding how the mysterious weapon then ap-

*Among them Grenville Clark, a lawyer and prototype of the Establishment man of influence, who was a prominent champion of conscription; and Stimson's old friend and legal protégé Justice Felix Frankfurter.
†HLS, Diary, vol. 51, May 9, 1945.

proaching readiness and still known only by its cover name, S-1, should be used. The committee was called, with deliberate obscurity, the Interim Committee. Stimson was in the chair. Three of the scientists who had taken the lead in establishing the Manhattan Project were there: James Conant, Vannevar Bush, Karl T. Compton. The other members were representatives of the State Department and the Navy, Will Clayton and Ralph Bard respectively; Stimson's deputy chairman, George Harrison, former chairman of the Metropolitan Life Insurance Company; and the President's personal representative. Stimson himself had tactfully suggested that this should be President Truman's close friend James Byrnes of South Carolina, soon to become Secretary of State.

At a later meeting of the same committee, on May 31, enlarged by a panel of scientists that included Enrico Fermi and J. Robert Oppenheimer, several of Stimson's hand-picked civilian associates from the War Department, as well as General George C. Marshall, chief of staff, and General Leslie R. Groves, who commanded the Manhattan Project, the issues were thoroughly thrashed out. At lunch a brief but intense discussion centered on an idea, put forward by the physicist Ernest O. Lawrence, that the terrifying destructive power of the bomb should be shown to the Japanese enemy in some harmless demonstration. That was soon dismissed. Stimson and the men around him, with very few exceptions, took for granted that the bomb would be used as an instrument of war, and by May 1945 that assumption had acquired a momentum that could hardly have been resisted. All that remained to be decided was how, where, and in precisely what circumstances the fateful explosion would take place. Before leaving the meeting in midafternoon, Stimson was able to sum up its sense: that the United States should indeed drop an atomic bomb on Japan, preferably on a "vital war plant" surrounded by workers' housing, and with no warning.

In May 1945 Henry Stimson was seventy-seven years old, a trim man of middle height, with a military bearing and a horseman's posture. His hair was white, and this somehow gave a curiously boyish aspect to his face, with its high, aquiline nose, firm chin, and eyes that were shadowed by insomnia and exhaustion yet could twinkle with intelligence and good nature. He was both fit and frail. He still made a point of riding as often as he could on his own eighteen-acre estate, Woodley, in the inner Washington suburb of Cleveland Park, or along the trails of Rock Creek Park, where he had embarrassed Theodore Roosevelt by his obedience more than forty years earlier. Until late middle age, he had loved to ride his big, hard-mouthed horses, Vanguard and Aberdeen, in the wooded Long Island countryside near the home he had built for himself, Highhold. In wartime, he often went home early to Woodley for an energetic game of deck tennis, the game played with a rope or rubber quoit on the ocean liners of his youth, with his aides or friends. He once challenged the scientist Vannevar Bush to a game of deck tennis. Bush said he couldn't. Stimson said it was because he was afraid he, Stimson, would trim him. No, said Bush, who was more than twenty years younger, that wasn't why. "If you will live the kind of moral life I have and avoid these dissipations," said the scientist, "when you get to my age you will be in as good condition as I am." Stimson loved it.*

Stimson had the excellent condition of a much younger man. On the other hand, he had been an insomniac for more than forty years, his digestion was poor, and he suffered from fits of weakness that may have foreshadowed the heart disease that was soon to strike him. Perhaps because of his insomnia and his indigestion, his temper was notoriously volatile. His office in the old State, War and Navy building, as one man who had occasion to know it recalled more than forty years later, was "an oasis of gentility," but it was not always an oasis of calm. If a paper was lost, Colonel Stimson was capable of bellowing so that he could be heard down the hall. If a paper was too long or too wordy, he was capable of throwing it on the floor.

This was a physically hard and courageous old man, who had shot his grizzlies and climbed his mountains in his youth, fought his war as a volunteer at the age of fifty, and now, in his seventies, had driven himself mercilessly for four years at the head of the greatest military machine ever assembled in the history of the world. At the same time, he was the very paradigm of the American gentleman. Not only had he attended all the best schools, the best universities, and belonged to the best clubs; he did not think such things unimportant.

He attended commencements and reunions at Andover, at Yale and at the Harvard Law School whenever he could, and was a loyal member of Skull and Bones, the secret Yale senior society of which many of his friends were also members. He was apt to attribute superior qualities to products of these institutions. On one occasion he was so impressed by the work of a new young lawyer at Winthrop, Stimson that he assumed the man had been educated at Andover and Yale, and

---

*Elting E. Morison, *Turmoil and Tradition: A Study of the Life and Times of Henry L. Stimson*, p. 600.

it was with some difficulty that partners persuaded him that, in spite of the man's excellence, this was not the case.

He was an assiduous clubman. In Washington, he ate lunch, as often as not, in the cavernous dignity of the Metropolitan Club, a block up Seventeenth Street from that glorious French Renaissance wedding cake, the State, War and Navy building, his official home in three different jobs. When he found time for a brief holiday, or when— as in the spring of 1945—he wanted to mull over an important question, he could escape to a hunting club in South Carolina or to the St. Hubert's Club at Ausable, New York, in the Adirondacks, a glorified summer camp for wealthy, old-family New Yorkers. In New York City, most lunchtimes, he would walk around the corner from his law office at 32 Liberty Street to the Ruskin Gothic splendors of the Down Town Association, and he also frequented the even more august premises of the Century Association. An appealing anecdote documents the respect in which Stimson held that institution.

Gentlemen of Stimson's generation took clubs seriously. Toward the end of his life, as a mark of high favor, he proposed to make a young colleague a member of the Century. The colleague, who was returning after the war to academic life, and not in New York, explained gratefully that he would not really be able to afford the membership dues or to get value for them.

"Young man," said Stimson severely, "when I was your age Mr. Root offered to put me up for the Century, and I said pretty much the same to him as you have just said to me. And Mr. Root said to me, 'Stimson, when a man offers to put you up for the Century, you join, even if it means writing for the *newspapers!*' "*

Stimson's marriage, to the former Miss Mabel White, of New Haven, was a relationship of unblemished happiness and reciprocal respect. A little before his seventy-eighth birthday he took time off from the great international conference at Potsdam, where the world was being partitioned by titans† under the shadow of the atomic bomb, to write her this letter:

Dearest little Misty,

This is a little token of the fifty-seven years of happiness we have spent together. No other man has ever received such happiness as I have with you.

*Personal communication to the author.
†HLS, *Papers,* Reel 113, p. 90, July 20, 1945.

Mrs. Stimson was not only a companion who could and did listen to his nightly conversation and that of his friends about affairs of state, but also a somewhat unlikely amazon, who shared his passion for riding and accompanied him on some camping expeditions in the Rockies. Their rectitude was total. It was also Victorian. Mr. and Mrs. Stimson did not entertain divorced persons. In sexual matters he was one of the pure to whom, as the Gospel says, all things are pure.

One of his law partners remembers an occasion when, as a very young man, he was helping Stimson to prepare the Blaustein case. An expert witness was required to testify as to the law of Texas on a particular point. A former attorney general of the Lone Star State was induced, in part with an offer of lavish expenses to be paid, to travel to New York to give evidence. He was late for the meeting, and when telephoned by the young lawyer protested vehemently that Northerners didn't understand how to live; he was in bed with a blonde at the St. Regis Hotel and would be along when it suited him. When he eventually arrived at the Century Association, where the legal conference was to be held, he entered the room, put his arm round Stimson—something in itself that brave men would hesitate to do—and expressed himself in such terms as it is likely no one had used to Stimson for forty years, if ever.

"Colonel," this unreconstructed man of law was bold enough to say, "I hope you spent last night in sin as I did!"

Stimson caught his young associate's eye and asked coldly, "What is this man talking about?" It was not a question that invited an answer, nor did it receive one.

That same young man had spent the whole night looking up cases. To do so he had to use initiative above and beyond the call of duty to persuade a law librarian to let him stay in the library after it was closed. It was not until four o'clock in the morning that he had found a book containing the relevant Texas cases, and it had no index. He just managed to find what he wanted in time for the conference at the Century. The cases were now put before the errant attorney from Texas, and later in the day he was successfully produced in court. The young lawyer felt proud of himself. Only at the last minute before going to court, however, did Stimson favor him with a word.

"You haven't shaved, have you?" he said.

The same lawyer recalls Stimson turning down what to any other lawyer would have been a tempting retainer from a major trade association because he thought what the association was doing was dishonest. He listened attentively to the would-be clients' presentation, and then told them, "Gentlemen, I think I can hear the sound of the jailhouse gates clanking behind you."* And that was that.

Forty years later, the young lawyer, retired after many years at Winthrop, Stimson, said of Stimson, "The most fantastic attribute he had was the total loyalty he inspired in other men. I have never met another man again who had that influence." What was the secret of that ability? "He was a man of such total uprightness that everybody with whom he worked had nothing but confidence in him and never had the feeling that the man would ever manipulate them, or betray them, or do anything for his own advantage."†

Certainly there have been few figures in American public life who inspired such unquestioning loyalty in men of such talent. In his first public office, as Theodore Roosevelt's trust-busting U.S. Attorney for the Southern District of New York, Stimson assembled an outstanding team of lawyers to work for him. Some, like Goldthwaite Dorr, Thomas Thacher, Emory Bickner, are now remembered only by New York lawyers, and not by many of them at that. One, however, Felix Frankfurter, has won universal fame wherever the writ of Anglo-Saxon law runs. They were all willing to work for Henry Stimson for all the hours that God sent, and many of them subsequently indicated that they looked back on their time in the U.S. Attorney's office as one of the most satisfying periods of their lives. In the War Department, even more conspicuously, he not only recruited men of great ability but welded them into a team who would do anything for their coach. They included George L. Harrison, Harvey Bundy, John J. McCloy, Arthur W. Page, Robert Lovett. In a very direct way, the men Colonel Stimson recruited and their friends became a nucleus of the foreign-policy establishment. But they came together because to each of them it was a privilege to work for Stimson, and when it came to working they gave him all they had.

As a young man, Stimson worked with that same intensity himself. The hallmark of his style as a trial lawyer was meticulous preparation. But by the time he was Secretary of State under President Hoover, he had learned that there was one thing even more important for a leader than being well briefed, and that was to find time to think.

Winthrop, Stimson, Putnam & Roberts: A History of a Law Firm, p. 23.
†Personal communication to the author.

Drew Pearson* thought he was "mentally and physically lazy." It wasn't that. Stimson had learned to save himself for the things only he could do.

Through the years of World War II he reflected on the implications of atomic energy and the atomic bomb. When, in the spring of 1945, it came time to take the fateful decisions on its use, he cleared his desk for a week and spent every day either rereading the record to clear his own mind or talking the issues through with one or another of his aides individually. His reflections were then carefully, if reticently, noted in his diary.

Stimson was far from insensitive to the moral burdens of war. He was appalled by the civilian casualties caused by the fire-bombing of Tokyo in 1944, and he intervened to order an end to it. He also stepped in to strike the ancient Japanese capital, Kyoto, the most precious shrine of Japanese art and religion, from the list of projected atomic targets. He was shocked by the vengeful character of the Morgenthau Plan for reducing Germany after the war to an agrarian society. That would be, he said, "just such a crime as the Germans themselves hoped to perpetrate on their victims . . . a crime against civilization itself." "Childish folly!" he scrawled in the margin of a Treasury paper on postwar plans for Germany. "A beautiful Nazi program! This is to laugh!"†

How did it come about that this champion of traditional American morality and civilized international behavior took the decision to drop an atomic bomb on the city of Hiroshima, in the full knowledge that tens of thousands of casualties would be the result? Then, when the worst was known, how could he have allowed a second weapon to be dropped on Nagasaki? Of course, the decision was hardly Stimson's alone. A Secretary of War may have full bureaucratic responsibility for developing and then ordering the use of a weapon, and Stimson was almost alone in having responsibility for every stage in the atomic-bomb project—from the theoretical research that made it

*Drew Pearson, *Washington Merry-Go-Round,* p. 109.
†The Secretary's comments are revealed in a memorandum from a civilian official in the War Department, R. A. Winnacker, to Harvey Bundy, Stimson's special assistant, tactfully suggesting a "personal" classification for this and other potentially embarrassing papers. HLS, *Papers,* reel 113.

possible to the operational decision to drop it on a certain target on a particular day. Even so, that responsibility was shared both with the President and with dozens, even hundreds, of more or less senior civilian officials and military officers who knew what was being planned.

I do not wish to exaggerate or to isolate Henry Stimson's responsibility for the decision to drop the bomb. It was not, however, a responsibility he was inclined to shirk. There is an apparent conflict between Stimson's concern for morality and his share of the responsibility for one of the most terrible single acts of war. What is interesting about that conflict, in the context of 1945, is that *even* Stimson, who repeatedly demonstrated a far from common sensitivity to the moral outrages of war, should have seen no objection to opening the atomic Pandora's box and loosing its demons on the world.

That decision, taken that day in Stimson's office at the Pentagon, two days after the last of Hitler's armies had surrendered and the day after the world celebrated victory in Europe, powerfully evokes the tragedy of the second half of the twentieth century. The very day after the grand Allied coalition had at long last and at fearful cost ended a cruelly destructive world war, the process began that replaced the specter of fascism with the even more terrible nightmare of nuclear war. When Stimson and his advisers were sitting down to determine the form atomic holocaust would take for Japan, he slipped away to learn in sickening detail of what had been done at Belsen, at Dachau and at Nordhausen. At the very moment when the victorious Americans had freed the world from terror in one form, they were getting ready to subject it to terror of a new kind.

Stimson was not naturally a squeamish man. He grew up in a tradition that accepted that life, land, civilization and freedom might have to be fought for, and that there would be casualties. As a hunter, he was untroubled by killing; indeed, he was unusually determined to make his kill once he had decided on it. But it would be a mistake to infer that Stimson was a cruel or crass man. Quite the opposite. He responded sensitively to the ancient lure of the military profession. As a young Secretary of War he loved the "long days in the saddle, a little hunting on the side, evening around campfires or in barracks with men who recalled the excitement and dangers of Indian fighting." Later he recalled with nostalgic pleasure the trips of inspection he made as Secretary of War with his friend General Leonard Wood, "the only white man," Stimson recorded admiringly, "who could run with an Apache

scout" and who "gloried in courage and fitness" as Stimson did himself. He looked back proudly on turkey shoots in Arizona and big
game fishing in the Philippines, and remembered proudly that though
the army was used to providing Washington visitors with a safe old
plug with a Western saddle no one could fall out of, when he visited
army posts in the West a cable was sent on ahead ordering "a real
horse and a flat saddle" for him. The regular army officer, he said at
the end of his life, was a man for whom he felt a natural sympathy,
because "the code of the officer and gentleman was my own code."*

Stimson grew up in admiration of a generation of men slightly
older than himself—men like Theodore Roosevelt, Elihu Root, Albert
Beveridge and Brooks Adams—many of whom were associated with
what was called the Progressive Movement, although they were not all
Progressives by any measure, and in any case the label can be mislead-
ing. What held them together was, rather, a militant nationalism. They
believed in the United States and its destiny to play a great part on the
world's stage. As a consequence, they wanted action to meet the chal-
lenges of sprawling city slums and mass immigration. They saw that
government must respond to the new scale of an imperial America.
But they also believed in the virtues of conflict and adventure, for
themselves and for the nation. Brooks Adams said that America would
do well to substitute the values of West Point for the values of Wall
Street. Henry Stimson, who spent his life on Wall Street, would not
have gone along all the way with that, but he would have felt some
sympathy with what Adams was trying to say. Herbert Croly, editor
of *The New Republic* and author of the Progressive best seller *The Promise of American Life,* said that the American nation "needs the tonic of
a serious moral adventure." Stimson came to know too much about
war to see it as the national equivalent of a regimen of jogging and
cold showers. But he shared the Progressive hankering for virility and
strenuous endeavor, strong leadership in America, and American leadership in the world.

Theodore Roosevelt died in 1919, Elihu Root in 1937. Henry Stimson was, almost uniquely, the connection between their early dream
of American power and its later fulfillment. Some of the values he
carried across the gulf of years between his Victorian upbringing and
the fierce conflicts of his maturity were not suited to the world of

*On Active Service, p. 40.

nuclear weapons that was coming into existence as he left the stage. For all his rocklike confidence in the lasting worth of those values, Stimson was, as we shall see, both a contradictory and a transitional figure. He personified, for a start, the contradictions of the Progressive Movement, led as it was by aristocratic reformers and capitalist trust-busters like him.

Stimson ran for Governor of New York in 1910. He wondered later, whether, if he had been elected then, he might not have been President of the United States in due course. "Victory," Bundy recorded him as believing, "would almost surely have opened to him a strong possibility of great advancement, even toward the White House."* The thought was not idle vanity. In the first third, even the first half, of the twentieth century, New York City and the Empire State dominated the country far more than they do today, and any competent governor in Albany was automatically a potential presidential contender. But Stimson did not win. He was not at ease in electoral politics. It is not too much to say that as a lawyer in public life, following an old American tradition personified by his patron and partner Elihu Root, Stimson was ambivalent about democracy. He was utterly committed to the system in theory, though he preferred to speak of "responsible government." In practice, however, he shied away from the uncouth manipulations of the political system. He found himself more comfortable in the quiet corridors of influence than on the hustings. In this, too, he certainly foreshadowed two generations of leaders in American foreign and national-security policy.

The Roman god Janus, god of doorways, is portrayed with two faces, and Stimson was in many ways Janus-faced. Each stage of his public career was characterized not by compromise or vacillation but by ambiguity.

His first major achievement as a diplomat was in Nicaragua. He was sent by President Coolidge to negotiate an end to a civil war there, which he succeeded in doing in just one month. He quickly achieved what he had been sent out to do, but his solution did not turn out as he had hoped. And an ambiguity lingers over his real purpose. Was he trying to extricate the United States from Nicaragua, or to shore up

*On Active Service, p. 25.

American interests there? His later term as Governor General in the Philippines, equally successful on the surface, raises similar questions. Was he preparing the Filipinos for independence, or trying to distract their attention from it?

As Secretary of State under Hoover and as Secretary of War under Franklin Roosevelt, Stimson bridged two sharply different ideas of what American foreign policy ought to be. For four years under Hoover, he kept his balance on the plunging circus horses of isolation and intervention, disarmament and collective security. And finally in his supreme job as the architect and arbiter of the American war effort in World War II, he had to balance atomic war and human decency, and the moment he had consummated victory with the ultimate weapon, he turned his attention to the ways in which a new international order might be built without atomic arms.

Nicaragua and the Philippines, China and Japan, disarmament and national security, the rival claims of the national interest and the world economy, isolation *versus* intervention: the specific problems with which Stimson grappled between 1927 and 1945 have an oddly contemporary look. There is nothing coincidental or accidental about that. The world has changed a great deal in the intervening years, but in important respects its shape is still the same. Henry Stimson was one of its designers. He was one of the small group of Americans who saw clearly, from the early years of the century, that the world would need American leadership and that, until others were ready to come forward, people like him were going to have to provide that leadership within the United States. They were prepared to act on those beliefs. Both their perception and their actions are relevant to any consideration of the way American leadership has been exercised since their time, and to whether it will be possible to exercise it in the future. We shall look at how Henry Stimson's ideas and his gifts as a leader were formed and developed, in a brief exposure to Latin America; in a substantial contact with the Far East; and in a long apprenticeship across the Atlantic. We shall see how they were used in the supreme test of war. But first let us turn back far into the past, to the education of a future American leader.

II

The Warrior
Dream

The central clue to Stimson's career is to be found in
the structure of American society. Born to respect-
ability, educated in schools that provided effective *en-
trées,* he quickly made himself a part of the group that
was not simply wealthy, but represented in so far as
any group represented it, the American aristocracy.

Eric F. Goldman, in *The New York Times
Book Review,* October 7, 1960

My father fought at Chattanooga, but these eyes have
seen nothing gorier than a presidential election. I have
never seen the lawless passions of men let loose on a
battlefield. And, as a stoodent of humanity, I hankered for the experience.

John Scantlebury Blenkiron, the American
agent in John Buchan, *Greenmantle*

Although it is less than ten thousand feet high, no more than
half the height of Mount McKinley, Chief Mountain has the aura of
peaks twice as grand. It is freestanding, rising from the plains of western Montana a few miles south of the Canadian border, like an officer
with drawn sword in front of the parading ranks of the main chain of
the Continental Divide. Lewis and Clark saw it, far to the north, in
1805,* and called it Tower Mountain. Later, in tribute to its domi-

*Or so Stimson believed. See HLS, *My Vacations,* p. 54. But my friend Dayton Duncan, who
has followed the trail of Lewis and Clark, does not believe this is possible. From studying the
map in Bernard de Voto's edition of *The Journals of Lewis and Clark* it would appear that, if
either of the two explorers ever saw the Chief, it must have been Meriwether Lewis on his
return from the Pacific in 1806, when he took a more northerly route than Clark and also made
a detour into what is now Glacier National Park.

nance, it was called the Chief. From the west, it rises steeply enough across a great hump, snow-covered much of the year, to a wall of rock. From the south, it looks like a jagged fang, the west side rising at about forty-five degrees, the east flank steeper than that up to the half-way mark, and almost vertical above. But from the east, it looms like the rampart of a fortress of the ancient gods, sheer and indomitable.*

Certainly in 1892, when Henry Stimson first saw it, it was thought to be both unclimbed and unclimbable. That alone was enough to make him, at the age of twenty-five, want to climb it. He made the attack with an older friend, a Dr. Walter James; with a cook and horse rustler called Fox, who had been with the Seventh Cavalry on the day of Little Bighorn and had survived only because he was with the wagon train that day; and with a pure-blooded Blackfoot Indian they called Indian Billy.

Sitting round the campfire the night before their ascent, Indian Billy told Stimson that only one Blackfoot had ever tried to climb the Chief. The Blackfeet were plains Indians, uneasy in high places. There was a story, though, that many years ago, before even the oldest brave was a boy, a great warrior from the Flathead tribe, who lived far to the west in the high Rockies, had climbed to the top of the Chief to sleep his warrior sleep. That was the special time when, according to Indian lore, he would dream the dream that would be his guide in life. For four days he had fasted at the top of the Chief, offering his pipe of peace to the spirit of the mountain to smoke. Since then, no other warrior had ever dared to venture there to meet the spirit.

The next day, young Henry Stimson and his friends decided to attack the Chief from the east, where the sheer face of the rock rose 1,500 feet from its forested plinth. Halfway up, the cliff was sliced horizontally by a broad shelf. There, after some hair-raising moments getting around a place where their ledge dwindled almost to nothing, 200 sheer feet up, the climbers ate their lunch below the second rock wall. Again, it was less formidable than it looked from below. One rock chimney led to a narrow ledge, then to a second chimney, 700 feet of almost easy staircase to the long, crumbling ridge of the summit. On the very highest place of all, wedged in the rocks, lay the small, weather-beaten skull of a bison. Even in the pure air of the

*Stimson's account of climbing the Chief was first published in *Hunting in Many Lands,* a publication of the Boone and Crockett Club, in 1895. He reprinted it in the privately published *My Vacations,* to which he added the tale of the 1913 sequel.

mountaintop it had rotted away until there was little left but the frontal bone and the horns.

The frontal bone of a buffalo was a sacred object to the western Indian tribes. The young warriors used a buffalo skull as a pillow when it came time to dream their warrior dream. Stimson and his friends did not move the buffalo skull. They respected the devotion of the warrior who had taken it to the top of the mountain all those years before. It did not take them long to reach safety, swinging hand over hand on a rope, the first any of the party had ever used, past the most dangerous places.

Twenty-one years later, in 1913, Stimson revisited the Chief. The West had changed, and so had he. The wilderness had become part of Glacier National Park, visited by hundreds of tourists every summer, and motorboats plied St. Mary's Lake. Stimson, now forty-six and one of the most distinguished lawyers on Wall Street, was accompanied by his wife, his cousin, his niece and two friends from New York. Yet Stimson decided to climb the Chief again "to see if it would bring back the feelings of old." As a concession to the years, though, he did agree to climb it from the easier western side. No one, it seemed, had climbed the steeper, eastern face since he and his friends had done so in 1892.

The afternoon before the climb, the Colonel, with his niece, rode up the creek looking for some fishing. Suddenly they came upon two young men who had just broken camp and were packing their horses. The older of them was a theology student from Princeton who had spent the summer across the Canadian border preaching, and had become fascinated by the silhouette of the Chief. The previous day, he and his friend had climbed it by the western route.

"That is a curious coincidence," said Stimson, and explained that twenty-one years before, almost to the day, he had made the first re-orded climb by the eastern side. And he asked the young theologian if by any chance he saw among the rocks on the peak a small buffalo skull.

The young man's face sparkled with interest, and lo and behold, he fished the skull out of his pack. So Stimson told him the story Indian Billy had told, and the upshot was that the student said that if he had known the story, he would have had too much respect for the Indian to touch the skull. So the next day Stimson reverently carried the skull and buried it so deep among the rocks that no future tourist would ever remove it.*

*During the 1988 presidential election there were reports that George Bush's father, Senator Prescott Bush, had in his youth stolen the skull of the Apache chieftain Geronimo and placed

•   •   •

There had been Stimsons in America for a long time. The first emigrants came from England and settled in Massachusetts in the middle of the seventeenth century. They were, as the tradition had been handed down to Henry Stimson, "sturdy, middle-class people, religious, thrifty, energetic and long-lived." They were also, if not pugnacious, at least accustomed to war. Stimsons fought in King Philip's War, in the French and Indian War, in the Revolutionary War, and in the Civil War.

In 1945 Stimson exchanged letters with a genealogist, Marjorie Rood, who reported that "a George Stimpson or Stimson came over from England before 1653" and that eleven of his children were to be traced in the records of Ipswich, Massachusetts. Stimson replied that "the traditions in my own family are that our first ancestor coming to this country was George Stimson who landed in Massachusetts about 1636. He or another ancestor was supposed to have been a soldier in King Philip's war . . . the family lived in Massachusetts until soon after the Revolution, when they moved to Albany and then to the Catskill mountains."

A later George Stimson, after carrying a musket in the Continental Army, moved some forty miles southwest from Albany to become the first settler in Windham, New York, in the Catskills. It was his grandson, Henry Clark Stimson, who moved—not out west as so many of the middling folk of New England, upstate New York, and Pennsylvania were doing in the middle years of the century—but off the land, first to take advantage of the industrial revolution that was transforming the eastern seaboard, and then to take his place in the very vortex of the capitalist excitement that in thirty years after the Civil War transformed New York City into the greatest marketplace on earth.

Henry Clark Stimson left the family farm at Windham and worked

---

it in the Skull and Bones hall in New Haven. Skulls of other famous Indian chiefs, it was reported, had also been stolen by Bonesmen. The reports are unconfirmed, and counterstatements were made that these exploits were imaginary. Still, the possibility is raised that the stealing of skulls, especially Indian skulls, was an admired exploit, possibly even an initiation test. It is tempting to wonder whether Stimson was intrigued by the discovery of the buffalo skull on the Chief because it had a special meaning for Bonesmen. Might he not have enjoyed the subtle amusement of telling an anecdote that would have one meaning for the general reader and a special meaning for the initiate?

first in a locomotive shop in Paterson, New Jersey. If to a modern reader that has overtones of proletarian deprivation, they are out of place. For Stimson's wife, Catherine Atterbury, had inherited a small trust fund, enough for him to wipe the oil off his hands for good and buy himself a seat on the New York Stock Exchange. In the hectic years during and immediately after the Civil War, he won a reputation as a broker with a cool head, which was rare enough, who was also scrupulously honest, which was rarer still. Winston Churchill's grandfather Leonard Jerome was one of his clients. The buccaneering Jay Gould was another, and a third was the imperious Commodore Vanderbilt. By 1867 the senior partner of Henry C. Stimson & Sons, of 8 Wall Street, was a known and, to all external appearances, a solid man; known, for one thing, for the imperturbability with which he had managed the legendary Prairie Dog Corner, a successful operation to drive up the stock of an obscure railroad called the Prairie du Chien.

The solidity was more apparent than real, at least in the psychological domain. Henry Clark Stimson hated the stress of the stock exchange and suffered from nightmares and what were probably psychosomatic ailments as long as he worked there. "He damned speculation," it is recorded, "and frequently said he wanted to get out." Before long, circumstances enabled him to do so. He lost much of his fortune in the panic of 1873 but was lucky enough to keep sufficient money, when added to his wife's trust fund, to enable him to retire from the market and still live in solid Victorian bourgeois comfort on East Thirty-fourth Street in Manhattan. If the future Stimsons were always a little better off than they pretended, it was in part because the founding grandfather had been careful not to risk everything in the market, partly because they were all as careful about what they spent as if they had been poor.

Henry Clark Stimson had four sons and three daughters. The eldest son, Henry, became a minister, like so many of his ancestors before him. Frederick became a lawyer, and John, in defiance of all Stimson tradition, became a painter of not particularly notable canvases. Kitty and Julia eventually married. Mary, known as Minnie, did not, with results that were fortunate for the subject of this book. Only the second son, Lewis Atterbury Stimson, had some difficulty in deciding what to do with his life. He had done well at Yale, then fought with distinction in the Army of the Potomac. Less than a year after

the Civil War ended, he met Candace Wheeler, the beautiful daughter
of a cultured though not opulent American family who were equally
at home in the artistic and intellectual elites of the United States and
Europe. Impetuously, Lewis Stimson followed his Candace when she
went to Venice like a Henry James heroine, impetuously wooed her,
and married her at the American embassy in Paris in November 1866.
Two children were quickly born: Henry Lewis Stimson in September
1867 and his sister, a second Candace, two years later.

Lewis Stimson's happiness was short-lived. He disliked being a
stockbroker even more than had his father, saying he would rather live
on "roots and berries." Shortly after the birth of her daughter his wife
became ill. To the doctors of the time the disease was mysterious; it
may have been diabetes. At any rate in 1871 Lewis Stimson sold his seat
on the exchange and on the proceeds took his wife to Europe. They
lived in modest hotels, first in Berlin, then in Zurich, finally in Paris.
In Switzerland, Lewis Stimson, perhaps impelled by a desperate wish
to alleviate or at least to understand Candace's condition, began to
study medicine. In Paris he worked with Louis Pasteur for a year. In
1873 he returned to New York to take a degree at Bellevue Medical
College and then worked as a surgeon, first at Presbyterian Hospital,
later as a professor at New York University Medical School and as
attending surgeon at the Chambers Street House of Relief. After his
wife's death in 1875 he sold his house, slept in a rented room, and
threw himself into "constant grinding work" in an emergency hospital, which brought him far lower rewards than a doctor of his ability
could have earned from private practice.

Dr. Stimson was a man of great sensitivity, which he protected
with an outer crust of hardness, even cynicism. One of his sayings, for
example, was that it was as well "to think evil of everyone and everything, and you will be more on a par with the rest of the world." He
never recovered from the blow of his wife's illness and death. One day,
fifteen years later, when his son was sharing his house, he announced
that he had to go out of town, and it transpired only later that he had
spent the afternoon visiting his wife's grave.

Henry Lewis Stimson and his little sister, then eight and six respectively, were sent by this grief-stricken father to live as orphans with
their grandfather and grandmother in the brownstone on East Thirty-
fourth Street. Their unmarried aunt Minnie looked after them with
selfless, overflowing affection. "She really mothered them," one of her

brothers remembered, but she had the tact never to try to be a substitute for their real mother. For all her good sense and kindness, though, the little boy must have been cruelly bewildered by the double shock of his mother's death and his father's apparent rejection. There can be little doubt that this event was one of the formative influences on his character; it may have contributed to a certain hard, reticent, stoical side of his personality and perhaps also to a timid, reticent search for affection. It may also have caused certain of his psychosomatic symptoms.

For five years Henry Stimson grew up in his grandparents' house, looking forward to his father's visits, surrounded by the austere comfort and reassuring certainties, the velvet upholstery and occasionally oppressive morality of such a home at such a time. He went first to various local schools, then to study Latin and Greek at the Sanver School of Languages in, of all places, Times Square. The school seems to have been unsatisfactory. Certainly, when he was thirteen, his father decided abruptly to send him away to boarding school, as it happened to the most patrician school in America.

Phillips Andover, then Yale College, then the Harvard Law School: the progression is the classic *cursus honorum* of the American upper class, and it came to mean much to Stimson. It is worth describing what those storied educational institutions were—and what they were not—at the time Henry Stimson attended them.

The Phillips Academy at Andover, Massachusetts, stands in a unique relation not just to the New England tradition but to the history of the United States as a whole. Sometimes called the American Eton, it is one of the best known of the expensive and famous boarding schools to which prosperous Americans have sent their adolescent sons for seven or eight generations.* For all the radicals it has turned out, however, from Percy Bysshe Shelley to George Orwell, Eton has always been an aristocratic school, a nursery of servants of Church and Crown, but also the traditional seat of education for those born to hereditary wealth. In practice, no doubt an almost equally high proportion of Andover students have come from comfortable backgrounds. But the tradition is very different, the American academy being revolutionary in its origins, Puritan in its

---

*And now their daughters. Early generations of Andover graduates might be more surprised to see young women on the campus than to see black students, since at least one of the handsome Federal houses there was a station on the Underground Railroad for escaping slaves.

instinct for "high thinking and plain living," downright Spartan in its habits.

As for its revolutionary credentials, George Washington, who met the founder, Samuel Phillips, during the Revolutionary War, sent his nephew Howell Lewis to Andover, the first of seven Washingtons to go there, not to mention the two sons of Richard Henry Lee. The song "My Country, 'Tis of Thee!" was written at 147 Main Street in Andover by the Reverend Samuel Francis Smith, and the silver seal of the Academy was made by Paul Revere. Two of the school's buildings were designed by Charles Bulfinch, the architect of the Massachusetts State House in Boston, who completed Benjamin Latrobe's design for the Capitol in Washington. Andover Hill is a spacious and a numinous place, and a boy would have to be thick-witted indeed who did not feel himself there to be in a special sense the heir of the founders and early champions of the United States, and in personal contact with its central tradition.

Ralph Waldo Emerson was an Andover boy and recorded in his journal "the debt of myself and my brothers to that old religion which, in those years still dwelt like a Sabbath peace in the country population of New England, which taught privation, self-denial and sorrow. . . . How dignified is this! how all that is called talents and worth in Paris and in Washington dwindles before it! . . . I value Andover, Yale and Princeton as altars of this same old fire, though I fear they have done burning cedar and sandalwood . . . and have learned to use chips and pine."* A garland of surnames suggests how the school's history was interwoven with that of New England at its richest for more than a hundred years. The school opened on April 30, 1778, less than two years after the signing of the Declaration of Independence and more than five years before the end of the Revolutionary War. Josiah Quincy, son of the famous patriot, was in the first class. Stephen Longfellow, father of Henry Wadsworth Longfellow, was a student. So were Charles Lowell, father of James Russell Lowell; Charles Pinckney Sumner, father of Senator Charles Sumner; Oliver Wendell Holmes, the Autocrat of the Breakfast Table (who was "subjected to the severest castigation . . . in the annals of punishment in that institution") and father of the Supreme Court justice; and Samuel Morse, the inventor of the telegraph. The famous first words Morse transmitted by this newfan-

---

*May 4, 1841, quoted in Bliss Perry (ed.), *The Heart of Emerson's Journals*. I am indebted to William P. Bundy for this reference.

gled technology from Washington to Baltimore breathed the very spirit of New England and of Andover: "What hath God wrought!"*

The inspiration for Samuel Phillips's two academies, at Andover and at Exeter, New Hampshire (founded three years later in 1781), was not in fact the great Anglican foundations in England such as Eton, Winchester or Westminster, all of which were in a state of more or less benighted decadence in the 1780s, but rather the dissenting academies founded in the course of the eighteenth century by English nonconformists, that is, non-Episcopalians, and Scots Presbyterians.

The physical conditions on Andover Hill, on the other hand, were quite as tough as those in any medieval English public school. Most boys, including Henry Stimson, boarded with approved families on the Hill, Stimson with the head of the classics department, Edward Austin Coy, known to generations of boys as "Eddie Greek." Others lived in two sordid ranges of buildings known as English Commons and Latin Commons. These weatherbeaten structures had, one nostalgic historian maintains, "an indefinable atmosphere of romance," especially when the wind howled through the cracks in the carpentry and boys huddled for warmth round the stove. "As the two rows of commons stood on the north-west slope of Andover Hill facing the distant New Hampshire hills on the horizon," Stimson himself recalled, "winter life there was neither soft nor enervating." Nor was it, by modern standards, hygienic. Before the 1890s there were no bathtubs, no showers and no washstands. "The care of the rooms is left to the boys entirely," wrote the great reforming principal Cecil F. P. Bancroft in 1879, just before Stimson arrived, "even to the removal of waste water and ashes, the sweeping, bed-making and cleaning. It is part of a boy's education to build his own fires, no doubt; it may be to black his boots, bring his water, and sweep his room."

The same principal was the recipient of a dubious compliment from "a prominent statesman" who was considering sending his boy to Andover. He "smelt the unedifying odors and saw the unattractive sights; then, turning to Dr. Bancroft, he said, 'Well, sir, this school is the place for my boy!'

*The ethos of nineteenth-century Andover is well, if a touch pompously, caught in two books by a twentieth-century headmaster, Claude Fuess, *Men of Andover* and *An Old New England School*. See also Scott Paradise, *Men of the Old School*. Fuess was a friend of Stimson's and a fellow member of the Ausable Club. He corresponded with Stimson in 1945 about writing his biography.

" 'Good,' replied the principal.

" 'Yes,' continued the visitor, 'any institution which can keep the fine reputation which Andover has, and yet lodge its students in such disreputable barracks, must have about it some miraculous quality which I want my son to learn to know.' "*

It was perhaps just as well that Dr. Stimson had arranged for his son to board. At thirteen, Henry Stimson was neither outstanding nor robust. When he left Andover, aged seventeen, he weighed no more than 120 pounds. But by that time a remarkable transformation had taken place in both school and pupil. Samuel H. Taylor, "Uncle Sam," principal from 1837 to 1871, was an "unmitigated despot" who literally flogged the Bible, Latin and Greek into the boys; dug a "deeply rutted route" from Andover to Yale because he suspected Harvard of being too Unitarian; and considered that "our vicinity to the city of Lawrence is one of the most fruitful sources of irregularity to which we are exposed."†

Narrow and old-fashioned he might have been, but it was "Uncle Sam" who established Andover as a national institution. By 1871, the year in which he collapsed in the middle of a Bible class, there were 228 boys in the school, 68 per cent of them from outside New England.

There followed institutional crisis and then institutional regeneration. At first, freed from Taylor's heavy hand, Andover floundered. The low point in numbers came in 1877, three years before Henry Stimson arrived, with only 177 students. Debts were growing. The future looked bleak.

Salvation came from Principal Bancroft, one of those brisk, effective High Victorians who were equally at ease preaching with a high moral tone and raising money or chairing a buildings committee. Bancroft had taught Latin at Phillips Academy, then went to study in Germany (like Daniel Coit Gilman, creator of the first modern graduate school at Johns Hopkins, and Charles W. Eliot, creator of modern Harvard). Wisely, the trustees brought him back in 1873. He raised money, put up new buildings, hired excellent new teachers, paid them well, and left them alone. The cornerstone of a new chapel was laid, and it was not long before a new chemical laboratory had been built as well. Enrollment grew, faculty grew, so did the endowment, the number of options in the curriculum, and the number of books in the library.

*Claude M. Fuess, *An Old New England School: A History of Phillips Academy, Andover*, p. 366.
†Fuess, *op. cit.,* p. 264.

At Andover, in fact, Henry Stimson was not only at a school whose ethos and traditions stretched back literally to the Revolution and to the Founding Fathers, but he was also being taught by men who were in touch with the roaring intellectual revolution of the late nineteenth century, with the onslaught of science on religion and with new ideas about economics and society.

Although Phillips Academy was one of the best-known schools in the country, the boys who went there were not for the most part rich. "School life," Stimson himself remembered sixty-five years later, "was extremely simple and inexpensive. The cost of tuition was sixty dollars a year."

> I was much younger than any other boy in the school, but the new surroundings were like heaven to a boy who craved escape from city life. I have heard the discipline of Phillips Academy of those old days described by an alumnus as "perfect freedom, tempered by expulsion." Of the outdoor life of the students that was a fair description. There was football, baseball [it replaced cricket at Andover in about 1860], skating, bobsledding and walking over the hills and woodlands of northern Massachusetts.

Henry Stimson enjoyed himself at the time. Once he built a specially perfected bobsled, and on another occasion an electric telegraph that sent messages across the campus. And he remembered Andover with an unusually deep affection for the rest of his days; he was a trustee from 1902 until 1947, and he described the school's welfare as "one of the greatest interests in my life." Such devotion to school days was unusual even in his generation. It is perhaps an illustration of a true judgment made by a very perceptive biographer* that "all his life he was to respect those in authority and to wish for their approval."

At Andover he studied effectively, and was graduated comfortably in 1883. He followed the "deeply rutted route" to Yale, where his father had been before him, but he did not feel ready to go there straightaway. He persuaded his father that he would be looked on "as sort of a kid"† and that it would be better to put off going to Yale for a year. He spent a month in the summer of 1883 in France with his father and sister, took special coaching in New York for several months,

---

*Elting E. Morison, *Turmoil and Tradition*, p. 60, to whose careful research and sensitive interpretations I am indebted throughout this book, and especially in this chapter.
†*Ibid.*, p. 28.

then went back to Andover as a special student, taking courses in scientific subjects, in the spring of 1884.

When Stimson finally reached New Haven, Yale, too, was in midstream. The "simple, bucolic Yale" of colonial and antebellum days was slow to pass away. It was, wrote one historian, "a place of arching elms . . . where the grass in the college yard was cut by scythe, so that the smell of new-mown hay drifted in at the college windows."* Its studies were as traditional as those at Andover under Uncle Sam Taylor, its recreations "sitting on the fence outside college hall" or, for the adventurous, the deliciously dangerous company of the college widow, a lady described as "an enchantress in illusion and a specialist in the heart."†

In the last third of the nineteenth century two great movements were transforming American higher education: the movement for elective studies for undergraduates, and the new idea of a university as a place of postgraduate specialist study, focusing on the respect verging on worship accorded in German universities to the doctorate, earned by the preparation of a dissertation based on original research. Yale was late in welcoming both.

In 1871 the fellows rejected Daniel Coit Gilman, who went off to Johns Hopkins, and chose instead as a new president Noah Porter, "a guarantee," it has been said, "that the college was still to preserve its conservative attitude in respect to all the educational questions."‡ Not until the year before Henry Stimson arrived as a freshman did the faculty, led by the social scientist and polymath William Graham Sumner, fight and win its battle with Porter over elective courses, and not until Stimson's junior year was the name of the institution officially changed from Yale College to Yale University. The election of Timothy Dwight, grandson of a former president of Yale, to succeed Porter in Stimson's sophomore year, 1886, meant that Yale came to adapt, slowly and gradually, to the profound changes that were sweeping through other American universities in those years. Overall, as George W. Pierson, one of the most eminent historians of Yale, records, "the picture of Yale College education remained depressing. The faculty except for

*Brooks Mather Kelley, *Yale: A History*, p. 224.
†*Ibid.*, p. 230.
‡*Ibid.*, p. 233 ff.

a few were aloof disciplinarians. The students betrayed many of the symptoms of a deeply disloyal subject population. They used 'ponies' [cribs] much of the time. They stole exams when they could and cribbed on them when they could not. Some later remembered their days at Yale with hot anger.''

What Yale and Yale men cared most about, at least after "God, country and Yale," was sports. Athletics and athletes still enjoyed high prestige at both Harvard and Yale until the 1930s, and official "de-emphasis" of football did not come until after World War II. But the age when athletics were held in highest esteem in what came to be called the Ivy League universities was between 1870 and 1917, before the pragmatism, professionalism and sheer numbers of the great Midwestern, Southern and Western schools took them out of serious competition. And in those years Yale was *"the* power in college sports"; Walter Camp was coach from 1885 to 1910; and especially in 1883–98 Yale was a phenomenon, with nine Yale football teams undefeated and three not even scored against! Against Harvard, Yale was so dominant that "Cambridge men began to think of Yalies as nothing but muckers, while Yale men had serious doubts about the manliness of the Harvards."*

Yale was above all a shrine to good fellowship and a school for success. "It is this marvellous *esprit de corps,* this habit of always pulling together," wrote Buchanan Winthrop in 1892. "Nothing could be more American than Yale," wrote George Santayana, a Spaniard from Harvard in the same year."† "Here is sound healthy principle but no overscrupulousness, love of life, trust in success . . . a democratic amiability." And the college inspired a loyalty in its sons, wrote Pierson, that was conspicuous and impressive. Yale men in post-college life made such records that it was suspected they were working for one another. In short, Yale in the 1880s was: "a thoroughly conservative institution; traditional in its habits, religious in its beliefs, earnest and moral in its atmosphere, conforming in its opinions, old-fashioned in its education. [Yale men were] open in their manners, square in their judgments, fiercely competitive but wholeheartedly loyal."‡

*See George Pierson's two-volume *History of Yale College;* Brooks Mather Kelley, *Yale: A History;* Reuben A. Holden, *Yale: A Pictorial History.* For the Yale ethos, I am indebted to Robin W. Winks, *Cloak and Gown.* For some hints about the senior (secret) societies, see Maynard Mack, *A History of Scroll & Key.*
†Quoted in Holden, *Yale: A Pictorial History,* introduction.
‡G. W. Pierson, *History of Yale College,* vol. ii, p. 9.

That passage might have been written with Henry Stimson in mind. While he was an undergraduate, his fierce competitiveness took the form of going out for any prize he thought he had any chance of winning. He won the Junior Exhibition, a prize awarded for composing and reciting a piece which began, apparently to the amusement of a less-intellectual roommate, "When men sang, they sang the songs of Béranger," and the next year he won the De Forest Prize for a study of the English seventeenth-century Roundhead (and governor of Massachusetts) Sir Henry Vane. He failed, however, to be elected to the most prestigious society, "The Lit," in spite of submitting careful articles on topics from Mazzini to Charlotte Brontë. Fifty years later, he wrote, he could "still feel the pang of that winter day when you rejected my suit."

The rejection was blotted out by a success, however, an acceptance that was to have an extraordinary effect on Stimson's life and perhaps a considerable effect on the future style, not to mention personnel, of the American foreign-policy establishment. He was elected to membership in the secret senior society Skull and Bones. It was, he was given to saying in later life, "the most important educational experience of his life."*

Few subjects have been wrapped in more mystification, not to say paranoia, than the Yale senior societies. To some extent this mystification is deepened by their members, who tend to react to any inquiry by simultaneously professing the supreme importance of membership for themselves, and the utter insignificance of the subject to anyone else. There is nothing new in this. As early as 1858 a Yale observer wrote of the secret societies there that "their great apparent desire to have their very existence ignored is only equalled by their intense desire to have their existence brought into view. . . . No reflection would strike a deeper pang into the hearts of members than the conviction that no one puzzled his head about them."

Ironically, in view of the affinity between the suspicion directed against them and the suspicion with which Freemasonry is regarded in many circles, the senior societies owe their origin to the Anti-Masonic movement that swept the United States in the 1830s. In 1832 the Anti-Masonic movement attacked the secrecy of the Phi Beta Kappa Society, and Edward Everett, a Massachusetts statesman whose obliterating fate

*Morison, *Turmoil and Tradition,* p. 34.

it was to speak first and at length before Lincoln at Gettysburg, was sent to Yale to argue against the academic fraternity. In protest, William H. Russell, valedictorian of 1833, persuaded Alphonso Taft and thirteen other members of his class to form Skull and Bones. The rival, Scroll and Key, came into existence in 1842 as a result of a feud between members of two junior societies, Alpha Delta Phi and Psi Upsilon. By 1856 the Bonesmen had their hall, much smaller than it is today, and the homes of Scroll and Key and Wolf's Head had also come into existence.

In the early 1880s—just before Henry Stimson arrived in New Haven—the junior class succeeded in prevailing on the seniors, who had previously held elections to their societies in private, to inaugurate the ritual of Tap Day. As the bell tolled five in the afternoon of the second Thursday in May, the juniors would mill around, and now and then a man would be hit between the shoulder blades and told, Go to your room! so that a formal offer could be made to him in private. "Keys" was supposed to pick social, convivial men, Wolf's Head "a congenial prep school crowd," which might or might not be a euphemism for boozy snobs. Bones, in one classic account, "almost invariably bet on achievement. It tapped the football captain for his prowess, the chairman of the *News* for his great accomplishment, a manager or two, the *Lit.* chairman and perhaps the *Record* chairman," and so on.* To be the last man tapped was the greatest honor of all, because it betokened sheer personal merit, undocumented by the winning of great prizes or the holding of significant office. If social connections counted for something in election to Skull and Bones, achievement counted for more. Although a Taft was one of the founders and President Taft a member, several Tafts, including Senator Robert Taft, Jr., were not tapped. Three generations of Bushes in Skull and Bones are an exception. The chance of being chosen by Bones drove many underclassmen, among them young Henry Stimson, to unremitting competitive effort. Years later, Stimson confessed to his fiancée that "the idea of a struggle for prizes, so to speak, has always been one of the fundamental elements of my mind, and I can hardly conceive of what my feelings would be if I ever was put in a position or situation in life where there are no prizes to struggle for."

Of course there are always prizes in life to struggle for, and Stim-

---

*Maynard Mack, *A History of Scroll & Key, passim*.

son won his share at Yale. The fiancée who was the recipient of that
confession, or boast, was one of them. She was Mabel Wellington
White, daughter of a socially prominent New Haven family* whom
he met in the impeccably correct setting of a whist party at Professor
Whitney's house. But the Whites were—to use a word such self-assured
provincial notables would have shrunk from, though it expresses the
New York attitude toward New Haven—not quite "grand" enough
for the Stimsons. Henry Stimson and Mabel White became engaged
in his senior year at Yale; but public announcement of the engagement
was to be deferred until the fiancé could prove that he could support
himself and a bride. It was to be more than five years before the couple
were married, and in that time, in a perfectly civilized way, Dr. Stimson made it plain that he would greatly prefer it if his son married
someone a little more sophisticated and a good deal better endowed
with the world's goods than the withdrawn, correct, provincial Miss
White. The son was unshaken, and the father eventually withdrew his
objections.

In the meantime Stimson had discovered the joy of another con-
test, different from both the manly emulation that could lead to being
included in the august company of Bonesmen and the genteel wooing
of New Haven drawing rooms. He discovered what was to be a lifelong
pleasure in the life and landscape of the West and in the rough self-
sufficiency of the Great Outdoors. He learned to love camping out,
following trails through rough country, riding and climbing and ca-
noeing in white water, and efficiently killing big game. "The slim city
boy" who went from Andover to Yale became a wiry, unsqueamish
man who was, in his own words, "at home in forest, prairie or mountain, could pack my own horses, kill my own game, make my own
camp and cook my own meals."†

At the end of his freshman year at Yale, when he was seventeen,
he met by chance an experienced hunter called Alden Sampson, who
took him to the Middle Park, as it was then called, in northwestern
Colorado. It was, Stimson remembered years later, "like an Eden into
which man had not yet entered." The deer were so tame that a doe
with a fawn would not bother to run away from them. Such trusting
animals did not long survive.

---

*According to Drew Pearson, *Washington Merry-Go-Round*, p. iii, Mrs. Stimson had an ancestor
on the *Mayflower*.
†*On Active Service*, p. xvi.

The next year he went into the New Brunswick wilderness with an Indian guide, living only off what they could fish or shoot, and there shot his first bear, "a great walloping he-bear." In 1887, back in Colorado, he sat up most of the night with a gun across his knees because a "tough or would-be tough"—a classic Stimsonism—drunk from Denver had threatened to shoot him during the night. Even more alarming, there was an outbreak of Indian fighting. A band of Ute had left their reservation, and the National Guard had to be called out to drive them back. There was a good deal of fighting and a number of ranchers and their families were killed. Stimson had met men whose friends and relatives had been tortured by the Ute and the Comanches. So it was frightening to learn that the Indian band was headed for the very spot where Stimson and his friend Sampson were hunting, and worse still to see four or five men approaching when one was hunting alone. Through his telescope Stimson could see they were Indians. He pulled out his rifle and stood behind his mule with the gun lying across its back. But if the Indians had planned to attack, they thought better of it.

In 1888 and 1890 he was back in western Colorado, and in 1889 he returned to the Nipisiguit. Then in 1891 he looked up George Bird Grinnell, editor of *Forest and Stream* and a great expert on the wilderness, to ask where really wild, unexplored country was to be found. Only two years later Frederick Jackson Turner was to celebrate the significance of the frontier in a famous lecture, taking as his text the official statement in the census report of 1890 that the frontier of settlement in the United States was closed for the first time. Inexorably, hunters were destroying the once inexhaustible resources of game in one part of the Rockies after another, and tourists, following them like infantry mopping up behind armor, were never far behind. True, untrodden wilderness was getting harder to find each year.

However, Grinnell told his young visitor, there was one area as yet unreached by the railroad which still had mysteries to yield up. This was the Blackfoot Indian reservation in Montana. Grinnell suspected that the source of the St. Mary's River might lie in the great glaciers there. (He was right; we know the area as Glacier National Park.) Grinnell was planning an expedition there that very summer. He took Stimson and another young man from Yale, William H. Seward, Jr., grandson of Lincoln's Secretary of State, and together they were able to explore glaciers previously untrodden by the foot of man

and climb mountains—including the one they called Mount Stimson*—whose mere existence was unknown to the white man until they
got there. As he left to go home, waiting in the early morning for the
work train carrying men and materials to build the Great Northern
Railway, which would take him to the passenger railhead 150 miles
away, Stimson first saw the jagged silhouette of the Chief and swore
to come back next year and subdue it.

The outdoor life not only transformed Stimson from an under-
weight weakling into a tough, self-reliant man, but gave him a passport
to a group of people who were to be something more than friends.
George Grinnell was one. The brothers Gifford and Amos Pinchot
were more important. And Stimson's relationship with General Leonard Wood played a crucial part at two turning points of his career.
Most important of all, of course, was his friendship with—indeed vir-
tual hero-worship of—Theodore Roosevelt. What these men and many
others in Stimson's circle had in common was that they were all Easterners of good family and education who had become fascinated with
the West and with the cult of toughness. Many of them were to be
members, as Stimson was, of the Boone and Crockett Club of New
York, which celebrated the bag of the big-game hunter. Some, like
Grinnell and Gifford Pinchot, later chief forester of the United States,
were among those who helped to found the movement for the protection of the environment.

It was natural that, as the tide of empire swept westward and steel
rails brought the imperial domain of prairie, mountain, forest and water ever closer to the growing cities of the East, city folk should want
to experience the adventure of the West. After all, the winning of the
West is the great American epic. It has always gripped the American
imagination, whether the story is told in the measured periods of Park-
man's *The Oregon Trail*, in the racy pages of Zane Grey, or on the
screen in countless Hollywood horse operas. What was different about
the appeal of the West to young men of Stimson's generation and class
was exemplified by the transformation of Theodore Roosevelt.

*Mount Stimson, 10,156 feet high, lies three miles south of Red Eagle Pass near Nyack Creek,
according to the National Park Service. There is doubt about whether this is the same peak that
in fact Stimson discovered. The first white man to visit the area, according to the Park Service,
was A. W. Tinklam, a government surveyor, who ascended Nyack Creek "by mistake" in 1853.
There was a brief rush of prospectors after copper was found in 1890. The land was not purchased
from the Indians until 1896, four years after Stimson's visit, and there were few visitors before
the National Park was opened in 1910.

He had originally been sent out West by his family because of his poor health. Rarely has medical treatment worked so well. An asthmatic, narrow-chested boy, brought up among worried females in brownstone luxury, was transformed into a young bull of a man who wrestled and rode, shouted and shot and reveled in every physical trial of strength. Roosevelt's friend William Roscoe Thayer could "recall my astonishment the first time I saw him, after the lapse of several years, to find him with the neck of a titan and with broad shoulders and stalwart chest, instead of the city-bred, slight young friend I had known."*

Roosevelt was nine years older than Stimson and was trying to make a go of ranching in the South Dakota Badlands when the younger man was still at Andover. In 1885, when Stimson was a freshman at Yale, Roosevelt published his classic *Hunting Trips of a Ranchman,* with its wonderfully appealing descriptions of life outdoors on the range in a Dakota summer, and life indoors in the ranch house "while the pine logs roar and crackle" in a Dakota winter; its monotonously complacent chronicles of the slaughter of wild creatures; and its steel engravings of encounters with grizzlies of legendary size and ferocity. Roosevelt's book, his example, and his idea of the West caught the imagination of a whole generation of more or less wealthy Easterners.

The other idea that obsessed young men too young to have fought at Gettysburg or Chattanooga like their fathers was that they were determined not to be soft. Hard, self-reliant Americans there have always been. What was new in the 1880s was a generation of young men—thoroughly versed in French symbolist literature and German idealist philosophy, with homes in Boston or New York that were proud of their luxury and refinement—who set out to make themselves *artificially* tough and self-sufficient. And nowhere was this cult of virility, Western-style, more influential than at Yale.

In his book *Old Money,* Nelson W. Aldrich, Jr., himself a scion of several plutocratic clans, talks of the American upper class's need to prove itself with three ordeals in particular: the ordeal of boarding school, the ordeal of nature, and the ordeal of battle. Henry Stimson passed unscathed through the ordeal of school. Indeed, having lost his mother at the age of eight, he probably found the companionship of school more than a compensation for his loneliness. If he was unhappy

---

*William R. Thayer, *Roosevelt.*, p. 57. See also David McCullough, *Mornings on Horseback.*

at Andover, he never said so, but then he wouldn't have said so; that wasn't his style or that of his class. He was eventually to encounter, indeed to invite, the ordeal of battle. The ordeal of nature, an essential part of the education of an American gentleman in his day, he underwent not only successfully but with real and lasting pleasure. This was a young man who found he did not mind killing beautiful animals or even gutting them. As his friend Amos Pinchot said, half-teasing, he must "continually be killing some poor damned animal or other, and when he was out after grizzly bear, the whole camp was subordinate to his paramount object—a dead bear. Nobody could rest till he got it."*

To see Stimson's passion for big-game hunting as evidence of mere insensitivity is too simple. Some of his contemporaries tested themselves by encounters with nature in small boats, as his father had done. Some climbed mountains, as he did. Some went exploring in places more dangerous and more exotic than the future Glacier National Park. Teddy Roosevelt himself, once freed from the cares of office, in 1909, went off to shoot big game in Africa. In a sense, too, as Aldrich acknowledges, these men were after even bigger game than could be bagged with Colonel Roosevelt's 45-75 Winchester or Colonel Stimson's favorite ammunition, imitated from a cartridge—he liked to recall—"recommended by Sir Samuel Baker, the Englishman who was famous for his shooting in Africa and Asia," and imported from Eley's in the English Black Country.† The romance of the West offered a whiff of the psychic satisfactions of empire. Indeed, in the late nineteenth century Americans freely spoke of their land empire. There was a sense of rivalry, too, and a whiff of envy, half-admitted, when the American upper class of Teddy Roosevelt's generation contemplated the European empires, whether the old, familiar British Empire, or the newer, brasher imperial enterprises of France, Germany and Italy. "I wish to see the United States the dominant power on the Pacific Ocean," wrote Roosevelt in 1900. "Our people are neither cravens nor weaklings and we face the future high of heart and confident of soul eager to do the great work of a great world power." The same love of adventure, the same desire to prove one was neither a craven nor a weakling, which after the Spanish-American War found imperial or quasi-imperial outlets, must in the 1880s send a young man West.

*Morison, *Turmoil and Tradition*, p. 89.
†*My Vacations*.

In yet another respect, young Henry Stimson followed his hero Roosevelt. Like others of their generation, they were fascinated and not at all repelled by war. "If it wasn't wrong," Roosevelt wrote in a private letter in 1896, "I should say that personally I would rather welcome a foreign war"; and again the next year, "in strict confidence . . . I should welcome almost any war, for I think the country needs one."* Independently, in the West, Stimson had come to exactly the same conclusion. A war "would be a wonderfully good thing for this country."† This was by no means an unusual opinion at the time.

As an ordeal in which he could prove his manhood, then; as the tournament lists in which he could prove his membership in the knightly class in America; and as the training ground in which America was being made ready for competitive struggle and, if necessary, war, the West was important for Stimson. At a deeper, more instinctive level, too, there was perhaps something about the heroic simplicities of the West that spoke to almost religious instincts in a young Puritan. In the end, life would make him draw on all these lessons he learned in the wilderness. But first he must take another tack, and submit himself to the hard discipline of a less romantic but still demanding school.

One "dreadful evening" three years before he climbed the Chief, Henry Stimson took "the most dismal, hopeless journey" from New York to Boston to study at the Harvard Law School.‡ His later career as a lawyer was so long and so distinguished, and he himself took on so many lawyerlike characteristics, that it is easy to forget that he was

*Howard K. Beale, *Theodore Roosevelt and the Rise of America to World Power*, pp. 49–50.
†Morison, *Turmoil and Tradition*, p. 40. See also Samuel P. Huntington, *The Soldier and the State*, pp. 270–88, a brilliant, all too short sketch of what Huntington calls "neo-Hamiltonianism." From roughly 1890 to 1920, he argues, the neo-Hamiltonian school flourished in America. So-called because it shared Alexander Hamilton's view of international politics as "basically politics among independent nations with interests which not too infrequently brought them into conflict with each other." Among the first generation Huntington counts Theodore Roosevelt, Henry Cabot Lodge, Elihu Root, Albert Beveridge, Alfred Thayer Mahan, Herbert Croly, Leonard Wood, Brooks Adams and Henry Adams. Neo-Hamiltonianism re-emerged briefly in 1940–41, Huntington says, in the persons of Henry Stimson, Robert Patterson, Grenville Clark and others; some would say the tradition is still alive.
‡For the decision to study law I have in the main followed Morison, *Turmoil and Tradition*, pp. 40–49. For the Harvard Law School and American legal education generally, see Arthur E. Sutherland, *The Law at Harvard;* Robert Stevens, *Law School;* and Lawrence M. Friedman, *History of American Law.*

initially reluctant to commit himself to the law, and all his life had ambiguous feelings about the private practice of law.

Twenty years after law school Stimson told a group of friends that "the profession of law was never thoroughly satisfactory to me, simply because the life of the ordinary New York lawyer is primarily and essentially devoted to the making of money." That was a considered judgment after two decades, but it is interesting that even before going to law school he had the same doubts. "The course which I think my father desires for me," he wrote to Aunt Minnie, "is precisely the one of which I stand in most deadly horror, viz that of a successful New York lawyer." Interestingly, like so many of his ancestors, he felt drawn to the ministry, but he was not sure that he had a strong enough vocation. Uncle Fred, the lawyer, thought he would make a doctor. His father did not think so and said, "We must not forget that the law is a noble profession," and so, reluctantly, it was to law school that he set out.

Many years later, Stimson's friend Harvey Bundy explained that the reason he went to Harvard Law School, rather than to any other, was quite simple: when one thought of law schools, one thought first of Harvard.* But in the 1880s Harvard's pre-eminence in this field was not universally acknowledged. Indeed, like Andover and Yale, the School was then in the middle of a drastic transformation. Between 1870 and 1910—under its first two deans, Christopher Langdell and James Barr Ames—one historian of legal education has said, "the School changed, in degree and kind, far more rapidly than it did between 1910 and 1967."†

It was not coincidence that each of the schools Stimson attended was changing rapidly. American education, like American institutions of every kind, was adjusting to the dynamic transformation of society and the economy during and after the Civil War, changes that can be labeled as expansion, the industrial revolution, urbanization, mass immigration and the triumph of capitalism, and that in truth scoured and invigorated every corner of the American world, from the Blackfoot reservation to the elm-shaded campuses of New England. Henry Stimson was a Victorian. But Victorians were not, as is sometimes imagined, stuffy, conservative people. They were the children and the worshippers of progress, their stern creed of self-denial and self-control

*Harvey H. Bundy, Oral History, Columbia Oral History Project.
†Sutherland, *The Law at Harvard*, p. 162.

a structure they felt they needed if they were not to be swept away by racing tides of technological and intellectual change.

Before the Civil War the vast majority of American lawyers were trained in the office of an established lawyer. Such law schools as there were, such as the Litchfield School in Connecticut, were little more than crammers. Harvard had its first professor of law as early as 1826, and undergraduate teaching of law there was popular in the 1830s. Yet it was Columbia University, under Theodore W. Dwight, appointed in 1858 to run the School of Jurisprudence there, that set the pace when university law schools began to expand in the 1860s; an eminent Yale professor went so far as to call it "the very West Point of the profession."* Harvard's pre-eminence dated from 1870, when the university's new president, Charles W. Eliot, appointed Christopher Columbus Langdell as dean of the Law School. Langdell is famous for inventing, or at least adapting, the "case method" of studying law. He and his disciple James Barr Ames—but not, for some years, their other colleagues at the Law School—abandoned the time-honored method of lecturing in favor of studying trial and appellate decisions in specific cases. As a method of teaching it was first derided, then widely and eventually universally copied in other American law schools. A senior member of the law-school faculty, Ephraim Gurney, wrote President Eliot after a sleepless night, to express his fear that the method, and Langdell's preference for inexperienced, academic law-school teachers, would bring judges into disrepute, and the Boston University Law School was set up as a response to the hare-brained methods in use on the other bank of the Charles River. Those methods, however, had one advantage of which President Eliot was well aware; the case method was cheap. It required only one professor for every seventy-five students!

That was not why Langdell was an enthusiast for the case method, however. He believed that law was a science, "and all the materials of that science are contained in printed books." The student's task was to isolate and analyze a few principles whereby he could master the infinite complexities of judge-made law. Paradoxically, at a time when more and more students were going from the Harvard Law School into the commercial practice of law on Wall Street or in Boston, the new method did not at first impress practicing lawyers. What it did do

*Benjamin Silliman, pioneer of the natural sciences at Yale.

was create a sense of great intellectual excitement and seriousness which Stimson, after a brief period of initial bafflement, was to share.

He arrived in the autumn of 1888, just over a year after the founding of the *Harvard Law Review*. Five years before, the Law School had moved into Austin Hall, built to the designs of H. H. Richardson with $135,000 given to Harvard by a Boston merchant. This was a massive stone castle in Richardson's bold Romanesque style, with a huge open fire in the library and wild boars and dragons luxuriantly carved on its hardwood beams. (What was the library is now used for "moots," simulated trials: the fireplace survives, though the fire, alas, does not.)

It would be another seven years before a college degree was required for admission to the Law School, though already in Stimson's time college graduates were beginning to predominate. That in itself set Harvard off from most of its rivals, since the typical law school until just before World War I was a "technical school serving undergraduates and usually with a second-class status."* And it was not until 1899 that Ames, Langdell's protégé and successor as dean, succeeded in imposing a three-year residential course for the Bachelor of Laws degree.

So Henry Stimson studied at Harvard for two years and left not with an LL.B. but with a Master of Arts degree. His first reaction was unfavorable. "They give you the best facilities," he wrote home, "and you have to study in self-defense for there isn't another blessed thing to do." Gradually, though, he began to join in the debates of an institution called the Pow Wow and to try his wits in moots against such men as Ezra Thayer, later dean of the Law School, and Louis D. Brandeis. He also found it possible to do what he would not have had the time to do in a later age, which was to take courses in philosophy—at the urging, if you please, of his roommate, who was the Harvard football captain—with such luminaries at the College as George H. Palmer, William James and Josiah Royce. He did not, however, allow himself to be distracted from his main purpose. He graduated high in his class in June 1890, with a grade point average of 76 (brought down by a 63 in equity pleading). In his memoirs, Stimson passed an interesting comparative judgment on the respective effects of his four years at Yale and two at Harvard. In the Law School, he wrote sixty years

*Stevens, *Law School*.

later, "the whole atmosphere was electric with the sparks of competitive argument," and the teaching, he concluded, "created a greater revolution in my power of thinking than any teaching that I got from Yale, while the faith in mankind that I learned on the campus at New Haven was greater and stronger than any such faith I achieved at Harvard."

His mind thus sharpened by disputation with some of the brightest minds of his generation and broadened by contact with the author of *The Varieties of Religious Experience* and the prophet of the Beloved Community, Henry Stimson now went home from Boston to New York to practice law. He began in the office of a Yale friend, Sherman Evarts, son of one of the greatest New York lawyers of the previous generation, William M. Evarts, who saved Andrew Johnson from impeachment and then served as his Attorney General. In spite of these antecedents, the young Evarts had a modest practice at 52 Wall Street. His chief client was the New York and Northern Railway Company, which owned the track from 155th Street to Brewster, New York; Stimson's first legal experience largely took the form of defending the railroad against suits brought by those involved in accidents on the right of way. The work was not intrinsically interesting to a student of Christopher C. Langdell. Being mainly the defense of a wealthy corporation against poor people, it was not edifying to the student of Josiah Royce, who had wanted to "do good work" in the world. And for an ambitious young fiancé with a special reason to be impatient, there was not enough of it.

For a moment Stimson was in the frustrating position of a Monopoly player who cannot throw six and has to watch others begin to zoom round the board while he is still immobilized. He was rescued, as so often in his life, by the providential intervention of a well-connected friend. Buried inside every successful career, like the chicken wire inside a plaster sculpture, lie networks of contacts. When, as was so often the case in Stimson's life, the opportune connection is with the bearer of a famous name or the alumnus of an elite school, the envious are apt to put success down to privilege, forgetting that not even the most august—indeed, least of all the most august—are likely to offer help unless they respect the beneficiary. In this instance, the help came from none other than William C. Whitney, then in the process of founding one of the great American fortunes in investment and street railways. Whitney was a friend of Dr. Stimson, who was well aware of his son's frustration, because Henry, since leaving Cambridge, had set up house with his father. Dr. Stimson confided in a Yale classmate, George Dimmock, who in turn talked to Whitney, who announced abruptly at a dinner party that he had the answer to young Stimson's problems: send him to work for Mr. Root.

Whitney happened to be Elihu Root's biggest client. His recommendation carried weight. On October 22, Stimson was interviewed, and on November 1 he showed up for work at the offices of Root and Clarke, looking out over "a beautiful sweep" of the city's rooftops to the Brooklyn Bridge from the fourteenth floor of the Liberty Mutual building at 32 Nassau Street.* He was to practice law in that building—with significant interruptions, as we shall see—for more than fifty years.

The office was high-ceilinged and old-fashioned. Its atmosphere was proudly said to resemble that of an eighteenth-century London lawyer's chambers. It was heated by cavernous coal fires and cooled in New York's steamy summer heat only by the breeze from the ocean. There was a large central room for the clerks, led by Joseph Kunzman, who used to express his contempt for the newfangled practice of paying wages to law clerks by shouting, "Now where is that *paid* clerk?" In even the most advanced Wall Street firms, wall phones only arrived in the early 1880s and desk phones not until nearly 1900. Most correspondence was in longhand until the mid-1880s, and women stenographers replaced male "type-writers" only around 1900.

Beyond the general office where these antiquated practices were still in force, young Mr. Stimson and another, slightly older law clerk worked in a way that had changed even less since the time of Alexander Hamilton—in the law library, studying for the New York bar exam, which they both duly passed with ease, looking up cases for Mr. Root and Mr. Clarke, and occasionally going to court with one or another of them to pass them references and learn how the craft was practiced by masters.

The other new clerk, also hired on the recommendation of Whitney, was Bronson Winthrop, who was to be Stimson's partner, trusted counselor and friend. On the same day, therefore, Stimson began relationships with the two people who, apart from his wife, his father

*See Morison, *Turmoil and Tradition; Winthrop, Stimson, Putnam & Roberts, A History of a Law Firm,* privately published, New York, 1980; Arthur H. Dean, *William H. Cromwell.*

and perhaps Theodore Roosevelt, would have the greatest influence on his life.

Elihu Root was, with Joseph Choate, the acknowledged leader of the New York bar, a man whose life exemplified Stimson's instinct that, while money and a great deal of it could honorably be made in the titanic struggles of corporate litigation, it was public service that yielded the true glory. Descended on his mother's side from John Burrick, the major of Minutemen who gave the order to fire the "shot heard round the world" at Concord, Root's family were long settled in Clinton, New York. His father, inevitably known as "Cube" Root, taught mathematics at Hamilton College there, from which his son graduated in 1845. Root then studied law at the New York University Law School before setting up his own law firm in 1868, the year after Henry Stimson was born. He rapidly established himself as a formidable and successful advocate at the bar in a Golden Age of advocacy, before many of the best minds of the legal profession had been tempted to the calmer and more lucrative practice of corporation counsel. Root was known for his prodigious memory, his meticulous preparation and, perhaps most of all, his grasp of every detail of an action.

No one held it against Root when he worked as an assistant for one of Boss Tweed's defense counsel, and in 1883 he served as U.S. Attorney for the Southern District of New York. In politics, he was that not uncommon hybrid of conservative Republican, opponent of the machine, and lawyer whose practice involved his representing many of those very corporate interests which younger, more progressive Republicans stigmatized as "the Trusts." By the time Stimson met him, Root had a craggy, deeply lined yet curiously boyish face, the face of a man who had spent all his time, not in law offices and courtrooms, but on the open range. What Stimson called his "constructive sagacity" was legendary, and not unpleasantly tinged with worldliness, as if he could not easily be surprised by anything men and women might do, and found their shortcomings on the whole amusing rather than tragic. When Stimson went to work for him, the most remarkable achievements of Root's life, as Secretary of War and Secretary of State, as senator and elder statesman, were all ahead of him. Stimson revered him and openly treated him both as fatherly adviser and as a role model. No man can be sure of following another man's career at the highest level in public life as closely as Stimson followed Root's. But the similarity was not perhaps wholly accidental. "Mr. Root," as Stimson called him meticulously, was the counselor to whom the younger man took every major decision of his life. He was also an exemplar of what the good and useful life might be and of what might be achieved by worldly wisdom, self-control and hard work.

There was, however, a less attractive side to Root's character, and that, too, was to be echoed in the most important and most controversial action of his protégé's life. When Root was sounded out on President McKinley's behalf about becoming Secretary of War in 1899, he said the appointment was absurd; he knew nothing about war and nothing about the army. McKinley sent word back that he didn't want anyone who knew about war; he wanted a lawyer to direct the government of the Spanish islands the United States had recently acquired: Cuba, Puerto Rico and the Philippines. Root was in favor of granting independence to Cuba, though he personally drafted, in a letter to the military governor, Leonard Wood, what became known as the Platt Amendment, which left the United States free to intervene in Cuba if it thought either Cuban independence or United States interests were threatened.

Root's experience of the Philippines soon corrected his ignorance of war and of the army in important respects. The United States was faced with a rebellion there, led by Emilio Aguinaldo, and in 1899 had sent out an army under General Arthur MacArthur to put it down. Soon disturbing reports of atrocities by the U.S. army began to filter back to the United States, through soldiers' letters home and to the newspapers. Root, as Secretary of War, was accused of covering up massacres, the killing of civilians and prisoners, torture (especially but not only the notorious "water cure"*), concentration camps and a policy that amounted to genocide in certain areas like Samar, the island that an American general swore to turn into "a howling wilderness." No one ever suggested that Root encouraged such atrocities. What he did do was to defend the army, and in specific incidents that meant defending the perpetrators of abuses.

In a speech at Peoria during the 1902 midterm elections Root, as his biographer Philip Jessup† put it, "rallied to the defense of his client, the army." Instances of torture had occurred, he conceded, but only as "exceptions in a uniform course of self-restraint, humanity and

*The victim's mouth was forced open with a gag and water was poured into his throat, making him feel he was drowning.
†On Root generally, see Philip Jessup, *Elihu Root,* 2 vols., New York, 1938; and James Brown Scott, *Elihu Root,* vol. ix in the "American Secretaries of State" series.

kindness.'' Democrats, anti-imperialists and those who were shocked
by the atrocity reports redoubled their attacks on Root. The most
effective was a pamphlet commissioned from Moorfield Storey and Julian Codman by a Boston committee headed by Charles Francis Adams
and Carl Schurz.* Root claimed that "substantially" every report of
atrocities had been promptly investigated and found to be "either unfounded or grossly exaggerated."

Storey maintained, persuasively, that on the contrary there had
been no serious effort to punish brutality in the army. The trials were
farcical, he said, and sentences, often a mere reprimand, derisory. Root
and the generals, he charged,

> had been more eager to punish informants than those on whom
> they informed; a war of terrorism and extinction was consistently
> waged; if Root was not aware of all that was going on, he grossly
> ignored his duty as Secretary of War; torture was applied system-
> atically to extort information, both by American soldiers and by
> the Macabebe scouts serving with the American forces. This and
> much more was supported by quotations from the testimony
> before a Senate committee which had investigated the conduct
> of the war. . . . Mr. Root . . . was silent in the face of certain
> knowledge and by his silence he made himself responsible for all
> that was done with his acquiescence. . . . Mr. Root, then, is the
> real defendant in this case.

Root's admiring biographer maintains that Root "neither inspired, nor approved, nor countenanced atrocities," but even he ad-
mits that the important question is whether he did everything possible
to check them, and that "the answer is probably no." It is hard to
avoid the judgment that Root did know that things had gone very
badly wrong in the Philippines, and that he used his lawyer's skill with
words to deny charges that were in substance true.

There is more to it than that, however. Root was an imperialist
who defended the United States' presence in the Philippines, and he
did not conceal that among his reasons for doing so was his conviction
that Filipinos were inferiors, "but little advanced from pure savagery,"
as he wrote to Senator John T. Morgan of Alabama in July 1902,
"[with] many of the characteristics of children."†

That was what Root believed; and with great hardness, willing the

---

*Moorfield Storey and Julian Codman, *Marked Severities in Philippine Warfare*, 1902.
†Quoted in Jessup, *Root*, p. 343.

end, he willed the means. It was this man who was for Henry Stimson more than a friend and a law partner; he was a *beau idéal*. When Stimson was put to the test in his second term as Secretary of War, he showed the same hardness, the same nationalism, and perhaps the same inability to think of Asian people as he would have thought of Americans. When he faced the army's demand for the forcible evacuation of the Nisei from California at the outbreak of the Second World War, when he confronted his supreme decision over the atomic bomb, as on so many previous occasions in his life Stimson was no doubt conscious of the spirit of Elihu Root looking over his shoulder. Where others later would ask, "What would Colonel Stimson have done?" no doubt Stimson asked, "What would Mr. Root have done?" The honest answer he would have had to give himself was that, if Mr. Root was the soul of Yankee sagacity and rectitude, he was also in his quiet way as hard as nails.

For three years after he was graduated from the Harvard Law School, Stimson kept house with his father and his sister, who never married. It was a pleasant household. Dr. Stimson still worked as hard as ever, but he found time to sail his boat, *Fleur-de-Lys,* and to accompany his son and daughter to the theater. Family tradition,* as we have seen, suggests that the doctor subtly tried to use his influence to persuade Henry to marry someone grander and richer than Mabel. Henry was firmly pushed into the world of the Four Hundred, of Astors and Whitneys, their excellent champagne and their marriageable daughters. "He can't bear for me not to be at the top of the heap," said the unsocial son, "irrespective of what kind of heap it may be." It was not the most respectful way to speak of Ward McAllister and Mrs. Astor.

Both Henry and Mabel, however, had made up their minds, and if there was anyone more determined than he, it was she. Counting the upsetting months when Henry had been persuaded by his family to withdraw his engagement, and then the two years' separation while he was in Cambridge, they had waited for five and a half years. During part of that time, Mabel had been ill with what was very likely a psychosomatic complaint. On January 1, 1893, Stimson was made a partner

*As recorded in interviews with members of both the Stimson and White families used by Morison, *Turmoil and Tradition,* pp. 50–61.

in the firm of Root and Clarke with a guarantee of $2,000 in annual income. (The previous year, the three partners had shared $98,000 between them.) At the age of twenty-five, he was in a position to support his wife, and he lost no time. He married Mabel in New Haven on July 6, 1893. Fifty-four years later Stimson wrote in the conventionally reticent style of his generation that she had been ''ever my devoted companion and the greatest happiness of my life.'' Literary and cultivated in her tastes, strict and formal in her social style and manner, Mabel Stimson was surprisingly active and adventurous. She enjoyed accompanying her husband on his expeditions to the West, Canada, Europe and the Orient. She trained herself to be efficient at both shooting and fishing, and she became an excellent horsewoman.

After ten years at the bar, Stimson could afford, with financial help from his father, to buy a hundred acres of land in Huntington Township on the North Shore spine of Long Island. He bought it for the view, which stretched from the Sound and the Connecticut shore to the shining ocean, just visible twenty-five miles to the south. At first they squatted in a little farmhouse on the property, which had no running water, no plumbing except a shallow well with a hand pump, and no telephone.* Over the years the Stimsons, with the help of a devoted farm manager, John Culleton, from County Carlow in Ireland, transformed what an early visitor proclaimed ''a desolate spot'' into a gentleman's country estate, complete with farm and stables. Stimson built a big, plain frame house which he called Highhold, and later extended it to accommodate his library.

At Highhold Stimson played the squire. He hunted with the Meadowbrook hounds from 1903 until well into the 1920s, shot pheasants, entertained lawyer friends and a growing band of nephews and nieces, and presided over the annual Highhold Games for his neighbors. It was an additional pleasure, and a consecration of his standing among the Long Island gentry, when Theodore Roosevelt hacked over, as he often did, from Sagamore Hill.

The Stimsons' marriage was idyllically happy in every respect—save one: they were unable to have children. Apparently this was a consequence of an attack of mumps that Henry had suffered shortly before the wedding. While they were the last couple in the world to discuss their feelings on such a matter, they overcame their disappointment

*HLS, *My Vacations*, pp. 165–80.

by becoming more and more closely involved in each other, and also, as the years went by, in entertaining a growing clan of Stimson and, especially, White kin.*

On January 1, 1893, Elihu Root had acquired not one but two new law partners. The other was Bronson Winthrop. He was in many ways an exotic creature. Lineally descended from that John Winthrop who urged his fellow colonists to remember that they would be "a City upon a Hill," first governor of Massachusetts Bay and described as "the first great American,"† Bronson Winthrop was born in Paris, educated in Britain at Eton and Trinity College, Cambridge, and so cosmopolitan and elegant that when he first met him, Stimson, no uncouth provincial himself, used to call him "the Exquisite." A bachelor, he entertained with "the silver of four generations on his table" and had a fastidious taste in literature and an encyclopedic knowledge of both American and European history.

At first the young partners did the hack work of general practice: drawing wills, drafting corporate agreements, collecting debts and defending accident cases. Later they graduated to doing the more routine work for the firm's many large corporate clients, including Continental Rubber, Astoria Power and Light, Mutual Life Insurance, and many, many others. As the law firm's privately published history delicately expresses it, this was the era of "trust-busting," and the recently enacted Sherman Act caused an array of legal and organizational problems for utilities, railroads and industrial companies.‡

Under Root's leadership, Winthrop and Stimson both became well-known Wall Street lawyers. Winthrop "became especially learned in the law of wills, estates and estate management," while Stimson specialized in major litigation.

Lawyers in every country play a prominent part in politics, but there are few parallels to the extraordinary dominance in American diplomacy of partners in a dozen or fewer Wall Street law firms and a handful of similar firms in other cities. Most of the great names in American international relations were lawyers from Wall Street or from

---

*For a cautious discussion of the possible emotional consequences of Stimson's infertility, see below, Chapter IX.

†By Hugh Brogan, in *Longman History of the United States*, p. 41.

‡For the history and practice of the law firm, I have drawn on *Winthrop, Stimson, Putnam & Roberts: A History of a Law Firm*, as well as on Morison, *Turmoil and Tradition*, on conversations with the late Kingman Brewster, a former partner, and on a lengthy interview with Peter Kaminer, former managing partner of the firm and now of counsel.

similar practice in Boston or Washington: one has only to think of Root, Stimson himself, Dean Acheson* and John Foster Dulles, not to mention dozens of lesser figures, from Cleveland's Secretary of State Richard Olney and Wilson's Robert Lansing to George Ball in the Kennedy and Johnson administrations, William Rogers in the Nixon administration, and Cyrus Vance under Jimmy Carter.

Of course not every qualified lawyer, not even every lawyer who has practiced in New York, ought to be counted as a "Wall Street lawyer" in the sense that Root, Stimson or the Dulles brothers merit that description. If one considers only those who practiced law in New York for a substantial period *before* going to Washington, the flow from the New York bar was limited but very influential until the beginning of World War II, then became a flood during the war, and has been steady since then, though less influential in policy-making since the time of the Dulles brothers.

When Stimson was working for Root in the Liberty Mutual building, the practice of law was undergoing a transition as marked as that which American higher education had passed through, more or less unremarked by young Stimson, a few years earlier. One key change was that law firms were starting out on that trajectory which has made them in some respects more important than lawyers. At the turn of the century, they were still small. The Cravath firm, for example, though its antecedents ran back to the 1820s and it numbered the Bank of England, the second Bank of the United States, John D. Rockefeller and the House of Morgan among its clients, had no more than five partners in 1900. As the banks, railroads and industrial corporations headquartered in New York became bigger (and incidentally from the 1890s began to hire their own in-house lawyers) the law firms that specialized in acting for them had to grow too.

So where once the *lawyer* was all-important, and law firms formed and dissolved according to the likes and dislikes or the career vicissitudes of individuals, gradually around the turn of the century the *law firm* began to be the primary entity to which lawyers felt loyalty and potential clients tended increasingly to turn. But that process was by

---

*Acheson was a partner in the Washington firm of Covington and Burling; Olney from Boston. Excluding men like James Rowe, Joseph Rauh, Clark Clifford, Lloyd Cutler, Harry McPherson and Joseph Califano, who came to Washington for government service in the first place and then stayed to practice law, the number of truly active Washington lawyers who have been participants in foreign-policy-making, other than Acheson and Paul Warnke, has been small.

no means completed when Stimson went to work. For example, after
Root and Clarke was transformed, as we shall see, into Winthrop,
Stimson, it was resurrected by Root's son as Root, Clarke, Buckner
and Howland, which was later transmogrified into Dewey, Ballantine,
another classic Wall Street firm.*

Since before the Civil War, men like William Seward or David
Dudley Field, to mention two names almost at random, had gone from
the New York bar to great offices in government. At the end of the
century those who were practicing law there included former President
Chester A. Arthur, former and future President Grover Cleveland, and
Speaker Thomas B. Reed, "Czar" of the House of Representatives,
who would have become a partner in Root and Clarke if Samuel Clarke
had not won his case for him and kept him in the House.

What was new was that where even the mightiest firms had once
stooped to legal drudgery, such as debt-collecting, a cluster of leading
firms were beginning to specialize in national and increasingly in international business. It was in part because they were at home in international affairs, as few if any lawyers who practiced in Chicago or St.
Louis could be, that partners in the Wall Street (and to a lesser degree
Washington) firms began to be natural choices for international work
in government.

Algernon Sydney Sullivan and William Nelson Cromwell, aged
twenty-five, formed a partnership in four rooms in the Drexel Building
at Broad and Wall streets in 1879. Before long they were acting for
J. P. Morgan, E. H. Harriman, Henry M. Flagler, and the power utilities.
But Cromwell's practice was also an international one. A high proportion
of the investment going into American expansion, especially into railroads, was coming from Europe, particularly from London. At an early
age, says Cromwell's biographer, Arthur Dean (himself director of the
Arms Control and Disarmament Agency under President Kennedy),

> he had gone to Europe to confer with leading lawyers and bank-
> ers. He became fully versed in English and continental under-

*For this account of the growth of the Wall Street law firms I have relied on several of their
house histories, e.g., Ralph Carson, Davis, Polk, Wardwell, Sunderland & Kiendl: A Background
with Figures; Arthur H. Dean, William Nelson Cromwell: An American Pioneer in Corporation,
Competitive and International Law; Otto E. Koegel, Walter S. Carter, on the founder of Hughes,
Hubbard & Reed; Robert T. Swaine, The Cravath Firm and Its Predecessors. See also Martin
Mayer, The Lawyers; Martin Mayer, Emory Buckner; Paul Hoffman, Lions in the Street; Charles
Warren, History of the American Bar.

writing and financing methods and the relevant law. In connection with the early financing of American railroads, utilities and industrial concerns he often represented Dutch, English, French and German banks or bond syndicates purchasing American securities. Cromwell also represented . . . sugar interests in Cuba, French interests in Brazil and Panama . . . [which] made him more conscious of the relation of developments in foreign lands to the interests of the American people.*

They certainly did. Stimson was one of those who was to criticize severely Cromwell's behavior in relation to Panama, but that was in the future. The point was that a group of lawyers was coming into existence who could earn a great deal of money, who were free to volunteer for public service in national or international affairs without having to depend on the exiguous salaries such service offered, and who had come to have an international perspective very untypical among Americans of their generation.

In 1899 Elihu Root received that "absurd" invitation to become Secretary of War. To their amazement he handed over his practice to his two young partners, Stimson and Winthrop. They were then aged respectively thirty-two and thirty-six, and Root had left them, as Stimson graphically put it, "pie-eyed with the best practice in New York and everybody trying to get it away from us." Stimson said he "never knew what the rough end of life in New York can be until I saw these people grab business away from us." In 1901 they changed the firm's name to Winthrop and Stimson. Deprived of Root's name but "sustaining the best of his reputation,"† the two young partners prospered modestly, grew in reputation and stature and became as close as two such reticent Victorians could bring themselves to be. Only on the fiftieth anniversary of their first meeting could Winthrop bring himself to write to Stimson of the "respect and love which somehow I never expressed before."

For fifty years, Bronson Winthrop was to remain faithful to the practice of law. But Stimson chafed. As a young unknown he had grumbled about "such a poky profession as the law in such a stationary place as New York." A dozen years of practice established his reputation as a lawyer and made him comfortably off; between 1898 and 1906

*Dean, *William Nelson Cromwell.*
†*Winthrop, Stimson, Putnam & Roberts: A History*, p. 19.

he earned between $8,000 and $11,000 a year,* which was far less than Root or the other leaders of the bar commanded. Charitable work for such good causes as the Workroom for Unskilled Women or the Lincoln Hospital, for which he was unpaid legal counsel, helped to alleviate his frustration with ordinary practice, which focused not so much on its tedium (he found it interesting enough) as on what he considered its lack of ethical purpose, its sordid selfishness. From about 1900, when he was thirty-three, Stimson began to suffer from lumbago and rheumatism and from the insomnia that plagued him for the rest of his life.

In 1898, when the great wave of patriotic excitement over the Spanish-American War had "caught me napping," Stimson had quickly joined Squadron A, Troop 2, of the New York National Guard. He learned to ride, and to love it, and in the horse exercise he also found relief from his physical symptoms, whether or not their origins were emotional. In due course he bought his first horse, Bouncer, from the Ninety-fourth Street Armory. Loving the companionship and the discipline of military life, he enjoyed his period of duty keeping order during a strike among the workers building the reservoir at Croton-on-Hudson, and took an almost boyish delight in the 1904 maneuvers on the site of the Civil War battlefield of Bull Run.†

From the routines as well as the dedication of the military life, he took, as some men do, profound satisfaction for the rest of his life. Unlike Elihu Root, Stimson knew something of the army, though nothing of war, and he was ready when the call to public service came.

A s it happened, it came first in civilian form—to be specific, in the shape of a Western Union telegram in December 1905 inviting him to "take lunch" with the President of the United States. After the meal, Roosevelt sounded Stimson out about taking the post of United States Attorney for the Southern District of New York. Stimson said straight out that he was interested in the job, but the President warned him that he could not yet make a definite offer. Others, including Charles Evans Hughes, a future justice of the Supreme Court and Secretary of State, and James Rockwell Sheffield, were under considera-

*Morison, *Turmoil and Tradition*, p. 75.
†HLS, *My Vacations*, pp. 114–23.

tion. And Senator Thomas Platt, whose approval, under the tradition of "senatorial courtesy," would be required, had a candidate of his own.*

Stimson's interest in the position was not something that Roosevelt could take for granted. The post of U.S. Attorney for the Southern District, including Manhattan, was then, as it is now, one of the key jobs in the entire American legal system. In one respect it was even more important than it is now: The problem of what were loosely called "trusts" was a key political issue of the day, and Roosevelt had staked much of his political credibility in his campaign speeches inveighing against the "malefactors of great wealth" who were widely seen as strangling the economy and bleeding the consumer. Prosecuting these malefactors fell to this particular U.S. Attorney; moreover, the job had been held by lawyers of great distinction in the past, including the President's kinsman James R. Roosevelt and Stimson's mentor, Elihu Root. But in recent years it had fallen on bad times.

Not that the incumbent whose impending retirement had created the vacancy was in want. Quite the contrary: Henry "Lighting Eyes" Burnett was reputed to have earned more than $100,000 a year in the job, a majestic income in those days, because the tradition had grown up of awarding the U.S. Attorney a substantial proportion of recoveries in customs cases. An attorney like Burnett, who took an easygoing view of the dictates of financial propriety and the public interest, could distribute the actual work of these lucrative cases to his friends, split the fees with them, and trouser the recoveries. The sheer volume of work was such that it was thought impossible for the Attorney to appear in court himself, so overladen with administrative work must he be. And the physical arrangements of the office were inadequate to the verge of squalor.

Roosevelt and his Attorney General, William H. Moody, a doughty trust-buster from Massachusetts, were determined to reform this bastion of *ancien régime* jobbery. It was essential to their strategy of compelling the trusts to obey the law that the job should be held by an energetic, skillful and high-minded young lawyer, and Stimson fitted the part perfectly. Roosevelt, one press service of the day commented, knew that he was choosing a clean-cut man of proven fidelity

---

*In my account of Stimson's term as U.S. Attorney I have used extensively an unpublished 1961 Yale A.B. honors thesis by John D. Viener, "A Sense of Obligation: Henry Stimson as United States Attorney: 1906–1909."

and integrity and ready acquaintance with the most intricate cases of legal practice. Stimson had that firmness of character, that general knowledge of affairs, and that ability to catch the significance of new questions steadily arising for the adjudication of the courts, that would allow him not only to maintain the high reputation of the office, but even to advance it.

This paragon took the oath of office on February 1, 1906. It was agreed that he would work for $10,000 a year. Unlike Burnett (or for that matter Root), he would take no commissions on work given to other lawyers and would do no private work while in the government service.

Stimson found the office in a deplorable state. It was "completely swamped," he wrote to one friend,* and to Moody he commented, "assistants, clerks, witnesses and criminals are necessarily jumbled together, and I am in constant anxiety lest valuable papers be lost."† Even more serious were the shortage in staff and its mediocre quality. For $750 to $1,500 a year you did not get the ablest and most dedicated men, even in 1906.

Stimson quickly installed a modern filing system, a card index, and dockets for witnesses and complaints. In time, he managed to find a bit more office space. But his key move was to introduce to public service the practice, well established in private law firms, of hiring bright young law-school graduates for very low wages, counting on their ambition and willingness to learn to get excellent work out of them for less than one would need to pay older but less talented men with family obligations.

Only a few years earlier the brilliant half-German British bureaucrat Alfred Milner had used the same principle to surround himself with a first-class staff when he went out to administer South Africa after the Boer War. Milner's young men, who went on to the highest posts in British politics, public life, journalism, business and the universities, came to be known as "Milner's Kindergarten," and they remained a cohesive and influential lobby in Britain for more than forty years.‡ Not only did "Stimson's Kindergarten" have a comparable

*Viener, "A Sense of Obligation: Henry L. Stimson as United States Attorney," P. 19, citing letter to J. Knox Taylor.
†HLS to J. Knox Taylor, December 12, 1906; to W. H. Moody, April 5, 1906.
‡See Sir Evelyn Wrench, *Alfred Lord Milner: The Man of No Illusions*. The Kindergarten included Geoffrey Dawson, editor of *The Times* of London; John Buchan, novelist and Governor General

continuing cohesion as a like-minded group of lawyers with much in-fluence in political and legal circles; but the *idea* of a public servant surrounding himself with a surrogate family of enthusiastic younger helpers was one that appealed to Stimson, the more so because of his own childlessness. In the Second World War much of his effectiveness in the War Department was to come from his ability to work closely with a group of men—Lovett, Bundy, McCloy and others—whom he trusted and with whom he could discuss troubling matters of policy and even ethics in the informality of his home, in the same way that he and Mabel opened Highhold to the young lawyers who came to work for the U.S. Attorney's office.

Soon after taking office Stimson wrote to several law-school deans, notably to Ames at Harvard, asking them for the names of their very best students and the very best of their recent alumni. From their suggestions and from his own contacts at the bar Stimson assembled a remarkable group of young men. Altogether he hired sixteen assistants, roughly half of them more or less straight out of law school. They included Emory Buckner (himself U.S. Attorney in the 1920s and one of the founders of the Dewey, Ballantine law firm), Thomas D. Thacher (later a partner in another major Wall Street firm, Simpson, Bartlett and Thacher, judge of the New York State Court of Appeals and a United States Solicitor General) and—last but not least—Felix Frank-furter. The future Supreme Court justice was to become one of Stimson's close friends and a devoted admirer, a self-appointed public-relations man and the marriage broker who made the last and most important stage of Stimson's career possible by introducing him to Franklin Delano Roosevelt and insisting, over Stimson's suspicions, that they must be friends.

Stimson's young men had a lot of fun. They went sailing off Fire Island, played baseball at Highhold, held play readings and wrote each other comic doggerel. They also worked furiously hard, and for far longer hours than the U.S. Attorney's office in the old Post Office building had been used to working. Stimson himself set them an ex-ample. He soon organized the office so efficiently that in his first year he collected nine times as much money in customs fines as his prede-cessor had collected in eight years. By 1908, in spite of the warnings

---

of Canada; Philip Kerr, later Lord Lothian, British ambassador to Washington; the political philosopher and student of comparative constitutions Lionel Curtis; and many, many others.

that he would never be able to get into court, he was able to boast in his annual report to Moody's successor as Attorney General that he had "tried personally during the past year seven important jury cases, personally prepared the briefs for and argued the six demurrers in the rebate cases, and argued the demurrer in the New York *Herald* case."*

James Gordon Bennett, editor and publisher of the New York *Herald,* was one of the most powerful journalists in what was perhaps the Golden Age of New York journalism. Unfortunately he had also allowed, if not encouraged, his paper to increase its very substantial profitability by accepting in its personal column small ads of a dubious nature. The ads might say: "Would young lady in blue suit who noticed gentleman at 53rd and Madison please write Herald 321. Admirer"; or "Will lady in blue on platform Broadway Car, 40th Street who noticed gentleman, address admirer, Herald 146." To a permissive or sentimental mind, there may be something poignant about the faint echo of those passing glances of almost a century ago. But Stimson was neither sentimental nor permissive. It is possible that the ladies in blue offended Stimson's sexual puritanism; it was in any case certain to his mind that the newspaper and those responsible for it had been breaking the law.

The *Herald* had been publishing such ads for years, but no one had cared or dared to prosecute. Stimson did, and he got a conviction from Judge Hough. The *Herald* was fined $5,000, and Bennett was fined $25,000, the judge remarking that he had maintained "for more years than I can remember . . . a potent aid to local libertines, and a directory of local harlots."

Stimson may have derived a certain pleasure from taking on so formidable an opponent as Bennett. Most of the U.S. Attorney's work, however, was far more humdrum. He argued successfully to sustain the conviction of a captain held guilty of negligence by a lower court in the case of the ferry *General Slocum,* concerning an accident in which close to a thousand New Yorkers died. He prosecuted smugglers, white slavers, counterfeiters and heartless immigration agents who brought aliens into the United States suffering from trachoma and other communicable diseases, as well as those who exploited immigrants on their way to the West. In one notable action he compelled the railroad magnate E. H. Harriman and his banker Otto Kahn to divulge information about their operations.

---

*HLS, *Report to the Attorney-General,* August 14, 1908. The Attorney General, after December 1906, was Charles J. Bonaparte, grandson of the Emperor Napoleon I's brother Jérôme, King of Westphalia.

The heart of the task Stimson had been set, however, was to assault the power and illegal behavior of the trusts. The process of combination that had dominated American business for more than forty years since the end of the Civil War was now reaching its climax.* In the first phase, up to about 1879, businessmen and their lawyer advisers got together in what were called "pools" and—less accurately, in view of the ethics of many of those involved—"gentlemen's agreements." Between roughly 1879 and 1896 they employed trusts, in the strict sense of the word, to own the assets of nominally competing companies. And from 1896 until about 1906 the fashionable device was the "holding company." In two years alone, from 1899 to 1901, more than two hundred large industrial combinations were formed, with an aggregate capitalization of ten billion dollars.

Against this titanic movement the efforts of the Progressives seemed feeble indeed. They were in any case divided between those who wanted to split the trusts up into their components and those who sought only to make them behave in a more restrained and public-spirited fashion. The 1887 Interstate Commerce Act, ineffective as it was, was then further weakened by the judgment in the *E. C. Knight* case of 1895, which held that commerce did not include manufacture, but "succeeds to manufacture and is not part of it." Three years later Congress passed the Sherman Anti-Trust Act, the charter of all subsequent antitrust action, but one that was at first rarely invoked and even less often effective. Indeed it has been said that the courts' interpretation of the antitrust laws had "more than established the legality of large consolidations; they had encouraged them."†

President Roosevelt had nailed his political colors to the antitrust mast. But at the time Stimson took over as U.S. Attorney in the district where the largest, most powerful and most flagrant consolidations tended to be concentrated, the Roosevelt administration had won only two significant victories. One was the Supreme Court's decision dissolving the Northern Securities Company, a trust put together by J. P. Morgan and James J. Hill to protect their northwestern railroad interests against the predatory ambitions of E. H. Harriman.‡ The

*See Purdy, Lindahl and Carter, *Corporate Concentration and Public Policy.*
†Ibid., D. M. Keezer and S. May, *The Public Control of Business,* New York, 1930, cited in Viener. *op. cit.,* p. 63.
‡Morgan went to the President and complained that he had not been warned of the suit. "That is just what we didn't want to do," said Roosevelt. "If we have done anything wrong," said Morgan, "send your man to my man and they can fix it up." Morgan assumed that the Attorney General of the United States would be available to come to New York and work out

Roosevelt government's only other significant victory was Congress's passage of the Elkins Rebating Act in 1903. It badly needed a victory in court to prove to the trusts that it meant what it said, and would not merely pass legislation against abuses of business combination, but press for and obtain convictions under the new laws.

As U.S. Attorney in New York, Stimson was bound to be the spearhead of that attack. Even so, of his three chief prosecutions, the litigation on which his reputation as a lawyer rests above all else, only one was an attack on trusts as such. The other two were prosecutions of frauds carried out under cover of the trust form of organization.

One of the ironies of Stimson's career as a trust-busting government attorney is that two of his major targets as a prosecutor had been clients of his law firm before he went to work for the government. To him, of course, this made no difference whatsoever. One was the American Sugar Refining Company, the other the National Bank of North America, controlled by Charles W. Morse, well known for his combinations in banking and as the organizer of ice and shipping trusts.

Morse's raiding of his two main banks, the National Bank of North America and the Mercantile National Bank, was thought to have contributed to the Panic of 1907. But bank inspection at the time was neither sophisticated nor tenacious. Inspectors went through the books of Morse's banks after the panic and found nothing. By November 1907 Stimson was writing to Attorney General Bonaparte that he was unhappy about "a number of acts of grossly bad banking, which run very close to the line of criminal misapplication of the bank's funds."* In January 1908 he reported that he had found evidence that the National Bank of North America, through several of its officers, "had gone into speculative enterprises beyond its corporate power, has concealed its interests in dummy loans, and has so reported them on its books." He put in a total of five bank inspectors of his own, who took more than a year to accumulate the evidence he needed for a successful prosecution.

There was a cumulative effect to Stimson's assaults on the misuse of trusts. In 1907 he had successfully prosecuted an associate of Morse's in the copper pool, one Fritz Augustus Heinze. In the process he had succeeded in getting the court to establish that "a loan made in bad

---

a compromise with his attorneys. See Andrew Sinclair, *Corsair: The Life of J. Pierpont Morgan*, p. 141.
*Viener, *op. cit.*, p. 67.

faith with intent to defraud or injure the association, is not an unwise act, but a fraudulent act and, strictly speaking, no loan at all but a misapplication of the funds of the bank."* Stimson found out that Morse had skimmed money for himself by making bogus loans to his broker's office boy and to his own secretary, as well as in more ingenious ways.

Alerted to the progress of Stimson's relentless investigation, Morse fled abroad; he was captured, and returned to face trial voluntarily when he learned of the arrangements Stimson had already made for extradition. He was indicted in August and convicted in November of misapplying the bank's and his depositors' money through improper loans falsely reported in the books. He was sentenced to fifteen years in prison, but subsequently contrived to be released by feigning ill health.

"I spent eleven months to get Morse copper-fastened," Stimson wrote proudly to his friend President Roosevelt, "when it would have been much easier to get the subordinates in the bank who acted under his direction." His satisfaction was justified. To have succeeded in collaring one of the wealthiest and most notorious of the malefactors was a substantial achievement, and it was noticed as such. Stimson's other two main cases brought him less public popularity, but even more solid recognition from Progressive Republicans and from the legal profession.

In the early 1900s most of the sugar consumed in the United States, whether on the table, in cakes or confectionery, as alcohol or in industry, came from the Caribbean and especially from Cuba. Bulk sugar, it was estimated, accounted for as much as 40 per cent of the westward freight out of New York.

Like other industrial giants, the Sugar Trust, controlled by the American Sugar Refining Company, was involved in secret rebating arrangements with the railroads. What happened was that the big shipper would work out a secret rebate with one or more railroads. He would then pay the full rate for freight; but he would be paid back a rebate by the carrier, which meant that he could effectively undercut smaller competitors in inland markets. Rebating was illegal under the Interstate Commerce Act of 1887, but it was not until the passage of the Elkins Act in 1903 that the government was able to exact fines large enough to deter a major trust.

As soon as his new antitrust bureau was working, in early 1906,

---

*Brief and argument by HLS in *U.S. v. Fritz Augustus Heinze,* cited in Viener, *op. cit.,* p. 68.

Stimson filed suits against both the American Sugar Refining Company, which controlled about half the market for sugar in the United States, and against nine railroads of which the mighty New York Central was the leader. The difficulty lay in proving instances of illegal rebating, because the company disguised the rebate by pretending that it was demanding legitimate repayments for sugar damaged in transit. By subpoenaing and correctly analyzing an enormous mass of freight records, bank drafts, board minutes and correspondence, Stimson was able to show how the Sugar Trust forced the railroads to agree to rebate. First he successfully prosecuted the nine railroads and one other carrier. Then he turned his guns on the Sugar Trust itself. Using an informer in the company's office, Stimson was able to prove, first, that its officers were well aware both of the lawful tariff for shipping sugar and of the illegal rebating arrangements. Then he painstakingly followed the money through the complex illegal system until it ended up with the American Sugar Refining Company. And in a steamrollering summing-up he laid the whole case out, starting with the reasons why equality is so important in commercial law, and arguing relentlessly through to the individual guilty responsibility of Heinze and his right-hand man, one Palmer. As he scrawled in his characteristic big handwriting in his trial notes, "Astonishing case, Secret crimes, Documentary evidence." Faced with this assault, as meticulously prepared and mercilessly carried out as a big German offensive on the Western Front in the Great War, the Sugar Trust fought for a while, then ran up the white flag. By December 1906 Stimson was able to inform the court that "I have been approached by the representatives of that Company . . . and have been informed by them that they are ready to plead guilty to all of the indictments."

A year later, reflecting on the implications of the case to Attorney General Bonaparte, Stimson concluded that

> the surrender of the American Sugar Refining Company upon all of the indictments pending was obtained by the policy of pushing to trial as rapidly as possible the successive indictments obtained. . . . The Sugar Company held out during three successive convictions by juries. It then came to me on the eve of the fourth trial and surrendered unconditionally.

Not content with operating a vast illegal scheme to pressure the railroads into granting them secret rebates and so give them a critical competitive advantage over all other refiners, the men who ran the Sugar Trust were also cheating the government. They did so on such a scale, over a period of time and by a method at once so bare-faced and so ingenious, that it became one of the classics of the age of the muckrake.

Shortly after the rebating convictions, Stimson was alerted by a newspaper investigation to the possibility that the Sugar Trust was defrauding the customs. United States Treasury agent Richard Parr became convinced that this was so, and Stimson put him on the case together with James O. Brzezinski and a former employee of the American Sugar Refining Company, Richard Whalley, as a special agent.

Sugar was weighed on the New York waterfront on seventeen large scales. At each one, a customs inspector and a company checker sat together in a little house, with the company man on the left and therefore next to the upright column of the scales. As Whalley, Parr and Brzezinski watched, they noticed that every time there was a load of sugar on the scales the company checker would drop his left hand in a strange motion.

It turned out that the Sugar Trust had been cheating the customs since the passage of the Dingley Tariff in 1897, ten years before. For the first four years, the company had stuck to conventional methods such as bribing customs officials, falsifying records and using light trucks to underestimate the amount of customs duty payable. In 1901 someone had thought up a better way. On each of the seventeen scales, a small hole, one quarter of an inch in diameter, had been bored, and into it was inserted a tiny piece of steel from a woman's corset, strong enough to counter the weight of the sugar. In this way, a tiny downward pressure of a few pounds' weight by the checker's left hand would register as several pounds less weight of sugar. By this simple trick, as Stimson was eventually able to prove in court from its own records, the American Sugar Refining Company had succeeded in selling to dealers far more sugar than it was on record as having imported into the country. In six years, Stimson demonstrated, 75 million pounds of sugar had escaped duty, and in the end Stimson collected $3.5 million in unpaid duty and penalties, the largest sum, it is said, ever collected by the government on a similar claim.

Stimson carefully defended the U.S. Attorney's office from political demands and pressures during his tenure. Some of these pressures were the traditional ones: for him to use his power of appointment to help deserving Republicans. "I would like you," wrote his friend Republican congressman Herbert Parsons, "in more ways than one to help the Republican party." "I do not intend to appoint anybody," Stimson replied a few weeks later, "on purely political recommendation. . . . I do not want you to recommend anyone whom I cannot implicitly rely upon to refuse a $10 bill when an Italian offers it to him, as will happen almost every day."* As we shall see, Stimson was not free from the conventional ethnic prejudices of his class and generation.

He can, however, be charged with yielding to a more insidious political pressure: the temptation to defend and support the President who had appointed him, whom he so much admired, and whom he wanted to count as a friend. In two incidents Stimson can be fairly charged with taking Roosevelt's side in quarrels where his usual caution might have urged him to stand aside.

The first incident arose out of reports published in Joseph Pulitzer's *New York World*. What happened was that the Indianapolis *News*, edited by one Delevan Smith, alleged that much of the $40 million that the United States had paid, at Roosevelt's insistence, to buy the right to build the Panama Canal, had gone, not to the French government or French holders of claims, but—indirectly, through the agency of the House of Morgan—to a syndicate of Americans, including William Nelson Cromwell (one founder of the august Wall Street law firm of Sullivan and Cromwell), Charles Taft and Roosevelt's brother-in-law Douglas Robinson. Challenged to reply to these charges, Roosevelt said they were "false" and "too absurd to be discussed." The letter in which he gave that reply was published in the *New York World*, which accused the President of "deliberate misstatements of fact in his scandalous personal attack on Delevan Smith." The issue, said the *World*, was not Panama but "the veracity of the President of the United States."

Roosevelt was furious, and he was right to be. No research has ever uncovered any support for the charges made by the Indianapolis *News* and endorsed by the *World*.† Where he was arguably less justified was in directing his Attorney General to bring suits for *criminal* libel against those responsible for the *News* and *World* attacks. The federal

*HLS to Herbert Parsons, April 10, 1906.
†See Elting E. Morison (ed.), *The Letters of Theodore Roosevelt* (Cambridge 1951–54), vol. vi, 1415–16.

government was able to act in this case only by claiming jurisdiction on the unprecedented and dubious grounds that the libel had been published on federal property, for example at West Point. The cases were never brought to court because the judges refused to accept the federal government's claim to jurisdiction.

Stimson was all in favor of the prosecutions to start with, in part apparently because he was resentful of the power of the press. (When he first became Secretary of State in 1929 he issued an order that no news could be released without his personal approval. Given the sanctity of his weekends, this did not work. Later in life Stimson earned the respect of reporters and developed respect in turn for some of the more cultivated and responsible members of the craft; nevertheless he was never enthusiastic about the barons of the yellow press, such as Pulitzer, Hearst and Bennett.) He does seem to have developed doubts about the wisdom of the prosecutions, and he did have the courage to write to Roosevelt warning him that they might look "queer" and to hint that they would be seen as reviving the crime of *lèse-majesté* or the Alien and Sedition Acts. Even so, he went along to a certain degree with the unwise attempt of an angry President, personally involved in the case, to go out of his way to punish a low blow by political opponents.

The other case reflects even less credit on both Roosevelt and Stimson. In 1906 three companies of black soldiers from the Twenty-fifth Regiment were assigned to Brownsville, Texas, where they were unwelcome to a section of the public. A number of instances occurred of harassment of the soldiers off duty, culminating in an incident on August 13 when shots were heard, one white man was found dead and another wounded. Suspicion fell on the black soldiers, and Roosevelt came to the conclusion that they were guilty. On November 5, after the elections, he delivered a message condemning them in strong terms and ordered the dishonorable discharge of the entire regiment. It appears from subsequent investigation that Roosevelt was wrong. The incident had been a provocation, and the soldiers were not guilty. Roosevelt eventually accepted that this was so, reinstated some but not all of the soldiers, and retracted some of his first statement. But he still insisted that he had acted rightly and constitutionally. An action—*Reid* v. *U.S.*—was brought to test the point. Although the incident had taken place far beyond his jurisdiction, Stimson agreed to act, more or less unofficially, as the President's lawyer. He based his case on the executive prerogative the Constitution gives to the President as Commander-in-Chief.* The subordinate's eager willingness to justify an ugly outburst of temper on the part of his leader leaves an unpleasant taste in the mouth.

The probable explanation for Stimson's actions is that the limelight that played on him in the U.S. Attorney's office had begun to awaken not only great admiration for Theodore Roosevelt but also an ambition of following him, if not as far as the White House, at least up the Hudson River to Albany. Stimson was surrounded by men urging him to run for this or that public office. Nor was he quite as indifferent to personal publicity as he liked to pretend. Stimson himself asked Roosevelt, now out of office, to draw what he called "the case of the seventeen holes" to the attention of the magazine which Roosevelt edited, *The Outlook.* Other papers took up the story about the sugar fraud, and Stimson became a celebrity, albeit one who behaved in anything but a flamboyant way. Although he often maintained at the time and later in his memoirs that he had no political ambitions, the fact is that within about a year of resigning as U.S. Attorney, he considered running for mayor of New York City, and agreed to run for governor of New York State.

In retrospect we can see that the fastidious Stimson was wildly unsuited for the cut-and-thrust, hail-fellow-well-met life of electoral politics. Still, he had been enthusiastically involved in the Good Government movement in New York. He had proved conscientious and effective in his work for his Republican club. And he had been a howling success, in both substantive and public-relations terms, as U.S. Attorney. His work in that office had been varied, but its main thrust was directly related to the hottest political issue of the day: the trusts and what should be done about them. He had made a good record. He had had a good press. And he had won the good opinion of powerful members of the Progressive wing of the Republican Party and of its leader, Theodore Roosevelt.

So it was entirely natural that his Republican friends should ask him to run. He personally disliked the idea of a political career. "From a purely personal view," he wrote to his father when he was canvassed about running in September 1909, it would be "a great misfortune to

---

*U.S. Constitution, Art. II, Sec. 2. But there is no explicit power there given to intervene in the manner in which Roosevelt did.

run for Mayor and still more to be elected." Dr. Stimson sympathized with his misgivings but thought it was his duty to run. "I would not choose this for you," was the message he transmitted through Elihu Root, who had come to consult him, "but when duties come to a man he must not dare to refuse them."*

Nothing came of the talk about the mayoralty: party workers wanted a man with a more common touch. But in 1910, after more party debate and further agonizing on the part of the prospective candidate, Stimson could not escape being chosen as the Republican candidate for the governorship of New York. It was clearly understood, by Roosevelt, by Elihu Root and by Stimson himself, that he was in for "a good licking." But Roosevelt wanted a liberal Republican to rally his men. As President William H. Taft said, "if you were to remove Roosevelt's skull now, you would find written on his brain '1912.'" Roosevelt had never been reconciled to Taft's occupancy of an office he thought of as his; Taft meant that everything Roosevelt thought or said or did, including his pushing forward Stimson to run for governor of New York, was conditioned by his unacknowledged ambition to run for the presidency in 1912. In the end, Roosevelt did run on the "Bull Moose" third-party ticket, further intensifying the deep divisions in the Republican Party between "regulars" and insurgent Progressives, and letting the Democrats into the White House. So Roosevelt argued to Stimson, in the self-interested way that the greatest political leaders have of convincing themselves that what they want is good for their friends, that "a good fight with a licking won't necessarily hurt him."

Stimson's style was not bespoke for the hustings. "His cultured accent," wrote one not unfriendly observer years later, "his uneasy platform presence, his cold personality, almost every detail of his manner betrayed his birth and breeding, gave his electorate an impression of a young aristocrat who condescends to rule, and who, though he may be a good ruler, condescends. . . . The opposition press called him 'the human icicle.' "† Unwisely, Stimson felt the need to spend much of his time assuring reporters that he was not an icicle—a self-defeating task. Party workers tried to inject "ginger" into his campaigning, but what he wanted to do was to talk about political theory and the need for reform.

The party was indeed hopelessly split. The regular organization

*Elihu Root to HLS, September 18, 1909, quoted in Morison, *Turmoil and Tradition*, p. 132.
†Cited in Drew Pearson, *Washington Merry-Go-Round*, p. 112.

was unavailable, so Stimson surrounded himself with young, able en-
thusiasts, some of whom—like Joseph Cotton, later Under Secretary at
the State Department, and Felix Frankfurter—were to become lifelong
friends. One of his friends supplied a little ditty in the cheerfully racist
manner of the day to sing at his rallies:

> If Stimson came from Africa
> If he was a Zulu chief
> If he wore a feather in his hair
> And dressed in a fig leaf
> We'd vote for Henry just the same
> And carry out the plan
> Because he's Roosevelt's man.*

His friends were right. Stimson did his best to put up a good
fight, but he did get a licking.

The Democrat, a paper-maker named John A. Dix, Jr., was a
"rough-and-tumble political fighter,"† and he won with 689,700 votes
against Stimson's 622,229. But the loss was not a disgrace, and it probably did not hurt him that much. I say *probably,* because ambition is
an unfathomable thing. Henry Stimson did not look like a man with
a private ambition for a career in elective politics. He did not act like
such a man. And one could even go so far as to say—in spite of
counterexamples such as two Roosevelts, Tafts, Wadsworths and Root—
that men of his class, in his generation, found it distasteful to offer
themselves to the approval or rejection of the electorate. Still,
there is a passage in *On Active Service* which may give a reader pause.

> Nothing about the campaign of 1910 in New York was so im-
> portant for Stimson's life as the simple fact that he did not win.
> *The defeat did not do him any important damage, but victory would
> almost surely have opened to him a strong possibility of great advance-
> ment, even toward the White House.* At the least it would have
> made him a commanding national figure at a very early age.‡
> [My italics.]

Whether or not Stimson nurtured a secret ambition of "great
advancement, even toward the White House," he did not have to wait

*I owe this endearing if lamentable doggerel to Morison, *Turmoil and Tradition,* p. 142.
†*Ibid.*
‡*On Active Service,* p. 25.

long for the call to national service in a form that was far more suited than Albany to his talents and his interests. President Taft was well aware that Theodore Roosevelt was preparing to attack him in 1912. It would be no bad move to break up the coming assault by bringing some of Roosevelt's bright young men into the Taft administration. So when the Secretary of War, Jacob Dickinson, resigned, the President offered the job to Henry Stimson, and Stimson, with very little hesitation this time, accepted.

He consulted just four people, in fact. One was his wife, one was his father, and one was his law partner, Bronson Winthrop. The fourth was Theodore Roosevelt. Stimson was aware, of course, that relations between Roosevelt and Taft were already hardening into something like enmity. But Roosevelt "warmly and strongly urged me by all means to accept the position," and later repeated his blessing in a letter.

Teddy Roosevelt, though, was a complicated human being, and he may not have been so delighted at his young friend's promotion as he said he was. It is the measure of how little Stimson had the political temperament that he may not have realized how much Roosevelt resented his going to work for Taft in 1911. Certainly in 1912 a strange episode suggested something of the kind. When the Bull Moose campaign was at last openly under way, Stimson, as a member of the Taft Cabinet, decided not to join Roosevelt. He felt obliged to make a speech in Chicago explaining his position. And with his usual scrupulousness in personal relations, he sent the relevant passage in his speech to Roosevelt, with an almost agonized letter:

> I am a poor hand at keeping quiet and balancing on a fence. But I feel very much as if the horizon of my little world was swimming a good deal and it is hard to look forward to a time when I am not working or thinking with you.

He received a bluff profession of untroubled friendship, beginning: "Dear Harry: Heavens' sake!" But in fact Roosevelt did not forgive. For the next three years the two men did not meet. In his memoirs Stimson used emotionally charged language to say how glad he was that eventually "a new common cause brought them together, and when the Colonel died, in 1919, Stimson lost a friend as close as the one he had lost in 1912."*

On Active Service, p. 52.

• • •

Stimson found the life of a Secretary of War pleasant. He moved into the old Shoreham Hotel at Fifteenth and H Streets, and every morning a black trooper from Fort Myer would bring over a Tennessee gaited horse chosen for its sedate manners by his predecessor, Judge Dickinson. Wishing for a more adventurous mount, Stimson would ride in Potomac Park or Rock Creek between six and seven in the morning. Almost the only other horseman out at that hour was a little man perched on a big horse. It was General Charles Francis Adams, grandson of one President, great-grandson of another, and a Civil War officer. Stimson would ride up alongside him, and Adams would say in his gruff voice, "Stimson, do you know any other man in Washington at the age of seventy-eight who is such a fool as to ride at this hour in mid-winter?"

After a time the Stimsons rented a house on Sixteenth Street, but the ritual of his morning ride continued, after which he would walk down the street and across Lafayette Park to the State, War and Navy building next to the White House with his Airedale terrier, Punch, who would spend the morning under his desk. When he went across the road to confer with President Taft, who did not like dogs, Punch would come too, and was supposed to be looked after by the reporters; but Punch knew his way to the President's room, and could not be kept away.*

The surface of life went on in Taft's Washington much as it had gone since the time of General Adams' grandfather. But under the surface the world was changing fast. There was political tension in the air as the Progressive Movement challenged both major parties, and as Roosevelt prepared to challenge Taft. The War Office was a specially tense place.

After the Civil War, the U.S. Army had retreated into peacetime obscurity so profound that the period has been called the army's "Dark Ages." But scholars have pointed out that this was also a period of great military creativity.† Abruptly driven back on the humdrum problems of the profession after the years of glory, American career officers in the last third of the nineteenth century laid the foundations on which it was possible to build the vastly expanded armies of 1917–18

*HLS, *My Vacations,* pp. 124–30, 144–45.
†See Samuel P. Huntington, *The Soldier and the State,* pp. 229–61.

and 1942–45. This was the period which saw the founding of the Engineer School (1866), the Artillery School (revived in 1868), the infantry and cavalry school at Fort Leavenworth (1881) and finally the Army War College (1901). Nevertheless, as the twentieth century approached, the old army that had patrolled the frontier and fought the Indian wars was all but obsolete in the world of Prussian militarism, British and French imperialism, and the United States as a major power.

Some of the army's internal troubles sprang from the rigid division between the staff corps and the general list of army officers of the line. While the line officers served in dusty forts in the West, the staff officers lived in some style in Washington and enjoyed a monopoly of promotions and power through their carefully cultivated relations with congressmen.

In the War Department, as earlier in the law and later in the State Department, Henry Stimson followed in the footsteps of Elihu Root, who had become Secretary of War in 1899. Root had led a partially successful fight against the staff corps system; in 1901, at his urging, Congress broke the staff corps' monopoly by legislating that officers from the line must be sent on four-year details to the corps, thus ending the privileged isolation of the staff corps. Impressed both by German military professionalism and by the writing of an American admirer of German methods, Spencer Wilkinson, Root set about introducing reforms, embodied in the General Staff Act of 1903, which reflected his thinking on these abstruse but important issues of military hierarchy. Abolishing the traditional direct-command relationship between the President, as Commander in Chief, and the Commanding General, the act substituted a system in which the President's command authority would be "exercised by or in the name of the Secretary of War, through a Chief of Staff." At the same time the chief of staff was given wider powers of supervision over the bureaus. As Stimson put it, Root struck the first blow in a campaign to end forever the grip on American military policy of armchair generals who had never commanded troops.* And as Stimson saw it, his chief task as Root's successor, ten years later, was to finish that job.

The two schools of military thought were personified in two officers, both of them, as it happened, former army doctors. The chief of staff, a man after Root's heart who was to become one of the objects

On Active Service, p. 33.

of Stimson's admiration, was Major General Leonard Wood, old Indian fighter and commander of the Rough Riders, as much an advocate of vigorous national self-assertion as his friend and singlesticks sparring partner Teddy Roosevelt.

The opposition was embodied in the adjutant general, Major General Fred C. Ainsworth, a master bureaucrat as much at home in the corridors and lobbies of Capitol Hill as Wood was fighting Comanches. Wood was determined to assert his authority, Ainsworth as determined to resist it. The confrontation came, as it so often does, on an obscure technical issue: Wood's proposal, supported by Stimson, that the bimonthly muster roll be supplanted by a more modern administrative system. Ainsworth rejected Wood's proposal in a memo that spoke of "incompetent amateurs." It was, Stimson decided, "so grossly insubordinate that as soon as he read it Stimson realized that the time for drastic action had come."*

The first person he consulted was the Judge Advocate General, General Enoch Crowder, who advised that General Ainsworth could be punished either by administrative action or by court martial, and recommended the former course as less explosive. No, said Stimson, he meant to bring him before a court martial. He consulted Taft, who said in his good-humored way, "Stimson, it has fallen to you to do a dirty job which your predecessors ought to have done." And he consulted one of those predecessors, Root, who said in his less easygoing fashion that "when a man pulls your nose there is nothing to be done but to hit him."†

Stimson called Ainsworth's bluff, and Ainsworth elected to retire rather than stand trial. Stimson learned of the news at a Cabinet meeting. The President asked him if this was acceptable. Stimson telephoned Root at the Senate and asked whether he should accept the retirement. "By all means," said Root. "Best possible result." The President came back into the room and said Ainsworth would retire but would not apologize. Stimson said he would waive the apology.

Stimson's victory was decisive in part because Ainsworth's supporters were demoralized by their leader's willingness to surrender. It also reveals a characteristic style with which Stimson was to handle himself in political fights for another third of a century. He was ada-

*Ibid., pp. 33–37.
†Ibid., p. 35.

mant on the point of principle, touchy on the point of honor, tactically flexible, but with a shrewd sense of who was going to come out of a confrontation looking best.

The Ainsworth fight did make trouble for Stimson on Capitol Hill, where the fallen hero still had powerful friends, and Stimson and Wood had to fight for the reforms they wanted and for their appropriations. But there were compensations. One lay in the fact that the Secretary of War was, in effect, America's colonial secretary. Stimson found himself responsible for the Panama Canal and for the Philippines, and so laid the basic foundations of his understanding of foreign policy and strategy in the empire-building tradition of Roosevelt and Root, of Leonard Wood and George W. Goethals. He traveled in the Caribbean, where he visited Cuba and Santo Domingo.

The travel he enjoyed most, though, was in his beloved West.* Stimson responded to the masculinity and companionship of Wood, who "gloried in courage and fitness," and to the reputation of his own aide, Captain Frank McCoy, who had killed the Moro leader Dato Ali in Mindanao with his own hands. He was delighted to make friends with young men like McCoy, who became his aide in the Philippines and a lifelong friend, and George S. Patton, then the boldest follower of the Upperville foxhounds in the Virginian Hunt Country and later celebrated for chasing bigger game. He was proud when he could match these military heroes in some of their own trials of strength. At Fort Sam Houston, in San Antonio, he insisted on galloping over the jumps with the cavalry, and he took a Springfield rifle from a trooper on the firing range and hit a disappearing silhouette target at long range. Best of all, out with McCoy and an Apache scout named Chow Big, he recognized the tracks of a grizzly and knew how to make the Indian sign for bear.

"The Secretary," said Chow Big, "he good scout," and thirty-seven years later the Secretary recorded proudly that at that moment, "I had won my spurs in the southwest!"

In 1912 came the break with Theodore Roosevelt. It was characteristic of Stimson that, although he idolized Roosevelt, he felt that, having eaten President Taft's political bread, he could not desert him. And it was characteristic of Roosevelt that, although he pretended to find Stimson's behavior correct and admirable, in his heart he regarded

---

*HLS, *My Vacations,* pp. 124–44.

it as ungrateful betrayal by a man he had thought of as one of his own. The episode also reveals another difference between Stimson and Roosevelt. Stimson was adventurous enough physically, happy to jump all the fences and hunt all the bears in creation, but politically he was cautious. Roosevelt, on the other hand, brought to his political campaigns all the dash and bombast of his outdoor exploits. Where Stimson watched the men he had to deal with carefully before making up his mind, Roosevelt hardly seemed to look before he leaped, taking it for granted that every man's eyes would be on him. In retrospect it seems likely that Stimson would not have got on as well with Theodore Roosevelt as he was to do with his cousin Franklin. But he regretted all his life that he never got a chance to try.

Stimson's unsuccessful campaign for governor of New York in 1910 was not the last of his ventures into state politics. In 1915 he played one of the leading parts in a drama of some lasting significance: the New York constitutional convention.*

The movement for constitutional reform, or "reorganization," as it came to be called, sprang from many sources. One was the frustration that reform-minded Republicans felt at the long domination of the state's affairs by the legislature, itself dominated by the Republican machine, inherited from Roscoe Conkling by Thomas Platt, who operated it with imperial authority from 49 Broadway for twenty years until his death in 1910. Another was the growing feeling that with the expanding complexity of government and the rapid increase in its budget, it was time for more effective power to be given to the executive. And a third was the resentment of the Democrats at their exclusion from the previous convention in 1894 and in particular at the way the resulting apportionment favored the Republicans. But in 1912, with the Republicans split by Roosevelt, the Democrats captured both the statehouse and the legislature, and immediately took action to move up the date of the convention.

The election of delegates, however, was a disappointment for the Democrats; 116 Republicans were elected, and only 52 of their stalwarts. The Republican delegates, moreover, were men of impressive quality. They included men like Taft's Attorney General, George Wickersham;

*See Thomas Schick, *The New York State Constitutional Convention of 1915 and the Modern State Governor;* also *On Active Service,* pp. 56–78.

the presidents of both Columbia and Cornell universities, Seth Low and Jacob Gould Schurman; and Elihu Root and Henry L. Stimson.

After his defeat for the governorship in 1910, Stimson had read widely and thought hard about state government. His central theme was what he called "responsible government." Responsibility, he said, could not be divorced from authority. "Irresponsibility was a direct result of scattered authority and divided power; fear of too much government had led to untrustworthy government." Elected officials must have "more power, not less—only so could they be held accountable for success or failure." In January 1911, in a McKinley Day speech in Cleveland, Ohio, he expounded his practical conclusions. State government should be reorganized in such a way as to strengthen the chief executive. Governors should be given a longer term, say four years; they should choose their own cabinets, and should be free to remove them, as was the President of the United States; and they should be expected to produce their own legislative program, which would have priority over other measures.

Some time in 1913, it seems, Stimson won Root over to his way of thinking about the need for reorganization, and in the event Stimson and Root came to work as a team, but now with Stimson as the moving spirit and Root, in a reversal of their longstanding relationship, as the lieutenant. There were three measures, in particular, that had long been advocated by the supporters of reorganization and that Stimson and Root were determined to get the convention to pass. One was the consolidation of the dozens of boards, commissions and other administrative agencies created by the legislature into a small number of agencies over which the governor could exercise control. The second was the "short ballot," meaning that the number of elected officials should be drastically reduced so as to weaken the hold of the machine and give power over the few offices that mattered to the voters. And the third was the introduction of an executive budget, necessary not only for executive control but also for reasons of efficiency now that the State of New York was spending close to a hundred million dollars a year.*

At the convention, the executive budget amendment passed easily. The most intense debate was on the short ballot, on which Elihu Root, speaking with a passion and an emotional eloquence that were

---

*$94 million in 1915, up from $24 million in 1901.

scarcely his usual style, carried the day. Altogether, Stimson and Root both had reason to be proud when the convention disbanded, on September 10, having approved a new constitution by the clear vote of 118 to 33. The Empire State, as Charles Wickersham put it, was the first to deal "intelligently, scientifically and courageously with this vast, complicated, inartistic, unscientific, expensive, wasteful system of government which has grown up in our midst."*

Up to this point Root and Stimson had every reason to congratulate one another on the skill with which they had managed the convention. Now reorganization had passed with flying colors. All that remained was to secure ratification by the voters on Election Day, November 2. One leading reorganizer guessed the new constitution would carry by 50,000 votes. Stimson himself wrote that "the chances of the constitution are rapidly improving with every day. I think it will carry, and very likely by a much larger vote than we expect."

He was wrong. The voters of New York rejected the constitution by more than two to one: 910,462 to 400,423. The detailed reasons for this stunning defeat are perhaps less important here than the light it throws on Stimson's attitude toward politics and toward mass democracy. In terms of what they would have called statecraft, Root, Stimson and their friends had done their work well. The convention had been meticulously prepared, skillfully managed, and finally carried by assault after a well-prepared oratorical barrage. In political terms, the story was very different. Too little trouble had been taken to publicize the convention, so that one delegate complained that his neighbor in New Rochelle, "not a particularly unintelligent or uninformed man," had not the faintest idea that a convention was taking place.† This public-relations failure was exacerbated by the great events that were taking place simultaneously in the world: President Wilson, for example, had declined an invitation to address the convention because the *Lusitania* had just been sunk, and the New York City newspapers were more absorbed by the war in Europe than by the convention in Albany.

With all the publicity in the world, however, Stimson and the champions of reorganization, "responsible government" and strengthened executive authority would not have persuaded the voters unless they had paid more attention to the realities of New York politics. For

---

*Quoted in Schick, *op. cit.*, p. 100.
†Charles H. Young to Herbert Parsons, Herbert Parsons papers, quoted in Schick, *op. cit.*, p. 64.

one thing, they made a tactical error in insisting that the voters accept or reject the amended constitution as a whole, thus ensuring a coalition of minorities against their handiwork. And a coalition of minorities is just what they found arrayed against them. The opposition in the convention had come mostly from upstate conservatives, led by Edgar T. Brackett, and opposition of that kind was to be expected from some voters. The Democrats, on the other hand, went along with the amendments to the constitution at the convention because the one issue that mattered to them was reapportionment—to give New York City political representation in proportion to its growing population. When it came to the vote, Tammany Hall had every interest in blocking the constitution, in the hopes of getting a new convention with strengthened Democratic representation at which reapportionment would be on the table.

Organized labor, with considerable political influence in New York at the time, had a specific reason for opposing the new constitution. The State Federation of Labor had asked the convention for various safeguards for trade unions, notably for a guarantee that where armed forces were brought in to break a strike, strikers would not be subject to trial by military tribunals. This concern may well have been exaggerated. But the convention, dominated by conservatives, showed little or no concern with labor's fears, and labor punished that indifference by using its influence against the constitution.

Yet another source of opposition to the reorganization forces came from those Republicans who were suspicious of Elihu Root and of his presidential ambitions for 1916. In the circumstances, it was unwise to allow Root to make a stem-winding speech the day before the vote on the second amendment, which sounded all too much like the opening salvo of a presidential campaign.

It is fair to say that Stimson, Root and the reorganizers of 1915 were in many ways ahead of their time. What they created became to a considerable extent a model for reorganization in other states, and for the new constitution which New York finally adopted in 1926. Beginning with Illinois, the convention's historian records, "state after state adopted some form of consolidation, short ballot and executive budget."* By 1929 every state but Arkansas had the executive budget, and by 1938 twenty-six had consolidated their agencies and in most

---

*Schick, *op. cit.*, p. 134.

cases also introduced the short ballot. Even so, with a little more sensitivity Root and Stimson might have neutralized or weakened each of the different kinds of opposition to reorganization. It is clear that they underestimated the need to do so. To the extent that the reorganizers were concerned with modernizing the machinery of government and making its functioning more rational and more effective, there can be no doubt that the defeat of the constitution was a misfortune for New York. Yet considered as an episode in Henry Stimson's political life, it does highlight what were to be flaws in both his and his followers' political personalities: an instinct to brush aside the complexities of legislative politics as obsolete and self-interested, and a certain impatience with the tedious business of electoral democracy.

General Adams was not the only Civil War veteran with whom the youthful Secretary of War made friends in Washington. At dinners there, Stimson used to see Adams with Mr. Justice Oliver Wendell Holmes. After dinner was over, when the smoking began, he would listen to the old men refighting their war.

Many years later, Holmes asked Stimson to tea. To break the ice, Stimson said something that is very revealing about the motives for his own decision to volunteer for the First World War. He recalled how he used to turn "green with envy" as he listened to Holmes and Adams reminiscing. "Now I have come to tell you that I have served in a bigger war than you have served in, and I am therefore as qualified to sit and swap yarns with you as you are with me."

The old judge roared with laughter, and said "Good man, good man, good man."*

In 1913, Stimson was forty-six. His party had split, Wilson had been elected, and there seemed no prospect of high political office for him in the foreseeable future. He was bored with the law. He had fallen in love with the army, and with soldiers. But the ultimate purpose of armies and soldiers is war, and of war he had no experience whatsoever.

The deficiency, however, was to be rather quickly made up. In 1914 Stimson's belligerent friend General Leonard Wood set up a camp at Plattsburg, New York, to train volunteers to eke out the pathetically

---

* My Vacations.

inadequate ranks of the regular army if war should come. Stimson's sympathies were with the Allies from the beginning of the war, and as it ground on, he became increasingly sure that the United States would have to become involved. He was appalled by the ferocity of German warmaking, and even more so by the ruthlessness of that Prussian statecraft which saw war as the ultimate justification of the almighty state. That philosophy, he believed, would have to be fought and beaten, and it was neither wise nor decent for the United States to count on others to fight it for her. "Into such a struggle," he said, "a man or a nation may well go with lofty faith and burning ardor."

Stimson visited Plattsburg in both 1914 and 1915, and in 1916 actually enrolled there. At the age of forty-eight he was proud that "he succeeded in shooting so well that the doctors, waiving both his age and his near-blindness in one eye, pronounced him fit for active service."*

The American declaration of war on April 6, 1917, found him on a speaking tour of the Middle West, the most isolationist section of the country, where he defined the issue as he saw it:

> America is not going to war with Germany merely because, as one of the accidents of the great struggle raging across the water, we have suffered an incidental injury [he meant German attacks on American shipping], gross and unbearable as that injury may be. It is because we realize that upon the battlefields of Europe there is at stake the future of the free institutions of the world.†

The moment war was declared, he threw himself into the not-so-easy task of getting into uniform, and not just into uniform, but into active service abroad. For this purpose he pulled strings shamelessly. Any ex-Secretary of War knows a lot of generals, but generals as a rule are not prepared to do favors for just any of their former political masters, so Stimson's success may be taken as an expression of the esteem in which he was held by the military. First he got a commission in the Judge Advocate General's department through the good offices of his friend General Enoch Crowder. Then he got himself assigned to the War College and spent a "strenuous summer" working in an office all day, getting up and drilling first thing in the morning, and then

---

*HLS, *My Vacations*. The sight defect seems to have been caused by a shooting accident out West when he was young.
†*On Active Service*, p. 89.

studying all evening. He got his name onto the list of officers for the artillery—his chosen branch of the service—only to have it removed personally by President Wilson's Secretary of War, Newton D. Baker, who explained somewhat insultingly, in a personal interview which Stimson demanded, that he did not want a lot of political generals like those in the Civil War. By chance, or perhaps, as children say, "by accident on purpose," as Stimson left Baker's office after a somewhat abrasive encounter, the door to the office of the chief of staff, Major General Hugh Scott, was open. He was a congenial spirit, "an old friend and fellow-lover of the West," and he promised to help. Through his intervention Stimson found himself, on the verge of his fiftieth birthday, training with the Seventy-seventh Field Artillery Regiment at Camp Upton, on Long Island, preparatory to going to France.*

In the event, he got there even before the Seventy-seventh, assigned to the school for general staff officers at Langres, in Burgundy. Before that, he was attached for a month in January–February to the British army's Fifty-first Highland Division, known to the Germans, for their kilts and their ferocity, as "the ladies from hell." The British officers, holding a sector they had just successfully defended in the battle of Cambrai, "had an attitude towards both bombing and shellfire which seemed to Stimson unreasonably casual." He found it "characteristic" that they took off their steel helmets just when they were needed. But "the Scots knew their trade." The Highlanders thought the sector of the line where they happened to be while Stimson was with them in the line "phenomenally quiet." But Stimson wrote back to his sister with satisfaction after five days in the trenches:

> I have seen the Boche popping his head up warily from his distant trench and seen him get hastily down again when our artillery was turned on him and I have flattened myself in turn against the front side of our trench when I heard the very unpleasant whistle of his approaching shell. . . .
>
> I have seen and felt real war now and been under more fire (little as it was) than many of the civil war "patriots" (GAR [Grand Army of the Republic] variety) to whom we have so long looked up.†

*On Active Service, p. 73.
†HLS, Papers, reel 50, pp. 363 ff.

The remark is revealing. Their father had fought in the Civil War, and men of Stimson's generation had spent almost fifty years, literally their whole lives, wondering how they would match up to the test of battle. Henry Stimson welcomed that test, and he passed it with flying colors. In July his battalion led the Seventy-seventh Regiment into the line with Colonel Stimson in temporary command.* "For the next three weeks," he confessed to his biographer, "he was wonderfully happy," because "the only thing worse than the fear that fills all battlefields is the fear of fear that fills the hearts of men who have not fought." His unit was only in the line for those three weeks, but in that time, he reckoned, "he saw enough of war and danger to be able to feel certain that he was a good soldier; this knowledge was important to him." For the rest of his life, he recorded with pleasure, " 'Colonel' was a title that his close friends often used," and it was one which gave him great pride.

In a longer passage in his memoirs he spelled out more fully his reasons for joining the army:

> . . . the basic one was that, after preaching preparedness for years and war for months, he could not in conscience remain a civilian. Though in some ways it might be quixotic for a man nearly fifty to become a soldier, it was the only way in which Stimson could feel comfortable in his mind. And of course it was also true that he had envied combat soldiers for many years; he realized that men like Justice Holmes and Gen. Charles F. Adams, whose Civil War reminiscences he often listened to in Washington, had known a part of life he wanted to know. For nearly twenty years he had felt a certain regret that he had not been free to go to the Spanish-American War, and this time he did not propose to be left behind.

Yankee boys from Phillips Academy, like the Flathead braves of the Continental Divide, dreamed their warrior dreams, especially if their fathers had fought at Petersburg. The modern history of the United States, after all, is so short. A single life spans the interval between Grant's Peninsular Campaign, in which Dr. Stimson fought and from which Henry Stimson derived his nostalgia for battle, and

*On Active Service, pp. 91–100.

the somber culmination of Hiroshima. Stimson had his fill of military virtue and military glory. He lived to see both of them devalued, by a mysterious transformation that he himself was one of the first to comprehend, at the end of his life: In one and the same moment the nuclear transformation conferred power and took away the possibility of using it—just as nature has ordained that if a bee stings, it dies.

III

The Latin Experience: The Thorn Tree at Tipitapa

On May 4, 1927, Henry Stimson sat down on the banks of the Tipitapa River in the remote Central American republic of Nicaragua to negotiate the surrender of a wild bandit army with a certain General José Maria Moncada. To escape the intense heat, they sat under the shade of a large blackthorn tree. The contrast between the two men could hardly have been greater. Stimson was a private citizen and the very model of the successful New York lawyer of his day, impeccably correct, invincibly conservative. Moncada was a backwoods schoolteacher turned banana-republic general with unusually loose morals even for that easygoing world. He called himself a liberal; but some of his followers were little short of revolutionaries and some little better than bandits. In a few hours' talk, Stimson persuaded Moncada and his ragged soldiers to turn in their arms. The meeting was a turning point for both men. In under two years, General Moncada, who had not previously been even the acknowledged leader of his own Liberal Party, became president of Nicaragua. Also in under two years, Henry Stimson, a fifty-nine-year-old lawyer in private practice who had not held public office for thirteen years, was sworn in as Secretary of State. The events that led to that meeting under the thorn tree of Tipitapa composed the first lesson in the postgraduate education of Henry Stimson: the southern chapter.

In the fall of 1911, on his way home from a tour of inspection of the western army posts as Secretary of War with his friends General Leonard Wood and Captain Frank McCoy, Henry Stimson stopped for a few hours in El Paso and crossed the Rio Grande to Juárez, "where the recent heavy fighting had taken place the preceding spring, resulting in the killing of a number of Americans in El Paso by stray bullets."*

That is the only contemporary reference in Stimson's diary to an event of incalculably great long-term significance for the United States: the Mexican Revolution. Between 1910 and 1920 Mexico underwent an extraordinary convulsion, sometimes heroic, sometimes comical, often brutal and always chaotic. It was, as the Mexican painter Miguel Covarrubias has written, "a sort of musical comedy nation, where browbeaten peons periodically rose in revolt against their Spanish grandee masters, and were led by bandit generals with magnificent mustachios and oily complexions, whose ruthless and sanguinary exterior concealed a patriotic heart of gold."† It was at the same time something more serious; the birth pangs of a modern nation, the painful initiation rites of a people growing up after the long enforced immaturity of colonial rule and postcolonial sloth.

The fighting in Juárez in May 1911 marked the fall of the dictator Porfirio Díaz and the opening of this struggle.‡ Like the reformist ministers of the last years of the tsarist empire, Díaz had impressed

---

*My Vacations.
†Miguel Covarrubias, Mexico South: The Isthmus of Tehuantepec, pp. xxi–xxii.
‡For this sketch of the Mexican Revolution I have drawn on a number of standard works, especially Peter Calvert, Mexico; Hubert Herring, A History of Latin America, pp. 299–375; Howard F. Cline, Mexico: Revolution to Evolution; Anita Brenner, The Wind that Swept Mexico.

foreigners with the progress he had made in modernizing his ram-
shackle domain. Public order was imposed, if necessary with some brutality. The currency was reorganized, and the national finances were
tidied up. Railroads and government offices and a magnificent opera
house were built. Yet this was a mere façade, or rather a shining crust
over stagnant and in certain respects poisonous waters. The country
was getting richer, but it was still desperately poor. The contrast between the bustling streets and elegant avenues of the capital and the
dusty plains of the countryside was no greater than the gap between,
on the one side, a few hundred *hacendados* who each owned from fifty
thousand to a quarter of a million acres together with a few thousand
científicos, millionaire industrialists with fat bank balances, and on the
other the millions of landless, hungry peons who had no alternative
but to work for them. Under Porfirio Díaz, what was more, that gap
was getting wider. Emiliano Zapata is said to have been driven to rebellion when he observed how much better housed were his master's
racehorses than his peons. It was a land divided racially, too, between
the few who were of European descent and the great majority who
were of mixed Indian and European or pure Indian descent. It was a
land where the hold of the Roman Catholic Church was deep but the
hold of pre-Columbian culture and religion even deeper. Finally, Mexico had been—before, during and ever since the Spanish conquest—one
of the most unpredictably but savagely violent societies on earth.*

Abruptly, in 1910, the year when Díaz celebrated the hundredth
anniversary of Mexican independence and his own eightieth birthday,
violence exploded in political upheaval. *Los de abajo,*† "those down
below," the landless peons of the southern provinces, rose without
warning under their leader Zapata. The next year Díaz fled to Paris
and was replaced by the idealistic but unworldly Francisco Madero.
Two years later a new dictator, Victoriano Huerta, took over. Madero
was shot by his guards, while *not* trying to escape.

This is not the place to trace the story of the Mexican Revolution.
Its plot is as complicated as a three-volume novel and as bloodstained
as a Kung-fu movie. But its course was a fiction that faithfully imitated
the reality of Mexican society. On the surface, politicians who looked
like the pieces on the chessboard of European politics made their moves
and countermoves: cynical men of the world like Porfirio Díaz, ideal-

*To this day Mexico has one of the highest murder rates in the world.
†The phrase was used as the title of a 1916 novel by the Mexican doctor/novelist Mariano Azuela.

istic radicals like Francisco Madero, proto-fascist men of violence like
Victoriano Huerta, parliamentarians, bankers, foreign concession-
hunters, and the eternal lawyers. But the game they were playing was
not chess. Mexico was not European, still less North American. Under
the crust of imitation politics, imitation law and imitation business
there lived the Mexican people, in their authentic suffering. Most of
the time the peons were fatalistic, unaware of anything that happened
beyond the boundary stones of their boss's *hacienda*. Long-suffering is
the word. Then suddenly, under their farouche, bewhiskered leaders,
stoically noble like Emiliano Zapata or cunning and savage like Pancho
Villa, they caught fire, and their tiny armies, in which even the generals
were mounted on burros, armed with stolen rifles and the machetes
they had used to cut cane, set the dusty plains alight like a match in a
strawstack.

So Porfirio Díaz's successor, the dictator Huerta, was left to cope
with his enemies in every quarter of the land: in the south Zapata, in
the north Pancho Villa, in the northeast Venustiano Carranza and in
the northwest Álvaro Obregón. From the jungles of Yucatan to the
deserts of Sonora, men fought, burned and killed, and their leaders
bargained, looted, crossed over and double-crossed.

The Rio Grande, across which those stray bullets had trespassed a
few weeks before Henry Stimson visited in 1911, marks the only frontier
the United States shares with a Third World country. To an American
like Stimson, born in the late nineteenth century, Mexico could hardly
have been a more exotic or distasteful place; a land of dirt, poverty,
violence and Roman Catholicism, a land unblessed by thrift, progress,
Puritan morals, democratic institutions or what William James called
the religion of healthy-mindedness.

Yet it was never likely that the United States would be able to
keep entirely clear of so chaotic an upheaval on her southern border.
For one thing, American business had become heavily involved in
Mexican investments and especially in Mexican oil. Petroleum production boomed at an exponential rate in the first fifth of the century,
from 10,000 barrels a year in 1901 to 13 million barrels in 1911 and almost
9200 million barrels by 1921.

In 1914, in characteristically moralistic fashion, Woodrow Wilson
helped to inflame the revolution south of the border. The United
States had imposed an arms embargo on Mexico. Wilson lifted it, and
thereby left Huerta naked to his enemies. That same spring Wilson

landed Marines at Tampico, and then when two of them were arrested, he sent the U.S. fleet to Vera Cruz. Two years later, in March 1916, when the fierce Pancho Villa invaded New Mexico, the President sent a lumbering column under General John J. Pershing, soon to be the national hero in World War I, to chase him back across the border.

There was nothing unprecedented or surprising about such punitive expeditions or operations to show the flag. Between 1898 and 1920, U.S. Marines or soldiers entered the territory of Caribbean and Central American states on twenty separate occasions.* After the war of 1898 with Spain, Cuba had been occupied for four years, then governed under the Platt Amendment by a species of "indirect rule" of the kind the British used to control princely states in India. This document, which the Americans insisted should be actually incorporated in the Cuban constitution, limited the power of the Cuban government to contract treaties or to borrow money, promised naval stations on Cuban soil to the United States, and contained a clause that baldly proclaimed, "Cuba consents that the United States may exercise the right to intervene for the preservation of Cuban independence, the maintenance of a government adequate for the protection of life, property and individual liberty."† On different occasions in the first quarter of the twentieth century, U.S. forces also landed and remained for varying periods in Haiti, Santo Domingo, Panama, Honduras, and Nicaragua.

While Mexico was undergoing a radical upheaval from the bottom up, in fact, the United States was both becoming more active in the Caribbean and Central America, and also staking bolder theoretical claims. Under Theodore Roosevelt the United States built the Panama Canal, appropriated a strip of land on either side of the waterway and asserted virtually sovereign rights there. Roosevelt justified this practice with a theory called the "Roosevelt corollary to the Monroe Doctrine." The argument went like this: Under the Monroe Doctrine, European powers were to be excluded from the Western Hemisphere. Unfortunately Central and South American governments were only too likely to behave in such ways that European powers had money

---

*Capt. Harry A. Ellsworth, *One Hundred Eighty Landings of U.S. Marines, 1800–1934,* 2 vols., mimeograph, Library of the U.S. Dept. of the Navy.
†The Platt Amendment, probably written by Elihu Root, was introduced by Senator Thomas C. Platt of New York and was enacted by Congress February 27 and March 1, 1899. A text is printed in Henry F. Guggenheim, *The United States and Cuba,* p. 58.

claims against them. The Europeans could vindicate these claims only by seizing territory. But only the United States was allowed to seize territory in the Western Hemisphere. It followed that, as TR put it to the Senate, "the United States then becomes a party in interest." Because the Monroe Doctrine, in other words, forbade European powers to collect debts or secure justice in the region, Roosevelt believed that it followed as a logical corollary, or obvious consequence, that the United States was entitled to intervene wherever and whenever it felt intervention was desirable.

It did so on various grounds. At first, one reason was to forestall interference by a European power, which might be either Britain, Germany or even France. As late as 1916, it was argued that Marines had to be sent to Santo Domingo for fear that otherwise some meddling European power might take advantage of chaos there. After the First World War, there was little fear of that.

Sometimes the Marines went in to protect the lives of American and other foreign nationals. (After 1918 most European governments were happy to let Washington perform this service on their behalf, though the British, with colonies throughout the Caribbean and with British Honduras and various trading interests elsewhere on the mainland of Central America, sometimes liked to send a warship of their own for old times' sake.) Sometimes they were there to protect local property, such as mines, coffee, banana and sugar plantations and other businesses. Sometimes it was a question of protecting loans made to the government or the collection of the customs dues on which the loans were secured. And then the Panama Canal itself became an additional argument for U.S. intervention. The point was powerfully urged—by Stimson when he was Secretary of War, among others—that it was imperative to prevent the canal's falling into hostile hands. Not until much later was it suggested that the United States had a general, strategic right to control what happened in its Central American "backyard," though some such assumption could well be inferred from the way Washington actually behaved in the region.

In this whole changing, dangerous world of Latin nationalism and rebellion and of growing *Yanqui* economic and military assertiveness, Henry Stimson took no part.

Yet this is strange. For Stimson was an intimate associate of the very men who had taken the lead in the new American imperialism in the Caribbean. His admired friend General Leonard Wood had been the American proconsul in Cuba after the Spanish-American War. The Platt Amendment was largely written by his partner and role model Elihu Root. And the hero of the Cuban expedition, the man who boasted, "I took the Canal Zone and let Congress debate," the author of the corollary in whose name the Marines were dispatched hither and thither, was the man Stimson idolized before all others, Theodore Roosevelt.

The explanation, no doubt, was simple; Stimson was otherwise preoccupied. Be that as it may, it was not until 1926 that the very first Latin American brief, so to speak, came his way. It could hardly have been more remote, in every sense of the word. But the client, this time, was the President of the United States.

From 1913, when he left the War Department, until 1926 Stimson scarcely mentions Latin American affairs in his diary and was certainly never involved there in any public or private capacity.

From 1913 until 1917, he was busy with the private practice of law, with New York state politics, and with the campaign for military preparedness. After his eighteen months in the army in France, he returned to the law, though now with less enthusiasm, his partners noticed.

Although it was well over a decade—what with war, politics and public office—since Stimson had practiced law, it did not take him long to re-establish his reputation and his practice. He was retained, in quick succession, in three important actions.* In the first, he represented the Cement Manufacturers Protective Association, which was prosecuted by the government under the Sherman Act. The cement-makers, said the government, used their association as a "gigantic scheme" for concerting action. Not so, argued Stimson. They were the victims of the public tendency, in a time of inflation, to look around for scapegoats. After his usual meticulous preparation, he came into court armed with elaborate charts showing the industry's production, finance and pricing. His arguments were good enough to overcome the presumptions raised by the cement industry's curious habit of always allowing Lehigh Cement to announce price changes and then gradually falling in behind it. The jury split seven to five in his

*See *On Active Service*, pp. 107–10; Morison, *Turmoil and Tradition*, pp. 253–66; HLS, *Diaries*, vol. vi, though these are unusually skimpy on this period.

favor. A year later, on this same record, the government brought a civil suit, and a judge ordered the association dissolved. (That order, in turn, was finally overthrown by the Supreme Court in 1925.)

Before then, Stimson had become involved in the celebrated Southmayd will case. Emily Southmayd was a wealthy old lady who in 1911 made a will leaving $150,000 to each of several nephews and nieces. In 1915, when her brother died, leaving $900,000 to be divided among them, Miss Southmayd made a new will without bequests to her nephews and nieces, to which in 1919 she added a codicil leaving $30,000 to her executor, Allen W. Evarts. When Miss Southmayd herself died in 1921 at the age of ninety-three, some of the nieces and a nephew disputed this second will on the grounds that she was "not of testamentary capacity" and that she was unduly influenced by Evarts. The law holds, as Stimson established in a preliminary memorandum, that provided a person demonstrates clarity of mind in relation to the nature of the act of bequest, the amount and character of the property to be bequeathed, and the identity of the potential beneficiaries, no amount of eccentricity in other respects may invalidate the will. Stimson's tactics were to admit, indeed bring copious evidence to prove Miss Southmayd's eccentricity. She disliked the telephone and central heating. She feared dogs and even cats. She burned her clothes and personal possessions, and liked to wash dollar bills. Very well. But she also understood her investments and business affairs, and wrote intelligent letters to her lawyer about how she wanted them managed and how she planned to dispose of her assets after her death. With remarkable single-mindedness, having prepared that position, Stimson stuck to it. He did not even bother to listen to his opponent's closing speech, for fear it might tempt him to depart from his plan; and he won. Much of the effectiveness of Stimson's method as an advocate came from his persistence. He gradually built up in the jury's mind that *his* version of the truth could be trusted.

The third major case was very different; in a way, it reverted to the sort of work Stimson had done for the cement-makers, except that now his clients were bituminous coal operators. There had been national shortages of coal, caused in part by bitter strikes in 1919 and 1922. President Harding had set up a United States Coal Commission, and Stimson's brief was to act as counsel for the coal industry and to prepare a report for submission to the commission. Stimson accepted in December 1922 on the understanding that his clients wanted "a constructive solution for all.'' In the voluminous briefs he submitted to the commission he argued that the bituminous coal industry would be stable and prosperous were it not for ''abnormal conditions and artificial obstructions'': the war, government interference, and above all the United Mine Workers. Stimson described the UMW in strong terms: as ''an arrogant minority—challenging the American Republic . . . by its attempt to fasten an irresponsible class supergovernment upon American political institutions.'' He chose to focus on Herrin, Illinois, a town where strikebreakers hired by the South Illinois Coal Company had been murdered by UMW gunmen. The Coal Commission did not wholly accept Stimson's argument, finding that the Herrin massacre was caused by a climate in the industry for which Stimson's clients were largely responsible. Stimson was outraged by what he saw as the undemocratic violence of the union, and also by the double standard applied by ''self-proclaimed 'liberals' '' who were quick enough to complain of force by the owners. But he seems to have felt that he had gone a little too far, to judge from a letter to his old friend George Wharton Pepper, in which he admitted that his friends might think he had become ''a hard-boiled old reactionary,'' and defended himself by saying that he had to make a lot of the Herrin massacre so as to keep his clients united, so that he could get them to accept ''progressive and constructive'' policies.*

The truth was that, although Stimson was not altogether enchanted with the practice of the law, and certainly liked to think that his cases related to public policy, he wanted to win them. His determination, as well as his perspicacity in thinking through his courtroom strategy and his passion for preparing his cases, made him one of the leading trial lawyers in New York within less than five years of his return to practice.

His practice brought him in a large income: on average, about $50,000 in the 1920s, whereas he had made some $20,000 a year before the war. (Winthrop, Stimson was, consciously, a gentlemanly firm where the partners did not work long hours and never interrupted their weekend sports and diversions. At certain other Wall Street firms partners earned many times more money.) Now Henry Stimson be-

---

*Letter to George Wharton Pepper, August 2, 1923, quoted in Morison, *Turmoil and Tradition*. A concise version of the Coal Commission's five-volume report is contained in *What the Coal Commission Found*, Baltimore, 1925. Paul M. Angle, *Bloody Williamson: A Chapter in American Lawlessness*, contains a fair-minded account of the Herrin disturbances and their causes.

came for the first time, in his own estimation, a rich man. This was
the result not only of his success at the bar, but of the benevolent
operation of the laws of capital and compound interest. In the 1890s a
wealthy patient of Dr. Stimson's, instead of paying his fee, had paid
the equivalent amount of money into a bank account in his name. The
doctor, treating it as capital and therefore untouchable, left it intact
until he died in 1917. It, and Stimson's other capital, was managed by
Stimson's cousin, Alfred L. Loomis, who had left the law firm to
become a partner in a firm of stockbrokers, Bonbright and Company.
One is reminded of the description given by Winston Churchill, at the
end of *My Early Life,* of how he handed over £10,000 he had earned
by an American lecture tour to Sir Ernest Cassel with a telegram reading, " 'Feed my flock.' He fed the sheep with great prudence. They
did not multiply fast, but they fattened steadily, and none of them
ever died." Alfred L. Loomis, too, was a good shepherd.

In the 1920s Stimson was in his fifties. He rode regularly, and
hunted birds, both over his own ground at Highhold and in South
Carolina, where he was a member of the Yeaman's Hall Club at St.
Stephen's. On a brief vacation there in 1931 he wrote in his diary, "Not
a thing had changed in the five years since I was here last. The same
old Negro servants were there ready to comfort you and make you
comfortable."*

Stimson used his new affluence to make himself comfortable, not
in the pursuit of stylish social ostentation. Mabel and he moved from
a rather cramped apartment on Lexington Avenue to a brownstone on
East Thirty-sixth Street. Both there and at Highhold, decor and diet
were comfortable rather than elegant. The drawing room at Highhold
was decorated with family portraits in paint and in photographs, and
with bound sets of the classics, opened, it was suspected, more often
by Mabel than by her husband. "At dinner there were things like clear
soup, roasts of beef and lamb, jellies and, often enough, ice cream and
chocolate cake. At tea there were cinnamon toast and little frosted
cakes. The people who cooked and served these meals had, ordinarily,
been in the house for years."† Stimson was a hospitable, but autocratic, host, capable of shaming even Felix Frankfurter onto a horse.
One of his joys was the annual Highhold Games, when the neighbors
came over to celebrate Thanksgiving. Squire Stimson would inaugurate

*Diary, December 30, 1931.
†Morison, *Turmoil and Tradition,* p. 195.

the proceedings by firing off his double-barreled shotgun. A Brooklyn newspaper reported how the festival went in 1910; the formula did not change until the second war:

> There was a barrel of new sweet cider on tap; there were any quantity of cigars much too good to use for campaign purposes, and any quantity of soda water, ginger pop, etc., for the ladies and little ones. There were sandwiches and cream cake, with cream from the Stimson dairy, and other kinds of cake and fruit in abundance.
>
> The sports began at 11 a.m. and consisted of clay pigeon shooting, riding across country after the anise bag, foot races, jumping contests and other sports, with suitable prizes to the winners. The straight-a-way race, in which the rider after going over the course had to dismount, put on a night shirt and open an umbrella, was the laugh producer of the day. . . .
>
> One of the most interested of the spectators was Col. Theodore Roosevelt, who came on foot from Oyster Bay, . . . wearing a broad-brimmed hat, leggings and walking clothes which showed much usage. . . .
>
> This annual fete at the hands of Mr. and Mrs. Stimson has endeared them greatly in the hearts of their neighbors. They look forward to this event just as eagerly as do children to their Christmas tree.*

Much as they entertained, and enjoyed entertaining, Mabel and Henry Stimson were probably happiest together pottering around their property, looking at the trees, the flower garden or the poultry, riding out together, or reading aloud to each other. He hated to be alone, and she made sure that he rarely was; but often he was alone with her, and one friend said that what they wanted most of all was "an open fire in their study with both doors locked."

In 1896 Stimson had done some adventurous rock-climbing in Switzerland which led to him being made, many years later, an honorary member of the Alpine Club of London; and until the war he and Mabel occasionally visited their beloved West. In the 1920s and 1930s, with the Stimsons' advancing age, their vacations became more stately. Sometimes they would go south to the Carolinas, sometimes north to the Maritime Provinces of Canada, in which case, if they

*Brooklyn Times, November 25, 1910.

traveled by sea, the Cadillac would follow on land. More often they went east, taking several young relatives in staterooms on carefully chosen liners and renting shooting lodges in the Highlands of Scotland from the likes of Mrs. Andrew Carnegie or the Duke of Sutherland only after meticulously checking the floor plans and the heating arrangements. But by that time Henry Stimson, trial lawyer with offices in Liberty Street, New York City, had been transformed into Colonel Stimson, statesman and public servant. The transformation began in one of the dustiest corners of the planet.

The story of the Tacna–Arica dispute sounds like something out of Voltaire's *Candide*, a parable of human stubbornness and folly. In 1879 the republics of Chile and Peru were sufficiently misguided as to fight what was rather grandiosely known as the War of the Pacific over the dusty towns and provinces of Tacna and Arica, between the Andes and the ocean in the far north of the one, the far south of the other country. The treaty that ended the conflict provided that Tacna and Arica should be governed by Chile for ten years and that their future should then be decided by a plebiscite. The trouble was that the two countries could not agree on the terms in which the plebiscite should be put to the voters of the two provinces. Negotiations broke down five times in the twenty-one years between 1893 and 1913. In 1922 the weary parties turned to President Harding an an arbitrator, and in 1925 a commission under General Pershing actually visited the area. Successive Secretaries of State, Charles Evans Hughes and Frank Kellogg, took up the tangled thread, and President Hoover finally won whatever glory was to be won from this ancient quarrel when Tacna went to Peru and Arica, not to Chile, but to Bolivia. In 1926, Stimson was asked to undertake an advisory brief for the State Department on the mediation process.*

Tacna–Arica was important in Stimson's life for two reasons. One was that the work he did on it left him with a lifelong conviction that— as he put it bluntly much later—"the notion of honest elections and plebiscites is not a fruitful one in most Latin American countries" unless those plebiscites and elections are "impartially" guided by an outside agency, meaning the United States.† And the second was that

*See *Foreign Relations of the United States*, 1926, vol. i, pp. 260–530.
†*On Active Service*, p. 110.

this dusty and futile dispute offered him, at an age when many successful corporation lawyers are looking forward to retirement, virtually his first responsibility in international affairs and absolutely his first opportunity as a diplomat. Within two years, he was to be Secretary of State.

The second break was not long in coming. On March 31, 1927, Stimson had just returned to his office in New York from a business trip to Philadelphia when he received a telephone call from Colonel Robert E. Olds, Assistant Secretary of State in charge of Latin American Affairs, asking whether he would undertake "a new mission of an important and emergent nature involving a trip of about one month." Stimson asked Olds whether it was political and was told, in effect, No, it is Nicaragua. He took the night train down to Washington, saw Olds and Secretary Kellogg in the morning, and lunched with President Coolidge at the White House.*

"I assume you want me to be your eyes and ears," Stimson said at the end of the meal.

"No," said Coolidge. "I want you to go somewhat further. If you find a chance to straighten the matter out, I want you to do so."

The next day Stimson told the White House he was free to leave in a week. He spent it, lawyerlike, in furiously reading up the brief. He devoured the State Department's papers on Nicaragua. He talked to anyone who could be found at short notice with special knowledge, from Elihu Root to Douglas Allen, the lobbyist for the "mahogany people," that is, the substantial American-owned lumber interests on the Atlantic coast of the country. Root suggested, as a "snap shot suggestion," inviting Mexico to supervise the next Nicaraguan election jointly with the U.S. Out of the question, said Kellogg the next morning.

On April 9, Mr. and Mrs. Stimson left for Central America from Brooklyn on board the S.S. *Aconcagua*. The first two days out were "cold and raw," but the weather improved and so did morale when on April 15, after lunching with a party of American officials in the Canal Zone, the Stimsons transferred to a 7,500-ton navy light cruiser, the *Trenton*, for the run up the Pacific coast of Central America. Their quarters were "comfortable," and the table "delicious," he noted;

*Stimon's first very full and lively account of his month in Nicaragua, starting with his account of this lunch with Coolidge, is contained in *Diaries*, vol. vii. He subsequently published another account in *American Policy in Nicaragua*, New York, 1927.

the voyage smooth and the moonlight memorable. Colonel Stimson was never unhappy to be back inside the certainties of naval and military order. On April 17 *Trenton* made Corinto, the chief Pacific coast port of Nicaragua, and the Stimsons went by special train to the capital, Managua. They traveled with a guard of Marines, and U.S. bluejackets could be seen at intervals guarding the track, with posts at bridges and the principal stations. These were not merely the honors due to an American proconsul. Nicaragua was in the grip of civil war.

If Mexico sometimes seems, even to Mexicans, a comic-opera country, Nicaragua at the beginning of the twentieth century was even harder to take seriously—for anyone who was not Nicaraguan, that is.* About the same size as Michigan, Wisconsin or Georgia, it had fewer than 650,000 people in the 1920s, more than half of whom were illiterate and fewer than 100,000 of whom were of European (that is, Spanish) descent. The national territory spreads like a fan, its short edge on the Pacific, the longer curve on the white sand beaches of the Caribbean; the west coast is more fertile and was a wealthy province of Spain with ancient cities whose origins date back even before the arrival of the *conquistadores*. Columbus himself explored the eastern, or "Mosquito," coast as early as 1502. But communications across the isthmus were so bad that even in the early twentieth century the Mosquito Coast, formerly under British protection, was a remote forest fringe, sparsely settled by Mosquito Indians and blacks of West Indian descent, many of whom spoke English until recently, and who were mainly occupied in cutting timber and exporting timber and fish to the United States. In the north, against the border with Honduras, the forested hills of the interior rose to form a rough barrier of mountain and jungle, long the refuge of bandits.

In the western coastal plain and around the great lakes of Nicaragua and Managua and below the mountain fringe around Matagalpa, Spanish, American and British planters owned coffee farms, or *fincas*. Most Nicaraguans were of Indian descent, owned no land, and worked

---

*Among the sources I found useful for the background to the Stimson mission and the subsequent political history of Nicaragua were: Rodolfo Cerdas, *La Hoz y el Machete;* Harold N. Denny, *Dollars for Bullets;* Richard Millett, *The Guardians of the Dynasty;* Dana G. Munro, *The United States and the Caribbean Area;* Gregorio Selser, *Sandino;* Bryce Wood, *The Making of the Good Neighbor Policy.* See also *Foreign Relations of the United States,* 1927, vol. iii.

for these foreign owners or for the descendants of Spanish landlords. In this microcosm, all the political passions of the twentieth century boiled as in a test tube. It might seem infinitely remote to most North Americans, but well-informed Americans knew that because of its geography, Nicaragua could not be forgotten entirely, as long as Americans had an interest in communicating between their Atlantic and Pacific coasts.

One of Stimson's rare comments on Latin American affairs when he was Secretary of War concerned the Panama Canal: The canal, he pointed out, shortened the maritime distance between the east and west coasts of the United States from 13,000 miles to 5,000 miles; the three months saved if a foreign fleet had to go round Cape Horn could make the difference between victory and disaster. "It is of vital importance to this country not only that the canal shall be open to *our* fleet in case of need, but that it shall be closed to the fleet of our enemy."*

Long before the canal was built, North Americans had been making similar calculations. In 1849, the year of the great California Gold Rush, with would-be miners dying of thirst in the Nevada desert or even reduced to cannibalism like the Donner Party, Commodore Cornelius Vanderbilt had his eye on an isthmian canal. By far the easiest route lay across Nicaragua; Vanderbilt obtained a charter for the Accessory Transit Company, which would use stagecoaches, lake and river steamers to cover the route. But the plan ran afoul of British interests established on the Mosquito Coast, and in 1850 the Clayton–Bulwer Treaty ordained that any future railway or canal across Nicaragua should be under joint United States–British control. The Nicaraguan government was not consulted.

For decades after the United Provinces of Central America, including Nicaragua, achieved their independence from Spain in 1821, "frank admiration" had been the predominant attitude of the Creole elites toward the United States. In Nicaragua, the elite were politically divided between the Conservative and Liberal parties. While, as the names suggest, the Conservatives were the party of the Church and of many big landowners, and the Liberals attracted anticlerical intellectuals and those sympathetic to nineteenth-century European liberal ideas, the party division also had a strong geographical logic. Each had

*Denny, *Dollars for Bullets,* p. 16.

its base in one of the two chief Spanish towns of the provinces that became Nicaragua: the Conservatives in Granada, the Liberals in León. There are those who say that the rivalry between the two cities goes back even before the Spanish conquest. It was in any case strong enough to cause the choice of the less historic and less attractive Managua as a compromise capital in 1857.

In 1855 the Californian "filibuster" William Walker, who was allied with both the Vanderbilt and Morgan interests, was invited to Nicaragua by the Liberals, routed the Conservatives, and became first the Master, then formally president of the country, recognized as such by U.S. President Franklin Pierce. Walker's precise motives are obscure, but it would seem that he dreamed of creating a great slave empire in the Caribbean allied to the American South. It is probable that among his supporters were some of the promoters and ideologues of nullification and secession. However that may be, he was overthrown in 1857 and eventually executed in 1860.

Walker's association with the Liberal party discredited it in Nicaragua for a generation. Until 1893 a more or less orderly succession of Conservative presidents followed one another in office. In that year a revolt by a dissident Conservative gave the Liberals their chance, and the Liberal José Santos Zelaya became President.

Zelaya was a tough, ruthless dictator, and he built up the Nicaraguan army to the point where he was not likely to be overthrown unless with the help of the United States. In the beginning, his relationship with Washington was good. This soon changed, however, with the U.S. decision to build the canal through Panama rather than Nicaragua, where the Nicaraguans had always assumed it would have to be. Zelaya canceled several American concessions and turned from Wall Street to a London syndicate for his next loan.

When revolution against his regime came in 1909, the United States openly supported the rebels. The real organizers were the Conservative leaders, but the nominal chief was General Estrada, governor of Bluefields, on the Mosquito Coast. Estrada was defeated by local government forces and had to take protection under Marine guns at Bluefields. When Zelaya sent troops against him, Estrada hired two American citizens (and one Frenchman) to blow up the troopships on the San Juan River. Zelaya imprisoned the Frenchman but executed the two Americans.

That gave the Taft administration the opportunity it wanted. In highly undiplomatic terms Secretary of State Philander Chase Knox came out against Zelaya. "The government of the United States is convinced," his note to the Nicaraguan government said, "that the revolution represents the ideals and the will of a majority of the Nicaraguan people more faithfully than does the Government of President Zelaya." President Taft and Secretary Knox, as *The New York Times*'s special correspondent Harold Denny later put it, "set about generally to run the country."

By the beginning of 1912, the moderate Conservative Adolfo Díaz, whom Washington supported, was President; negotiations were proceeding for a new loan from the New York bankers Brown Brothers and J. and W. Seligman*; and the United States was pressing for first the police, and then the army, to be put under American officers.

Liberal risings outside the capital were successful. President Díaz was compelled to call for American help, and in August 1912 the U.S. Marines landed at Corinto. The American force soon built up to 2,700 men, commanded by Marine Colonel Joseph Pendleton. At the Battle of Coyotepe, near Managua, the Marines easily routed the Liberal troops, and the Liberal commander, General Zeledon, was killed. Gradually the Marines withdrew, leaving only a hundred-man "legation guard" behind them, symbolic affirmation of American military power in Nicaragua and American willingness to use it. Its presence kept the minority Conservative party in power until 1925, and its removal in that year not surprisingly acted as an invitation to the Liberals to bid for power.

Between 1912 and 1925 American interests tightened their grip on Nicaragua's vulnerable economy. The main cash crops and export industries were almost all in the hands of American, British or German entrepreneurs, with the former out in front in terms of numbers and size of investments. The legendary United Fruit Company, "the Octopus," had few investments in Nicaragua. But another American firm, Standard Fruit, together with its wholly owned subsidiary the Bragman's Bluff Lumber Company, was worth $8 million in 1929. Cuyamel Fruit in Bluefields was American-owned, and so was the La Luz y Los Angeles gold mine. With the exception of the loan Zelaya had nego-

*Both banks transferred their interests to the Mercantile Bank of the Americas. In 1924, caught by the fall in sugar prices, which acted as security for many of its loans, the Mercantile Bank collapsed, and Guaranty Trust took the place of Brown Brothers as partners with J. and W. Seligman in financing the Nicaraguan government.

tiated in London, Nicaragua's public finance was wholly in American hands. New York bankers had first charge on the customs revenue and half of the government's income, and an American citizen was Collector of Customs. The National Bank of Nicaragua was incorporated in Connecticut, and its manager, L. G. Rosenthal, was an American and an ex-employee of Guaranty Trust. The Pacific Railroad of Nicaragua, owned by the National Bank, was managed by the J. G. White Company of New York City.

That was how American imperialism worked in the early twentieth century. As President Taft explained with superb candor, it was a system that aimed at "substituting dollars for bullets." Unfortunately, it did not altogether eliminate bullets.

Adolfo Díaz, the Conservative leader in the coup of 1912, was a mild-mannered gentleman whose benevolence beamed out from under his straw skimmer and from behind his wire-rimmed glasses. He was so pro-American that he not only did all he could to push for a new American loan to refund the London one, but actually cabled President Woodrow Wilson in 1914 asking for money and proposing as a *quid pro quo* that the Platt Amendment should be extended to Nicaragua. Even Elihu Root thought that was steep. He pointed out that "The present government with which we are making this treaty [it was in the end defeated in the U.S. Senate] is virtually maintained in office by the presence of U.S. Marines."* For Root, dollar diplomacy might be acceptable; the conflict of interest involved in Díaz asking to be paid to invite U.S. domination of the country of which he was President was too much.

Behind Adolfo Díaz in the Conservative ranks there stood the more military figure of Emiliano Chamorro. In 1924 Chamorro lost the election to the Liberals, led by Juan Bautista Sacasa, head of one of Nicaragua's oldest grandee families. Chamorro claimed he had been cheated. Still, in August 1925 the Marines finally withdrew, to be replaced by a "constabulary" trained by U.S. officers. In their absence peace in Nicaragua lasted just twenty-five days, ending in the finest *opera buffa* manner. A Conservative editor, waving two large pistols, gatecrashed a champagne reception at Managua's International Club. While timid members of Managua's elite cowered under the billiard tables, Conservative gunmen frog-marched Liberals to the door. The scene in contemporary descriptions has a certain Marx Brothers qual-

*Harold N. Denny, *Dollars for Bullets*, p. 130. Denny was *The New York Times*'s correspondent to Nicaragua at the time.

ity—one can imagine the gunmen slinking away, utterly discomfited by a rebuke from Margaret Dumont—but it must have been frightening enough at the time. Emiliano Chamorro was behind this comic-opera scene too. As a result of it, he became Commander-in-Chief, virtually dictator. But, in order for his power to be secure, he needed American recognition. And that he would not get.

The American minister, Charles Eberhardt, left Managua for Washington to avoid the hottest months of the summer of 1926. He left the legation in the hands of a *chargé d'affaires*, Lawrence Dennis, who was described by Harold Denny as a "hard, youngish man." (Less than a year later he was to go to work for J. and W. Seligman in New York. He had rather sinister political views; he wrote for the ultraconservative *American Mercury* and in 1936 published a book called *The Coming American Fascism,* not as a warning but as a welcome. Later still, Dennis was to be indicted with other American fascist sympathizers for conspiracy to commit sedition.) At that point, Dennis seemed no more than a brusquely dedicated supporter of constitutionalism. He would regularly call up General Chamorro and say, "Good morning, General, now how about that resignation of yours?" After the explosion at the other end of the line subsided he would say, "But you know you'll have to do it eventually. Better do it now!"*

In May a new civil war broke out. This time it was the Liberals who landed at Bluefields; two American adventurers and one German were killed fighting for the Conservatives. Two freelance American pilots, working for the Conservative cause and for a wage of $500 a month, bombed the Liberal positions in Managua. So little do things change in Nicaragua!

In October 1926, in the continued absence of Minister Eberhardt, Dennis called a conference on board the U.S. cruiser *Denver* at Corinto and proceeded to make Adolfo Díaz President of Nicaragua. On November 14 he was inaugurated. (One of his first acts was to send Emiliano Chamorro off as ambassador to Britain, France, Spain and Italy all at once!) So now Nicaragua had two Presidents: the Liberal, Juan Bautista Sacasa, duly elected and then pushed aside by Chamorro; and Adolfo Díaz, imposed in place of Chamorro by the U.S. legation. Worse, the Conservative incumbent was backed by the United States, the Liberal by Mexico.

Sacasa, in a long career in Nicaraguan politics never notable for

*Denny, *op. cit.,* p. 222.

personal courage, established himself at Puerto Cabezas, on the Mosquito Coast, with General Moncada and an army of some three thousand straw-hatted soldiers as his military protection, their weapons and ammunition coming from Mexico. And at the end of the year, Mexico formally recognized Sacasa when the United States recognized Adolfo Díaz as President. The tangled affairs of Nicaragua were now getting mixed up in the conflict between the United States and the Mexican revolution.

The State Department, after World War II, justly or unjustly acquired a reputation for liberalism. It had no such reputation in the 1920s, least of all where Latin America was concerned. It treated Mexico, in particular, under Presidents Obregón (1920–24) and Plutarco Elías Calles (1924–28) with deep suspicion. One major cause of this was oil. Article 27 of the revolutionary Mexican Constitution of 1917 vested in the Mexican nation all oil and mineral rights. If Article 27 was to be interpreted retroactively, then all foreign investments in Mexican oil and mining, including copper, would be confiscated. The prudent Obregón refused to commit himself on this crucial point of interpretation, and the Harding administration therefore withheld recognition of his government, demanding that Obregón affirm that United States interests would not suffer. This Obregón regarded as an insult to Mexican sovereignty, and he refused. After two years of deteriorating relationships, the Mexican Supreme Court in 1923 fortunately held that Article 27 was not retroactive, and so averted a crisis.

President Calles, however, was both more radical and less cautious than Obregón. He liked to be seen as the "heir of Zapata." He favored the retroactive interpretation of Article 27, and in December 1925 the Mexican Congress, at his instigation, declared that the oil companies would have to exchange their holdings for fifty-year concessions. He also proposed agrarian legislation that alarmed American landowners in Mexico, who included the newspaper magnate William Randolph Hearst, owner of some 300,000 acres in Chihuahua. Calles also found himself in a tense confrontation with the Church. Each of these components of his policy meant trouble in the United States. American Catholic organizations such as the Knights of Columbus held protest meetings and raised money for Calles's opponents. The Hearst newspapers denounced him and printed documents purporting to show that the Mexican President had bribed American supporters, including four senators. The oil industry was the most influential of all. The principal American oil interests in Mexico (competing with the Mexican Eagle company owned by the Englishman Weetman Pearson, later Lord Cowdray) were Sinclair and Doheny, the same two companies that were compromised in the Teapot Dome bribery scandal of 1924, when it was shown that they had bribed Secretary of the Interior Albert B. Fall, who gave them valuable government-owned oil properties.

The State Department was extremely responsive to all these American interest groups. So too was the embassy in Mexico City. Ambassador James Sheffield was a stern upholder of American interests, and at times he sounded contemptuous, almost racist, in his remarks about Mexicans. In a letter to his friend William H. Taft, for example, he said that they "understand and respect only force." As for him, he said, "I have tried to be a red-blooded American south of the Rio Grande," and in that he certainly succeeded.*

In 1925 Secretary of State Kellogg protested the lack of protection accorded to American interests in Mexico. He added on the record that he had read in the press of another revolutionary movement coming forward in Mexico, and that he hoped this was not true. This kind of comment was of course blatant interference in internal Mexican affairs, and it was criticized in most American newspapers. Indeed, American public opinion was increasingly skeptical of the idea that the United States should engage in confrontation with Mexico and perhaps even resort to military force, all to protect a handful of American oil, mining and land companies and a few of the wealthiest men in America. The Supreme Court, upholding the conviction of Edward Doheny and Harry Sinclair in the winter of 1926–27 and the subsequent conviction and imprisonment of Albert B. Fall, reinforced this new mood.

In August 1927, recognizing the unpopularity of the hard line on Mexico, President Coolidge changed tack. He replaced the red-blooded Ambassador Sheffield with Dwight W. Morrow, a Morgan partner and a classmate of the President's at Amherst.† Morrow saw his task as heading the United States and Mexico off from a dangerous confron-

---

*James R. Sheffield, letter to W. H. Taft, March 27, 1927, quoted in Robert H. Ferrell, "Frank B. Kellogg," in *The American Secretaries of State and Their Diplomacy,* vol. xi, pp. 31, 32.
†Morrow was the father of the poet Anne Morrow Lindbergh, mother of the baby taken in the famous kidnapping (1932).

tation. His skillful diplomacy marked the beginning of a new period of greater sensitivity in relations between the United States and its neighbors to the south and an approach which Franklin D. Roosevelt later called the Good Neighbor Policy. As a Wall Street banker, Morrow was known to Stimson, and they were friendly. Later, Morrow was to work with Stimson when the latter was Secretary of State.

The Morrow mission was still in the future when Henry and Mabel Stimson rode the train from Corinto to Managua in the spring of 1927, but the ideas that led to Coolidge's change of policy toward Mexico was very much part of the background to Stimson's mission to Nicaragua. The Nicaraguan crisis cannot be understood except in the context of American responses to the revolution in Mexico.

Before American policy softened, it hardened for a while. Conscious that defending Sinclair and Doheny was unpopular with American voters, President Coolidge and his State Department had started denouncing the Mexican government as the exporter of Marxist revolution to Central America, a charge which, they believed, would be a more acceptable criticism of the neighbor to the south than that it was opposed to U.S. business interests. On November 17, 1926, Assistant Secretary of State Olds briefed the Associated Press to this effect; specifically, he told the wire-service reporter, the Mexican government was "seeking to establish a Bolshevik authority in Nicaragua to drive a 'hostile wedge' between the U.S. and the Panama Canal."*

In making this claim, Olds committed a major blunder. Senator George Norris of Nebraska moved for an investigation into his statement and was defeated only by five votes to eight in the Senate Foreign Relations Committee. Others charged that Olds was trying to justify war with Mexico over oil. Senator William E. Borah charged the "oil interests" with trying to get the United States into a "shameless, cowardly little war with Mexico."

Yet Olds was not discouraged. On January 2, 1927, he wrote a confidential memo arguing that the Mexican involvement in the Nicaraguan crisis was

> a direct challenge to the United States. . . . We must decide whether we shall tolerate the interference of [Mexico] in Central American affairs or insist upon our dominant position. . . . Until now Central America has always understood that governments which we recognize and support stay in power, while

*Denny, *op. cit.*, p. 243.

those which we do not recognize and support fail. Nicaragua has become a test case. It is difficult to see how we can afford to be defeated.

That was blunt enough. Coolidge at first intended to follow this line, which was also that of other powerful figures in the State Department—Secretary of State Kellogg and Under Secretary Joseph Grew (later ambassador to Japan).

On January 10 he sent a message to Congress stating that crisis conditions in Nicaragua "seriously threaten American lives and property" and in general interpreting developments there as a mere episode in a larger crisis vis-à-vis Mexico. Noting that arms had been shipped to the Nicaraguan "revolutionists," as he called the Liberals, he pointed out that Sacasa had used Mexico as a base to raise his standard at Puerto Cabezas, and that he had been promptly recognized by Mexico. "It has always been and remains the policy of the United States," the message concluded ominously, "to take the steps that may be necessary. . . . In this respect I propose to follow the path of my predecessors."*

For a couple of weeks, Coolidge's message set off a scare that the administration was indeed planning war with Mexico. The reaction from Congress, the churches, the newspapers, and European and Latin American opinion was all but unanimous: the Republicans must put away Teddy Roosevelt's Big Stick, which seemed to be wielded only on behalf of such greedy and unappealing figures as Sinclair, Doheny and Hearst. The President and his conservative allies were taken aback by the breadth and indignation of the opposition, and decided it was time to back off.

One of the more powerful opposition voices was again that of Senator Borah, chairman of the Senate Foreign Relations Committee. In February he suggested that the entire committee should visit Nicaragua to see for itself how matters stood. The very thought must have been a nightmare to Coolidge. Preposterous as Borah's suggestion was, it may have been the seed of the President's decision to send the sagacious and reliable Colonel Stimson.

S̲o far as ignorance could free it from prejudices and commitments," Stimson said later, "my mind was a clean slate." In other

*Denny, *op. cit.*, pp. 250 ff.

respects, his disqualifications were impressive. He had never been in Nicaragua or indeed in Central America. He did not speak a word of Spanish. When he did try to say two or three sentences in Spanish by way of a toast, he wrote the words out in phonetic spelling on a scrap of paper which survives: *Amigos, brindo por una paz pronta, husta y henerosa.** (My friends, I toast a prompt, just and generous peace.) The imagination boggles at how this actually came out, because we know that Stimson stubbornly mispronounced the name of the country as "Nic-a-rag-yew-a," in place of the liquid native pronunciation.

What is more, Stimson was not to be relied on to avoid heavy-handed racist humor, which must have made him sound like the most pompous of *sahibs* lecturing the natives. In a talk with the Nicaraguan foreign minister, Dr. Cuadro Pasos, for example, he "said jokingly Nicaraguans ought to play more football, baseball etc."† Dr. Cuadro Pasos "referred to the role of the umpire," and Colonel Stimson "remarked jokingly that the players at times tried to kill the umpire." Again a couple of days later he "urged the necessity of better sportsmanship" to a delegation from Granada, "giving the analogy of baseball and cockfights [*sic*]."‡

This was not conventional diplomacy or even common tact. But Colonel Stimson brought to Nicaragua three qualities more valuable than those he seemed to lack: a lawyer's trained intellect, which enabled him to grasp the realities and the possibilities of the situation with remarkable speed; a man of the world's shrewd understanding of what the various parties might be prepared to settle for; and unmistakably disinterested integrity within the limits of his patriotic Americanism.

At breakfast with the minister, Eberhardt, on the third day of his visit, he suggested there were strategically three alternatives. The first was "an indefinite succession of sanguinary revolutions." That was to be avoided at all costs. The second was "what I would term barren or naked American intervention." That, too, was undesirable and to be avoided if possible. The desirable third alternative was "constructive American intervention which would endeavor to lead the country nearer to self-government." That meant many things. Certainly, as Stimson planned his campaign, it meant that the United States must

*I.e., *justa y generosa*.
†HLS., *Diary*, April 17, 1927.
‡*Ibid.*, April 19, 1927.

supervise the Nicaraguan elections in 1928 and perhaps for some time after that.

There were to be three stages to the negotiations which Stimson now conducted. First, he had to deal with the Conservatives, reassuring them that Washington would stand by its recognition of Adolfo Díaz. It also meant making them see that they could not simply count on the Americans to take their side, but must make compromises. Second, he must see whether Sacasa and the various factions of Liberal politicians could be brought to accept an agreement that would leave Díaz as President. Third, he had to agree on terms with the Liberal armies in the field and with their chief leader, General Moncada.

Getting the Conservatives on board was the easiest part. Even Stimson, when he met them on their ground, was surprised how willing they were to put everything in American hands. After an expedition on the lake to Granada, which he found a "much higher class city than Managua," he jotted in his diary: "All Conservatives, wealthy, dreadfully frightened of Liberal success. Fairly turned on me for US intervention"—he means, demanded it—"wanted us not only to give military protection but to run their finances in absolute US control. Were very frank in admitting Nicaraguan incompetence and corruption."*

In short, the Nicaraguans of 1927 anticipated all those other elites, from the Philippines by way of Vietnam to Iran, not to mention other parts of Latin America, who during the next fifty years chose to count on the United States to protect their pleasant and privileged way of life, rather than share their power with their fellow countrymen.

After negotiating with Adolfo Díaz through the foreign minister, Cuadro Pasos, Stimson was able to write by the fifth day, "got Díaz in writing on terms agreed with Cuadra [*sic*] Pasos": an immediate peace, with both sides surrendering their arms into American custody, followed by a general amnesty; Liberal participation in the Díaz Cabinet; the organization of a Nicaraguan constabulary under American officers, with in the meantime enough Marines staying in the country to keep the peace; and American supervision of the Nicaraguan elections in 1928 and succeeding years. The same conditions were cabled to Sacasa in Puerto Cabezas. "Then," Stimson wrote that night, "I felt we had accomplished something."

*HLS, *Diary*, April 23, 1927.

That was April 22. For the next few days, while he waited for Sacasa's answer, Stimson, who had been interviewing at a furious pace, could slack off a little and enjoy a dove shoot with Marine General Logan Feland, hero of the battle of Belleau Wood in World War I, who was commanding the Marine brigade in Nicaragua, and a visit to U.S. Admiral Latimer's "very attractive den in a beautiful garden on edge of lake."

On April 29 the delegation from Sacasa finally arrived. (Since, as Stimson reported to the State Department, "the country is full of armed men . . . rapidly approaching anarchy," the Liberals were sped round through the Panama Canal by the U.S. cruiser *Tulsa*.) Their temper was more amenable than Stimson expected. At a "very hilarious and jovial" lunch, Stimson made a speech saying that there were two pleasant surprises: one was to find that the Liberals exhibited no anti-American feeling, and the other was the unanimous agreement that "the root of Nicaragua's political evils lay in government control of elections." This was Stimson's pet theory. Since whoever was in power controlled the outcome of elections, he argued, the losers were left with no option but armed rebellion. Only outside intervention could break the cycle of revolution and revenge. The theory was a good enough observation on what had been happening in Central America. In the short term, American intervention might be the only way out. But Stimson for once did not look far enough ahead. He did not grasp that American intervention would in time become part of the system. Those who wanted reform and were denied it by the beneficiaries of American aid would sooner or later have to make the United States the target of their revolution.

A couple of days after the pleasant lunch with the Sacasa delegates, Colonel Stimson enjoyed his first meeting with a "very frank, friendly, likeable young liberal" whose attitude "impresses me more favorably than almost any other."* The name of this rising Liberal hope was Anastasio Somoza Garcia. Stimson was so impressed with his fluent English that, it appears, he took young Somoza with him as his interpreter for a few days.

What quickly became clear was that Sacasa's delegates wanted a deal but did not want to commit themselves to one until they knew what General Moncada had to say. Moncada was the key. It was plain,

---

*Diary, vol. vii, p. 99–102, memorandum of conversation with Anastasio Somoza, morning of May 3, 1927.

too, that he was not merely a general subordinate to the civilian authority of Dr. Sacasa, but an independent player in the political game, and one with high ambitions of his own. On May 3 he agreed to meet Stimson, and they met—as we have seen—the next day on the Tipitapa River, between the Lake of Nicaragua and the Lake of Managua. Five hundred Marines lined the river, a summer trickle in its parched bed, when General Moncada arrived the next morning and disappeared into a dingy inn to be briefed on the preliminary negotiations. When he emerged after a quarter of an hour, Sacasa's delegates faded into the background.

Then General Moncada and Colonel Stimson sat down to talk, man to man and soldier to soldier, on the riverbank under the thorn tree. In the background were the well-fed, spick-and-span Marines, newly armed with the Thompson submachine gun. All around the wild soldiers of the Nicaraguan revolution sprawled in the shade: wiry, undernourished men in straw hats with ancient rifles who had nevertheless shown that they could fight with desperate courage. They were led by a mixed bag of "generals," some city-bred politicians on horseback, some backcountry Indian and *mestizo* rebels, some, to North American eyes at least, indistinguishable from bandit chiefs. The condition of Moncada's army can be judged from the fact that before the negotiations were over their general had successfully obtained for them pants, shirts, rice, flour, beans, coffee, sugar and salt.

Moncada was ready to allow his men to be disarmed by the Marines, he said. It was agreed that American forces would be interposed along the line of the Tipitapa and would collect arms from both sides. What Moncada could not accept was the retention of Adolfo Díaz as President. Men had died for that, Moncada said; therefore it was an issue of honor, and not negotiable.

Stimson records laconically in his diary that he "gave Moncada a letter explaining the point about Díaz so General Moncada could explain it to his men." He makes it sound so easy—a miracle of negotiating skill. The truth was that Stimson understood that he had the ace of trumps in his hand. He also knew that because Moncada understood the point perfectly, he would not need to play it. Stimson had superior force: in pure numbers, Moncada had two or three thousand men, roughly the same strength as the Marines, but the Marines were incomparably better armed, with heavy and light machine guns, artillery and even bomber aircraft. They were also better trained and better led. Moncada knew that his men would stand no chance at all in a pitched battle with such forces; he also knew that if he simply ordered his men to accept Díaz as President and hand over their arms to his American backers, they would see him as a traitor who was selling out the revolution.

Nor would they have been entirely wrong. One of the factors in the situation, which Stimson did not have the background or perhaps the imaginative sympathy to understand, was that however conventional the Liberal leaders and however scrappy the Liberal generals, the Liberal party and Moncada's army were nonetheless the only hope of change for the *campesinos,* the hungry and angry who had been effectually excluded from all political power by the play of party politics in Managua. Stimson was too discreet to mention it, but what he was offering Moncada was what that cynic wanted: his turn in the political square dance. And he eventually got it. On January 1, 1929, José Maria Moncada was inaugurated President of Nicaragua.

Moncada, in other words, needed to be threatened so that he could come in, and he needed to let his followers know that he had been threatened. That was the function of the letter which Stimson dictated under the blackthorn tree.

Tipitapa, May 4, 1927

Dear General Moncada,

Confirming our conversation of this morning, I have the honour to inform you that I am authorized to say that the President of the United States intends to accept the invitation of the Nicaraguan government to supervise the election of 1928: that the retention of President Díaz is essential to that plan and will be insisted upon: that a general disarmament of the country is also regarded as necessary for the proper and successful conduct of such an election; and the forces of the United States will be authorized to accept the custody of the arms of those willing to lay them down, including the government, and to disarm forcibly those who will not do so.

Very respectfully,

Henry L. Stimson

The last sentence, Stimson subsequently explained, was added "not as a threat to Moncada's organized and loyal troops . . . but as

a warning to the bandit fringe.'' That was not, however, Admiral Latimer's understanding, as he testified to the Senate Foreign Relations
Committee the following February. This tough old officer, known in
the navy as Rosie Poker Face, was asked by Senator Swanson:

> Did you understand, and did General Moncada understand from
> the statement made by Mr. Stimson that if he did not acquiesce
> in the continuance of Mr. Díaz until an election was held, force
> would be used to disarm him and compel him to acquiesce?
> ADMIRAL LATIMER: Yes.
> SENATOR SWANSON: You understood that and so did he?
> ADMIRAL LATIMER: Yes.

A week after their first meeting, Stimson sat down for a second
time with General Moncada under the thorn tree. Stimson transmitted
to the Liberal general the Díaz government's willingness to pay $10 for
every weapon handed in. (The Nicaraguan treasury being empty, the
money was to come from a loan of $1 million helpfully arranged by
Seligman's and the Guaranty Trust.) That night Moncada and his
troops entered Managua, where they were treated as heroes, and so
treated themselves, though the wine shops were closed as a precaution.
Moncada and his officers, it seems, neither handed in all their personal
weapons nor denied themselves the warrior's traditional repose. ''They
set up in a hotel,'' one eyewitness reported, ''as if they had conquered,
while the Indian servant girls giggled and whispered at their pistols.''*

On May 15 Stimson felt justified in cabling the State Department
in triumphal language. ''The civil war in Nicaragua is now definitely
ended,'' it began. There also seemed ''less danger of banditry and
guerrilla warfare than I at first feared. . . . Almost the only malcon-
tents are the extremely small group of personal associates of Sacasa who
through their well-organized press bureaux in Mexico, Costa Rica,
Guatemala and the United States have sought to convey an entirely
false impression of the situation.''†

It certainly seemed a remarkable feat of mediation and diplomacy. Stimson had been given less than ten days to brief himself about

*See Denny, *Dollars for Bullets*, pp. 298–311.
†HLS, *Diary*, vol. vii, p. 179, text of letter sent by HLS to Under Secretary (R. E. Olds), May 15,
1927.

Nicaragua. He then spent less than a calendar month in the country. Yet by masterly diplomacy, direct yet tactful, all parties seemed to have been brought to accept American supervision of Nicaraguan democracy for the foreseeable future. Nor was this an isolated episode in American foreign policy. Stimson's achievement, anticipating that of his friend Dwight Morrow in Mexico, was to make possible a new era in American relations with the Latin American republics. The Peace of Tipitapa, as the historian of President Franklin Roosevelt's Good Neighbor Policy toward Latin America put it, was a turning point.* It was the start of thirty years in which the United States refrained from using arms in Latin America for whatever reason.

Yet a closer look surely compels a more critical judgment. The skill with which Stimson handled the negotiations was impressive, yet his success depended to a great extent on the presence of superior American military force and the administration's willingness in the last resort to use it. It was not really even true that the civil war in Nicaragua was over, only that it was moving into a different and in some ways more ominous phase. The very day that he sent his victory cable to the State Department, Stimson recorded in his diary the "sad news" of a "bandit" attack at La Paz Centro in which "our men accounted for 14 of the bandits." The next day, Mr. and Mrs. Stimson left Corinto on their voyage home. (Stimson played with the idea of visiting Sacasa at Puerto Cabezas but was apparently rather easily talked out of it by Admiral Latimer.) That same day Captain Richard B. Buchanan and Private Marvin A. Jackson of the United States Marine Corps were killed when guerrillas attacked a Marine post near León.

More important, Stimson seriously underestimated the only one of Moncada's generals who had not accepted the cease-fire: Augusto Calderón Sandino.† Immediately after the peace of Tipitapa, even this most resolute of the guerrilla commanders seems to have flirted with the idea of giving in, and in what is thought to be, but may not be, a genuine letter to Moncada he said he would disarm his forces. But instead, he rode north with his men—only sixty of whom were said to have rifles—into the wild mountains of the department of Nueva Segovia, near the Honduran border, and on July 16 attacked a mixed garrison of Marines and the new Nicaraguan constabulary, the Guardia Nacional, at Ocotal, capital of Nueva Segovia. He was driven off with

*Wood, *The Making of the Good Neighbor Policy.*
†Gregorio Selser, in *Sandino,* gives his middle name as "Calderón"; others give "César."

heavy losses, thanks largely to the Marine aviation forces. Sandino learned his lesson, and for the next six years, by adopting classic guerrilla tactics, made himself a thorn in the flesh to the Marines, the Guardia, and the Nicaraguan government. In 1934 he was betrayed and murdered on the orders of Stimson's "frank, friendly, likeable" young friend Anastasio Somoza.

It suited the Marines to call Sandino a "bandit," and Stimson accepted their classification. General Feland showed him a memorandum written by an American engineer, John Willey, who owned a mine near Matagalpa, the chief town in Sandino's operating territory. Willey had seen Sandino and his force, and Stimson records reading his account with "great interest."

So why did Stimson make the mistake of thinking that it didn't matter if Sandino were left out of the deal with Moncada? It is hard to avoid the impression that there was an element of class consciousness in Stimson's evaluation. For him, General Moncada was an officer and a gentleman, even if one with a regrettable taste for "good wine and bad women."* Sandino was a man of the people, and therefore nothing better than a bandit.

After his death, Sandino became a hero to radicals, nationalists and anti-*gringo* intellectuals from the Rio Grande to Tierra del Fuego. In his own country he came to symbolize the struggle not only against the United States but against dictatorship and corruption of the kind that came equally to be associated with "Tacho" Somoza and his two sons. Sandino, the "hairy little warrior" with his "crazy little army,"† is seen as a hero, a martyr and a revolutionary pioneer. Today the ruling party of his country is called after him. All over Latin America, there are those who revere him as a cross between George Washington and Robin Hood.

The reality was different, but on the other hand, to dismiss Sandino as a bandit, with the implication that he was interested only in making money by robbery or blackmail, is totally to misunderstand how dangerous he was because of what he stood for. Sandino was not only interested in loot. The son of an Indian woman and a small coffee farmer, he went to work abroad, first in Honduras, then for United Fruit in Guatemala, and later at the Huasteca Petroleum Company, Doheny-owned, in Tampico, Mexico. He is said to have been anti-

*Selser, *Sandino,* quoting "a journalist," probably Denny.
†The title of an admiring study by Gregorio Selser: *"el pequeño ejército loco."*

American since as a boy he saw the body of the rebel commander Zeledón, shot at Coyotepe in the rising of 1912. However that may be, Sandino was certainly exposed to leftist ideas in the Mexico of Plutarco Elías Calles. Being half-Indian, he was excited by the way the Mexican Revolution was reviving the Indian roots of Mexico's history, giving the long-despised Indian peoples an honored place in Mexican society.

Sandino joined a labor union; he became a Freemason. And in 1926 he took his savings and offered his services to General Moncada. Moncada did not accept them. Sandinista legend relates what may be an apocryphal exchange:

> MONCADA: And who made you a general?
> SANDINO: My comrades in arms, señor. I owe my rank neither to traitors nor to invaders."*

Caramba!
Sandino himself wrote later that at the time of the Peace of Tip-itapa he spent three "wretched, depressed days" trying to make up his mind whether to join Moncada in surrendering his arms. "I . . . realized with bitterness that the Nicaraguan people had been swindled. . . . Finally I broke the chain of reasoning and decided to fight."

By May 21, five days after Henry Stimson sailed from Corinto as the pacifier, Moncada marched out against Sandino. First, though, the old cynic sent Sandino's father this message: "In this world, saviors end up on crosses, and the people are never grateful."

Sandino, in fact, was no sophisticated revolutionary, let alone a Marxist. He was, rather, an excellent example of what the British historian Eric Hobsbawm has called "primitive rebels," like the guerrillas of Spain or southern Italy in the nineteenth century, and like so many other brave and desperate people throughout history. Such rebels have no carefully worked out revolutionary program. They have their pride and their anger. By courageous, determined action they express the anger of the landless, impoverished masses and give them the courage to help themselves. In Sandino's case he had been exposed to revolutionary nationalist ideas in Mexico, in particular to the teaching of APRA, a group of revolutionary intellectuals which subsequently became the ruling party in Peru. Alive, he was Public Enemy Number

*Selser, *Sandino*, p. 72.

One to the settlement Stimson negotiated. Dead, he became the national hero.

When Sandino was a guerrilla fighting the Nicaraguan government, the State Department accused him of adopting "the stealthy and ruthless tactics which characterized the savages who fell upon American settlers in our country 150 years ago." Sandino did not have a monopoly of stealthy or ruthless tactics in the Nicaraguan civil wars; if that had been the case, he would not have met his death as he did. But the charge does reveal how little, for all its expertise, Washington understood about the underlying historical dynamics and the emotional climate of Latin American politics. For the *mestizo* Sandino had chosen the path of rebellion in part precisely because he identified, not with European conquerors, but with the "savages." Almost everywhere from Brazil north to the United States border, a greater or smaller proportion of the population is proud to be descended, in whole or in part, not from European "settlers" but from the "savages" they dispossessed and kept in peonage.

By any count, it was a disastrous mistake to underestimate Sandino as Stimson did, just as it was a catastrophic mistake to be taken in by Somoza. Stimson had read the personalities and politics of the gentlemen politicians of Managua. The only two men he got hopelessly wrong were the two who would define the political future of the country.

In 1929, the year when General Moncada succeeded to the presidency of Nicaragua, Colonel Stimson became Secretary of State. The Nicaraguan presidential election had been held successfully, without serious interference from the Sandinistas, but only because of the presence of 5,000 heavily armed U.S. Marines, not to mention 2,000 of Somoza's national guards. In July Sandino went into exile in Mexico, but before long he was back. By 1931 he had plunged the country into chaos again. He and his soldiers sacked Bragman's Bluff and massacred American and British employees of the lumber company there. The U.S. legation in Managua asked the navy to send a Special Service Squadron cruiser to Puerto Cabezas, and this was done. But Stimson complained that the navy had sent the ship and landed armed sailors without consulting him. The Secretary of State made it plain that he would approve such landings in the future "only when it was absolutely necessary" to save the lives of American and foreign people excluding property.

At a press conference on April 15, 1931, Stimson reflected aloud, "This administration will hesitate long before becoming involved in any general campaign of protecting with our forces American property throughout Nicaragua." The contrast with President Coolidge's message of January 1927, promising to follow the path of his predecessors by protecting both American life and American property, could not have been more plain.

Guerrilla activity reached a peak in the summer of 1931. Even with Marine air support, the Guardia were hard-pressed to contain the guerrillas; there was no question of suppressing them. In June 1932, General Matthews and other Americans in Nicaragua argued that fifty Marine officers should continue to serve with the Guardia after the new Nicaraguan and American presidents were inaugurated in the early months of 1933. Stimson would have none of it. He felt strongly that to prolong the Marine presence would convince many people both in the United States and in Latin America that the United States was trying to hang on to power over Nicaragua at any cost.*

His attitude made it possible for the incoming administration of Franklin D. Roosevelt to enter upon its Good Neighbor Policy with one embarrassment the less. But Stimson's change of heart had a more immediate, less happy effect. It removed the last remaining obstacle between Anastasio Somoza Garcia and the totalitarian power he and his family were to exercise for the next forty-five years.

It would be unjust to reproach Stimson with any significant fraction of responsibility for this outcome. He had gone to Nicaragua and decided that American military force might, by guaranteeing free and fair elections, help the Nicaraguans to govern themselves. Later, responsive to the rising opposition in Congress and the country to the use of American forces to prop up favored regimes in the Caribbean, he had changed his mind. The first course was honorable, the second prudent.

There was, though, something arrogant, even frivolous about

---

*An additional motive may have contributed to Stimson's change of attitude. When news of Stimson's appointment as Secretary of State broke, newspapers all over Latin America had denounced him as Coolidge's representative in Nicaragua. Given the dangerous situation in Mexico, he may have wanted to minimize his personal unpopularity south of the Rio Grande. See Pearson, *Washington Merry-Go-Round*, p. 104, for a characteristically highly colored but shrewd account.

Stimson's efforts to save the Nicaraguans from themselves. Those efforts were doomed—it is easy for us to see now—by his failure to recognize that the inevitable consequence of American involvement was that the conflict in Nicaragua must sooner or later be transformed. It would become not a confrontation between Conservatives and Liberals, but a conflict between a certain kind of fascism, established by the young man Stimson found so likeable, and a revolutionary movement whose leader Stimson found too insignificant to include in his settlement. As a consequence, the United States became the guarantor of one side in that conflict for the future of Nicaragua, and therefore the implacable enemy of the other.

In the Nicaraguan experience, in fact, there was evidence of a certain amateurism, and of that lack of imagination that can sometimes be more dangerous than any miscalculation. More important, Nicaragua illustrated the limitations of Stimson's foreign policy: carrying forward the instincts of Teddy Roosevelt into the age of Franklin Roosevelt, he willed the ends when he did not will the means. It was gratifying and profitable, that is, for the United States to play the imperial role in Central America. But where Teddy Roosevelt would have accepted the consequences and sent the Marines, his less aggressive disciple wanted a "liberal" imperialism, where the United States relied on local auxiliaries to maintain its supremacy. The apparently inconsequential episode that ended under the thorn tree at Tipitapa cast a long shadow over the future of American foreign policy, just as Henry Stimson, in his very first venture in foreign affairs, can be seen as a link between the unselfconscious expansionism of 1898 and the reluctant, self-doubting imperialism of the 1950s and 1960s.

IV

The Oriental Experience

The Philippines

Take up the White Man's burden—
  Send forth the best ye breed—
Go bind your sons to exile
  To serve your captives' need;
To wait in heavy harness
  On fluttered folk and wild—
Your new-caught, sullen peoples,
  Half devil and half child.

Rudyard Kipling, *The White Man's Burden*, 1899
The poem is subtitled "The United
States and the Philippine Islands"

In the summer of 1926 Henry and Mabel Stimson visited what they called "the Orient." It was, according to the fashion of those days of steamers and steamer trunks, a leisurely trip. It began with the overland train journey by Canadian Pacific from New York to Vancouver, with a stop for a little golf at Banff, in the Rockies, and then continued by ship, with "rather interesting company . . . an assortment of Yanks, British, Chinks and Japs,"* to Yokohama and Kobe before they sailed for Manila. In the Philippine Islands, as guests of the Governor General, the Stimsons made leisurely expeditions. Sailing to Cebu in the government yacht, Stimson's host found time to catch a large pom-

*HLS, *Diary.*

pano and Stimson a small barracuda. They visited the villages of the Moros, the Filipino Muslims, and put in at the exquisite bay of Zamboanga, nearest point of American territory to the island world of Joseph Conrad.

In the villages of Apa and Iloilo there were native dancers to be admired, though in contrast the Stimsons found the dancing of the "American *mestizo* girls" at the Manila Hotel "disagreeable." It was a relief to escape from the steamy, multiracial world of the capital to the cool, Anglo-Indian–style hill station at Baguio, in northern Luzon, where the Colonel played a little more golf. The return journey was even more leisurely, with stops at Hong Kong and Shanghai before a day's sightseeing at Kyoto, a city rich in centuries of art and the home of many emperors. In the strange workings of history, it may be that Henry Stimson was the most important visitor Kyoto ever had.

The Stimsons' luxurious progress around the westernized fringes of "the Orient" was a holiday of a kind that is not possible, even for wealthy New York corporation lawyers, in a world of jumbo jets, mass tourism and national sovereignty. Theirs was a *Madame Butterfly* world of hot nights and cool drinks, of submissive native houseboys and confident, red-faced white men bearing their distinctly agreeable burden in stiffly starched white ducks.*

Sightseeing, however, was not the purpose of Stimson's journey to the Philippines. He went at the invitation of the Governor General, none other than his old friend General Leonard Wood. Stimson's shrewd observations on his visit to the Islands, and the report of them that he made to President Coolidge at lunch in the White House, led directly to his being appointed Governor General in succession to Wood two years later, and indirectly to his becoming President Hoover's Secretary of State in early 1929. To be viceroy of America's oriental empire was a job that made everything possible. Wood went there from being a presidential candidate, and Taft went from there to the White House.

From 1898 until the "snap revolution"† that brought Corazón Aquino to power in 1986, it was axiomatic with most Americans that,

*Stimson's account of his 1926 visit is in HLS, *Diary*, vol. vi(a). He also gave his views on the Philippine situation in an article in *Foreign Affairs*, February 1927.
†James Fenton, *The Snap Revolution*, Cambridge, England, 1986.

whatever the United States was doing in the Philippines, it was not there as a mere imperialist power. This, however, was not necessarily so apparent to the Filipinos. Certainly many Filipinos of the political class greatly admired the United States. Many appreciated what Americans had done for the Islands. Yet they also resented American dominance and the behavior of many Americans. Similar mixed sentiments were common among *assimilés* in French Africa or among the "brown Englishmen" who prospered under the Raj. Colonel Stimson's future Assistant Secretary of State and intimate, Harvey Bundy,* visited the Islands on a world tour before World War II, and remarked on how much more easygoing the atmosphere was there than in British India, from which he had just come. But in the same breath Bundy quoted a little ditty that was popular among the Americans in Manila at the time:

> Damn, damn, damn the Filipino
> He may be a friend of William H. Taft
> But he ain't no friend of mine;
> Civilize him with a Krag!†

No wonder Manuel Quezon, of all the Filipino leaders the one most admiring of the United States, said that he would prefer "a government run like hell by Filipinos to one run like heaven by Americans."

The history of the United States presence in the Philippines up to the decision in 1933 to grant independence in ten years' time can be

---

*Young Bundy, unhappy as a schoolmaster at St. Mark's School, in Massachusetts, had accepted a fee of $3,000 to escort around the world a well-heeled but imprudent young Bostonian who had married an unsuitable young person at sixteen and then been divorced by nineteen. Of this fee he was able to save $2,000. H. H. Bundy, *Columbia Oral History Project*, pp. 27 ff.

†*Ibid.* But according to Stanley Karnow, in *In Our Image,* there were two separate ditties:

> Damn damn damn the Filipinos!
> Cut-throat khakiac *ladrones!*
> Underneath the starry flag,
> Civilize them with a Krag,
> And return us to our beloved home.

The other was:

> They say I've got brown brothers here,
> But still I draw the line.
> He may be a brother of Big Bill Taft,
> But he ain't no brother of mine.

The Krag-Jorgensen rifle was introduced into the U.S. Army, replacing the single-shot Springfield, in 1893. Michael, Lord Carver, *Twentieth Century Warriors,* p. 266.

divided into four periods. In the first, the Islands were Americanized, initially by force of arms and then by wise and generous policies. In the second, from 1913 until 1921, they were re-Filipinized. Then, from 1921 to 1929, under Republican administrations, an attempt was made to stabilize American sovereignty more or less permanently. Only with the onset of the Depression, after 1929, and the intensified pressures to eliminate both American expenditure on the Islands and any competition from Filipino products within the American tariff wall, did a Democratic Congress get around to promising eventual independence.*

The legislative history of the Jones Act of 1916 displays the American ambivalence about the idea of Philippine independence. When in 1912 Congressman William Atkinson Jones introduced a bill calling for complete independence by 1921, it failed to reach the floor of the House. When he reintroduced the bill with no set date for independence, but with a simple preamble to the effect that independence would be granted as soon as a "stable" government could be established, the Republicans killed it in the Senate. In 1916, Senator James F. Clarke's amendment promising full independence in between two and four years passed the Senate by a single vote, but the Democrats killed it in the House. Even so, the Jones bill did become law in 1916, and its preamble did promise to withdraw American sovereignty and to recognize the independence of the Philippines "as soon as a stable government can be established therein."

Congressman Francis Burton Harrison, Democrat of New York, was appointed Governor General by Woodrow Wilson in 1913. Wilson was committed in theory to "deprive" the United States of the Philippines. He sent his close colleague and friend Henry Ford Jones of Princeton to assess the Filipinos' capacity to govern themselves, and Jones reported favorably. Wilson then proposed that "step by step we should extend and perfect the system of self-government in the islands."

The question of how fast the Philippines should move to inde-

---

*For the background to Stimson's time in the Philippines, see Teodoro Agoncillo and Milagros C. Guerrero, *History of the Filipino People*; Renato Constantino, *A History of the Philippines*; Romito V. Cruz, *America's Colonial Desk in the Philippines*; Theodore Friend, *Between Two Empires*; Hermann Hagedorn, *Leonard Wood*, vol. ii; Philip Jessup, *Elihu Root*, vol. i, pp. 304–71; Stanley Karnow, *In Our Image: America's Empire in the Philippines*; Peter W. Stanley, "The Forgotten Philippines 1790–1946," in Ernest R. May and James C. Thomson, Jr., *American–East Asian Relations: A Survey*. I have been helped in my study of Philippine history by Dr. Peter Carey, of Trinity College, Oxford; any mistakes are, of course, my own.

pendence was not a simple party question; there rarely have been simple party questions in the United States Congress. Many southern Democrats had doubts about granting early independence, and some northern Democrats who were Catholics had been influenced by their bishops into taking a similar line. Still, it was a Republican administration that had taken the islands; the Republican President Taft had governed them, and the expansion of American power in the world was the policy of both the Taft and Roosevelt wings of the Republican Party.

And now Harrison arrived in Manila as the agent of a Democratic President who was committed to anticolonialism in principle and to early independence for the Philippines in particular. He shared Wilson's commitment, and he set to work with a will to do what he had been sent to do. He announced in his initial message on Wilson's behalf that the United States hoped to move toward Philippine independence "as rapidly as the safety and the permanent interests of the islands will permit."

Harrison swiftly made Filipinos the majority on the Commission, giving them full control over the legislature. He increased the number of Filipinos in the civil service and reduced the number of Americans, so that by 1919 he had transformed a government of Americans "assisted by Filipinos to a government of Filipinos aided by Americans." By the same date he had reduced the Governor General's control over the Cabinet to "matters of general policy," and the Cabinet had become in effect responsible to the legislature on the parliamentary model. He created a Council of State which "brought about a centralized Filipino leadership responsible to the electorate through the majority party." Sergio Osmeña, Speaker of the House, became vice chairman of the Council (the Governor General was Chairman *ex officio*) and so officially the second-highest official in the government.

The *políticos* who were the primary beneficiaries of this political Filipinization used their new power to create Filipino-owned economic institutions: a Philippine National Bank, the Manila railroad, a hotel, and several important sugar *centrales* and development companies. Both the Filipinization of the government and these economic ventures infuriated the American business community in the Islands, which mobilized to denounce Harrison and his policies. The attack was the more successful because while real progress was made in many respects under Harrison (for example in transport, irrigation and education), mismanagement and corruption were real too. By 1921, with Warren Gamaliel Harding in the White House, the Philippine treasury had been seriously depleted by graft, the Philippine National Bank was bankrupt, and the Philippine government was "on the brink of total economic and financial collapse."*

The problems were not in truth wholly the fault of Harrison's administration. Commodity prices, inflated by the World War, had broken sharply in mid-1920. The price of sugar, in particular, which had risen to astronomical heights during the "dance of millions," as it was called in Cuba, fell from 45 cents per pound in mid-1920 to less than 2 cents by the end of the year.†

Since many of the National Bank's loans were ultimately secured against the sugar crop, the most prudent managers in the world could hardly have averted trouble in these circumstances. Still, the American business community in Manila was so hostile to the Harrison administration that any stick was good enough to beat it with. Harding's Secretary of War, John W. Weeks, appointed a commission to visit the Philippines in 1921. Its members were both prominent Republicans who knew the Islands: a former Governor General, Cameron Forbes, and General Leonard Wood, once governor of Moros province and commander of the Philippine division. The commission's report was partisan, but devastating.

The Harrison administration was uncompromisingly criticized. Under Harrison's "incompetent direction," the report said, the quality of public service had deteriorated. Withdrawal from the Philippines would be "a betrayal of the Philippine people." It recommended formally that "the present general status of the Philippine Islands continue until the people have had time to absorb and thoroughly master the powers already in their hands." That came close to asserting that the Filipinos were unready, not merely for independence, but for the limited participation in government they had already achieved.

The second formal recommendation was that the Governor General should have "authority commensurate with the responsibilities of his position." If the Philippine legislature refused to act, then the United States Congress should nullify any Philippine legislation that "diminished, limited or divided" the authority conferred on the Governor General by the Jones Act.

*Agoncillo and Guerrero, *History of the Filipino People*.
†I am indebted to Dr. Laurence Whitehead of Nuffield College, Oxford, for this information.

Filipino historians have generally acknowledged that the Forbes-Wood report was a true bill as far as conditions under the Harrison administration were concerned, though Harrison continued to be held in high regard for his commitment to equality, Filipinization and independence. "That there were mistakes committed under the Harrison regime," wrote Maximo Kalaw in 1929, "the writer, a Filipino, will not deny. That there was more democracy in the Islands during that period than during any of the subsequent periods, no impartial observer can deny."*

What Filipinos objected to about the report was not its description of conditions, but the strong implication that those conditions demonstrated that they were not ready for self-government. That, however, was precisely the conclusion that was drawn in the Washington of "normalcy" and nationalism. President Harding appointed General Wood as Governor General.

In 1886, when he was serving as an Indian fighter in Arizona, Leonard Wood gave it as opinion that even Geronimo, the most feared and most elusive of the Apache chiefs, could be hunted down if only "the right kind of white man" could be found for the task. Much of Wood's formidable energies was devoted to proving himself the right kind of white man.

Trained at the Harvard Medical School, Wood had to leave the Boston City Hospital, where he was an intern, in 1885 because he had carried out minor surgical operations that an intern was not supposed to do. He joined the Army Medical Corps, but soon found himself involved first in combat and then in command in Indian wars. His courage and energy were both legendary. During the Geronimo campaign he carried on, riding dozens of miles in a day, after being severely bitten by a tarantula.†

In 1898 he was one of the remarkably motley band of adventurers who volunteered for service in Cuba; they ranged from Harvard-educated polo players to wranglers, roustabouts and roughnecks of all kinds, as well as regular Army officers. In fact, Wood was the colonel of the First United States Volunteer Cavalry, universally known as the Rough Riders, and as such the nominal superior of Theodore Roose-

*Maximo Kalaw, "Governor Stimson in the Philippines," *Foreign Affairs*, April 1929, pp. 372–83.
†Jack C. Lane, *Armed Progressive: General Leonard Wood*, p. 10.

velt, whose protégé he became and whose philosophy of life and politics he uncritically adopted. It was typical of Wood that when his Rough Riders first came under fire in the Santiago campaign, he refused to take cover and stood up, exposing himself to heavy enemy fire, until an enemy bullet shattered his cuff links, and his brother officers screamed at him to take cover. Stephen Crane, author of *The Red Badge of Courage,* who was there, was favorably impressed with Wood's performance on this occasion. Wood and Teddy Roosevelt, when the latter was President, used to wrap themselves in padding and towels and thwack each other with heavy singlesticks, until Wood hurt the President's arm so badly that he couldn't sign bills for a while. Virile, hearty, he was a man after Teddy Roosevelt's heart, though he lacked both the President's culture and his political talents.

Wood showed great energy as a military governor in Santiago and later in Havana, using his medical knowledge to cope with an outbreak of yellow fever; with the help of energetic lobbying from Elihu Root, he was soon promoted over 509 senior officers to brigadier general. Politically, he was in the conservative wing of the Republican Party. In spite of the Foraker Amendment of 1899, which forbade the American military government in Cuba to grant economic concessions, Wood tried to bring in capital from American entrepreneurs like James J. Hill and Thomas Fortune Ryan to develop Cuban railways. He was also a convinced annexationist where Cuba was concerned.

In short, Wood was a leading member of the group who shared Teddy Roosevelt's dream of an American empire. It was natural enough that he should be sent to the wildest new frontier of that empire, Moros province in the Philippines, where he became governor in 1903. Wood specialized in mounting sanguinary punitive expeditions from his headquarters at beautiful Zamboanga, at the southwestern tip of Mindanao; "the only way to deal with these people," he said, "is to be absolutely firm." In the execution of his conception of firmness, he destroyed several hundred Moro *cottas,* or fortified villages. In 1906 there was something of a scandal in the United States about one of these expeditions, dignified as the "Battle of Mount Dajo." Chasing one Moro who had run amok in Borneo and was wanted by the British authorities there, Wood ended up storming a Moro stronghold in a volcano crater and killing six hundred men, women and children, for the loss of eighteen American dead. TR sent a cable congratulating him on what he called this "brilliant feat of arms."

The uproar over the Mount Dajo incident did not harm Wood's

slow-starting but now accelerating career. After a period as commander
of the Philippine division, he was appointed in 1910 to the comparatively new office of chief of staff of the U.S. Army. There, as we have
seen, Wood found himself allied with President Taft's young Secretary
of War: Henry L. Stimson.

Wood, Teddy Roosevelt and their friends, of whom Stimson was
one, were, Samuel Huntington has written, "the first important
American social group whose political philosophy more or less consciously borrowed and incorporated elements of the professional military ethic."* The political beliefs of the group were not uniform;
Huntington called them "a peculiar amalgam of liberal-conservative
values." They ranged from the active Progressivism on social issues of
a liberal journalist like Herbert Croly of *The New Republic* to the
conservatism of Admiral Mahan or the brothers Brooks and Henry
Adams, self-conscious heirs of an American political and intellectual
aristocracy. What brought them together was their belief in the United
States' destiny as a world power, and the need for the United States
to accept that destiny and to learn to wield military force in pursuit of
it. These men called themselves "expansionists," but the school to
which both Wood and Stimson belonged may be more precisely seen
as both militarist and nationalist; in the European experience it most
closely resembled the liberal imperialism of Joseph Chamberlain and
his friends.

It is worth pointing out that most members of this school were
unmistakably racist in their cast of thought, though in this respect
individuals varied, to be sure. Stimson was accustomed to refer to
himself as "an old abolitionist," and he certainly saw himself as enlightened in racial matters, although the evidence suggests he was less
enlightened in his instincts than he thought he was. Wood, on the
other hand, sometimes spoke in terms that would not have provoked
disagreement from Houston Stewart Chamberlain, his American contemporary who was one of the fathers of pseudoscientific racial theory
and the grandfather of Hitlerism.

In 1926, for example, Stimson made this record in his diary of a
talk with Wood (without dissent):

> The Governor-General thinks pure Malays (Filipinos) superior
> to *pure Mexican Indians* (Chihuahua and Sonora) in self-governing

*Huntington, *The Soldier and the State*, p. 270.

capabilities, *but probably inferior* to Porto Ricans [*sic*] and Cubans owing to white blood in the latter; thinks them *far* superior to Negro and probably far simpler here [in the Philippines] owing to lack of Negro blood.*

After Stimson left Taft's Cabinet in 1913, Wood's career was disappointing. The top command in France, which he coveted, went to his zealous former junior in the expeditions against the Moros, John J. Pershing. In 1920, Wood went into the Republican convention as the heavily financed front runner for the party's presidential nomination, but, in part because of his own ineptness, he lost the prize to the imposing but shallow Senator Warren Harding of Ohio. Once in the White House, Harding gave him as a consolation the Governor Generalship of the Philippines.

As might be expected of this whiskered buffalo of a man, Wood did not stoop to diplomacy in his determination to undo the harm, as he saw it, that had been done by Governor Harrison. Roaring like an old bull, he put his head down and charged. He swiftly replaced the Filipino head of the National Bank with an American. He cut the budget and campaigned successfully against graft. But he also moved to reverse Filipinization both in the economy and in the political system.

The tone of Wood's official biographer, Hermann Hagedorn, is revealing. According to Hagedorn, the two most prominent Philippine leaders—Manuel Quezon, Speaker of the House, and Sergio Osmeña, President of the Senate—were "the crux of the problem" for Wood. They had "organized a Philippine national bank, purchased a railroad, a hotel and countless sugar centrals, organized a coal company and a cement company . . . in order to forestall the intrusion of American capital. Rape, adultery, seduction, unlawful marriage had been left practically unpunished during the later years of the Harrison regime." And then he sums up what can surely be taken to have been Wood's own view of the two nationalist leaders he had to deal with. "Astute and brilliant as they were," says Hagedorn, "they were like children."†

Wood plowed ahead. Alleging graft (perhaps truthfully, but when have legislators ever skimped on their travel expenses?), he did his best

*HLS, *Diary,* August 22, 1926.
†Hagedorn, *Leonard Wood,* pp. 382, 409.

to cut off the money from the Independence Fund, which was used to finance delegations to Washington to lobby for independence. He abolished the Council of State, and insisted that Philippine government must follow the American, not the British model; that is, that the Cabinet must not consist of members of the legislature. Finally, he interfered in a case involving the alleged bribery by Chinese gambling-house operators of an American detective with the Manila vice squad, Ray Conley.* The rights and wrongs of the original case were obscure, but Wood made his attitude all too plain. "Mr. Secretary," he told the Philippine Secretary of Justice, "this question is one between Americans and Filipinos. Naturally I have to be with the Americans."

Not long afterward, the entire Cabinet resigned in a body, and the Philippine legislature passed a formal resolution calling for Wood's recall. No Republican administration in Washington, however, was going to abandon the leader of so significant a fraction of the Grand Old Party. The general response was not very different from Wood's attitude to the Conley case. At the height of the furor, Calvin Coolidge became President upon Harding's death. Through the Secretary of War, Coolidge backed Wood and snubbed a delegation led by the new Speaker of the Philippine House, Manuel Roxas. The U.S. Attorney General found that the Board of Control was contrary to the Jones Act, and the Supreme Courts of the Philippines and the U.S. agreed.

The economic situation was chaotic, and the tone of Filipino leaders sharpened dangerously. This was the time when Quezon made his remark about preferring "a government run like hell by Filipinos to one run like heaven by Americans," though he added hastily, "because no matter how bad a Filipino government might be, it can still be improved." Later Quezon went further, on one occasion telling the Governor General to go to hell and on another calling him a "tyrant" and a "usurper."

It was at this juncture, in the summer of 1927, that Leonard Wood left for surgery in the United States, where he died on the operating table. Honorable and brave, but incapable of criticizing either himself or his assumptions, and therefore doomed to be misunderstood and to become obsolete, Wood was a tragic figure, as men are always tragic

*See Carlos Quirino, *Quezon: Paladin of Philippine Freedom,* p. 157 ff.; Hagedorn, *Wood,* pp. 428–29.

whose lives have outlasted their beliefs and whose tasks are too great for their abilities.

Those tasks now fell to Henry Stimson.* With his Progressive credentials and his nationalist instincts, Stimson might have been expected to follow a middle course between Harrison's Democratic anticolonialism and Wood's bluff imperialism. That is not what he did, however. He had already visited the Islands as Wood's guest in the summer of 1926, and had defended him in articles in *Foreign Affairs* and *The Saturday Evening Post.*† He shared Wood's basic philosophy, the creed of strenuousness, imperial responsibility and dedication to national destiny. He also shared Wood's contempt for the mess Harrison had left behind. Since he held no exaggerated opinion of elected politicians in the United States, it can be guessed that he privately despised the *políticos* of the semifeudal Philippine system. And he opposed independence. There is, in fact, no evidence that Stimson's views on independence had changed substantially since 1912, when he wrote: "Until our work in the archipelago is completed, until the Filipinos are prepared not only to preserve but to continue it, abandonment of the Philippines under whatever guise, would be . . . an abandonment of our responsibility to the Filipino people and of the moral obligations which we have voluntarily assumed before the world."‡

On his 1926 visit, he told Sergio Osmeña "frankly that I personally believed it to be for the interests of both the United States and the Philippine Islands that there should be permanent association." And he was even more frank in the course of a three-hour lunch with Quezon:

> The "false issue of independence" had made it impossible to perfect the system. On the contrary, said Quezon, he was more

*There is an interesting account of Stimson as Governor General in Lewis E. Gleeck, Jr., *The American Governors-General and High Commissioners in the Philippines: Proconsuls, Nation-Builders and Politicians.*

†He wrote in his February 1927 *Foreign Affairs* article that in the Harrison period "the Malay tendency to backslide promptly made itself felt with disastrous consequences. The sanitary service became disorganized with resulting epidemics of smallpox." It is perhaps going too far to call Stimson a racist, but he shared the weakness of his Anglo-Saxon contemporaries for unsustainable racial generalizations. No doubt this perception followed General Wood's table-talk, yet Stimson chose to incorporate it in a serious academic article.

‡*On Active Service*, p. 120.

sure that there must be independence than he had been in 1913.
The U.S. must stop talking about the "unfitness" of the Filipinos to govern themselves, and [he said] that he was in favour
of a Filipino as Governor-General.*

Stimson was no less direct on the taboo subject of race. He admitted
that Americans were prejudiced on the subject, and he said he was
aware of the danger of provocation by "thoughtless Americans."

Given these fairly unbending views,† and given Stimson's close-
ness to Wood and the way he insisted on identifying himself with his
ham-handed predecessor, it might have been expected that Stimson
would arouse equal, perhaps even greater hostility.

That, however, is not what happened.

From the start, Stimson deployed great tact and charm. In his
inaugural speech, as one Filipino wrote, "he gained our souls. He
called us fellow-countrymen."‡ It was appreciated that Mrs. Stimson
wore Philippine national dress on formal occasions at Malacañan, and
danced the national dance, the *rigodón*, with grace. (The Governor
General's efforts on the dance floor, though equally valued for the
spirit in which they were undertaken, were apparently less successful.)
It was also noted with approval that where Wood never met a Filipino
without a witness in the room, Stimson habitually met Filipino leaders
alone, and soon established relations of trust with most of them. With
Manuel Quezon in particular he developed a close personal friendship
which lasted for the rest of their lives. Quezon remarked in his autobiography that "there was never any mental reservation" when Stimson talked to him, and that from the days of his Governor Generalship
"he gave me his entire confidence exactly as . . . if I had been an
American."

Most of Stimson's inaugural speech was devoted to economic development. "I lay particular stress upon industrial and economic progress," he said. And by economic development Stimson the Wall Street
lawyer, devoted believer in the benefits of American corporate capital-

*HLS, *Diary*, August 10, 1926.
†Elihu Root held even stronger views. He called General Aguinaldo, the leader of the Philippine
independence movement, a "Chinese half-breed," and said in a political speech: "Government
does not depend on consent. The immutable laws of justice and humanity require that people
shall have government, that the weak shall be protected, that cruelty and lust shall be restrained,
whether there be consent or not. . . . There is no Philippine people." Quoted in Philip Jessup,
Elihu Root, vol. i, p. 329.
‡Morison, *Turmoil and Tradition*, p. 285.

ism, emphatically did not mean government-owned, Filipino-operated public enterprises. Many years later in his autobiography he wrote, "It was a necessary condition of economic growth in the Philippines that large quantities of foreign—presumably American—capital be attracted to the Islands."*

American investment meant revision of the Philippine corporation laws on foreign investment, and of nothing in his term as Governor General, Stimson wrote, was he prouder than of winning Filipino approval for more "liberal" treatment of American capital. His inaugural, in fact, accurately foretold his strategy. He intended to divert attention from the divisive and dangerous issue of independence and to direct it instead to practical objects, such as the economy, health, education.

In political terms, Stimson's policy was to oppose independence flatly but at the same time to improve the workings of responsible government under the Jones Act. He disposed of the bad blood over Wood's "cavalry Cabinet"† by securing passage of the Belo bill, which gave the Governor General a fixed annual appropriation to pay assistants and advisers. He accepted that members of the Cabinet should be chosen only from the Nacionalista party and after consultation with its leaders. He amended the rules of the legislature so that Cabinet members could address both houses from the floor. And the Council of State was revived, not, however, as the powerful body of Harrison's time, but as a forum for friendly consultation between the American Governor General and the Filipino legislative leaders.

Stimson's tenure at Malacañan was brief, but his involvement with the Islands did not end with his removal to Washington. As Secretary of State, his was a powerful voice in the discussions on the Timberlake Resolution, which threatened an American tariff on Philippine goods. Stimson three times went to Capitol Hill to testify on matters affecting the Philippines. In April 1929 he gave evidence against the Timberlake Resolution, and in October of the same year he opposed a measure to extend American coastal shipping regulations to Philippine waters. But by August 1930, the interests affected by Philippine exports—cordage, copra, but above all sugar—had shifted their policy; cynically, they came out for independence, because an independent Philippine Re-

---

*On Active Service, p. 140.

†Two of Wood's officers, as we have seen, were intimate friends of Stimson's: Frank R. McCoy and George S. Patton.

public would have no case for demanding that its products should be admitted to the United States duty-free. Ever since annexation, Philippine products had enjoyed, not free, but preferential treatment in the United States, while the United States had enjoyed protected access to the Philippine market. As a consequence, Philippine industries, especially sugar, had become heavily dependent on the U.S. market and would do nothing that might deprive them of it. The combination of residual Wilsonian idealists with the representatives of the sugar interests was enough to guarantee independence within five years—and decades of enhanced suspicion and resentment of the United States among many Filipinos.

On both emancipative idealism and manipulative commercial cynicism, Henry Stimson characteristically turned his back. His policy, in fact, epitomized the Theodore Roosevelt tradition. Let us unpick its several threads and see what held it together.

One element was pure American nationalism and a strong sense of imperial mission. Stimson's imperialism was less rambunctious than Roosevelt's, let alone Wood's, but its essential principles were the same. TR's view was accurately expounded in an "intimate biography" by Roosevelt's friend William Roscoe Thayer before time and political fashion had softened the outlines of that virile creed:

> Roosevelt embraced imperialism . . . boldly, not to say exultantly. To him imperialism meant national strength, the acknowledgment by the American people that the United States are a World Power and that they should not shrink from taking up any burden which that distinction involved. . . . Having reached national maturity we must accept Expansion as the logical and normal ideal for our matured nation.*

Stimson would not have put the thought so plainly. He was not a man for banging drums and sounding trumpets. ("Darn it, Harry," Roosevelt used to tell him, "a campaign speech is a poster, not an etching!") But essentially his convictions were the same.

The justification, though, was not in the satisfactions of victory and glory alone. Both Roosevelt and Stimson believed that the United States had been given power in the world to protect the powerless. "Having destroyed Spanish sovereignty in the Philippines," Roosevelt

*Thayer, *Theodore Roosevelt*, p. 172.

believed, according to Thayer, "we must see to it that the people of the Islands were protected." Stimson used the same language, speaking of the American duty to protect the Philippines as a "moral obligation."

This is the pure milk of "liberal imperialism." It is the language of the great lines in Virgil's *Aeneid* in which the spirit of Anchises charges his son Aeneas, the founder of Rome, with a double duty. Even in Roman times it was assumed that Virgil meant them to be an exhortation to Octavian, who as "Augustus" was to become the founder of the Roman empire. This climactic passage in Virgil's great national epic was learned by heart by Roosevelt's and Stimson's contemporaries in late Victorian schools and taken as the motto and justification of their conception of imperialism. And even if Stimson did not have to recite it out loud at Andover, it comes close to expressing his feelings about America's destiny in the world. Let others, says Anchises contemptuously—for he means his enemies the Greeks—beat out bronzes more softly, or carve marble faces. Rome's destiny was different:

> tu regere imperio populos, Romane, memento
> (hae tibi erunt artes), pacisque imponere morem,
> parcere subjectis et debellare superbos.

> [Roman, do not forget to rule the peoples in your sway;
> those will be your arts, to impose the habit of peace;
> to spare the subject, and beat down the proud.]

Influenced by contemporary British experience in Australia and Canada as much as in India, Stimson was attracted to the idea of "dominion status" for the Philippines. In this liberal variant of imperialism, the mother country would grant self-government but would continue to enjoy the strategic advantages and psychic comforts of dominion.* But Stimson was not able to sell dominion status either to Filipinos or, with a few exceptions, to Americans. (One of the exceptions was Elihu Root.) In part this was because, in the Depression, Americans did not want to be burdened with the cost of a continuing connection with the Philippines. More important, it was hard to reconcile a continuing relationship with the growing protectionism of the sugar and other lobbies in Congress. The fact remains that Stimson's

---

*The British Parliament granted dominion status to Canada in 1867, to the Commonwealth of Australia in 1901, to New Zealand in 1907, to the Union of South Africa in 1910, to the Irish Free State in 1921, to Southern Rhodesia in 1923, and to India, Pakistan, Ceylon and Burma after 1945. Ireland left the British Commonwealth in 1949, South Africa in 1961 and Pakistan in 1972.

ideal for Filipino-American relations was an imperial one, though one updated on the latest Westminster model of the time.

There were other elements to this American creed of empire. One was the belief that economic development would come from investment by American business, and that it was therefore right that American businessmen should be given inducements to bring the benison of their enriching presence to developing societies like the Philippines. Another was the easy assumption of cultural, if not racial, superiority. We have seen how in a man as wise and as courteous as Stimson, this assumption did not express itself as bullying or arrogance and was compatible both with the ability to form genuine friendships (as with Quezon) on a basis of something like genuine equality, and with a theoretical recognition, at the level of philosophical or religious belief, of human equality. To men like Stimson, there was no reason to glory in, still less to deny, what seemed clear to them: it was obvious that for all practical purposes, Filipinos were inferior. They needed protection, instruction and example from Americans, and therefore they should count themselves lucky to be allowed to purchase those advantages with the surrender of their independence.

Sometimes Filipinos shared, or affected to share, this assumption that they needed American protection. Quezon, in particular, was concerned about the danger his country faced from Japan. Time was to prove him right about that: only a dozen years after Stimson and others were arguing that the Filipinos should defer independence in return for American protection, General Douglas MacArthur was feverishly, and unsuccessfully, struggling to put the Islands in a state of defense.

No doubt, too, Americans often believed this compliant attitude was more widespread among Filipinos than it actually was. It is significant that virtually every American discussion of the American role in the Philippines makes a point of the superiority of American imperialism to all other brands. Yet few Filipinos seem to think the point worth making as most Americans did. A comparison of two historians illustrates the point rather neatly. Even the liberal Theodore Friend feels the need to begin his study of the Philippines by asserting that "the question of independence, elsewhere a matter of grievous dispute on principle, was for the United States and the Philippines only a question of 'when.' "* Whereas a Filipino historian stresses, not the

*Theodore Friend, *Between Two Empires*, p. 1. The point is, in any case, debatable. Britain was unmistakably committed to granting responsible self-government to India by the Montagu-

differences between American and other forms of imperialism, but the similarity: "American imperialism in the Philippines is as genuine a fact as the imperialism of other western powers at the turn of the nineteenth century in Asia, Africa or the Middle East."*

It is time to draw the threads together and to see why Henry Stimson's year in the Malacanan palace was so significant for the evolution both of Philippine politics and of American policy.

In terms of the former, Stimson's achievement was that he cemented the good relations between the Filipino elite and the United States. Later in life, giving his advice to President Harry S. Truman about how to deal with Stalin, he made his famous remark that the only way to make a man trustworthy was to trust him. The phrase itself may have been borrowed from his successor as Philippines Governor General, Dwight Davis, who said of Quezon that he was "absolutely trustworthy as long as he feels that he himself is being trusted," but the perception was probably Stimson's. Certainly by the urbane and generous way he behaved toward individual members of the Filipino elite, he administered tannic jelly to the raw burns left by Leonard Wood. On his way out to Manila in the S.S. *President McKinley,* Stimson had written in his diary that the job would require "the patience of Job and the wisdom of a serpent." Stimson had both. If Wood's successor had been less diplomatic, the animosity that was building up under Wood might have poured into open rebellion.

In March 1929 Stimson returned to the United States from Manila to be sworn in as President Herbert Hoover's Secretary of State. He had been a popular Governor General, and the Filipinos thronged the streets and packed the pier to see him and his wife off. Both Manuel Quezon and Manuel Roxas brought silk flags made by Filipino ladies as parting gifts. A crowd Stimson estimated "conservatively" at ten thousand people came to see him depart, and as the boat pulled out "the entire pier, both upper and lower, was lined the entire length with friendly brown faces."† When Stimson reached home, with this

---

Chelmsford Report of 1918, twenty-nine years before independence. (See P. Moon, *The British Conquest and Dominion of India*, pp. 944–56, pp. 972–85.) The future in which Stimson contemplated granting independence to the Philippines may have been at least as distant.
*Romeo V. Cruz, *America's Colonial Desk and the Philippines*, 1898–1934.
†HLS, *Diary*, March 7, 1929.

comforting testimony to his popularity still ringing in his ears, *The New York Times* added an even more gratifying tribute. His comparatively brief tenure as Governor General in the Philippines, it said in an editorial, had been "brilliant."* The adjective is too fulsome from any point of view. Stimson's few months in the Malacañan palace were in effect an interlude, both in his life and in the political history of the Philippines' progress towards independence.

Stimson did not succeed in delaying Filipino independence. Nor did he succeed in protecting the Philippines either from being excluded from the American market or from being invaded by the Japanese. What can be claimed is that he was one of the first American statesmen to think of American foreign policy in global terms. In this he was a true disciple of Theodore Roosevelt. Even before he became Governor General of the Philippines, he was far more aware of Japan than most of his American contemporaries. (That was presumably because he had visited both China and Japan, as well as the Philippines in 1926.) But it was his interest in the Philippines that led him to make those brief, exploratory journeys, and it was his experience of the Philippines that gave him a wider perspective on Asia than any other American leader of his generation enjoyed. That understanding was about to be brutally reinforced by the experience of dealing with the Japanese in the Manchurian crisis of 1931–33.

Stimson, in fact, forged the link between the global thinking of the expansionists of 1898 and the new "globalism" of 1945. There was more than a difference of individual style between the raw, assertive nationalism of Theodore Roosevelt and Elihu Root's generation, and Stimson's world view. Stimson shared his mentors' conviction that America was destined for leadership, but he polished it and made it acceptable to a generation of Americans more and more of whom were offended by colonial empires, their own or anyone else's. Stimson is a key figure in the process by which the "new nationalism" of the first decade of the twentieth century made the traverse between two Roosevelts and emerged transformed into what might be called the "new internationalism" of World War II.

More than that: Stimson's experience of the Philippines confirmed him in the doctrine that the United States was justified in using its military and economic strength to protect those who might want

*Cited in Morison, *Turmoil and Tradition,* p. 298.

to go to hell in their own way but ought not to be allowed to do so. The Philippines, after all, were not the only smithy in which the assumptions of American world leadership were forged. But they were one such forge, and Henry Stimson labored mightily there.

Spears of Straw and Swords of Ice

> The road to World War II is now clearly visible; it has run its terrible course from the railway tracks near Mukden to the operations of two bombers over Hiroshima and Nagasaki.
>
> Stimson and Bundy, *On Active Service in Peace and War*, p. 221

Early in June 1931 a Japanese army officer, Captain Nakamura Shintaro,* obtained a permit from the Chinese authorities in Harbin, in Manchuria, to travel in Inner Mongolia. He gave a false name and stated that the object of his trip was to carry out an agricultural survey. When the permission was given, he set out with one Japanese assistant and Russian and Mongolian interpreters along the Chinese Eastern Railway. On June 27 the party arrived at a lonely inn on the road near Solun, in the Hinganling Mountains. There they were stopped and questioned by Chinese soldiers, who soon found a Japanese army map, survey instruments, six revolvers, and a supply of narcotics, presumably intended for bribery. Captain Nakamura and his men were arrested, escorted to the Chinese army post and there, after a few days, taken out to the hill behind the barracks and shot.†

The Nakamura incident was the latest in a series that had inflamed, in the Japanese army and in many of their civilian supporters,

---

*I have followed the Japanese practice of putting surnames—*e.g.*, Ishiwara, Tatekawa—first.
†David Bergamini, *Japan's Imperial Conspiracy*, p. 412; Edwin P. Hoyt, *Japan's War*, p. 81. Takehiko Yoshihashi, *Conspiracy at Mukden*, chapter 6.

what was called "the Manchuria fever." For years Japanese military figures had dreamed of invading the provinces north of the Great Wall of China. Indeed the great division in Japanese military circles was not between those who favored and those who opposed an invasion of Manchuria. It was between the so-called "Strike North" faction, who wanted to take Manchuria as a prelude to an invasion of Siberia, and the "Strike South" advocates, who accepted the need for a Manchuria operation but only to free Japan's elbows for a march on the rich resources of Indochina and the Dutch East Indies. The hottest heads were to be found in the small elite force—it numbered fewer than 20,000 men at this time—known as the Kwantung Army. Since Japan's victory over Russia in 1905, Japan had kept troops not only in Korea but also in southern Manchuria and in the peninsula jutting into the Yellow Sea which the Chinese call Liao-tung and the Japanese Kwantung.* For months there were hints and rumors that the Kwantung Army or perhaps some of its junior officers, unknown to their senior commanders, were planning some incident or provocation that would enable them to start a major offensive against the Chinese and eventually take over Manchuria.

Much historical controversy has swirled about the part the Emperor Hirohito played in the decision to invade Manchuria. One school of thought portrays him as doing his best to restrain the officers, though he was necessarily obliged by the strength of Japanese militarism to use the greatest subtlety. This interpretation was reinforced after World War II when the United States, committed to maintaining the Emperor as a key component in the postwar democratization of Japan, needed to dissociate him from his generals and admirals. The veneration in which the Emperor was held by Japanese, his own modesty, and the growing power and reputation of his country in the world, inclined Western public opinion and even many scholars to give him the benefit of the doubt.

There is, however, another view. Some scholars† bluntly portray Hirohito as encouraging his army and navy officers to plan wars of conquest, while cloaking himself in the mystery of his quasi-divine of-

---

*Not to be confused with the province that used to be given the same name by westerners, and is now known as Gwangchou, in the south of China, around Canton.
†Notably and, for me, persuasively, Bergamini, *Japan's Imperial Conspiracy*, especially pp. 322–60 and pp. 411–31. The critical view of the Emperor has also been robustly adopted by Edward Behr in *The Last Emperor*.

fice to hide the tracks of his own involvement. According to this school, the Emperor actually ordered a secret operational plan for the invasion of Manchuria from a brilliant young officer, Ishiwara Kanji, as far back as 1928. Ostensibly filing it as a contingency plan, the Emperor ordered his great-uncle, Field Marshal Prince Kanin, to make preparations to put the plan into operation. The murder of Captain Nakamura, on this interpretation, was one successful consequence of a campaign of provocation secretly mounted by Japanese military intelligence and secret police to provide a pretext for putting the Ishiwara plan into effect.

The state of tension in Manchuria was so great, in any case, that the Chinese scarcely needed specific acts of provocation. And on either interpretation, by mid-July 1931 the Japanese Kwantung Army was ready to strike. Field artillery was deployed the length of the South Manchuria Railroad, from Dairen to Mukden, the capital of southern Manchuria. And on July 25 Lieutenant Colonel Ishiwara finished the job of giving himself a secret weapon for the capture of Mukden, where Chinese troops, though admittedly of indifferent quality, outnumbered the 20,000-man Kwantung Army by ten to one. Two 9.5-inch siege guns, abandoned by the Russians after their surrender at Port Arthur a quarter of a century before, were installed in a gun pit concealed as a swimming pool, one trained on the main Mukden police barracks, the other on the airfield.

The war minister, General Minami, called a meeting of senior officers of the Imperial General Staff at his home. Was there any chance that the Kwantung Army might act without consulting Tokyo? he asked. One by one the officers—most of whom already had more or less precise knowledge of the Kwantung Army's conspiracy—said it was impossible.

Then Major General Tatekawa Yoshitsugu, chief of operations on the general staff, known to his friends from his sexual exploits as "the Peerless Pimp,"* looked up from scraping out his pipe.

"There is no need to worry," he said. "The Kwantung Army is not that stupid."

Tatekawa strenuously denied that he had any inside information,

---

*Bergamini, *Japan's Imperial Conspiracy*, p. 363. Tatekawa was a protégé of Prince Kanin and a former head of European and American intelligence on the general staff. He was responsible for an unsuccessful attempt to assassinate Chang Tso-lin, the warlord of Manchuria, in 1916, and for another, successful attempt in 1928. See Yoshihashi, *Conspiracy at Mukden*, p. 156.

but his tone gave him away. There was something about the way he had spoken that made it plain he knew more than he admitted.

The subsequent maneuvers of everyone, from the Emperor down to the field commanders of the Kwantung Army and the intelligence operatives on the ground in Mukden, make sense only if there was indeed a concerted plan to take advantage of recent provocations, themselves in all probability deliberate, and take over Mukden.

Again, the Emperor's role is hotly disputed. Because of the veneration in which he was held, Hirohito was obliged not to commit himself publicly to any course. His own actions and words can be made compatible with either interpretation. Did he struggle quietly, and unsuccessfully, against the army's determination to invade Manchuria? Or did he merely pretend that the operation was against his wishes, when he had secretly encouraged it all along? Given the Emperor's power and position and given the history of the next ten years of Japanese aggression—given, above all, the complex network of connections binding the known plotters and firebrands to the Emperor and the imperial family over the previous decade—it is hard to believe that the Emperor did not know and approve of, even if he did not order, the attack. At the same time he kept his balance by maintaining to Prince Saionji, the *genro*, or elder statesman; to Prime Minister Wakatsuki; to Baron Shidehara, the foreign minister; and to other members of the peace faction, that he wanted to restrain the impetuous Kwantung Army.

Whatever the precise nuance of the Emperor's foreknowledge or responsibility, the Manchurian operation was finally set for September 28. It was General Tatekawa, chief of operations on the general staff, who devised a plan of characteristic cunning for moving the action up and heading off a possibility that the peace party would succeed in getting it stopped. He summoned his subordinates and explained that it was up to every loyal Japanese to lighten the Emperor's burden now that he had decided to act. He then sat down and drafted a cable to Lieutenant General Honjo Shigeru, commanding the Kwantung Army; he announced his intention of visiting him, in Mukden of all places, in three days' time. It was a broad enough hint that he expected Honjo by that time to have advanced the timetable for his coup and taken Mukden.

One of the two subordinates to the political ''commissar'' of the Kwantung Army, Colonel Itagaki Seishiro, who had been in on the plot from the start (and who was to be hanged by the Allies as a war criminal in 1945), also received a cable from the General Staff in Tokyo. It repeated Tatekawa's schedule and added: HOSPITABLE TREATMENT WILL BE APPRECIATED; HIS MISSION IS TO PREVENT THE INCIDENT.

Another general staff officer also sent a cable, to a friend who was an aide of Colonel Ishiwara. PLOT EXPOSED, it said. ACT BEFORE TATE-KAWA'S ARRIVAL.

General Tatekawa proceeded slowly by train across Japan and Korea, taking three days for a journey that could be done in one. The plotters agonized over the meaning of the two cables. In the meantime, though, General Honjo had received a visitor, an elderly officer who was an intimate of Prince Kanin. After talking to him, General Honjo told his young men to go ahead with the operation they had planned, and took another train away from Mukden, to Kwantung Army headquarters at Port Arthur.

Two hours out of Mukden, General Tatekawa's train stopped for water at the village of Pen-hsi-hu, where it was boarded by Colonel Itagaki, an aristocratic young man with a moustache like a seal's.

After an hour and three quarters of cautious doubletalk, the colonel reassured the general that all was in readiness and promised to take him to a good inn; business could wait till the morning. When the train reached Mukden, it was met by a young major, who drove the two officers to the best teahouse in town, the Literary Chrysanthemum. After his bath, the Peerless Pimp settled down to enjoy himself with the *sake* and the geishas. Itagaki, after a single toast, excused himself and hurried off to the concrete headquarters of the Special Service Organ, the Japanese army's Secret Service.

With characteristic Japanese indirection, these courtly maneuvers had provided everyone with a cover story. Thus Prince Kanin covered for the Emperor, Tatekawa for Kanin, Honjo for Tatekawa and Itagaki for Honjo.*

At 10:20 an operative of the Japanese Special Service Organ pushed a plunger and exploded forty-two charges carefully placed to shower with dirt the railroad tracks north of Mukden. The phony attack was

---

*In the main, I have adopted Bergamini's interpretation, which is based on the Japanese sources. "The multiplicity of cover stories would convince Western historians that junior officers had acted on their own. . . . The reality, in which every man on the ladder conspired to deceive, knowing exactly what was afoot, is demonstrated by Lieutenant General Honjo's diary." Bergamini, *Japan's Imperial Conspiracy*, p. 422. Other interpretations, such as that of Yoshihashi, seem to me less persuasive.

to be blamed on the Chinese, and was the pretext for a general assault on the Chinese garrison.

At about 9:00 Tatekawa had retired to bed with one of the geishas. At 10:30, when the big guns hidden in the "swimming-pool" opened up, she woke her companion up and said she was frightened. He went into the lobby, clad only in his sleeping kimono, to be told politely by armed guards that they had been ordered to prevent him going out as it was dangerous. The Peerless Pimp announced that he and his girlfriend were going back to bed, though later that night he was seen in uniform, sword in hand, leading the assault on the Chinese police barracks.

At three o'clock in the morning in Tokyo the war minister, General Minami Jiro, was woken by a night duty officer who read him a telegram from army intelligence in Mukden. At 10:30 the previous evening, the telegram said, a unit of the Northeastern Frontier Defense Army of the Republic of China had dynamited the tracks of the South Manchurian Railway and attacked the Japanese guards. The second battalion of the Mukden garrison had come to their support and annihilated the enemy.

Still later, as the rising sun circled the globe, Henry Stimson was awakened at Woodley and told that the Kwantung Army had moved out of its cantonments along the South Manchurian Railway and was proceeding to occupy southern Manchuria, sweeping before them like so much dust the large but ill-equipped Chinese armies that stood in their way. (These were commanded by Chang Hsueh-liang, the "Young Marshal," who ruled the province as a warlord in loose alliance with the Chiang Kai-shek government in Nanking.)

Colonel Stimson's idea of the military code was very different from that of General Honjo or Colonel Itagaki, just as General Tatekawa's pleasures were even more foreign to his Puritan soul than those of the former Texas attorney general.* Still, a lifetime of practicing law had taught him something about the human capacity for duplicity. Although most of the Western embassies in Tokyo, including the American one,† had refused to believe reports that the Kwantung Army was

---

*Cf. p. 16.

†Ambassador Cameron Forbes had arranged to return to Washington for consultations on the very day of the attack, something he would never have done if he had believed it was imminent. And Nelson T. Johnson, U.S. minister in Peking, sent a memo from an American adviser of Chiang Kai-shek, warning him of the Kwantung Army's plans only twenty-four hours before, minuted it as "incredible, fantastic," and sent it to Washington by the slow pouch.

about to move, Stimson was skeptical. "The situation is very confused," he dictated for his diary later that day, "and it is not clear
whether the army is acting under a plan of the government or on its
own." Later, however, he observed that the dynamiting incident on
the railroad tracks at Mukden, which was claimed by the Japanese as
justifying their attack, "diminished to such small proportions as
strongly to suggest its nonexistence." Both the American and the British military attachés, in fact, rightly believed that the Japanese had
provided their own pretext for war by themselves blowing up the railway tracks.

What neither Colonel Stimson nor any other responsible Western statesman or diplomat could understand was that the Japanese
coup against Mukden was no trivial incident, but the opening of a
Japanese war of conquest that would test the collective security system
established after the First World War, destroy it, and in the end make
another world war inevitable.

From Washington, and perhaps even more from Europe, Korea
and Manchuria seemed as obscure as they were remote. Until the 1890s,
Korea was a "hermit kingdom," Manchuria a little-known province
of China beyond the Great Wall. Unnoticed by all but a few of the
self-absorbed and supercilious watchers in Whitehall and Washington,
however, four of the great events of the late nineteenth century had
transformed the strategic situation of both Korea and Manchuria. From
the remote periphery they moved to what would in time become the
very center of the world power struggle. The transformation of Japan
under the Meiji emperor (1868–1912) from a medieval to a modern society; the awakening of China; the eastward expansion of Tsarist Russia
across Siberia to the Pacific and Vladivostok, "Lord of the East"; and
the emergence of the United States as an Asiatic power with the acquisition of the Philippines in 1898: these four processes meant that
Korea and Manchuria were destined to be a cockpit where the influences of the four greatest powers of the late twentieth century would
meet and conflict. In its early years, in the meantime, other significant
powers, too, such as Germany, ensconced at Tsingtao and on the
Shantung Peninsula on the southern shore of the Yellow Sea, and
Britain, with concessions at Hong Kong, Shanghai and Weihaiwei, in
the north, kept one eye on events around the Yellow Sea.

Korea felt the rise of Japanese naval and military power first. In a short, conclusive war in 1894–95 the Japanese defeated the paralytic Manchu empire and seized Korea. During the Boxer Rebellion of 1900, Japan offered to send in an army of 30,000 and would undoubtedly have taken advantage of the situation to claim at the very least a sphere of influence in northern China. The Western powers declined this kind offer, though, and restricted the Japanese to 10,000 men in the Kwantung Peninsula. Practicing their traditional self-restraint, the Japanese had to watch, outwardly civil but inwardly seething, as the Tsar's armies marched in and occupied Manchuria, with its valuable farmlands, its timber and coal, its future industrial potential and strategic importance.

In 1904–5, Japan had her revenge. The Japanese army, proving itself a match for the Russians in courage, equipment and generalship, besieged and captured the great Russian naval base at Port Arthur, on the tip of the Kwantung Peninsula, then smashed the Russian armies in the field at the battle of Mukden in February 1905. Three months later, in the Tsushima Strait, the Japanese attacked the Russian battle fleet which had been dispatched around the world to cut off the Japanese army in Manchuria. The Russians lost thirty-four of their thirty-seven ships, and 4,830 men drowned; the Japanese losses were three small boats and 110 men killed.

This decisive Japanese victory was an event of great significance in world history. For the first time a major European power had been defeated, in a major engagement and in fair fight, by a nonwhite nation. In India and China, as well as in Japan, the lesson was duly committed to memory. The fall of Port Arthur and the battle of Tsushima did not strip the Western nations of their power in the Orient, but they did strip them of their mystique, and of the reputation of invincibility they had earned over more than a century of one-sided encounters since the days when Clive and Dupleix won battles in India over armies that outnumbered them by ten to one.

At the peace talks under American auspices in Portsmouth, New Hampshire, the Russians were pushed out of Manchuria, and the Japanese acquired rights in the Kwantung Peninsula and along the South Manchurian Railway. While millions of Chinese migrated into prosperous Manchuria, a few hundred thousand Japanese established themselves as railway employees, shopkeepers and farmers.*

* According to Stimson, *The Far Eastern Crisis,* p. 17, only 230,000 Japanese and nearly 30 million Chinese.

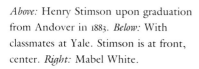
Above: Henry Stimson upon graduation from Andover in 1883. *Below:* With classmates at Yale. Stimson is at front, center. *Right:* Mabel White.

The lifelong outdoorsman Stimson indulging his love of big-game hunting *(above)* and opening the annual games at Highhold.

Above: Stimson whistlestopping as Republican nominee for governor of
New York in 1910. *Below:* In his artillery officer's uniform during World War I.

Stimson with his friend the fierce
nationalist General Leonard Wood,
whom he succeeded as Governor
General of the Philippines in 1927.

Henry and Mabel Stimson.

Secretary of State Stimson (right) with President Hoover (left) and Italian Foreign Minister Dino Grandi. *Below:* Conferring with Mussolini in 1931.

Stimson (seated at center) with his State Department staff, 1933.

Left: Stimson as FDR's Secretary of War with Department staffers John McCloy (center) and Robert Lovett (right). *Above:* With Eisenhower in 1944.

Stimson in 1945, at the end of his War Department tenure,
with Truman *(above)* and with General George Marshall.

In the First World War, Japan sided with the Allies, and so was able to pick up some of Germany's lost chips in the Far East, including the German concessions around Tsingtao in Shantung and the former German-held islands of the Marianas and the Caroline and Marshall archipelagos in the northern Pacific. In 1917, after the Russian Revolution, the British government pressed the Japanese to secure the Trans-Siberian Railway, and later Washington asked the Japanese to help the hard-pressed Czechoslovak "legion," strung out by the hazards of revolution and war along the railroad. In the event, the aggressive spirit of the army triumphed over the vacillations and reservations of the civilians, and by the time the Allies met in Paris to negotiate the peace treaty, there were more than 100,000 Japanese troops in Siberia. They held the Trans-Siberian Railway as far west as Irkutsk. And Japan had annexed the maritime province of the Russian empire and the island of Sakhalin.

Before the end of 1914 the Japanese government had presented China with its outrageous Twenty-one Demands. These were listed in five groups. Group One claimed the German interests in Shantung. Group Two covered claims to concessions in Manchuria, and Group Three dealt with Mitsubishi iron and steel interests there. Group Four forbade China to grant any coastal concessions of the kind she had given to Western powers. And Group Five, the most insolent of all, demanded for Japan the right to propagate in China the Shinto faith, to appoint Japanese advisers to the Chinese government, to share control of the Chinese police, and to operate vast economic concessions all over China. The combined effect, in the opinion of Paul Reinsch, U.S. ambassador in Peking at the time, would have been "to place the Chinese state in a position of vassalage." Appropriately, he noted, the paper on which the demands were presented bore the watermark of a machine gun.

Eventually, the demands were watered down. But this was seen by a growing segment of Japanese opinion as a scandalous betrayal. It was the same with every issue. Whenever a Japanese government stepped back from the most extreme demands of the expansionists, the cry of treason was raised.

Japan had staked her claim to be considered one of the front rank of naval powers in 1905. At the Washington Conference of 1921–22, Westerners thought this had been acknowledged when Japan was allowed to build warships in a ratio of three Japanese to every five British and five American. The rationale, for Westerners, was that the United

States Navy had two oceans to be concerned about, while Britain had to cover her major European rivals and at the same time protect the far-flung lines of imperial communication. The Japanese, however, interpreted the ratio as nothing more than an insult. A split developed in the Japanese navy between the "treaty faction," who were willing to accept limitation of warship building, and the "fleet faction," who wanted unlimited building to create a navy capable of taking on the United States.

Japanese nationalism in the early twentieth century was rampant but not confident; it was a sour and rancorous patriotism full of fear and resentment. The Japanese resented their exclusion by the Western powers. They read with bitterness of the way Japanese settlers were treated in Hawaii and California, and their anger was fanned to white heat by the specific exclusion of Japanese immigrants from the United States in 1924.

Although under the leadership of the *zaibatsu*—huge economic empires like Mitsui, Mitsubishi or Sumitomo, originally controlled by a single family or even an individual but spreading their interests into many different kinds of business—the Japanese economy was expanding and modernizing, the 1920s were a time of hardship. There was recession in the early postwar years, and the worldwide depression that elsewhere followed the New York stock market crash of 1929 began in Japan in 1927. Even if the economy had performed as well as anyone dared to hope, millions of individual Japanese would still have suffered the hardships and the social and psychological upheavals inseparable from rapid transformation from a rural to an urban society. And in the background there was the fear of overpopulation as a result of Japan's limited area of arable land and rapid population increase.

In 1918 it looked as though Japan had successfully weathered the passage from the paternalism of the Meiji period to something like parliamentary democracy when Prince Saionji, the last of the *genro*—the aristocratic elder statesmen who held real power in the Meiji period—handed over power to Hara Kei, known as the Great Commoner because it was so unusual for a Japanese politician not to have a feudal title, and to the first true Cabinet on the Western pattern. Hara's Seiyukai Party government rapidly introduced universal manhood suffrage and withdrew from the former German possessions in Shantung and the former Russian maritime province of Siberia. In the 1920 elections it won some 60 percent of the vote, and in 1925 another government reduced the standing army by four divisions. But in 1921 Hara was assassinated—by a railway worker, not by an army officer, as would be the fate of so many Japanese politicians in the next fifteen years. The political parties fell more and more under the influence of the *zaibatsu*. Japanese political life became a grim wrestling match between the politicians, liberal or conservative, who wanted to preserve at least the forms of the newly imported parliamentary democracy, and the grand coalition of those industrialists, soldiers, sailors and nationalists who sought to build a greater and more glorious Japanese empire on the ruins of Western-style democracy. Within a few years, it was plain to those who could see beneath the decorous surface of Japanese political life, with its Diet and its Cabinets, its princes and marquises, its Lord Keeper and its Prime Minister, that the forces of democracy were in undisguised retreat.

In 1921 three young majors* from the Japanese military academy met in, of all places, a Turkish bath in Baden-Baden, in southwestern Germany, and formed the Double Leaf Society, one of a long and baleful series of secret nationalist societies that sported romantic names like the Black Dragon Society and even the Cherry Blossom Society.† But there was nothing even faintly effete about them. Their members were junior officers burning with resentment over the humiliations they saw heaped on the army and the nation. Their goal was, first, power at home, then empire in Asia. Their methods were conspiracy, provocation, assassination. They were capable of tearing out the tongue of a senior Chinese civilian official, as happened in Shantung in 1927, in the hope of provoking a reaction from the Chinese which would give a pretext for further Japanese aggression. Men who thought such cruelty justified were unlikely to shrink from the string of assassinations, in Tokyo and north China, that in the late 1920s and early 1930s eliminated or intimidated moderates and helped to channel the streams of

---

*The three, known as the Three Crows, were all military-intelligence agents, Nagata Tetsukan from Berne, Obata Toshiro in Moscow, and Okamura Yasuji at large. Dedicated to reducing the aristocratic, *samurai* tradition in the army, which was identified with the Choshu clan, and allied with the imperial house against the old aristocracy, they were all closely identified with Prince Higashikuni. They and their associates, who included the wartime Prime Minister Tojo Hideki, also present in Baden-Baden, played a leading role in transforming the Japanese army into a modern fighting force. Hoyt, *Japan's War*, p. 57; Bergamini, *Japan's Imperial Conspiracy*, pp. 322 ff.

†Black Dragon, because the Chinese characters for those two words are the same as those for the Amur River, which the Japanese wanted to make their boundary. Cherry Blossom, because it symbolized the short life of the military hero.

Japanese political life toward the waterfall. At home liberal or left-wing ideas were more easily repressed after the passage of the euphemistically named Peace Preservation Laws of 1928, and radical thought was stamped out in a whole generation of young workers and students by random police arrests and routine torture.

The partisans of *kodo ha,* the Imperial Way, were careful to clothe themselves in the language of loyalty to the Emperor and in the silken trappings of feudal *daimyo* and their *samurai*. They spoke fervently of *bushido,* the knightly code of the medieval Japanese warrior, and claimed they wanted to restore *Showa,* the Emperor's goal of Enlightened Peace. There can be room for argument about how much self-deception there was in all this, how much romanticism and how much conscious cynicism. Certainly the officers who claimed to be restoring the Emperor's vision of peace knew perfectly well that it was war they were preparing. As one of the greatest of American students of Japan once put it, "after all the curious Oriental detail, such as Shinto mumbo-jumbo, 'Imperial will,' and samurai prestige have been removed, the stark outlines of the picture bear an all too clear resemblance to the major outlines of Western history in recent decades."* Specifically, the political history of Japan in the 1920s and 1930s bears a close resemblance to the rise of fascism, especially in Germany. A striking number of similar elements were present: the same psychological and social turmoil resulting from rapid industrialization and urbanization; the same alliance between big business, seeking new markets and fearing socialist criticism and labor unrest, and a military class that exulted in its past conquests, was horrified at the loss of them and all too ready to blame it on a stab in the back by the liberals; the same tendency for self-interested groups and psychotic individuals to wrap themselves in a toga woven from loyalty to the throne, medieval warrior mysticism and nationalist hokum; the same ruthless use of violence and intimidation to shut the mouths of anyone who dared to laugh at the dangerous absurdities that were being codified as a new national religion.

Manchuria, geographically hemmed in by China, Japan and the Soviet Union, and a tempting honey pot for each of them, was the logical place for the Japanese militarists to pursue their strategy, which was to commit the reluctant civilian governments in Tokyo to expansion by taking actions of their own accord which Tokyo would not dare to disavow. So in 1928 the Kwantung Army blew up the train in

*Edwin O. Reischauer, *The United States and Japan,* pp. 202–3.

which Chang Tso-lin, the "Old Marshal" who was the warlord of Manchuria, was finishing a game of *mah-jong*. They plotted to pin the blame on three wretched Manchurian dissidents who had been suborned to go in and finish the Old Marshal off if the explosive did not kill him (as in the event it did). One of the three escaped to tell the tale.*

In the spring of 1931 they tried again unsuccessfully to provoke the Chinese into starting major hostilities. And so in September the explosion on the railway near Mukden was both one episode in a long campaign to militarize Japanese society at home, and the long-heralded opening of a grand campaign of conquest on the Chinese mainland.

There was one specific dimension to the ferment of nationalism in Japan that was not fully understood in the United States: it was increasingly anti-American. Reports of discrimination against Japanese in the United States lost nothing in the telling in the nationalist Japanese press. The *zaibatsu* saw the Open Door Policy, by which the U.S. since 1900 had proclaimed the Chinese market open to all exporters, as a threat to their more mercantilist ambitions there. Many Japanese considered the 1922 naval treaty not just a reverse for Japan's legitimate ambitions, but a racially motivated denial of Japan's right to be treated as an equal. The last straw, for those who regarded the United States in these terms, was the London naval treaty of 1930. The Japanese wanted to increase the ratio between their fleet and those of the United States and Britain from 3:5:5, that is from 60 percent of the size of the U.S. and Royal navies, to 70 per cent. Overall, they almost got what they wanted. But within the set overall figure (69 per cent of the American and British levels) the Japanese were constrained to accept a low ratio for cruisers and an actual reduction in the number of submarines. The "fleet faction" in the navy, on this issue allied to the *kodo ha* faction in the army, was furious and leaked the draft treaty to put pressure on Prime Minister Hamaguchi. Hamaguchi stood firm, backed by the Emperor. But on November 14, 1930, he was murdered at the Tokyo railroad station by a young member of the Love of Country Association.

A few days after the Mukden Incident, Henry Stimson confided to his diary a brief statement of his policy, which was at once highly

---

*Bergamini, pp. 363–66; Hoyt, pp. 68–69.

shrewd within the terms of the conventional wisdom and at the same time quite innocent of the ferocity and ruthlessness of the human typhoon he was shortly going to have to deal with. "My problem," he wrote, "is to let the Japanese know we are watching them and at the same time do it in a way which will help Shidehara who is on the right side and not play into the hands of nationalist agitators."*

Baron Shidehara Kijuro, the foreign minister, and his Prime Minister, Wakutsuki Rejiro (whom Stimson had met during the London naval talks in 1930, at which Wakutsuki was the chief Japanese delegate), were among those in Japan who favored maintaining good relations with the United States. At this juncture, they were both less than two months from being forced to resign by the "nationalist agitators" against whom Stimson hoped to prop them up. (Both Wakutsuki's predecessor as Prime Minister, Hamaguchi Osachi, and his successor, Inukai Tsuyoshi, were gunned down by "agitators," that is, by assassins associated with the secret nationalist societies backed by the army.)

Even so sagacious a diplomat as the Boston Brahmin Joseph Grew, who arrived in Tokyo a few months later to begin ten years of yeoman service as U.S. ambassador there, started out by thinking that the Japanese army's "operations are really aimed at Russia—not at present but at some time in the future. Japan is afraid of Bolshevism and feels that it must drive Bolshevism out of Asia." And Stimson, who had taken the trouble to think about the Far East more than most American statesmen of his generation and had visited Japan more than once, utterly underestimated the political and psychic convulsions that were taking place there, and the ruthless determination of the Japanese to seize an empire for themselves.

The Manchurian incident, by no means the first illustration of that purpose, was the first that positively demanded a firm reaction from the rest of the world. But Stimson held no cards in his hand.† Formally, as he analyzed it later, the situation was governed by certain

---

*HLS, *Diary,* September 23, 1931.
†For the following interpretation of Stimson's handling of the Manchuria crisis, I have relied, *inter alia,* on Stimson's own three accounts, in the *Diary,* vols. xix and xx; in *The Far Eastern Crisis;* and in *On Active Service,* pp. 220–81; A. Whitney Griswold, *The Far Eastern Policy of the United States;* Armin Rappaport, *Henry Stimson and Japan 1931–1933;* Joseph C. Grew, *Ten Years in Japan;* and League of Nations Publications No. C 663 M. 320 1932 VII, Report of the Commission of Inquiry (the "Lytton Report"). See also Richard N. Current, *Secretary Stimson: A Study in Statecraft.*

treaties: by the Covenant of the League of Nations, by the Nine-Power Treaty of 1922 that bound its signatories (including the U.S., Britain and Japan) to respect the "sovereignty, independence and territory" of China and to uphold the free-trade principles of the Open Door; and by the Pact of Paris, the so-called Kellogg Pact, of 1929, by which the United States, Britain, France, Germany, Italy and again Japan promised "to renounce war as an instrument of national policy."

The reality was very different. The League began by siding *with* Japan. So did Britain, because of her fear of Chinese Communism. In 1928 Chiang had turned in friendship toward the Soviet Union, and for the time being, the Communist generals Chu Teh and Mao Tse-tung seemed to be gaining in the Chinese civil war. France and Holland tended to favor Japan likewise. As for the United States, many American diplomats shared Grew's initial perception that Japan would be a bulwark against Communism. The far more salient fact, though, was that American public opinion, in the very trough of the Great Depression, and with the isolationists riding as high in Congress as ever, was simply not ready to contemplate effective action in the Far East or anywhere else.

Although much later Stimson argued that the road was straight and clear from the Japanese aggression in Manchuria in 1931 through Pearl Harbor to the dropping of the atomic bombs, it is not certain that he understood straightaway the full implications of the Mukden Incident. In a letter at the time to the British Prime Minister, Ramsay MacDonald, he did not mention it. On September 22, four days after the Kwantung Army took Mukden, he refused to send an American member along with a proposed League of Nations fact-finding mission unless the Japanese agreed. It was not perhaps until around October 19, when he wrote in his diary that "the Japanese government with which we have been dealing is no longer in control," that he fully came to terms with the dangerous realities of the crisis.

We should think of Stimson's response to the Manchurian crisis as evolving in a series of phases. In the first three months, Stimson was alert and alarmed, but he was constrained by the limits of what the United States could do through "collective security"—given the lack of enthusiasm in the League of Nations for bold action, the lack of enthusiasm in America for the League, and the preoccupation of all the powers with the miseries of the Depression.

As early as September 29 the influential commentator Walter

Lippmann wrote in his newspaper column that he could sense "the end of isolationism." It was, however, a long time a-coming. In his Armistice Day speech in 1929 President Hoover said of Japanese infringements on Chinese sovereignty, "Neither our obligations to China, nor our own interests nor our dignity require us to go to war over these questions," and two years later a massive preponderance of American public opinion would have agreed. There was not even support for the United States to cooperate with the League in peaceful diplomacy. When, in mid-October, the League Council invited the U.S. to participate in talks about how the Kellogg Pact, with its renunciation of war, might be applied to the Manchurian situation, Stimson reluctantly allowed the U.S. consul in Geneva, Prentiss Gilbert, to sit at the Council table for a single day; the result was outraged fury in Congress.

In any event it was not at all clear that the United States, in 1931, had the physical capability to do anything, even supposing the political climate and the political will for drastic action had been present. As a result of years of cuts in the naval budget, the United States had one more battleship than Japan but far fewer cruisers, and one fewer aircraft carrier; in the Pacific, Japan was then the stronger naval power.

Over the course of the autumn, however, Stimson's personal attitude gradually hardened. At a press conference on November 5 he pointed out that public opinion was pro-Japanese in Britain and France, and in the U.S., though there was a special sympathy for China, people were "overwhelmingly against going to war or risking it." Such cautious words did not necessarily reflect his private instincts. Harvey Bundy, who had just come down to Washington from practicing trust law in Boston to be his Assistant Secretary and increasingly his confidant, recalled many years later of this time that Stimson, "brought up in the Teddy Roosevelt tradition and believ[ing] in the exercise of power and not waiting to listen to the country," had "a lot of the soldier in him," and was "on his horse and ready to shoot the Japanese at sunrise."* But, as the loyal but cautious Bundy pointed out, Stimson had not only the Congress against him, but the President too, and for good measure his Under Secretary, William Castle. Castle had undercut him on other issues, and he had access to Herbert Hoover.

Over the course of the autumn the Japanese made it all too plain

*H. H. Bundy, *Columbia University Oral History Project*, pp. 105 ff.

they were embarked on a war of conquest that would not end until they had made Manchuria into a subject province like Korea. At the end of September, General Honjo of the Kwantung Army withdrew Japanese recognition from Manchuria's ruler, the Young Marshal, Chang Hsueh-liang. On October 8 Japanese aircraft first bombed the Young Marshal's stronghold at Chinchow. By the end of the month the Japanese had launched an expeditionary force against the northern province of Heilungkiang, of which Harbin is the capital. Two days before Christmas the Japanese armies were closing in on Chinchow, southwest of Mukden, which fell during the night of January 2–3.

Stimson was shocked by the bombing of Chinchow. The man who was to order the atomic bombs dropped on Hiroshima and Nagasaki sent a protest note to Tokyo saying that "bombing of an unfortified and unwarned town is one of the most extreme of military actions, deprecated even in time of war." He was outraged by what he perceived as Japanese perfidy and, worse, as the betrayal of a personal promise to him. "For all their promises," he wrote, "the Japanese army was expanding rather than contracting its operations." Later he wrote bitterly that "the Japanese had joined in the post-war treaties, but they did not mean the same to them." He became ever more sure that something must be done to stop them. But what could be done?

One idea was to call a conference of the signatories of the Kellogg Pact. There was not much in that. Another, proposed by the newspaper magnate Roy Howard, was to recall the U.S. ambassador from Tokyo. Privately, Stimson called Howard a "damn fool" for that. Economic sanctions sounded more promising. But the President was against them, so was Castle, and even Stimson was concerned at the possible consequences. After all, when the U.S. did finally impose oil sanctions, the decision provoked the Japanese to go to war for the oil of the Dutch East Indies; Pearl Harbor, from their point of view, was an operation to clear their left flank for the drive south. At a meeting at Woodley the Secretary reluctantly sided with his Under Secretary, against his friend Allen Klots* and other officials for whom he had a higher regard than he did for Castle.

*Klots was a partner in Winthrop, Stimson who had come to Washington to work as Stimson's special assistant. A special favorite of Stimson's, he had been the "class boy" of Stimson's class at Yale, that is, the first son born to a member of the class, whose members contributed to sending him through Yale.

Another idea, however, was gestating. A letter from Walter Lippmann played some part in its genesis, and so did a suggestion from an able official in the State Department, Stanley Hornbeck. By November 19 the Secretary was talking it over on the transatlantic telephone with Charles G. Dawes in Paris. He also took counsel of his old mentor, Elihu Root.

The new measure was the Doctrine of Nonrecognition, or the "Stimson Doctrine," one of Stimson's claims to fame as a diplomatist. Stimson himself never claimed it as his, though it was generally credited to him at the time. Herbert Hoover claimed that he "first proposed this idea (originally Bryan's).* Much praised at the time, in retrospect it has to be tested in terms of its consequences, and by that test, it has to be said that it failed.

On January 2, learning of the imminent fall of Chinchow, the Secretary rose at six o'clock and wrote a first draft of a nonrecognition statement. This was refined into two identical notes, delivered through the U.S. ambassadors in Nanking and Tokyo to the governments of China and Japan on January 7, 1932. The key phrase was that the United States "did not intend to recognize any situation, treaty or agreement which may be brought about by means contrary to the Pact of Paris"— that was to say, by war, declared or undeclared.

It didn't work. As one historian unkindly put it, Stimson "had reflected superbly the sentiments of a majority of Americans. He had voiced the revulsion . . . yet had made no commitment to aid the victims of aggression. He represented the outraged conscience, but at no cost."† That judgment is unfair, because as we have seen, Stimson had few practicable alternatives to nonrecognition. But it is hardly untrue.

The same day as his nonrecognition notes were delivered in Nanking and Tokyo, Stimson asked the British and French to join him. The British, in particular, he expected to "repair to the standard." They did nothing of the kind. Later Stimson pressed the British foreign secretary, the able lawyer Sir John Simon, to make a joint *démarche*. Nothing doing. Many Liberals in Britain shared Stimson's outrage at what the Japanese were doing. The leading Liberal newspaper, the *Manchester Guardian,*‡ with characteristic waspishness said

---

*dH. Hoover, *The Memoirs of Herbert Hoover,* vol. ii, *The Cabinet and the Presidency,* pp. 372–73.
†Armin Rappapport, *Henry Stimson and Japan,* p. 95.
‡As it then was. It moved its editorial offices to London and changed its name to *The Guardian* in 1960.

that Sir John was behaving like "a lawyer picking holes in a contract in the interests of a shady client." The client, so to speak, was himself; Simon wanted to be Prime Minister in the National (coalition) government in succession to MacDonald, and that could happen only with the approval of his Conservative colleagues. To join with the Americans in some madcap adventure in or about Manchuria would do him no good whatever with those pragmatic patriots. British Tories were suspicious of American ambitions in China and of the Open Door, which they saw as a formula for pushing American business interests at the expense of Britain's. They thought it would be a far better thing if peace in the Far East could be guaranteed by Anglo-Japanese, rather than United States–Japanese, cooperation. And if all failed, they felt Manchuria would be a far preferable outlet for Japanese expansionism to the Yangtze valley, still largely a British sphere of influence, let alone Southeast Asia, Australasia, or—God forbid!—India.

As early as November 8, 1931, a Japanese colonel virtually abducted the last Manchu emperor of China, Henry Pu Yi, from Tientsin to Mukden, and held him in residence to be elevated as the ruler of a puppet Manchurian state. The move was preplanned, part of a plot by high Japanese officers to create an "independent"—in reality Japanese-controlled—state of "Manchukuo," or Manchu-land.

Then in January 1932, with surprising speed, the focus shifted, from the north to the great international port and business center of Shanghai. The Japanese community there was the largest in the international concessions, and it was protected by the most powerful of the foreign forces: twenty-three warships in the Huang-pu River, against five British, two French and one American, and 2,500 Japanese marines, compared to 2,300 British, 1,250 U.S. Marines and 1,050 French. About 30,000 Chinese soldiers of the Nineteenth Route Army, one of the more determined of the Kuomintang units, were stationed in and around the Chinese quarter of Chapei.

When the Chinese in Shanghai, of course the overwhelming majority of the population, heard the news of the Japanese invasion of Manchuria, they started a boycott of Japanese goods. This gave the Japanese commanders the excuse they wanted. On January 18 Japanese priests from an extremist Shinto sect started a riot with Chinese outside a Chinese factory in Chapei. Later the same sect set the factory on fire and fought the Chinese police. But the Japanese consul general promptly demanded a formal apology, punishment of those (Chinese) responsible, and an end to the boycott.

The mayor of Shanghai said he would meet all but two of the Japanese demands; he could not end the boycott. On January 28 the Japanese admiral gave the Chinese just half an hour to remove all their troops from Chapei. But the Nineteenth Route Army held firm and dug in. The next day, January 29, Admiral Shiozawa sent in the bombers from his carriers, using incendiary bombs. Much of Chapei was burned to the ground. Thousands of Chinese men, women and children were killed. The Shanghai incident was the sinister forerunner of the infamous war that was soon to engulf all China, swallow millions of Japanese soldiers and earn Japan nothing but a reputation for ruthlessness she would take decades to live down.

World opinion, not least opinion in the United States, always sympathetic with the masses and the missionaries of China, began to turn sharply against the Japanese, and so did the American Secretary of State. Even before the bombing of Chapei he put it to the British that he would send the U.S. Asiatic fleet to Shanghai if they would send their powerful China Squadron from Hong Kong. The British government refused, and much of the British press—largely Conservative-owned—still openly preferred Japan's case to U.S. criticism of it.

The most Stimson could do, after a meeting with President Hoover, was to send the cruiser *Houston,* six destroyers and one infantry regiment, with 400 Marines, to Shanghai, where they could do little more than reinforce the defense of the International Concession; though simultaneously the U.S. Pacific fleet maneuvered in great strength off Hawaii. In Tokyo, the Japanese government asked the U.S., Britain and France to use their good offices to work for peace in Shanghai. But by February 18 peace talks with the Chinese had broken down after the Japanese once again produced an ultimatum that could not be met, and 20,000 Japanese troops, backed by artillery, aircraft and naval gunnery, moved in to the attack, surrounded by millions of civilians in the middle of one of the half-dozen biggest cities in the world. The next day, in Geneva, the Council of the League voted to call the Assembly into emergency session.

Stimson was more outraged than ever by the way the Japanese had behaved, and more at a loss than ever as to what could be done about it. Once again he looked to Britain, in the far from Churchillian shape of Sir John Simon, for solidarity; and once again he looked in vain. He complained bitterly on the telephone to Ray Atherton, U.S.

minister in London, that Britain "has let us down." But the complaint reflected Stimson's frustration as much as anything; he knew as well as anyone that the President was opposed to cooperating with the League, let alone to any direct military action, and so were all but two members of the Senate.

A number of impressive figures in American public life—including the president of Harvard University, A. Lawrence Lowell; and the former Secretary of War, Newton D. Baker; Nicholas Murray Butler, president of Columbia University; and the young John Foster Dulles— came out for an economic boycott of Japan. Though Stimson had reluctantly accepted that a boycott was not a realistic option, he was pleased to have such pressure from highly respected public figures, if only because it kept the Japanese guessing about what costs their actions might bring them.

On February 24, despairing of organizing an international *posse comitatus* to cut out the rustlers of the Orient, Stimson fell back on another of his masterly strokes of traditional diplomacy. He adopted a time-honored device, the open letter: in this case, addressed to Senator William E. Borah, the isolationist chairman of the Senate Foreign Relations Committee. After a "refreshing" game of his favorite deck tennis at Woodley, he sat down with Allen Klots and James Grafton Rogers* at his side and dictated the whole letter, some 2,500 words long, "almost as it stood, with occasional suggestions and corrections from the others." By midnight it was finished. (A self-styled "lark" rather than an "owl," the Secretary liked to get his important work done early in the day; a midnight session indicated the importance he attached to the Borah letter.) President Hoover approved the result, and even asked, "with one of his rather shy smiles," whether it could be said that the nonrecognition notes had been sent at his instructions, though later he became nervous, and had to be restrained from putting out a statement saying that the United States would not join in a boycott.

The letter, Stimson wrote later, was "intended for the perusal of five unnamed addressees": it was intended "to encourage China, enlighten the American public, exhort the League, stir up the British, and warn Japan." The way Stimson did this was by retracing the his-

---

*Assistant Secretary of State James Grafton Rogers was a Westerner, the only one to serve on any of Stimson's staffs. He did not, however, represent a total break with tradition: he was a graduate of Yale and of the Harvard Law School.

tory of American policy from John Hay's Open Door Policy at the turn of the century, through the Nine-Power Treaty of 1922, the Washington disarmament treaties and the Kellogg Pact, which he called "a program for the protection of China." "That is the view of this Government," the letter concluded. "We see no reason for abandoning the enlightened principles which are embodied in these treaties. We believe that this situation would have been avoided had these covenants been observed."*

In effect, what Stimson told the world, through the dignified periods of his Borah letter, was that American policy since the Boxer Rebellion had had as its grand object the preservation of the integrity of China as a nation. To this great end, he reminded readers, the United States had involved the other nations in a series of binding treaties. With the same purpose in mind, the United States had taken risks and made sacrifices under the naval treaties and by, for example, agreeing not to fortify Manila or Guam. But all these international agreements hung together, Stimson was saying, addressing the Japanese in particular. Japan could not claim the advantages to be won from them while at the same time it shrugged off the agreements' solemn obligations. If they went on breaking the treaties, including the naval treaty—Stimson was reminding them with elaborate politeness—then in the end the United States would feel free to do the same. Once again, the letter was hailed as a diplomatic masterpiece, and indeed—unlike the nonrecognition statement—it did appear to have the desired result on the ground. For in March 1932 the Japanese decided to pull out of Shanghai. The Borah letter, in consequence, was universally popular in the United States. It seemed to show that a tough stance could bring the Japanese to heel, without fighting or even spending money on improved military readiness.

It is very doubtful whether that was the right lesson to draw. The Japanese withdrew from Shanghai in part because of the unexpectedly tenacious resistance of the Nineteenth Route Army, which pulled back twenty miles from Shanghai in February but continued to fight stubbornly; and in part because Japan wanted recognition for Manchukuo, which was to say for her *de facto* conquests in Manchuria, from the League if possible and especially from Britain. On March 11 Britain, France and all other members of the League except Japan and—under

*On Active Service, pp. 249–54.

Japanese pressure—China duly voted against recognition of Manchu-kuo, thus appearing to vindicate Stimson's original nonrecognition policy. But there was not much comfort to be taken from such real or apparent diplomatic victories.

Hard facts remained. Over the longer term the Japanese military were determined to expand, starting with Manchuria and China. The very day before the Borah letter was published, the Japanese government, in a formal answer to an official approach by the League of Nations, stated that it did not and could not "consider that China is an 'organized people' within the meaning of the Covenant of the League of Nations." China has, it is true—the Japanese note went on—been treated in the past by common consent as if the expression connoted an organized people. But fictions cannot last forever.

The Japanese military were in effective control of the government in Tokyo. (In May, Prime Minister Inukai Tsuyoshi was assassinated. A few weeks earlier the chairman of the board of Mitsui was murdered; even the *zaibatsu* were not warlike enough for the young officers.) And no amount of skillful expression of American disapproval was going to stop men who had now drawn the sword. By the ancient samurai code, once the blade has been withdrawn, even by an inch, from the scabbard, it must be wet with the enemy's blood.

On April 8, 1932, the Secretary of State left for Geneva, arriving there by way of London and Paris on April 15. He explained to as many delegates as he met his view that the Japanese were adopting "the old Spanish ideas of exploitation of foreign peoples." If no more effective action could be achieved, at least let the nations pass moral judgment on Japan. At best, that might deter Japanese aggression; at worst, it would lay a foundation for concerted action at some more favorable time in the future. In return, the Secretary of State was asked by the Europeans whether, if the League were to brand a country such as Japan as an aggressor, the United States would stay neutral. It was not a question that an honest Secretary of State could answer in the negative, and it was painful for Stimson—who would have been only too happy to put the United States at the head of a world crusade to make the Japanese obey their treaties—to have to answer that, for the foreseeable future, the United States was rock-solid for neutrality. If he had been in any doubt about that, his Under Secretary, in collusion with his President, reminded him of the realities by making two statements to the effect that the United States would join in no boycott of Japan. It was true. But it was the last thing Stimson wanted to say.

He made one last attempt to draw a credible line in the sand and tell the Japanese not to cross it. In a speech on August 8 he put Tokyo on notice that the United States was committed to consult the other signatories of the Kellogg Pact.

> Henceforth when two nations engage in armed conflict . . . we no longer draw a circle around them and treat them with the punctilio of the dueller's code. We denounce [the wrongdoers] as lawbreakers. . . . A nation which sought to mask its imperialistic policy under the guise of defense of its nationals would soon be unmasked.*

But Japan scarcely tried to mask its imperialistic policy. On September 15 it finally recognized the puppet government of Manchukuo, set up over more than 20 million Chinese by a blatant mixture of fraud and armed force.

At the beginning of October the Lytton Report was published, the work of a commission of inquiry sent by the League of Nations to report on the facts about Manchuria. The chairman was Lord Lytton, a former British governor of Bengal and acting viceroy of India; one of the other members was Colonel Stimson's old friend from happier days inspecting army posts in the Southwest and from both Nicaragua and the Philippines, General Frank McCoy.

The Lytton Commission originally intended to set out the facts in a balanced fashion, favoring neither one side nor the other. So unambiguous did its members find the record, however, that the report turned into a lapidary indictment of Japan. When the League's Assembly met in Geneva in December 1932 to consider the report, the smaller powers, such as Sweden, Ireland and Czechoslovakia, insisted that the League must accept the report, censure Japan, and refuse to recognize Manchukuo. If not, they saw clearly, the League's future power to protect them from other predators and bullies, indeed its very existence, would be at risk.

Sir John Simon would have none of it. He succeeded in getting the report referred to a committee, which promptly appointed a subcommittee and then adjourned! On January 3 the Kwantung Army

*The New York Times, August 9, 1932.

took another bite out of China. It invaded Jehol, the province immediately north of the Great Wall. If the League objected, Article XVI
of the Covenant, which called for collective action against aggression,
would almost certainly have been invoked, and that would have meant
war. No one wanted that. All the League was willing to do was to
condemn the aggressor, and that it finally did. On February 24, 1933,
the Assembly in Geneva adopted the Lytton Report forty-two to one,
with Britain, in the person of Sir John Simon, abstaining. Shrilly calling down imprecations on the world, the Japanese delegate, Matsuoka
Yosuke, later foreign minister, led his country out of the League of
Nations. (To argue Japan's case at the League, Matsuoka was accompanied by General Tatekawa and Colonel Ishiwara.*) The world community had failed to find the will to restrain Japan by force. And Japan
had made it painfully clear that she was not to be restrained by anything less.

A̱fter 1933 moderates had little room for political maneuver in
Tokyo, and the voice of Western reason reached fewer and fewer re-
ceptive ears. The army and navy high commands pressed ahead with
their plans for a great Japanese empire, stretching from the gates of
India to the island fringes of Alaska, and transforming China and her
more than 400 million "unorganized people" into a captive market
for the Japanese *zaibatsu.* The atmosphere in Tokyo was feverish. The
February 26 incident, in 1936, when military conspirators murdered
Viscount Saito and only failed to kill the Prime Minister because they
killed his brother-in-law instead by mistake, was only a particularly
horrible example of the paranoia and violence that had now become
endemic.

The universally respected Prince Konoye, who became Prime
Minister in the spring of 1937, could no more control the military than
his predecessors had done. On July 8 came the so-called China Incident. The Japanese North China Army wanted a base with an airfield
at the Marco Polo Bridge at Lukouchiao, on the south side of Peking,
covering both the Peking-Hankow and Peking-Tientsin railroads, and
so potentially cutting the city off from outside help. An incident was
engineered on the railway, almost a carbon copy of the Mukden In-

*Hoyt, *Japan's War,* p. 108.

cident six years before, and predictably having the same effect. Military
historians date the beginning of the general war between Japan and
China, which lasted until 1945, from the repulse of the Chinese Nationalists' Twenty-ninth Army, which tried to relieve Peking. From
now on, Japan was committed to the invasion and—as far as possible—
the occupation of the most populous country on earth, with a land
area virtually as large as that of the continental United States. Before
the end of that year Japanese generals had carried the war up the
Yangtze to Nanking, where Japanese troops were allowed to commit
unforgivable atrocities. An American gunboat, the *Panay,* was sunk by
Japanese aircraft.

In 1938 Hankow fell, in spite of the flooding of the Yellow River,
which caused millions of casualties. Canton was taken by a naval expedition. Japan had an army of more than a million men on the Chinese mainland, and they had driven Chiang Kai-shek back as far as
Chungking, in Szechuan, the remotest corner of China.

For seven years after the failure of the League, and of the United
States, to stop Japan over Manchuria, the progress of Japanese conquest, and the evolution of Japanese paranoia, did not concern Colonel Stimson. After November 1932, the month in which the League
wrestled with the implications of accepting, or rejecting, the Lytton
Report, he was a lame duck. Thereafter he was removed to the private
practice of law, interrupted by increasingly Cassandra-like warnings of
the dangers of drift in world affairs, and by his and his wife's ever more
stately vacation progresses to Maine, to the Carolinas or to Scotland.

On January 9, 1933, however, six days after the Japanese invaded
Jehol, Stimson met President-elect Franklin D. Roosevelt at the ances-
tral Roosevelt home at Hyde Park, New York. Strangely enough, given
their respective relationships with Theodore Roosevelt, the two men
had never met before. For Stimson, the meeting was a pleasant surprise
and a revelation, all the more so because it could not come about until
clouds of mutual suspicion had been dispersed. It was, not surprisingly, Felix Frankfurter, whose admiration for Stimson was only exceeded by his idolatry of Roosevelt, who suggested that it might be a
good thing, especially in the context of the debt negotiations then
proceeding with Europe, if the outgoing Secretary of State could brief
the President-elect.* To members of the defeated Hoover administra-

*See *On Active Service,* pp. 289–95.

tion, many of whom regarded FDR as a monster of duplicity as well as a traitor to their class, the very idea of such a meeting was alarming as well as shocking. Ogden Mills, Secretary of the Treasury, was dead set against it. President Hoover said that Roosevelt was "a very dangerous and contrary man and he would never see him alone."* In the end, Stimson went to Hyde Park, and was seduced by FDR's charm as so many others had been and would be again.

The lessons of the Manchurian crisis have been much debated. Some have blamed Henry Stimson for his initial caution, others for taking a moralistic position that was bound to provoke and antagonize Japan and yet one that the United States had neither the means nor the will to back up.

Stimson was pitiless in his judgment of the League of Nations in general and the wretched Sir John Simon in particular. In private he said he was "disgusted." He called the leaders of the League in general "damn mushy cowards"† and singled Simon out for "weasling." Simon's performance was in all truth not inspiring, but Britain was passing through economic depression and political crisis, and her military capability to influence the situation in China was very limited. The week before the Mukden Incident, Britain went off the gold standard. The week after, there was a mutiny in the Royal Navy at Invergordon, the first for more than a hundred years. But Simon's resistance to Stimson's appeals to, figuratively speaking, wave a bright saber in the air and charge the Japanese, was not due to weakness or even cowardice alone. They could also have been quite rationally premised on the Secretary's own position, which was in truth scarcely stronger than Sir John's. The spirit might be willing. Henry Stimson's always was. But the political flesh was weak.

In the history of world affairs, the Manchurian crisis was an episode of the first importance. It demonstrated the weakness of the cobweb of collective security built around the League of Nations and the treaties. It taught a lesson that was learned by the dictators before the democracies absorbed it: that only force could stop a nation or a leader who was willing to use force and use it ruthlessly. It showed beyond a doubt that the Japanese were determined to conquer China and such

---

*HLS, *Diary,* January 3–4, 1933.
† *Ibid.*

other territories as would give them the markets and the raw materials they believed they needed. And, last but not least, though few recognized the fact at the time, it meant that the United States, and the United States almost alone, would have to fight to defend the integrity of China—even though in the event that happened only after an attack by the Japanese provoked by their fear of running out of oil before they could accomplish their designs for expansion.

Finally, the crisis had consequences in the mind and spirit of Henry Stimson. It taught him the greatest suspicion, if not of Japan, at least of Japan's leaders. As early as September 1932 he had a long talk with Admiral Hepburn, commanding the U.S. Pacific Fleet, about the "underlying danger in the Far East and the absolute necessity of keeping the Navy in such a condition in which it would be airtight against any sudden attack by the Japanese."* There, looking forward to Pearl Harbor, was prescience. Most important, the Manchurian affair led Stimson to meditate about how international security was to be maintained. He had always been a soldier at heart—he said so himself—more than a lawyer or a diplomat. In his heart, even while he invoked it, he had never trusted the Wilsonian ideal or had confidence in the litany of treaties by which the international order was to be maintained. Certainly, without the means and the determination to fight in the last resort, those imposing structures would indeed prove as light as cobwebs. Or, as Stimson's friend, the great French poet Paul Claudel, who was ambassador of France in Washington at the time, put it, they would be "spears of straw and swords of ice."†

Colonel Stimson never supposed that the only potential aggressors were the Japanese. In his seven years of absence from the public arena he came to fear and dislike the European dictators as much as he feared and despised their counterparts in Japan. He set himself to try to persuade the American people that they, too, might have to fight, and that when the time came they had better be ready. It was not the easiest brief an advocate ever gave himself.

---

*Armin Rappaport, *Henry Stimson and Japan,* pp. 170 ff.
†*On Active Service,* p. 256. The phrase is an old Chinese one, which Stimson learned from Claudel.

V

The Atlantic
Experience:
The Suicide
of Europe

If the European Civil War is to end with France and
Italy abusing their momentary victorious power to
destroy Germany and Austria-Hungary now prostrate, they invite their own destruction also, being so
deeply and inextricably intertwined with their victims
by hidden psychic and economic bonds.

J. M. Keynes, *The Economic Consequences of the Peace*, 1923

A political arithmetician would predict that, in the circumstances of 1931, the American people would throw
themselves into the task of salvaging the economic world
order, with which their own material fortunes were
bound up, with ten times the energy that they had
thrown into the task of winning the World War in
1917. . . . Yet the *a priori* calculations of theory were
completely contradicted by the facts of observation.

Arnold Toynbee, *Survey of International Affairs*, 1931

I said that the time had come when somebody has
got to show some guts.

Henry L. Stimson, *Diary*, November 30, 1932

Millions of Americans to this day cherish a dark hostility to
the New York legal and financial establishment in which Henry Stim-
son lived. Part of that hostility comes from a suspicion that men like
Stimson and his friends have focused on Europe to the exclusion of
American interests in Latin America and the Pacific. Indeed, in its
more conspiratorial and virulent form, the suspicion alleges that the
Eastern Establishment cannot be trusted not to prefer the interests of
Europe, and of Britain especially, to those of the United States.

In recent years, for example, the Trilateral Commission, an attempt nurtured by David Rockefeller among others to bring leaders

from the United States, Western Europe and Japan together to discuss
world problems, evoked fierce anger from Southern and Western conservatives. After World War I, however, this suspicion of New York
and its secret entanglements with Europe in general and London in
particular, was far more intense. Many were the Americans, especially
those of German or Irish descent, who believed that the United States
had been manipulated into taking part in World War I by the insidious
wiles of the Lion. Men like Stimson, who became convinced that
America had no alternative but to fight, were often seen as mere cat's
paws of the British. After the war, and after the rejection by the Senate
of the Versailles Treaty, that sentiment only grew. A large majority of
the American electorate, and a formidable body of opinion in both
parties in Congress, was determined that the United States must never
again be entangled in what they saw as the ancient and irrelevant quarrels of Europe. After 1929, as the icy fingers of the Great Depression
paralyzed most of the economies of Europe, the general reluctance to
become involved in international politics was embittered by passionate,
if ill-informed, resentment on the subject of Europe's debts to America
and the efforts of some Europeans to avoid repaying them.

Right up to the eve of Pearl Harbor, as we shall see, a body of
opinion in the United States powerful enough to compel the most
gingerly respect even from such a master politician as Franklin D. Roosevelt angrily denounced any suggestion that the United States should,
in its own interests, act to prevent Europe being dragged into war for
a second time under the weight of its ancient rivalries, and its new
economic quarrels.

Henry Stimson believed, as early as 1931, if not before, that America and Europe were inextricably entangled, whether anyone liked it
or not. But, as his involvement in policy toward first Central America,
then the Far East, makes clear, this did not mean that he was "Euro-
centric." Throughout his public life, from 1911 to 1948, Stimson was
actively concerned with how the United States should deal with Asia
and Latin America. Nicaragua and the Philippines were the first the-
aters of his international activity. His diaries show that as Secretary of
State he found at least as much of his time taken up with the affairs of
Latin America and with areas of interest to the United States, such as
the Caribbean, the Philippines and even Liberia, as was occupied with
Western Europe. He treated the Manchurian crisis as at least as serious as the contemporaneous problems over European debt and
disarmament.

Still, between 1911 and 1941—that is, from the date of Stimson's first involvement in international affairs until the moment of the United States's final commitment to global conflict and global power—it *was* primarily Europe that threatened to draw the United States into war and economic disaster. The threat from Japan was serious, but less immediately dangerous. Moreover, it can be argued, and Stimson almost certainly would have argued, that if Europe had been healthy, sufficient pressure could have been brought to bear through the League of Nations, backed by the threat of naval and economic sanctions, to make Japan cease and desist from her schemes of conquest.

It is also true, however, that Americans of Stimson's class and generation, like the independently wealthy, well-educated Americans in the novels of Henry James and Edith Wharton (whom Stimson's parents greatly resembled) were far more at home in London or Paris than in Omaha or San Diego (a city which Henry James, in his 1882 story "The Siege of London," located in New Mexico!). When Stimson acknowledged that his sympathies were strongly on the side of the French and the British, he pointed out that he had lived in Paris as a boy and that his father had left Berlin and moved to Paris not only to study under the great Louis Pasteur, but also because he was "disgusted by the martial swagger of the youthful German empire." He learned from his father, he added, to mistrust the Germans and admire the French.

There was in this, too, more than a trace of racial superiority. Stimson and those who shared his education and background instinctively thought themselves the equals of the British and the superiors of everyone else. Such assumptions scarcely needed to be expressed, but in the privacy of his diary Stimson from time to time allowed his ethnic prejudices to show through the boiled shirt of formal good manners. "The Haitian Minister came in to present the new Haitian minister," the Colonel recorded in his diary on January 29, 1931, and then added, apparently in surprise, "who was a fine fully fledged Negro." (When in 1932 he was asked by Franklin Roosevelt about Haiti, he replied, "I did not think it would stay permanently put and I asked him whether he knew any self-governing negro community which had stayed put, and he could not suggest any.")* Again, a couple of months later, when he was asked whether the funds of a bequest called the Parker Trust should go to Princeton, Duke, Yale or Columbia, he

*HLS, Memo of conversation in HLS, *Diary,* vol. XXIV, p. 101.

noted in his diary that he did not like the "atmosphere" at Columbia. It was not just the "bad influence" of radical thinkers like John Dewey and Charles Beard that he distrusted, he added, but also "the tremendous Jewish influence."* In the Philippines, too, he was quite easy with Leonard Wood's robust assumption of the inferiority of Malays to Americans, even though he was free enough from racial hostility to have social relations with upper-class Filipinos, most of whom were not of pure Malay descent, of course, but had at least some Spanish blood, and, as we have seen, he enjoyed a real friendship with one, Manuel Quezon.

The point is not that Stimson was unusually prejudiced against black people, against Jews, or against Orientals, though not all of his contemporaries displayed his racial biases. It is that he shared with most white Americans of his generation a hierarchical view of the world's nations and peoples, a view clearly evidenced by the various immigration acts, and most clearly of all by the National Origins Act of 1929, enacted while Stimson was Secretary of State, which discriminated flagrantly in favor of migrants from northwestern Europe over other Europeans, and in favor of Europeans as a whole against all others.

When war came, Stimson had gone overseas and fought alongside the British and the French. He was especially impressed with the Scots officers and men of the Fifty-first Highland Division, with whom he received his own baptism of fire. During his month with the Highlanders he wrote home again and again to Mabel and to his sister Candace describing his hosts' kindness and imperturbability under fire. Some of them were professional soldiers. Most were volunteers like himself. As it happened, one of them was a London lawyer who had done a lot of business with Stimson's own partner, Bronson Winthrop.

Like many officers in the American Expeditionary Force, Stimson believed it would be up to the wartime Allies, especially to the United States and Britain, to secure the peace. In this simple emotional assumption lay the seeds of what was to become a commitment to opposing isolation and a policy of preparing the United States for war at Britain's side after the defeat of France. "If we ever get through this," he wrote to Mabel on January 31, 1918, "we shall have a lot of good

*Diary, March 19, 1931.

friends in England to look up when you and I go over! and this is only an instance of what I hope the war will do in bringing the two nations together."*

By the two nations, needless to say, Stimson did not mean the Two Nations of Disraeli's prophetic novel *Sybil,* the rich and the poor. Americans of Stimson's background (and income) instinctively got on with wealthy Englishmen, whether or not they had titles, like Lord Hugh Cecil, whom Stimson made friends with on the troopship that took him to Liverpool, or Virginia-born Nancy, Lady Astor, whose husband had emigrated to England and who was the first woman to be elected to the British House of Commons. Stimson records in his diary how she always made Mabel's dinner parties go with a swing.

After 1918, indeed, the friendly relations between upper-class Americans and their British counterparts in banking, law, diplomacy, and academia were beginning to be institutionalized. Rhodes Scholarships, founded by the will of Cecil Rhodes, who died in 1902, brought young men from Germany and the white British Dominions (Australia, New Zealand, Canada and South Africa), as well as from the United States to study at Oxford. The scholarships wove a network of relationships between the British Foreign Office and the State Department, as well as between the banking worlds of New York and London. The Pilgrim Trust, founded in 1930, brought powerful opinion-formers in the two countries together for charitable enterprises and occasional political initiatives; the Pilgrims' Society was already in existence. In 1929, when Stimson wanted to give a fair wind to a new international agreement on naval disarmament, it was arranged for the American ambassador to the Court of St. James, Charles Gates Dawes, to speak at a Pilgrims' dinner at which he could be certain that his listeners, in their white ties and tailcoats, would include a good proportion of those in London whose ideas on imperial policy were listened to in Whitehall. And when Stimson and his delegation arrived in London in search of a naval treaty, as a matter of course they were welcomed to dine in the Temple with the leaders of the British bar, a confraternity who greeted these Americans with a great deal more warmth than they would have extended to most British politicians.

The First World War, in fact, had not only imbued the political and business elites in London and New York with a new comradeship,

*HLS, *Papers,* reel 119, p. 381, January 31, 1918.

forged on the battlefield, or at least in wartime committee rooms, but it had made the British highly conscious of the relative decline of their economic and military power; did a wag not call it the War of the British Succession? In a world full of enemies—from the new Indian nationalist movement to Japanese manufacturers of cheap bicycles and cotton-spinning machinery, from the insurgent Irish to resurgent German militarism, from Soviet Russia on the northwest frontiers of India to socialist coal miners in the northeast of England—British leaders of all political parties instinctively turned to the United States for sympathy and support. They often exaggerated the amount of sympathy there was for them in American public opinion. All the more welcome, therefore, was the bond with those, like Stimson, Dawes, and many State Department officials and New York bankers, who shared their view that they were the embattled and unappreciated defenders of a civilization threatened by barbarism, and who were appalled by the isolationism of what H. L. Mencken called the *booboisie* in their own country.

The interwar period was the time when the tight, sharply defined ruling class in England and its more diffuse but still recognizable counterpart in the United States, after a century of mutual dislike, began to make friends. Very often they did so as individuals. These were the years of the improbable friendship between Oliver Wendell Holmes, the Yankee from Olympus, and a middle-class Jewish socialist at the London School of Economics, Harold Laski. In 1934 Felix Frankfurter fell in love with Oxford, where he was a visiting professor, and extended on the eastern side of the Atlantic those networks of information and recruitment which he had already knitted among his friends in Cambridge, New York and Washington. Before commercial transatlantic flight (which became routine only in the 1950s), few Americans knew Europe well, but those who did found few doors closed against them. There was fundamental common ground between, on the one hand, the world of the Middle Temple in London, the common room at All Souls' College, Oxford, and Lady Astor's weekend house parties at Cliveden on the Thames, and the New York and Boston lawyers and bankers at home at the Down Town Association or the Century in New York or at the Metropolitan Club in Washington.

Socially, these two elites shared tastes, values and prejudices. Politically, there was no longer any real rivalry between them. After 1918 the United States had become unarguably the ascendant, the British Empire unmistakably the declining power. American internationalists believed that their country was bursting with youthful strength, but many of them saw themselves as still green and ignorant of the world in comparison with the heirs of a century of empire. Their British counterparts were all too conscious of their country's faltering economy and declining power. The relationship, as both sides saw it, echoed the old French proverb: *si jeunesse savait, si vieillesse pouvait*—"if only youth had the knowledge: if only old age had the strength."

Every year between 1925 and 1939 (and again for a few years after World War II) the historian Arnold Toynbee divided his time between what he and his family called his "nonsense book," *A Study of History*, and editing for the Royal Institute of International Affairs at Chatham House in St. James's Square, London, a survey of the year's events. In late 1931 he sat down to write the Survey in a mood that was somber, even for the student of the mortality of civilizations. In this year of grace, he reflected, for the first time in more than two hundred years, all over the world thoughtful men and women were seriously contemplating and soberly discussing the possibility that the great liberal civilization that had spread over the world from Western Europe and North America might not survive. Why, Toynbee went on to ask, had the United States not acted more energetically to save the economic world order in which they had the biggest stake? In 1917 they had overcome their natural reluctance to become entangled in the affairs of the rest of the world. "In 1931, they had the double incentive of averting a great national disaster and winning a great national reward."* Puzzled, Toynbee retreated from the enigma of isolationism into one of his more obscure classical references; "in the crisis of 1931 the American Jeshuron," he shrugged, "was playing as negative a part as the German Sisyphus."†

In the 1920s few members of the Royal Institute of International Affairs ventured far into the American Middle West. It was perhaps just as well; for few Englishmen had any but the vaguest idea of how unpopular‡ they were in the American heartland. Isolationism, that

---

*Arnold Toynbee, *Survey of International Affairs*, 1931, p. 20.

†Jeshuron "waxed fat and kicked." Deuteronomy xxxii.15. Sisyphus was a legendary king of Corinth condemned in the underworld, in punishment for his avarice, to roll a huge stone uphill for all eternity.

‡Englishmen, however, may have been less unpopular than other Europeans, at least in 1937. In that year, when the American Institute of Public Opinion found that while 69 percent of Americans were in favor of stricter neutrality, 55 percent chose England as their favorite Euro-

most complex episode in the history of American attitudes toward the outside world, was not confined to the Middle West, yet it was essentially a Middle Western phenomenon, deeply rooted in that section's interests, political consciousness and ethnic composition. For isolationism was only in part opposition to American involvement in the business of the world overseas. Few isolationists were opposed to all forms of U.S. military intervention abroad. Most of them objected, not to intervention as such but to intervention in Europe, as opposed to the Caribbean or the Far East, and to intervention on behalf of Britain and France in particular. Isolationism meant, to the isolationists, not the limiting of American freedom of action, but the freeing of America from entangling alliances, avoidance of commitments, a refusal to limit American sovereignty or share it with any political "superauthority" such as the League of Nations or the World Court. It meant not friendlessness but "an ideal interpreted to the nation by Washington as 'the command of its own fortunes.' "* Finally, isolationism was intimately bound up with domestic American politics, and especially with the divergent interests and competing ambitions of the East and the Middle West. In the last analysis it was not about world politics, but about American politics.

The idea of a "special relationship" between the United States and Britain founded in kith and kin and in the shared principles of Anglo-Saxon democracy and the common law is largely a myth, invented by publicists for the Anglo-American alliance in both world wars, and kept alight by those members of the British elite who prefer to have a share, however small and dependent, in American power rather than feel without power in the world at all.† Before 1914, most Americans focused far more on the differences between revolutionary, democratic, republican America and conservative, imperial, monarchical Britain.‡ As a corollary, in the nineteenth century it was British

pean country. In contrast, 11 percent chose France, 8 percent chose Germany, and 4 percent chose Ireland. American Institute of Public Opinion Survey, October 1937. The archisolationist Senator Burton K. Wheeler once said, "Next to being pro-American I am pro-English."
*Albert K. Weinberg, "The Historical Meaning of the American Doctrine of Isolation," *American Political Science Review*, vol. xxxiv, June 1940, p. 547.
†See Max Beloff, "The Special Relationship: An Anglo-American Myth," in Martin Gilbert (ed.), *A Century of Conflict*, essays presented to A. J. P. Taylor.
‡The British journalist David Watt, in his definitive essay on the history of Anglo-American relations, pointed out the contrast between its coolness for most of its duration and its warmth in modern times. "Only for a mere forty-five years in total . . . has it amounted to what might be called an 'alliance.' . . . A shared language and a joint adherence to the common law did

radicals, not—as was to be the case increasingly after 1945—British conservatives who most admired the United States.

For more than a century before the United States found itself fighting side by side with the British Empire against Germany, Austria-Hungary and Turkey, the predominant American attitude toward Britain was coolness, interspersed with brief periods of acute resentment whenever Britain appeared to show signs of interfering in the Western Hemisphere, for example, over Oregon in 1846, over British complicity in Confederate blockade-running during the Civil War, and over Venezuela in 1895. Toward the end of the nineteenth century, this age-old suspicion of John Bull was sharpened by the identification made by Western farmers and radicals between Eastern and British capital. And whereas in the nineteenth century Middle Westerners shared the national interest in a worldwide struggle against tyranny, in the early years of the twentieth century a great many of them "decided that the rest of the world was beyond redemption."*

There were many reasons for this. The two political parties, for one thing, both came to what amounted to an isolationist position—even if by very different routes. On the question of the Philippines, Republicans tended to see American expansion as an opportunity for business and labor alike, and therefore to oppose the British and French empires as rivals. Democrats, on the other hand, saw any kind of colonization as immoral, and also as a cynical attempt by Republican businessmen to undercut American wages. Hard times between 1873 and the 1890s bred the Free Silver insurrection. Free Silver men believed that the end of inflation condemned the farmer to an uphill struggle against debt and impoverishment and could be blamed on Eastern and British capitalists, two wings of a single "money power." Nor was this notion wholly fantastic. Billions of dollars of British capital had been

---

not make our nineteenth-century forebears feel any very close affinity. The average Englishman, right up to World War II, regarded the Americans as surpassingly strange and largely irrelevant. . . . The general American image of the British for 150 years was of a nation of more or less menacing snobs." See W. R. Louis and Hedley Bull (eds.), *The Special Relationship,* especially introductory essay by David Watt, "The Anglo-American Relationship," pp. 1–14; David Dimbleby and David Reynolds, *An Ocean Apart;* Godfrey Hodgson, "Britons, Americans and Europeans," *The Politician Quarterly,* vol. 59, No. 3, July–September 1988; D. Cameron Watt, *Succeeding John Bull: America in Britain's Place: A Study of the Anglo-American Relationship and World Politics in the Context of British and American Foreign-Policy-making in the Twentieth Century;* Beloff, in Gilbert, *A Century of Conflict.*
*The historian Ray Allen Billington has shown how complicated were the roots of Middle Western isolationism. See his "Origins of Middle Western Isolationism," *Political Science Quarterly,* vol. lx, March 1945.

invested in American stocks and bonds, especially in the paper of the Western railroads, which were the bane of the farmers, who saw their differential freight rates as one of the most painful of the thorns pressed down upon their brow. ("You shall not press down upon the brow of labor this crown of thorns," said William Jennings Bryan in the speech to the Democratic convention in 1896 which won him his party's nomination not once but three times, "you shall not crucify mankind upon a cross of gold.")

Paradoxically, if hard times bred fear of the arcane power of the City of London, growing prosperity in the Middle West did nothing to soften attitudes toward Britain. In the first quarter of the century Midwestern farmers were putting the raw, precarious pioneer days behind them and building a confident, resourceful society with a culture of its own; and Midwestern cities, with Chicago and St. Louis in the lead, were evolving into metropolitan societies not wholly different from Boston or Philadelphia, with their suburbs and street railways, their great universities and educated patricians, their newspapers and their art museums and their symphonies increasingly unashamed to challenge comparison with those of the East or of Europe. While it built a great new inland empire around the Great Lakes and across the Plains, the Middle West could afford to ignore the rest of the world even while its poets and its editorialists asserted a sense of equality, or more than equality, with the ancient empires of Europe.

Middle Westerners, even more than other Americans, had a special motive for rejecting the claims and quarrels of Europe. In 1900 more than four million of them were foreign-born, and half of those came from Germany or from the other German-speaking lands of Central Europe. In addition, many of the native-born Midwesterners were of Irish Catholic descent. As the second and third immigrant generations rose to political power, new Midwestern leaders of German or Irish or Slav descent were able to represent their voters' distaste for involvement in the quarrels of the Old World. They were also able to insist with some success that, if the United States must get involved, it should not be on behalf of England, rival of Germany and oppressor of Ireland.

The "hyphenated Americans," as they were called to their own intense disgust, were only an active minority within the Middle West. The region as a whole, in spite of its prairie radicals and "Sons of the Wild Jackass," was essentially conservative, because it was preoccupied with the excitement and the problems of economic development. It clung to the traditional American aloofness toward Europe longer than any other region for this reason. For a short time, that tradition weakened. Then came Woodrow Wilson's ill-judged and disastrous effort to impose the League of Nations. By insisting that the Senate pass the Versailles Treaty intact, he made certain of its failure. The Senate rejected the treaty, and the nation rejected its author. For years after that, as two eminent historians of isolationism have written, "it was regarded as politically impossible to induce the American people to subscribe to any form of political commitment beyond that of the Monroe Doctrine. There were those who never abandoned the campaign for collective action. But public opinion was against them and became rabidly so."*

One of those who never quite abandoned the quest for collective action was Henry Stimson. Public opinion, however, was not rabidly against him in the 1920s, only because he did not take a prominent part in the fierce battles over the Versailles Treaty and the League. For a man who had held Cabinet office and run for governor of New York, he took remarkably little part in public life or debate between his return from France in 1918 and his visit to Nicaragua in 1926. He concentrated on his law practice, though he repeatedly told his friends that he found the private practice of law tedious and even sordid compared to public life. He was earning a large income in his law practice—over $50,000 a year. In addition, he had the legacy left by his father, which by the shrewd investment skills of Alfred Loomis had turned into a very substantial sum of capital. Colonel Stimson, who had never been poor, was now a rich man. It is hard to avoid the conclusion that the reason he took little part in the debates over the postwar relations between the United States and Europe, one of the great questions of the hour, was because he was shrewdly aware that in the age of isolationism his own instincts were so far out of touch with those of the majority.

In fact his position, in the 1920s, if logical, was perhaps excessively lawyerlike. It rested, that is, on certain distinctions rather too subtle for the politics of the hustings. He believed, as he wrote in his autobiography, that "the great lesson of [World War I] was that the United States could not remain aloof from world affairs and still keep the

*William L. Langer and S. E. Gleason, *The Challenge to Isolation.*

world 'safe for democracy.' " He was "unequivocally in favor of American participation in the League of Nations."* But he was also opposed to unreserved ratification of the League Covenant, and in particular to Article X, the famous proviso that bound member states "to respect and preserve as against external aggression the territorial and existing political integrity of all members"—in plain language, to go to war to defend a member threatened by either invasion or revolution. His position was similar to that of Elihu Root, which was not surprising, because the two men talked the question over incessantly. In 1920 he first became involved in the presidential campaign of his old friend General Leonard Wood. Then he publicly threatened to leave the Republican Party if it adopted the views of the hardline "irreconcilables" who would not have the treaty at any price. And finally he committed what he himself described thirty years later as a "blunder" by signing, along with thirty other notables, a letter saying he could support Harding because he would favor a "loose association" with the League of Nations and a world court. (Harding did nothing of the kind.)

Stimson's position in the debate over the League of Nations was not clear. The Senate majority leader, Henry Cabot Lodge, needed to hold together the two wings of his party, moderates and "irreconcilables," but he moved in the irreconcilables' direction by hardening up Root's reservations and by putting them in a way that Stimson found "harsh and unpleasant." Democrats who might have had similar worries about Article X rallied around President Wilson. Dragged into naked partisan politics, the treaty was doomed. The United States, having imposed a settlement on Europe, now refused to guarantee it, indeed washed its hands publicly of the continent it had only so recently intervened to save. Europe was left to its debts, its reparations, its fears and dreams of revenge, and to the memory of its millions of dead. American reluctance to become involved is very understandable, yet the rejection of the treaty by the United States Senate made a second European civil war all but inevitable.

B efore the age of strategic bombing, the first line of defense and the strong right arm of power for a nation, like the United States, that lived behind barrier oceans must be the navy.

---

*On Active Service, pp. 102–3.

Nothing more clearly marked the American challenge to a century of British hegemony than the American demand, not only for naval disarmament, but also for naval parity with Britain. And nothing more clearly revealed the decline of both British power and British morale than Britain's willingness to concede it. Britain was impoverished both by her exertions in the war and by the huge sums she had lent to her allies. Her export industries—coal, cotton, shipbuilding and heavy engineering—were the key to her whole trading system and guaranteed the position of the pound sterling at the heart of the world's financial system, but after the war those industries never fully recaptured their markets. Along the Clyde, the Tyne, the Tees and the Mersey, soldiers came back from France not to "a land fit for heroes," as they had been promised, but to silent mills, empty yards and motionless winding gear above the pits where before the war more than a million miners had worked. Industrial strife was frequent and bitter, with miners' strikes in 1920 and 1921 and a General Strike in 1926. So at the Washington naval conference of 1921, Britain accepted both a limitation of her right to build capital ships (battleships and battle cruisers) and parity with the United States. The Washington Treaty, signed in February 1922, ended a century and a half of British naval dominance, and more than a hundred years in which American security and American trade had been guaranteed by the Royal Navy. Japan, too, secured international recognition of her elevated status; the ratio to the U.S. and British navies at which she was allowed to build capital ships was highly favorable, given that both Britain and the United States might have to face battle in more than one ocean, whereas the Japanese were free to concentrate on the northern Pacific alone.

The Washington Conference had not been able to go beyond establishing a ratio for the capital ships of the main naval powers (including France and Italy as well as the United States, Britain and Japan) because the problems of negotiating agreed limits on the next-largest category of warships, cruisers, were even more difficult. The first problem arose out of the different strategic needs and purposes of the United States and Britain. There were two kinds of cruisers in the world's navies in the 1920s: heavy cruisers of 10,000 tons or more, armed with 8-inch guns, and smaller cruisers armed with 6-inch guns. The United States, with virtually no overseas bases, favored big cruisers that could sail without refueling from home bases in the continental United States to wherever they might be needed. Britain, concerned about patrolling the thousands of miles of sea lanes between Australia, India, the Middle East, the Caribbean and Southern Africa, not to mention with keeping open the lifeline to North America, wanted as many cruisers as she could afford, and did not mind if they were smaller and had a shorter range. Moreover, the Royal Navy had far more cruisers than the U.S. Navy, so parity would imply a far more painful sacrifice for Britain, one which many British naval experts thought would endanger her imperial sea routes.

Even if the Anglo-American difficulties could be solved, other problems would remain, in particular the rivalry between Mussolini's Italy, determined to turn the Mediterranean into an "Italian lake," and France, which had been less afflicted by the Depression in 1929 than either Britain or the United States and could therefore well afford a big naval building program to match her claim to be a two-sea naval power, able simultaneously to fight Germany in the North Sea and Atlantic, and Italy in the Mediterranean.

Germany had been forbidden by the Treaty of Versailles to own capital ships, a prohibition the German navy was already evading, long before Hitler came to power, by building a class of "pocket battle-ships," under 10,000 tons but with heavy guns and great speed. Even before the Depression had taken hold in Europe, and long before Hit-ler's rise to power, the fear of Germany lurked in the back of British and French minds. Stimson's eventual experience of the difficulties of naval disarmament negotiations in 1929–31 contributed powerfully to his growing pessimism about the prospects for avoiding another war, and to the conviction that the United States could not keep aloof from the affairs of Europe, however much she might yearn for isolation.

Five times between 1922 and 1927 the powers tried to solve the cruiser puzzle, without success. At Geneva in 1927 the atmosphere deteriorated further, and Stimson, on his return from the Philippines two years later, found that Britain and the U.S. "were really at each other's throats."* At Geneva, the United States, under pressure from the navy, demanded twenty-five to thirty 10,000-ton cruisers with 8-inch guns. Britain was willing to settle for only fifteen big cruisers, but wanted fifty-five light cruisers. By 1929, too, the puzzle was made even more difficult by the fact that Japan was demanding a more fa-vorable ratio. Slowly, inexorably, the Japanese admirals were putting themselves in a position where—as events would show two years later—

---

*Tate, *United States and Armaments,* p. 164, quoted in Morison, *Turmoil and Tradition,* p. 319.

neither Britain nor the United States could, short of a world war, stand between Japan and her dream of empire on the Asian mainland.

In May 1929 resuming progress toward naval disarmament was high on the Hoover administration's list of priorities. This goal was, however, somewhat confused. In theory, the Republicans wanted disarmament. The trouble was that they also wanted parity with Britain. Since the British navy was in fact larger than the U.S. navy, obtaining parity meant that others, and in particular the British, should disarm more than the United States.

Stimson privately believed that naval parity between Britain and the United States was dangerous, because Britain needed a larger navy to fulfil her double responsibilities, in Europe and in Asia. But as Secretary of State he went along, though in his memoirs he was scathing:

> The American delegation was sent to London to get parity. A more ridiculous goal can hardly be imagined. On every ground, the United States should have been happy to see the British fleet just as big and strong as the British pocket-book would permit— excepting of course as this size might stimulate rival building. That America should have no other important object than a fleet as big as the British was utter nonsense.*

Nonsense it might be. But the fact was that the British pocketbook did not permit a navy big enough to defend Britain's traditional obligations. And Britain was about to re-elect as Prime Minister a man who represented a consciousness and a philosophy very different from that of nineteenth-century imperialism.

In the British general election of 1929 the Labour Party won 288 seats to 260 for the Conservatives and only 59 for the Liberals, who were being squeezed between the other two parties. The new Prime Minister, Ramsay MacDonald, lost no time in conveying the message to Washington that he wanted to solve the naval question in order to let him tackle the Labour Party's priority agenda of economic recovery and social reform. Stimson and the State Department had, of course, been well aware that this election was likely from the time the Hoover administration took office, and they also knew that a Labour administration, particularly one headed by MacDonald, would look far more kindly on naval disarmament, and on parity for the U.S. navy, than

*On Active Service, p. 174.

the Tories would. Stimson therefore waited for the result of the election before making his move, and when it came he was well prepared. He sent to London as U.S. ambassador a man after his own heart: Charles Gates Dawes, who had been Vice President under President Coolidge. Dawes, a brigadier in the American Expeditionary Force, had won the Nobel peace prize for his 1924 "Dawes Plan" for "solving"* the reparations problem. An Ohioan of Yankee stock, Dawes had made a large fortune in Midwestern gas and electric utilities and banking before becoming Controller of the Currency in the ultraconservative McKinley administration. Yet oddly he got on well with MacDonald, the illegitimate son of a servant girl from the far northeast of Scotland and an idealistic, indeed almost mystical, believer in socialism. Within days he had established a warm relationship with MacDonald and was seeing the Prime Minister sometimes as often as three times a day.

Even before the Labour election victory, Dawes had been appointed and confirmed and had visited Washington to work out in detail with Hoover, Stimson and the British ambassador, Sir Esmé Howard, the key sentences he would make in a speech to the Pilgrims' dinner. Dawes arrived at Southampton on June 14, and two days later met MacDonald at Forres in Morayshire, in the far north of Scotland. By the end of June the Labour Prime Minister had proposed a five-power naval conference if substantial agreement could be reached on cruisers, and the British had accepted cruiser parity in principle. He also told Dawes he would like to visit Washington: no British Prime Minister had ever visited the United States up to that date.

Both the French and the Japanese were worried by the idea of this trip, which confirmed their suspicions that the Anglo-Saxons were allied against them—and so, in a sense, they were. "The mind of our European neighbors is not tranquil," MacDonald wrote at one point to Dawes, "but is suspicious that we are to come to some bargain with the United States against them."†

Certainly MacDonald was forcing the pace. As Dawes reminded Hoover when the President, who in spite of or because of his years in London was something of an Anglophobe, jibbed at some British reluctance to accept one of his proposals, MacDonald had to scrap real,

---

*The Dawes Plan allowed German reparations to be funded over an extended period; it was replaced by the "Young Plan," named for Owen D. Young, in 1929.
†Charles G. Dawes, *Journal*, p. 73, September 24, 1929.

steel cruisers, and face the Tories in the House of Commons when he did so; all Hoover was being asked to do was to scrap unbuilt paper ships. But MacDonald was determined to save money on the navy. He was a lifelong pacifist. And he had a Labour Party behind him that was chafing to spend money on domestic programs that would help its working-class voters, not on guns and glory. But the core of his motivation in pressing for progress in disarmament was the conviction he had expressed in his election broadcast: that the world was drifting toward another war in which civilization itself might be destroyed. MacDonald did not say so, but he also believed that the drift could not be halted until Britain and the United States ended their naval rivalry and acted as trusting allies. He was all the more sure that this was the only solution because he saw, more clearly than men from the traditional ruling class, that Britain no longer had the sheer resources to hold the balance of power or lead an alliance for peace on her own. In both of these perceptions, Henry Stimson agreed with him.*

A few days after their meeting at Forres, the Prime Minister hinted broadly to Dawes that he was ready to slow down the building of two cruisers and that it would "have a fine effect" if Hoover would agree to do the same. Stimson read the signals from Dawes. On June 24 MacDonald announced to the House of Commons that he accepted parity with the United States in cruisers and that he was slowing down the building of two of them; the very next day Hoover reciprocated. But from Stimson's point of view, it was time to put the brakes on the process. He could not afford to seem to Congress too keen to reach a deal with the British. On August 15 he announced that the United States could accept fifty British cruisers in all, but insisted that the U.S. must have twenty-three large cruisers with 8-inch guns. That presented the British with a serious problem. Since the Japanese were demanding a ratio of 10:10:7, twenty-three American heavy cruisers would mean the Japanese could have sixteen. Yet if the British were to have all the light cruisers they needed for their empire's sea lanes, they could only have fifteen heavy cruisers, one fewer than the Japa-

---

*There is a convincing account of MacDonald's attitude, and a clear account of the London conference, in David Marquand, *Ramsay MacDonald.* Charles G. Dawes, *Journal,* is also very useful on the personalities and the atmosphere of the conference and of the negotiations leading up to it. Giovanni Engely, *The Politics of Naval Disarmament,* is an interesting analysis by an Italian journalist, highly critical of the French role in the naval disarmament process. Stimson's diaries are of course an essential source, and his retrospective view in *On Active Service* is especially illuminating.

nese in total; in the Pacific that limit on heavy cruisers would strip Australia and New Zealand of reliable British naval protection, and the Australian and New Zealand governments would make trouble over that.

For a few days the prospects for a disarmament conference, let alone for progress, seemed to be slipping away. Then the U.S. Navy said it could accept twenty-one big cruisers, and the ingenious suggestion came from the British side that some of them might be armed with 6-inch guns only and counted as light cruisers, though their size, engines and armor meant they could be quickly upgraded. That did it. On September 17 MacDonald issued invitations to France, Italy and Japan, as well as to the United States, to meet in London for a naval disarmament conference the following January. Eleven days later, with his daughter Ishbel (Mrs. MacDonald had died a few years earlier) the British Prime Minister set sail for the New World on the Cunard Line ship *Berengaria,* and by October 5, after a tumultuously friendly ticker-tape welcome in New York, he was conferring with Hoover and Stimson in Washington, whence he accompanied the President to his camp on the Rapidan, in the Blue Ridge foothills, a sort of Virginian precursor of Camp David. The atmosphere, again strangely, given the gap between MacDonald's political philosophy and Hoover's, was so harmonious that the papers were full of rumors that the British Prime Minister and the American President had decided to fuse their two navies.

It had not come to that. The ghosts of John Paul Jones and Admiral Rodney could slumber undisturbed. What the Americans and the British had begun to fuse was their policies. When the Navy Board suggested that he put a certain negotiating position forward "only as camouflage," Stimson replied with one of those superbly seigneurial aphorisms that became his trademark: "Gentlemen, the United States in its international relations is not in the habit of camouflaging."* The tone of a cable Will Rogers sent to his friend Dawes in the London embassy was a bit less grand: DON'T SINK ANYTHING UNTIL YOU SEE THEM SINK FIRST! But in truth it was the British, not the Americans, who were being asked to sink existing ships.

MacDonald's visit to the Rapidan has been forgotten, obliterated from the memory of history by the square figure of Winston Churchill

---

*Dawes, *Journal.*

greeting Franklin D. Roosevelt on the deck of a cruiser in the St. Lawrence River. Yet it deserves to be remembered as a moment of some significance in both British and American history. As his biographer puts it, MacDonald came "in pursuit of an agreement which was intended to confirm the end of British supremacy at sea. His visit was a milestone in British foreign policy; it was an even greater milestone in America's hesitant emergence as a world power."*

The Five-Power Conference assembled in late January 1930. Stimson led the U.S. delegation in person, which arrived at Plymouth aboard the S.S. *George Washington*. In London, Stimson went straight from his special train when it arrived at Waterloo Station to see Mac-Donald at Number Ten, Downing Street, and he went with a high-powered team. Avoiding the disastrous mistake Wilson had made in Paris in 1919, Secretary Stimson brought with him two able and powerful senators, the Republican David Reed of Pennsylvania and the Democrat Joe Robinson of Arkansas. Stimson was also accompanied by the Secretary of the Navy, his old friend Charles Francis Adams, and by two exceptionally able ambassadors, Hugh Gibson from Belgium and Dwight Morrow, of the House of Morgan, whose tact and skill had defused the crisis in relations with Mexico.

Stimson easily led this team of heavyweights. Dawes's description in his *Journal* offers a fine portrait of the man at the height of his powers, newly ascended at the age of sixty-two to the very summit of international affairs.

> Stimson has studied with care the technical naval questions involved. Because of this knowledge, gained through many months of intensive investigation as well as because he is a good tactician, he has placed the United States in a position of leadership in this conference.†

Of course it could be argued that what had placed the United States in that position was sheer economic preponderance. But if Stimson had a winning hand he played it like a master, and his mastery was as freely acknowledged by the Europeans as by his colleagues. It was enhanced by the fact that MacDonald, chairman of the conference,

---

*David Marquand, *Ramsay MacDonald*, p. 506.
†Dawes, *Journal*, p. 145.

was sketchy on details because he was fighting late every night in the House of Commons to keep his minority government alive.*

The only other figure of comparable authority at the Five-Power Conference was the French foreign minister, Aristide Briand. But he was aging and played second fiddle to his Prime Minister, André Tardieu, and it was an open secret that the French government, like the British, could collapse at any moment, as indeed it did on February 17. Stimson was the dominant figure in the conference as no American had been since Woodrow Wilson in Paris; and if Stimson lacked Wilson's philosophical bravura, he had twice Wilson's skill in negotiations, as Dawes observed:

> He is patient and extremely considerate with his delegation. He keeps them all satisfied; but also keeps firmly in hand the control of negotiations. In these he uses the members of his delegation when they may be useful, but always directs and co-ordinates their activities. He is a safe leader, not afraid to take individual responsibility where necessary, without hesitation, and yet wise enough to patiently explain all he does to his delegation. As a result he has a united delegation behind him.†

The negotiations proceeded in the leisurely style of the last age of classic diplomacy. Each country had fielded its first team. MacDonald conducted the British delegation in person, backed by his foreign secretary, Arthur Henderson, and the First Lord of the Admiralty, A. V. Alexander,‡ later "ruler of the King's Navee" again in Churchill's war Cabinet in 1940–45. France was represented by Briand and Tardieu, Italy by Dino Grandi, who was to become something of a friend of Stimson's.

The social background to the conference was in the grand manner. Stimson, accompanied by Mabel, was accommodated in a suite in the Ritz Hotel in Piccadilly with, for weekend repose, a leased eighteenth-century country house at Stanmore, a few miles northwest of London, with its own nine-hole golf course. The Stimsons were deluged with invitations: to a banquet in Guildhall, to lunch at *The Times* and again

---

*HLS, *Diary,* Jan 22, 1930. The only member of the British delegation who had really mastered the details was a civil servant, R. L. Craigie (later, as Sir Robert Craigie, British ambassador in Tokyo), who amazed the American delegation by the frankness with which he revealed his distaste for the Labour government.
†Dawes, *Journal,* p. 145.
‡Henderson began life as an apprentice iron molder in Newcastle; Alexander left school at thirteen in Sheffield to become a blacksmith.

tête-à-tête with the Prime Minister at the Athenaeum Club (traditional haunt of bishops), to a visit with the headmaster of Eton College, and to dinner and a weekend at Cliveden with the Astors. The entire delegation was asked to dine by the "benchers" of the Middle Temple, one of the four Inns of Court.* All of this was, in more senses than one, meat and drink to Colonel Stimson. He was, one American diplomat accurately reported, "essentially a grand seigneur and proceeds about his high duties with the pageantry and suite that such high duties conventionally call for."† He was also not unhappy to be performing those high duties in London, where—at least in the 1920s—pageantry and suite were more abundantly available than on the banks of the Potomac.

Mr. and Mrs. Stimson took tea with King George V and Queen Mary at Buckingham Palace, where Stimson was "taken aback" when the monarch, who had been a naval officer and commanded a battleship in 1908, "suddenly said he was in favor of immediate abolition of battleships," which he called "expensive monsters." Think of seven or eight million pounds being wiped out in one minute at Jutland, he said, and repeated, "One minute—I tell you!" Stimson duly reported this outburst to Ramsay MacDonald, who said, "the King had no business to talk politics but he was constantly doing it."‡

The King, nevertheless, opened the conference on January 20 in the House of Lords. Outside, London was shrouded in an old-fashioned pea-soup fog, and for many days the Five-Power Conference's proceedings were equally opaque. It developed into an unfinished symphony in three movements. The first movement, in which the United States and Britain reached agreement on parity, was harmonious, if long drawn out, and ended with a trio as the Japanese joined the dance. In the second movement, *agitato*, the French, nervous now of Mussolini's Italy as well as of some future revival of German aggression, did their best to buy with the price of their adhesion

---

*Medieval institutions where barristers, one of two branches of the British legal profession, must "eat dinners" to establish pupilage before being called to the bar, and where many barristers have their chambers; the benchers, senior members of an Inn, are successful lawyers and judges. The "livery companies" started life as guilds, but have long since been social and charitable associations, not dissimilar from Masonic lodges, made up of successful bankers and other businessmen from the City, the London financial district. Their dinners and their wine are a byword for excellence; their conversation less so.

†Hugh Wilson, *Diplomat Between Wars*, p. 236.

‡HLS, *Diary*, March 25, 1931.

to a cruiser agreement some form of political commitment—if possible from the United States, failing that from the British. The third movement was a long and in the end abortive negotiation between France and Italy, with both America and Britain kibbitzing, encouraging and trying to help things along.

By February 15 Charles Dawes was writing a paper which spoke of "our acute and dangerous position." In fact, it was the French whose position was most acutely dangerous, and it was on the French that suspicion and hostility from all the other participants fell. Yet France was in many ways in a position of strength. With America disarmed of her own free will, Germany disarmed under the terms of the Versailles Treaty, and Britain finding it hard in the postwar recession to generate the resources needed for maintaining a worldwide empire, France was in many respects the strongest of the powers: strong in the numbers and equipment of her army, navy and air force, strong above all financially. But this military strength, even this hoarding of gold, could be construed as the manifestation of a national psychology deeply traumatized by a war whose terrible destruction had taken place largely on French soil, and in which more than 1⅓ million Frenchmen had been killed and more than 3 million wounded.* And the trauma in turn explained the attitude of the French delegates in London: jealous of the pretensions of Italy in the Mediterranean, always on the lookout for signs of a revival of militarism in Germany, and at the same time constantly fearful that the Anglo-Saxon powers were ganging up on them. And, indeed, Stimson and MacDonald did to some extent coordinate their policy without including the French and shared an uncomprehending, faintly contemptuous attitude toward France's preoccupations. On March 20 Stimson confided to his diary that MacDonald had told him that "France wanted to be the biggest military power in Europe, and that she wishes to be able to fight any two nations in Europe successfully, and rather expects to fight Italy and Germany." In view of the fact that nine years later France was actually at war with those two nations, this calculation appears not so much "militaristic," as MacDonald called it, as merely prudent. Reading the memoirs of the time, including Stimson's, it is hard to escape the impression that they were unfair to the French delegation and its concerns; the French were certainly suspicious of them.

---

*Journal Officiel, Documents parlementaires, session extraordinaire 1920, annexe 633, séance du 29 mars 1920, proposition de la résolution Marin, quoted in Winston S. Churchill, The Great War, vol. iii, p. 1642.

The French also tried to improve their security by drawing either the British or, better still, the Americans into some kind of political guarantees as a condition of accepting naval disarmament. The idea was not in itself unreasonable; but it was treated with the greatest skepticism by British and Americans alike. Tardieu proposed to Mac-Donald a military alliance, something, as David Marquand points out, that MacDonald had opposed for thirty years. Then, on February 17, Tardieu's government was defeated in the Chamber of Deputies on a financial issue and fell. Tardieu and Briand left for Paris. After the formation of a new government, they returned to London on February 26 and tried to get Stimson to agree to a "consultative" pact, meaning that if France were attacked the United States would agree to discuss possible military support. Stimson promptly rejected the idea: he realized that it would be interpreted both by the French and in Congress as a commitment to something more than mere consultation; and while the French would have liked that very much, Congress would have regarded it as a sin against the Holy Ghost. In a dispatch to his deputy and friend Joseph Cotton, who had been left behind in Washington to mind the store as acting Secretary, Stimson put it on record that the objection of the United States was not to a consultative pact as such, but to one given "in circumstances where it would seem a *quid pro quo* for a reduction in French armaments." In truth, the objection was to anything that could be represented in Congress as an "entangling alliance" of the kind George Washington had warned against.

So events moved toward success in the naval negotiations between the U. S., Britain and Japan, and toward failure in the bargaining with France. On February 27, the day after the French delegation returned to the conference, Stimson was able to record, "We finally reached agreement with the British on figures,"* and a week later in a meeting with MacDonald in the latter's room at the House of Commons he proposed for the first time that if France wouldn't go along, the U. S., Britain and Japan might sign a three-power pact without her or Italy. When a couple of days later Briand, now Prime Minister, brought up the idea that the United States should promise to back the Kellogg Pact (which outlawed aggression) with military sanctions, Stimson concluded with uncharacteristic cynicism that the French were either trying to entangle the Americans or maneuvering to blame them if the conference failed, and he suggested to a newspaperman he trusted,

*HLS, *Diary,* February 27, 1930.

John Owens of the Baltimore *Sun,* that the French might be trying to break up the conference. By the third week in March, the French were indeed despondent. One member of their delegation revealed to Dwight Morrow what was probably an important part of their thinking: that the value of a consultative pact would be as a clear indication that the United States was not trying "to draw Britain out of the European system."*

That same day, March 22, MacDonald called Stimson "in considerable excitement" to say that he had heard from the British ambassador that "the French have quit the conference." His news was premature. On March 30 talks were renewed in London, but the French insisted in inserting language into the draft treaty text committing Britain to military sanctions in the event of any breach of the Kellogg Pact. When Foreign Secretary Arthur Henderson refused to accept that, the Five-Power Conference was for all intents and purposes at an end.

The Japanese trumped the last remaining French card, the threat to break up the conference, by agreeing to accept a three-power treaty. On April 10—international diplomacy still danced to a stately measure in those days—it was agreed by the five powers that there was no further point in pursuing an agreement among them all, and on April 22 the United States, Britain and Japan signed a treaty without France and Italy. It remained in force until December 1936, and, apart from the painfully hammered out agreement on cruiser strengths, it decreed what was called a "holiday" in the building of capital ships and restrictions on the building and use of submarines. Having appended his signature to that text in the morning, Henry Stimson, with Mabel, caught the boat train for home that same evening to board the S.S. *Leviathan.* The ship itself was something of an object lesson for the times. For once she had been, as the *Vaterland,* the pride of the Hamburg-Amerika line. She was in American registry now (incidentally experiencing difficulty in attracting passengers who were not, like the Secretary of State, obliged to travel on a "dry" ship). Thousands of Germans had lined the banks of the Elbe to watch as she was towed away to America—part of the great tide of reparations that impoverished Germany without enriching her victors, and bedeviled all attempts to restore the economy of Europe and build a stable peace.

*The same idea was the key to General de Gaulle's thinking about Anglo-American relations in 1958–63, leading up to his veto of British entry into the European Economic Community.

• • •

For a year, French and Italian delegations continued to slog away in the hopes of reaching a naval agreement, but without success. In Rome in March 1931, according to an Italian source, they were close to agreement when a special messenger arrived from Paris and the French delegation immediately drew in its horns. There were rumors that France had been pressured by her ally, Yugoslavia. Other sources attribute the breakdown of the talks to the news of a customs union between Germany and Austria, which sent waves of apprehension through official and political Paris. At any rate, by the summer of 1931, French, Italians, Germans, Austrians and certainly Henry Stimson had something else to worry about that made even naval disarmament seem less urgent.

Neither the economic system of Europe nor the stability of economic relations between Europe and the United States had recovered from the world war when, in 1929, the fragile prosperity of the later 1920s collapsed. Money is fungible, and the nations of the world are economically independent. Nevertheless, it is easier to understand the crisis that burst on the world in 1931 if one breaks its origins down into three parts: the problem of reparations, the problem of debt, and the problem of the international banking system.

The story of German reparations is well known,* though the degree of its responsibility for the economic and political crisis of the 1930s is not always fully appreciated. It was understandable that the nations that had suffered from German aggression in the First World War should have wanted to be repaid in money. After all, as was ceaselessly repeated by French, Belgian and British politicians, the Germans themselves, in obliging the French to pay after the war of 1870, had established the principle. The Allies' insistence on reparations was understandable, because the war had killed and maimed millions of the Allies' men, inflicted unimaginable desolation on whole provinces of France, flooded Belgian coal mines, shattered factories, uprooted great systems of transportation, sunk 2,479 of the merchant ships on which Britain's trade depended, and destroyed the fabric of Russian civilization and society, perhaps forever. But it was unwise. For one thing,

---

*I am particularly grateful to J. M. Keynes, *Economic Consequences of the Peace;* H. G. Moulton and Leo Pasvolsky, *War Debts and World Prosperity;* and Sir John Wheeler-Bennett, *The Wreck of Reparations.*

just before they imposed the burden of reparations on Germany, they
went out of their way to reduce Germany's capacity to pay. For that
was the effect of those clauses in the peace treaty that returned Alsace-
Lorraine, with its iron mines and steel production, to France, gave
German coal fields in Silesia to Poland and in the Saar to France,
stripped Germany of her overseas colonies, and gave away all the larger
and half the smaller ships in the German merchant marine.

It did not take long for the folly of this policy to become clear.
At first the subject of reparations was a minefield of conflicting claims
and counterclaims. The German army collapsed in 1918 with bewilder-
ing suddenness, and its surviving soldiers in their hundreds of thousands marched home leaving behind them all the impedimenta of a
great military machine, from thousands of tons of food to whole railway systems. No one ever figured out the value of the "reparations"
the Allies simply helped themselves to as spoils of war. Then came the
Treaty of Versailles in 1919, which merely repeated the demand Woodrow Wilson had made in his address to Congress about peace terms in
January 1918, and the actual terms Wilson put on behalf of the Allied
governments in November: the demand that "compensation will be
made by Germany for all damage done to the civilian population of
the Allies and to their property by the aggression of Germany by land,
by sea, and from the air." Government lawyers, notably the French,
vied with one another to think of the highest possible number at which
to value that damage. Already by 1921 it was clear that the claims made
far exceeded any amount Germany could hope to pay. In London in
that year a first attempt was made to draw up a credible schedule for
German reparations. They were set at 2 billion gold marks, or about
$500 million a year, plus 26 per cent of the value of her exports in each
year.

By 1924, after the spectacular collapse of the German currency in
the hyperinflation of 1923, that schedule was seen to be beyond Germany's strength. The Dawes Plan, worked out by a committee of experts in Paris, assumed that Germany could pay a flat 2.5 billion gold
marks a year, but only after five years in which the obligation rose by
gentle steps. It also sought to help Germany to pay by arranging a £40
million ($160 million) loan at 7 per cent, which interested New York
bankers as well as making available a pot of hard currency with which
to meet reparations obligations.

The Dawes Plan did not solve the problem of reparations, however, and in 1929 it was followed by the Young Plan, named for a new American negotiator, Owen D. Young, former president of General Electric. The Young Plan limited the amount Germany had to pay to £5.5 billion ($22 billion) payable in sixty annuities, of which the last one would have fallen due in 1988. The Young Plan proposed the end of the occupation of the Rhineland, something Hitler was to bring about by force in 1936; the setting up of a new Bank for International Settlements in Basel (where it still survives); and a new loan of £70 million ($280 million) at 5½ per cent. That was all very well; but it assumed a rising volume and value of world trade and at least sufficient economic buoyancy in Germany that money already lent to German borrowers would remain there. Instead, the Wall Street Crash of October made the Young Plan unworkable within weeks of its being published.

If Germany was burdened with reparations that she could hardly hope to pay, her conquerors, except for the Americans, were burdened with debt that they could no more hope to repay. Making the mistake of seeing Europe as a single unit, and so ignoring vital complications of the real position, American commentators on postwar debt, and American politicians, tended to lump all Europeans together as debtors lucky to have been bailed out by Uncle Sam.

The real position was more complicated.* War debts were incurred in three distinct periods. Between August 1914 and April 1917, Britain was the main lender and France also lent money, especially to Russia, a major client of French capital markets before 1914. In the second period, from April 1917 until the end of the war in November 1918, Britain and France continued to lend, but their loans were dwarfed by the enormous credits made available by the United States. These American loans were extended to individual Allied nations and only for the purpose of meeting payments due in dollars in the United States. Altogether, between April 1917 and late 1920, when Europe was considered to have returned to normal, these loans totaled $13.7 billion. Of that, $2.7 billion was spent for munitions; $3 billion for cereals and other foodstuffs; and $2.6 billion for cotton. During 1917 and 1918, then, Britain and to a lesser extent France continued to extend loans to Italy, Serbia and Belgium while racking up debt to the United States

*I am indebted to John Maynard Keynes's classic account in *Economic Consequences,* pp. 252–65, but I have also relied on the numbers in Moulton and Pasvolsky's 1932 study for the Brookings Institution.

Treasury to be used to finance purchase of American munitions, food-stuffs and other goods. After Armistice Day, the United States, now alone, lent a further $3.4 billion in various "Liberty" and relief loans to help tide Central Europe, in particular, over the chaos and near-famine left by the war as well as by the collapse of the German, Russian and Austro-Hungarian empires.

The United States, alone, had lent and not borrowed. Of the total of about $10 billion it had lent, roughly $4 billion had gone to Britain, $2.5 billion to France, and the rest to Italy, Russia, Belgium, Serbia (which became part of Yugoslavia) and other Allies. Britain, on the other hand, with at the time about half the population of the U.S. and about one-third the national income, had lent almost as much money—$8 billion—to her other Allies. France, too, while borrowing $5 billion, had lent $2.5 billion, almost half of it to Russia, whence there was small chance of seeing any come back.

Just as there was a difference between the financial position of the European Allies, including Britain, who all owed money to the United States and were all beneficiaries of reparations, so there was a psycho-logical gap as wide as the Atlantic. The Europeans all linked the twin problems of reparations, which were squeezing the German economy, and debt, which were squeezing theirs—if these were not, indeed, two aspects of the same problem: how to pay for the war. The Americans, with only a few exceptions, one of whom was Stimson, saw the two issues as separate. "They hired the money, didn't they?" was how Calvin Coolidge put it, and his fellow countrymen applauded. In truth, the debts were more like a slate run up at the store than a bank over-draft. And besides, as a Brookings Institution study put it,

> while there is no legal connection between the two sets of ob-ligations [reparations and war debts] . . . there is between them so important an economic relationship that the legal aspects of the problem have very little realistic significance. . . . The Allied governments have assumed since the early post-war years that receipts from German reparations would furnish the means with which to liquidate their international war debts.*

With one exception, this was a correct assumption. Between Sep-tember 1924, when the Dawes Plan went into effect, and June 1931,

*Moulton and Pasvolsky, *War Debts and World Prosperity,* p. 296.

when Stimson found himself faced with the breakdown of the whole system, France received a total of 6 billion gold marks ($1.5 billion) in reparation payments; the British Empire $600 million, Italy a little over $200 million, and so on. The United States, incidentally, received 450 million gold marks ($110 million), about the same as Yugoslavia. But at the same time between the end of the war and July 1, 1931, the United States was repaid $2.6 billion by fifteen European debtor nations, of which $1.9 billion came from Britain. Britain, in fact, had the worst of both worlds, receiving only 42 per cent of the loans and accounting for 74 per cent of the repayments. On aggregate, Britain was down $240 million on the whole balance sheet of reparations and debt, Belgium and Italy were slightly ahead, and France was up by a cool billion.

Opinions varied at the time, and experts still disagree today, on how great a part reparations played in the coming drama of German finance. But it is certainly true that reparations, returning prosperity, and uneven but rapid economic growth in the later 1920s were financed by massive borrowing, mainly from New York. Between 1924 and 1931, Germany paid 11 billion gold marks in reparations, and received 18 billion in loans, about half from New York banks.

Germany's economy, relying as it did on paying for massive imports of food and raw materials by roughly equal exports of steel and machinery, was badly hit by the world recession, but it was not hit all at once. After the bubble of the New York Stock Exchange burst in the fall of 1929, the world economy ground unevenly to a halt. Throughout what were then primary producing countries—Australia, Argentina and Brazil, not to mention colonial territories such as India, the Dutch East Indies and French Africa, and the countries of southeastern Europe that normally supplied Germany with food and raw materials—prices collapsed and hardship was acute, with consequent political unrest in various forms. The United States, Germany and Britain, the major industrial and exporting nations, were first and worst hit. Unemployment in Britain, which had not fully shared in the boom of the 1920s, nearly doubled in the course of 1930, from 1.5 million to 2.75 million. In Germany unemployment rose in the single month of January 1930 from 1.5 million to 2.5 million. By the end of 1931 there were almost 6 million German workers out of work, and in 1932 that figure, too, would be exceeded. In the United States, with at that time roughly three times the population of Britain and one and a half times that of Germany, 4 million people were unemployed in March 1930, and 8 million out of work a year later.

The economies of all the industrialized nations, in other words, were fragile, and Germany's, because of the losses of territory and industry in the treaty and because of reparations, not to mention the political instability already visible in the rise of both Communists and National Socialists, was the most fragile of all.

In March 1930, Heinrich Bruening became German chancellor. This intelligent and conscientious conservative was very different from the German industrialists and other once respectable men of the Right who were already making their peace with Hitler. In personality, indeed, Bruening had certain traits in common with Stimson, as they discovered when they met at a dinner at the Carlton Hotel, London, in 1931 and fell to talking about the war. They soon discovered that they had been on opposite sides at Bourlon woods, near Cambrai, when Bruening had been a machine gunner and Stimson on secondment to the Scottish Highlanders. Stimson was intrigued and impressed. Bruening, he decided, was "a very careful, sincere and strong man." Indeed, years later, when Bruening was living in exile on Long Island, they became good friends. Frederick Sackett, the able American ambassador in Berlin, whom Stimson trusted, described Bruening in glowing terms: ". . . the discovery of Europe, a really great man, about forty-seven years of age, a profoundly religious man, belongs to the Catholic Center, thinks he is under a mission to save his country, very thoroughly patriotic, and who thus far has not made any serious mistakes."*

In fact, however, Bruening had already made at least one serious mistake—namely, to institute a *Zollverein,* or customs union, with Austria, which the French immediately interpreted as directed against them, and which even dispassionate observers like Stimson saw as an attempt to set up a competing economic system, led by Germany, to break the "encircling" French policy, started by Raymond Poincaré,† of using French loans to build an alliance among countries such as Poland, Czechoslovakia and Yugoslavia, which feared Germany. The customs union led directly to the breaking-off of the Franco-Italian naval talks; worse, in the desperate financial crisis that was now approaching for Germany, it both poisoned French attitudes toward Ger-

*HLS, *Diary,* May 4, 1931.
†Raymond Poincaré, cousin of the great mathematician Jules-Henri Poincaré, was President of the French Republic from 1913 to 1920 and prime minister from 1922 to 1924.

many and handed the French a weapon. In truth Bruening, while an attractive and even a noble figure, was both doom-laden and doomed. His political epitaph was written in a brilliant simile by the German historian Golo Mann:

> Like the knight in Duerer's engraving who rides on bravely in spite of the gruesome figures following behind and who already sees his native castle in the background, Bruening thought that he could see the castle, he wanted to reach it, but the road became increasingly bleak and horse and rider increasingly weak.*

On May 21 Henry Stimson was first made aware of the approach of the tempest that would for a while put him at the center of world politics as no American had been since Woodrow Wilson. That day he was contemplating a quiet visit to Europe, and his friends Dwight Morrow and George Rublee came round to Woodley urging him to go. They were, he noticed, "rosy with a good mint julep which they had received from Judge Covington."† (Dean Acheson's senior partner, the most distinguished private lawyer in Washington, did not let Prohibition stand in the way of his hospitality.) That was when the telephone call came. It was from George Harrison, governor of the Federal Reserve Bank of New York. There was, he said, a "bad situation" in Austria, "which may spread to the rest of Europe and cause trouble."

What had happened was that early in 1930 a real-estate finance house in Vienna, the Boden Kredit Anstalt, had failed and had been taken over by the Kredit Anstalt, the biggest commercial bank in the country, which financed 70 per cent of Austrian industry. The Kredit Anstalt's 1930 balance sheet showed heavy losses, and by May 1931 these losses became known. The rumors Harrison reported to the Secretary of State went beyond the precarious condition of one Austrian bank, however. They went on to say that the French had brought on the crisis by putting pressure on Germany and Austria to break off their proposed customs union, which might or might not be true; and that the Germans might be forced to declare a moratorium on their reparations payments, which turned out to be all too true.

For on top of the underlying economic crisis, Germany also faced

*Golo Mann, *The History of Germany Since 1789*, p. 398.
†HLS, *Diary*, May 21, 1931.

a financial panic. In the course of 1930 some 900 million gold marks ($180 million) had left Germany; this was money belonging to either Germans or foreigners who had lost confidence in the future of the German economy and the stability of the mark; much of it had been invested by Americans in German stocks and bonds, and as they were sold American money began to leave Germany at the rate of several million dollars a day. Moreover German public finances depended on about a billion dollars of short-term credits, more than $700 million of which had come from the United States. The fall of a bank in Vienna would produce panic in Berlin. The Americans would call in their loans, and Germany could face—as Stimson put it to the British ambassador, Sir Ronald Lindsay—real bankruptcy and default.

This process now seemed unstoppable. About May 10 the Reichsbank's reserves began to melt away. In the second week in June George Harrison told Stimson that the Germans had lost $107 million in three or four days. Altogether between May 10 and June 6 the central bank's reserves fell from $613 million to $445 million.

On June 2 the Bruening government announced new taxes in an attempt to restore confidence. It had already, in an honorable, if vain, effort to spread the misery more equitably, cut civil servants' salaries in Germany by 10 to 13 per cent in the first half of 1931. Unfortunately on June 5, the day the new measures were announced, the German government also issued what amounted to a manifesto, blaming the troubles of the German economy on reparations and intimating that Germany would no longer be able to pay.

That same day Bruening was due to meet Ramsay MacDonald at Chequers, the British Prime Minister's official weekend retreat northwest of London. The German chancellor found himself in the economic equivalent of the plight of the man in Edgar Allan Poe's nightmare story "The Pit and the Pendulum": the only movable piece of his prison was reparations. "The economic and political situation of the Reich," he told MacDonald, whose own position was hardly any better, "which is menacing in the extreme compels the relief of Germany from the intolerable reparations obligations."*

On that same day, before the news from Germany arrived, for the first time, Herbert Hoover wavered in his rigid adherence to financial orthodoxy and informally sounded out Stimson and the Treasury Sec-

*J. W. Wheeler-Bennett, *The Wreck of Reparations*, p. 42.

retary, Ogden Mills, on the wisdom of a moratorium on repayments of both reparations and American debt.

This was what Stimson wanted. Almost alone in the circle around Hoover, he had understood all along that it was not possible to draw an artificial wall of separation between debts owed to the United States and the reparations with which the European Allies proposed to pay them. So it was a "facer . . . a bombshell," when at ten o'clock in the morning the next day, June 6, Ogden Mills telephoned to say that the United Press was reporting that the German government had said that Germany could no longer pay reparations. Hoover relapsed into one of his moods of introspective inaction. Two days later Stimson stopped off at the White House on his way to the State Department to find the President "swinging away from the thought of any action" and insisting on two rigid principles: the United States should deal with each nation individually, which didn't trouble Stimson; and "that we should keep reparations absolutely separated from debt," which Stimson thought was unrealistic.

Whether Hoover liked it or not, the United States could not remain isolated from Europe's problems. On June 14, Hoover set off for the Middle West and saw for himself the distress that was being caused by a bumper crop that had driven prices down to the floor. Wheat was 44 cents a bushel, cotton a nickel. For once, the Midwestern farmer and the Wall Street banker shared a common predicament: if Germany collapsed, bringing the whole Central European economy down with it, those crops of wheat and corn could never be sold, and farm foreclosures would follow; and if that happened the greatest financial houses of New York would ultimately be threatened with bankruptcy.

All this Henry Stimson, the Wall Street lawyer with his own network of contacts in New York and Europe, understood better than Hoover. He threw himself into the vacuum left by presidential hesitation. He got together with Ogden Mills to write a paper showing that to do nothing was more dangerous than to propose a moratorium. He helped the President to explain individually to twenty-one senators and eighteen members of the House of Representatives why a moratorium was necessary. On his own initiative he got up at 5:45 A.M. and telephoned his friend Ramsay MacDonald to ask whether "a general postponement of all debts, and obligations, and claims by all nations, for say one year would be helpful," to which MacDonald, no financier, and himself only hanging on to power by his eyebrows, could say only, "I really have no reply to that offhand."* The moratorium came to be known as the Hoover Plan, even though Stimson had to talk the President into it and his part in the whole process was so great it should perhaps have been called the Stimson Plan.

Stimson moved to the center of the stage not only because of his superior abilities in a complex crisis, but also because the problem was one of diplomacy as much as finance. First he tried to help Montague Norman, the imperious governor of the Bank of England, save Austria with an emergency loan. France insisted on tying their share of the loan to dissolution of the customs union, so Norman found the money on his own, and that was a respite.

Stimson was getting more and more irritated by the French. They had wrecked the naval agreement, as he saw it, and now they were trying to make petty capital out of a world crisis. He and MacDonald referred to France in their talks on the trans-Atlantic telephone as "the fussy nation." "Little Austria stood up like a man," he wrote in his diary, "and told France to go to hell."† Yet he cultivated what he called an "intimate" relationship with Paul Claudel, the poet who was also France's reliable ambassador in Washington, and on one occasion drafted language for Claudel to pass to the French government to express its reservations about Hoover's moratorium in a more moderate fashion so as not to upset the delicate negotiations that were under way for bailing out the Germans. "I am taking every step possible to avoid any misunderstanding with the French," he wrote in his diary on June 22, "because the great trouble is going to be with them."

By then Hoover had made his move, stirring himself from the mood that made being with him, as Stimson put it, like "sitting in a bath of ink." On June 20 it was announced that the United States was declaring a moratorium on all debt repayments for one year. Stimson had won his point. Hoover had made a generous and statesmanlike gesture. But he had waited too long. Stimson, however, had the satisfaction of knowing that he had been proved right. The Europeans, even the French, eventually accepted the moratorium, and there was surprisingly little objection from domestic American public opinion. On June 22 Stimson noted justifiably in his diary that "the President

*HLS, *Diary,* June 13, 1931.
†*Ibid.*

is showing a dependence on me ever since my judgment on this thing has proved to be correct.''*

At this point, with superb audacity Stimson announced to an ''uproarious'' press conference that he was going to Europe after all in just two days' time. Once again he took Mabel, and once again his journey was an almost royal progress. The latent power of the United States and panic in Europe, combined with the stature he had earned by his presence and wisdom, made Stimson for a few weeks, at the height of the crisis, the arbiter of Europe.

In the summer of 1931 an action he had taken quietly two years previously came back to haunt him. It was to be the foundation for one of the best remembered, most misunderstood of all the Stimson legends. In 1929 it had been brought to Stimson's attention by his Under Secretary, Joseph Cotton, that a team of code-breakers in New York, picturesquely known as the Black Chamber, was deciphering and reading incoming messages for foreign ambassadors in Washington. It was even said, though Stimson said he could not believe it, that during the 1922 Naval Conference the American delegates were presented every morning with the instructions sent to the British, French, Japanese and Italian delegates they were negotiating with. The code-breakers were controlled by the War Department's Division of Military Information, but Stimson discovered that the State Department had been contributing the substantial sum, for those days, of $40,000 a year to them. He and Cotton agreed that it was ''a highly unethical thing'' for the government to be reading the incoming traffic to ''our diplomatic guests.'' That was how Stimson put it in his diary in 1931. In 1946, when he was interviewed by McGeorge Bundy for his memoirs, he put it more graphically: ''Gentlemen do not read each other's mail.'' After Stimson withdrew State Department funding, the leader of the Black Chamber, Herbert Yardley, was fired. He proceeded to write a book spilling the beans, which naturally caused the Japanese and others to change their codes. However, the Army moved most of the code-breakers into the office of the Chief Signal Officer, where under the leadership of the great cryptographer David Friedman they went on reading other gentlemen's mail, to such good effect that they eventually cracked the Japanese ''Purple'' code—an achievement that would eventually prove of immense benefit to Stimson and the nation.†

*Diary, June 22, 1931.
†On Active Service, p. 188; Diary, June 1, 1931; Ronald W. Clark, The Man Who Broke Purple,

The Stimsons left New York on June 27 on an Italian ship and visited Gibraltar, Palermo and Naples, not to mention Old Capua, almost as if he were a retired lawyer taking his wife on a leisurely cruise rather than a Secretary of State trying to stave off a world crisis. In Rome, he conferred with his friend the Italian foreign minister Count Grandi, and with Mussolini, who turned up on Sunday at the shore and gave the Stimsons a run in his new speedboat! "He showed his attractive side," Stimson recorded in a memorandum after this meeting, "and we both liked him very much." Then the Secretary went to Paris, where the serious business of his tour began.

The French government had invited to Paris both Bruening and his foreign secretary, Dr. Curtius, head of the People's Party, and it seemed intent on upstaging the meeting MacDonald had convened in London. While Stimson was on the high seas the U.S. published a memorandum urging France to take part in a loan to bail the Germans out, but Paris would play only if the Germans accepted political conditions: end the customs union; end building a second pocket battleship; accept the eastern frontier decreed by the Versailles Treaty, which handed tens of thousands of square miles of German-occupied territory to Poland; dissolve the *Stahlhelm*, the paramilitary veterans' organization allied to the political conservatives; and stop agitating for revision of the treaty. Bruening refused these terms and was backed by the German parliament, the Reichstag. So the statesmen and the powers moved on to London for MacDonald's conference.

Time was running out. On July 11 the president of the Reichsbank returned empty-handed from Paris. The next day the German government guaranteed the liabilities of all leading banks. But it was too late. The day after that the Darmstaedter-und-Nazional Bank went into bankruptcy, and within days the Reichsbank's own reserves had fallen below the statutory minimum level: Germany's central bank was literally bankrupt. To all intents and purposes, the parliamentary regime that had staggered on through hyperinflation, prosperity and back to crisis again was bankrupt too. The way was cleared for the fall of Bruening in May 1932, for the sinister farce of the "barons' Cabinet,"* and—only eighteen months away—for the coming of Hitler.

---

pp. 115–117; personal communications to the author from McGeorge Bundy, William P. Bundy and Walter Isaacson.

*This was the name given to the administration of Baron Franz von Papen. The minister of defense was General Kurt von Schleicher, who had secretly agreed with Hitler to back von

On July 20, Stimson took the boat train from Paris to attend the Seven-Power Conference in London.* Here again he was at his very best, using his negotiating skills as a lawyer to put together a "standstill agreement" that staved off abject panic and gave the Germans, and the New York bankers, valuable time. Five days later he was in Berlin for the first time since early childhood. He walked about in the holiday crowds with his new friend Bruening, hating the "Wilhelmine" architecture and the "frightful" statuary, but impressed by the Pergamon Altar and the other Oriental treasures of the imperial museum. At a dinner at the American embassy he berated Bruening and General Wilhelm Groener, minister of defense, about German militarism. He passed through London, where he saw MacDonald several times, Henderson and other leading British statesmen. Then, on August 1, he was off to the Highlands to catch a few salmon and trout, stalk some deer and shoot some grouse.

Stimson's journey to Europe in the summer of 1931 shows him at the height of his powers and reputation. It also reveals certain limitations in his personality. Practically, he had conducted the naval disarmament negotiations on his own. In the financial crisis of 1931 he behaved almost as an assistant President, converting Hoover to his view that a moratorium was necessary, giving the President crucial help in building congressional support for it, carrying through the ticklish process of announcing it in such a way as to involve the Europeans without panicking or infuriating Congress. In short, he displayed his touch at its surest. It is not too much to say that for a few weeks he was the most important statesman in Europe—for the experts. What he did not possess was the temperament or personality to appeal to the mass of men and women, in the United States or in Europe, as his contemporaries Hitler and Roosevelt, Mussolini and Baldwin and Churchill and even poor Ramsay MacDonald could do.

In this critical period, with Europe and East Asia both spinning toward an abyss of hatred, folly and destruction, dragging the United States with them, Stimson was too unemotional, too rational to comprehend the cataclysmic forces, the anger, the fear, the desire for re-

---

Papen in return for a free hand and new elections. Von Papen inspired a grim but not unpleasing jest from the French politician Édouard Herriot: "The more I study the face of a German cavalry officer, the more I admire his horse." Otto Friedrich, *Before the Deluge*, p. 365.

*Volume xvii of the *Diary* covers Stimson's visit to Europe in July and August 1931. I have drawn on it in what follows.

venge and the search for scapegoats that had been released. For all his intellectual comprehension of the most complex interactions, he failed to grasp the nature and scope of the crisis that he, perhaps more than any other individual statesman in Europe, might have been able to make the decisive contribution to resolving.

For while Stimson was somewhat complacently enjoying his rich man's holiday, the world was falling apart. Even while the London conference was in session, the panic shifted from Germany to London. Speculators and timid investors withdrew £200 million (then worth about $1 billion) in gold from London between July and September. The Labour government responded with expenditure cuts. In early September the incident of the Royal Navy "mutiny" at Invergordon— in reality little more than an insubordinate demonstration against pay cuts dictated by the crisis—was reported in France and elsewhere as if it were the beginning of a Red revolution and the end of two hundred years of British naval power. That was the last straw as far as the money markets were concerned, and on September 21 Britain was forced to go off the gold standard,* with catastrophic consequences for her own and her neighbors' economies.

Truly, as Ramsay MacDonald said a year later in his speech to the Lausanne Conference, "nothing smaller than a world, nothing less than a system . . . [was] crumbling under our feet."†

That the financial and diplomatic crisis was serious, no one understood better than Henry Stimson. What seems to be lacking, on a reading of his diaries, is a full sense of the historical dimensions of the disaster that was in the making. And this overall failure of imagination is strangely counterpointed by odd errors of judgment about people, all the more strange in one so widely esteemed as a judge of men.

In Nicaragua, he had judged that the "bandit" Sandino was an unimportant element in the equation and that Anastasio Somoza was the best of the younger liberals. Now, in Rome, he found Grandi reliable and Mussolini likeable. In Berlin, he lectured Bruening, the last bastion against Hitler, and Wilhelm Groener, the soldier who had made Weimar democracy possible by assuring the Social Democrats of the army's loyalty to the constitution, against the dangers of milita-

---

*That is, to rescind the promise to make paper currency redeemable for gold and in effect to devalue the British pound sterling against currencies, like the dollar and the franc, that continued to be backed by gold.

†Wheeler-Bennett, *op. cit.*, p. 211.

rism. The man who impressed him, on the other hand, whom he described in his diary as "a true democrat," was General Kurt von Schleicher, archintriguer and demagogue, who offered Hitler a job as his deputy and who was murdered by Hitler for his pains.

Stimson went along too easily with the prevailing Francophobia of his British friends. The French politician he most admired was Pierre Laval, who later collaborated with the Nazis and was convicted of treason and shot in 1945. It was not easy, McGeorge Bundy, in *On Active Service in Peace and War,* recorded Stimson as saying, "to look back fairly at the Laval of 1931 and 1932, across years in which he recorded himself as a villain like Iago, glorying in unrepentant treason." There is a whiff of special pleading about this ingenious argument. It was frank of Stimson to admit after the war that in July 1931 he found Laval "an able, forceful and I think a sincere man." But the Laval of 1931 was the Laval of 1941.

Again, he was capable of telling his friend MacDonald that "America was watching to see which of the two nations, France or Germany, would again permit the military authorities to get the upper hand"*; this a fairly staggering misjudgment if one reflects that within eighteen months Feldmarschall von Hindenburg handed power first to General Schleicher, and then to Hitler, while France remained for the next nine years firmly in the hands of the all-too-civilian politicians of the Third Republic.

Stimson's grasp of British politics was not much subtler. He took the view that the Labour leaders, unlike their followers, were not "socialistic," when it would have been truer to put the proposition the other way around and to say that millions of rather conservative British working-class voters were being led by a handful of middle-class socialists. And he seemed to have little understanding of the personal and political tragedy through which his friend Ramsay MacDonald was living during those very weeks. For on August 24, only a few days before Stimson left for home, the Labour government fell and MacDonald accepted the King's invitation to form a "national" coalition government. MacDonald even visited Stimson in the Highlands during August; but Stimson appeared to have little understanding of how fateful a decision it would be for his friend to stay on as Prime Minister of a national government. By so doing MacDonald abandoned his party

*HLS, *Diary,* August 1, 1931.

to ignominious defeat and a decade in the political wilderness, and condemned himself to be despised and abhorred as a traitor by his own friends and the movement he had led for so long.

Worst of all, Stimson did not at first seem to grasp the enormity of the disaster impending in Germany. It was hard for a man of his probity and rationality, not to mention his Victorian upbringing, to imagine that one of the great countries of Europe, one, to be sure, at which he looked askance for its militarism, was on the very brink of falling into the hands, not of militarists—indeed a time was coming when the "militarists" would be seen as the only hope of salvation in Germany—but of gangsters led by a half-educated psychopath.

Of course Stimson's diary, like his public utterances, is full of warnings of the dangers to be feared if the financial crisis could not be alleviated. But he seemed not to comprehend the sheer enormity, the unredeemed blackness, of the approaching catastrophe. Instead, lawyerlike, he seems to have taken his clients as he found them, happy to establish with them relations of friendship or even something like intimacy, but feeling no more than skin-deep curiosity about the ideas that drove them or about what might be their fate; picking up his brief, mastering it with rare application and perception, but not quite understanding, until much later, that in this trial not just the parties, but counsel, spectators, judge and courthouse were all equally at risk.

If Stimson did not penetrate far below the surface of the great tragedy at which he had a seat in the front row, he did not, however, altogether miss the lesson of the play. In November 1932 Adolf Hitler's barbarian chariot had rumbled to within two months of power. But it was some comparatively minor irritation over financial negotiations that drove Stimson to pronounce, to a group of his advisers, the epitaph of the Versailles years:

> In a nutshell, the experts seem to know what ought to be done; but in every case it runs into a vicious circle controlled by political factors, and nobody dares to break that vicious circle. . . .
>
> I broke out and said that I was living in a world where all our difficulties came from the same thing, not only in finance but in all matters, where we are constantly shut in by the timidity of governments making certain decisions, for fear that some admin-

istration will be overthrown. . . . I said that the time had come
when somebody has got to show some guts.*

Whatever the limitations of his imagination or the foibles of his
judgment, no one ever doubted Colonel Stimson's guts.

The story of reparations came to an end at Lausanne in 1932.
Months before the conference opened it was widely understood that
the Germans neither could nor would pay reparations for much longer.
The French asked for seven billion marks in settlement of reparations
for good; the Germans said they could pay no more than two. The
French reduced their demand to four; the Germans said it would bring
Hitler to power. In the end the Germans agreed to pay three billion
marks. MacDonald tried to get the French to agree to drop from the
treaty the clause insisting on German war guilt, but the French were
unyielding. Instead, the conference did state that the payment of reparations was at an end. It was too late. Hitler was indeed on his way
to power.

The European Allies had at long last given up their demand for
reparations; but the Americans, still insisting that there was no connection between reparations and war debt, had not given up their
insistence on being repaid. In the drama of war debt, there was one
more big scene to be played. By a curious twist, it was a scene that
would have an effect on Henry Stimson's life long after he left the
State Department.

On November 8, 1932, Herbert Clark Hoover was defeated by
Franklin Delano Roosevelt in the presidential election. Stimson had
worked for two Presidents who had been defeated in running for a
second term. He consoled Hoover, for whom he had developed a half-
contemptuous affection, by reminding him that Grover Cleveland had
been elected to a second term after an interval. The best thing, he
urged Hoover, was to acknowledge that the tides of American politics
were running against you and to wait until those tides turned.

The night after the election, Stimson, who had been an insomniac
for years, "had a good sleep and woke up . . . feeling a greater sense
of freedom than I have for years." His future, as he wrote in his diary,

---

*HLS, *Diary*, November 30, 1932. The first paragraph was his view confided in his diary; the
second his summary of his own outburst to Bundy and others earlier in the day.

was "all up in the air." He was sixty-five years old, and he had not practiced his profession for five years. He supposed he would have to go back to the law or be "completely lost," but privately he now regarded it as "drudgery."*

At that moment, it looked as though his public life would end with the new President's inauguration on March 4, 1933. But already the hand of Providence, nudged by the loyal friendship and nimble brain of Felix Frankfurter, was making sure that when he went home to Highhold, it would not be forever.

Preoccupied by the election, the Hoover administration had not focused on the fact that the half-yearly deadline for the payment of war debts was approaching, and that both France and Britain might default. Both France and Britain delivered Notes that seemed to imply as much, and Hoover sent a message to Roosevelt about the situation which, Stimson felt, would arouse resentment in Europe. Congress, on the other hand, had come back "red-hot" against any weakening of the American position. They were a "hard-boiled lot," Stimson judged after a meeting with congressional leaders. The British, who after the run on the pound and the abandonment of the gold standard, were genuinely short of gold to pay the debt installment, and the French, who were not, must pay in full or face the consequences.

The problem of debt could not be solved by a lame-duck administration. It would be for Roosevelt to solve. What made its solution so difficult was the degree to which Hoover mistrusted his successor. He agreed to see Roosevelt on November 22, but Roosevelt wanted to see him alone, and Hoover didn't want that. "He has been warned by so many people that Roosevelt will shift his words," Stimson wrote, "that he wants some witnesses."† The meeting came. Hoover told Stimson arrogantly that he had spent "most of their time educating a very ignorant and . . . well-meaning young man." Then FDR made a statement to reporters that the debt problem was the incumbent administration's doing and that he was not going to coerce Congress on it. Hoover was furious. That was just what he had feared from Roosevelt: that he would offer his cooperation in private, then go outside and repudiate his offer for the benefit of the press. Even Stimson, who did not share Hoover's extreme suspicions, said that Roosevelt's behavior "makes a very unpleasant impression." Years later he scrawled

*Diary, November 9, 1932.
†Ibid., November 16, 1932.

against this in his diary in pencil: "FDR welches." Stories of Roosevelt's untrustworthiness, as Stimson called it in his diary at the time, seem to be pretty well founded. In the same entry he repeated his favorite aphorism, that the only way to make a man trustworthy is to trust him.

Both Hoover and the Treasury Secretary, Ogden Mills, were sure that both the French and the British would default. Stimson was not so sure. "At the last moment" he came to the belief that "when the British actually reached the brink of the chasm they would stop." Working quietly through telephone calls to his friend Thomas Lamont at the Morgan bank, Stimson suggested that a compromise might be worked out to make it easier for the British to pay. His instinct proved right. When December 15 came, Britain paid. France, with far less to pay and far more reserves to pay it out of, defaulted. And Italy paid; "cagey little Italy," Stimson wrote in his diary, "waited to see what would happen to the other nations."

A week later his old friend and former assistant Felix Frankfurter, now working for Roosevelt, called from Albany. "Roosevelt suddenly out of a clear blue sky said, 'Why doesn't Harry Stimson come up here and talk with me and settle this damned thing that nobody else seems able to.'"* There was a certain magnanimity about this offer. In the campaign, Stimson, together with Ogden Mills and Secretary of War Patrick Hurley, had made speeches attacking corruption in Democratic-controlled New York City. Roosevelt, in a brilliant speech, had ridiculed these charges: "I say to these gentlemen," he had said in his best mock-heroic manner, "We shall be grateful if you will return to your posts in Washington, and bend your efforts and spend your time solving the problems which the whole nation is bearing under your administration. Rest assured that we of the Empire State can and will take care of ourselves."† But the President-elect was not a man to bear a grudge; and if Stimson was annoyed, he did not show it. FDR volunteered to meet Stimson either in New York or on his way south to his polio treatment at Warm Springs, Georgia, over the Christmas holiday. Stimson talked to Hoover, who repeated that Roosevelt was a "very dangerous and contrary man." After some hesitations, and some discreet lubrication by Frankfurter in the background, Stimson traveled up and saw Roosevelt on January 9 at his Hudson

*HLS, *Diary,* December 22, 1932.
†The speech is analyzed in Samuel I. Rosenman, *Working for Roosevelt,* pp. 43–45.

Valley home. "Mabel would not have approved of the furnishings" of Hyde Park, Colonel Stimson commented severely. But he acknowledged that FDR received him with great cordiality and that their interview, which lasted from eleven in the morning through luncheon and during their drive through snowy weather to New York, was "very pleasant."

The conversation ranged far beyond the immediate question of debt that had occasioned it. In effect the outgoing Republican Secretary of State was briefing the incoming Democratic President on the whole range of American foreign policy, from Manchuria to disarmament and back by way of Cuba and Haiti to the Philippines. Roosevelt, as always, was as interested in the man as in the subjects he discussed, and was impressed. A seed had been planted that was to grow into the last and most important political relationship in Stimson's life.

The tides of American history washed Herbert Hoover up on the shore as a castaway in perpetuity. But for Henry Stimson they would eventually turn. That day at Hyde Park, without knowing it, as the snowflakes drifted against the limousine's windshield, he had begun the long, improbable traverse from one administration to the next.

VI

The
Organizer of
Victory*

> *Gabriel,* lead forth to Battel these my sons
> Invincible, lead forth my armèd Saints
> By Thousands and by Millions rang'd for fight.
>
> Milton, *Paradise Lost,* Book VI, ii. 46–48

> Geographically and historically Bolero [the code name
> for a frontal attack on Germany across the English
> Channel] was the easiest road to the center of our
> chief enemy's heart.
>
> Henry L. Stimson, *Diary,* June 19, 1942

> My faith rests upon my belief that there is a Power
> in the universe that makes for righteousness and that
> Power cannot allow such a clear issue of right and
> wrong to go the wrong way.
>
> Henry L. Stimson, *Diary,* July 1942

In the fateful month of June 1940, as German *Panzers* entered Paris and Marshal Pétain formed a government and went to Hitler for an armistice, Henry Stimson took a week off from his legal work that, at least for him, was also to be fateful. On June 12, which was a Wednesday, he took the train from New York via Boston to his old school at Andover, Massachusetts. The next day he wrote the commencement address he had been asked to give, and on Friday he delivered it to an audience of boys who included the future President George Bush. He told them that a civilization built up over four centuries was under

*Lazare Carnot, one of the members of the Directory which governed France from 1795 to 1797 was known as *l'organisateur de la victoire* after his arrest was ordered and a deputy cried out in the Assembly: "Will you dare to lay hands on the man who has organized victory?"

attack, and that in particular the Christian principle of the equal value
of every human personality was in danger. But, he said, when he looked
at their faces, he was filled not with pity but with the desire to congratulate them that they had been placed at a moment of great opportunity to choose between good and evil.

That night Stimson flew back to Long Island and worked on an
address for the students at Yale on compulsory military training. On
Sunday he and his wife went to New Haven, where they stayed with
Mrs. Stimson's niece, Mrs. Daggett. On Monday he gave his speech
and began work on a talk to be broadcast on Tuesday over NBC radio
from the Daggetts' house on Prospect Street. This radio speech on
"America's Interest in Britain's Fleet" developed Stimson's by now
well-worn theme that the United States could not afford to let Britain
follow France into defeat, not for any sentimental reason but because
America would then be the Nazis' next target. On Wednesday June 19
the Stimsons were driven back to New York, to their rented apartment
in the Hotel Pierre, looking out over Central Park from Fifth Avenue.
It was at his office, at three o'clock that afternoon, that the new call
to duty came.

It was the President of the United States on the phone. FDR came
straight to the point and offered Stimson the job of Secretary of War
in his Cabinet. As usual, he was pleasant, even ingratiating. He needed
Stimson in his Cabinet as a stabilizing influence, he said, because "everybody in Washington was running round at loose ends." He did not
add that the reason they were doing so lay in his own inspired system
of intentional confusion, which made everyone compete with someone
else and no one feel safe in his job.

Stimson asked for time to consult a few close friends, and discussed the offer with his wife and with his partners Bronson Winthrop
and George Roberts. They all urged him to accept. At about seven
o'clock he telephoned the White House and asked the President three
questions.

Had he heard the New Haven radio speech? The President said
he had already read it and agreed with it. Did he know that Stimson
favored compulsory military service? He did, and he conveyed, with
Rooseveltian evasiveness, the notion that he was "in sympathy" on
the issue. Finally Stimson asked the President to confirm that Frank
Knox, another strongly anti-isolationist Republican to whom the President had offered the Navy secretaryship, had accepted. Roosevelt said

he had, and Stimson then said yes, too. For good measure, he also indicated that he had no objection to Judge Robert P. Patterson* as his Assistant Secretary. Those were the circumstances in which Colonel Henry Stimson, a lifelong Republican, became—at the age of seventy-two and in a Democratic administration—Secretary of War, a job he had last accepted twenty-nine years before.

In the summer of 1940 Henry Stimson was a tired and troubled grandee. Since 1936 he had been involved in the biggest and longest lawsuit of his legal career. This was *Blaustein* v. *Pan American Petroleum and Transport Company*. Stimson's client was Jacob Blaustein, who, with his immigrant father Louis Blaustein, had founded the American Oil Company, which marketed petroleum products under the Amoco trademark, but which was dependent on the major oil-producing companies for those products. The Blausteins had therefore sold their stock to Pan American Oil. It would be an integrated oil company; they would be minority shareholders, and Standard Oil of Indiana would hold the majority of the stock. An elaborate contract was drawn up to give effect to this plan, but the moment it was signed, Standard Oil of Indiana in effect tore it up, arranging for oil to be shipped and refined not by Pan American Oil, but by Standard Oil of New Jersey (ancestor of the modern Exxon).

The Blausteins retained Stimson, who for technical reasons advised that, while there was little hope of winning an action for breach of contract, the Standard Oil of Indiana management might be successfully sued for breach of their obligations as directors. Standard was represented by one of the leaders of the American bar at the time, John W. Davis, also counsel to Standard Oil of New Jersey and Democratic presidential candidate in 1924. (The judge in the case, incidentally, was Samuel I. Rosenman, President Roosevelt's close adviser and favorite speechwriter.)

The case took four years to come to trial. That was hardly surprising, since it involved more than 1,000 exhibits, 2,686 printed pages of pretrial examinations and 2,900 pages of printed briefs.† When it

*Patterson, a robust opponent of isolationism and a man of the "neo-Hamiltonian" tendency, had fought in France in World War I and wore around his waist as a memento the belt of a German soldier he had killed there.
†On *Blaustein*, see *Winthrop, Stimson, Putnam and Roberts: A History of a Law firm*, pp. 35–37. I

did come to court, the trial lasted for seventy days and filled 10,631 pages of stenographic notes. In 1944 Stimson's clients won $250 million. Though that judgment was later overruled by an appellate court, Jacob Blaustein was eventually vindicated. His stock increased in value enormously, and he became chairman of Standard Oil of Indiana. The award was the largest ever made up to that time, and in every way the *Blaustein* case was the biggest that had ever then been tried at the common law.

Before it was over, Stimson had become heartily tired of *Blaustein*. By 1940, he was seventy-two years old, and—to use a homely phrase— he was feeling his age. He was tired by the long days in court. He still exacted the most rigorous preparation for his examination of witnesses, but he found the work more and more fatiguing; and by midafter- noon, he found it impossible to concentrate as he had once been able to do. The pretrial depositions of Standard witnesses had been espe- cially irksome, because Stimson was constantly interrupted by defense counsel. Cross-examination, which he had once enjoyed so much and brought to such a pitch of art, became more difficult for him than for the witness. He feared that he was squandering his opportunities and fluffing his carefully prepared *coups*. He wrote to Felix Frankfurter that he had become "a slow old man and this trial work is out for me." One day he could stand it no longer and simply handed over responsibility for the case to his partner and old friend Allen Klots. "I can't go on," he told Klots, and from then on, though he sat in court and offered Klots advice when asked, the young lawyers in his firm assumed that he was more or less finished as a lawyer and as far as active life was concerned.

Stimson's failing powers in court, his irritation with the Blaustein case, and his fatigue, not to mention his chronic insomnia and a long series of minor ailments, were no doubt symptoms not only of his age, but of the anguish he had felt about the condition of the world ever since he left office in 1933. In July 1939 he wrote, "Outside this profes- sional burden there has constantly overhung the burden of the events in the world at large—the cloud over Europe; the barbarity of the Japs in the Far East. Ever since the British cabinet pledged itself to defend Poland, I have felt that war might come at any moment. That was an immensely fateful step."*

He had watched with pained incredulity and intermittent anger as the League of Nations and its chief backers, the European democ-

---

was also greatly helped by an interview with Peter Kaminer, one of the partners who worked with Stimson on *Blaustein*. See also HLS, *Diary*, vol. xxix.

Diary, vol. xxix, p. 15. (The first six months of 1939 were written up by HLS retrospectively.)

racies, failed to stop Japan's cruelty in China, Mussolini's barbarous invasion of Ethiopia, Hitler's defiant invasion of the Rhineland, his gangster methods and concentration camps at home, his forced take-over of Austria in the *Anschluss,* and his barefaced invasion of Czecho-slovakia. In 1931–32 Stimson had been in a real sense the arbiter of Europe, courted and deferred to by the rulers of Britain, France and Germany alike. But now he watched the crisis in Europe with the knowledge that there was nothing he could do to resolve it.

The failures of American policy were even more frustrating be-cause less wholly beyond his power to affect. It was plain to Stimson that the United States could not shut itself off from the world, that a policy of neutrality and nonintervention simply handed over the keys to the enemies of everything the United States stood for. In early 1939, as the fortunes of the Spanish Republic dwindled away, he wrote, "It became more and more evident what a disaster the non-intervention agreement had been and how it had played into the hands of the Axis powers."*

For isolationists in Congress and elsewhere he had nothing but contempt. When invited to testify to the Senate Foreign Relations Committee by Senator Key Pittman of Nevada, he referred by name to William E. Borah, Hiram Johnson, Tom Connally, Alben Barkley and Robert LaFollette, Jr., as "that hostile group of cynical-minded men," even though for some of them—notably Borah—he had felt respect in the past and would feel respect again in the future.

In that climate it may have seemed that an aging ex-Secretary of State—a Republican conservative, moreover, who was almost as much out of sympathy with the New Deal's domestic policy as he was with the instincts of the majority of his own party in foreign affairs—would have little more sway over American public opinion than he had power to stem the tide of fascist aggression in Europe. Yet Stimson knew that he was not wholly without influence. During the seven years from 1933 to 1940 he doggedly took advantage of speaking engagements, invita-tions to speak on the radio and access to papers like *The New York Times* to sound his warning call. At first his was a lonely bugle, and it sounded harshly in a world where the Nye Committee† had persuaded many that war was the fault of "merchants of death" in the interna-

---

*Ibid., p. 3.

†The congressional committee, chaired by Senator Gerald P. Nye of North Dakota, in 1934, drew attention to the profits of munitions manufacturers and contributed to the climate of opinion that led to the Neutrality Act of 1935.

tional arms industry, and where isolationism and national self-absorption were in the ascendant.

As Stimson persevered, his isolated utterances began to form into a coherent alternative policy, a plan for national defense in a world threatened by fascism. When he had lunch with New York Governor Thomas Dewey on October 11, 1939, for example, he was able to hand him a package of speeches and writings in which his policy was argued. On September 16, just after the outbreak of war in Europe, when it was proposed to repeal the neutrality legislation by which the United States was not permitted to sell arms to belligerents, Senator Borah spoke on the radio against repeal. Stimson answered him in a powerful letter in *The New York Times*. He did not differ from the senator about ends, he wrote, but only about means:

> Senator Borah evidently thinks that the repeal of the automatic arms embargo provision of the so-called Nye legislation would inevitably drag us into armed participation in the present war. I think that the repeal of those provisions constitutes perhaps the last remaining hope of our avoiding being so dragged in.

In controversy, as in morals, timing may be everything. It may be that in September 1939 Stimson still believed that the Neutrality Acts should be repealed for the reason he gave. Certainly he believed that it made sense for the United States to sell arms to those European democracies that might do her fighting for her. But from the start he must have suspected, and after the fall of France in May 1940 he knew, that eventually the United States would have to fight for herself. By October 1941 he was confiding to his diary his gloomy view that the President "is entirely in the hands of people who see only the side of other nations and who are wedded to the idea that with our weapons they can win the war. I am perfectly certain they cannot and perfectly certain that eventually we will have to fight."

Where Stimson was at all times consistent was in his belief that the Axis powers must be stopped, or civilization itself, including American civilization, would eventually be destroyed. In the privacy of his diary, he left no doubt about the contempt and loathing he felt for Hitler. During the "Phony War" in the winter of 1939–40, when the British and French were cautiously mobilizing their strength, Stimson wrote that it was a new kind of war with our civilization hanging by a thread. The aim of the Allies should not be to crush Germany indiscriminately but to oust the Nazi system as recreant to and destructive of the Caucasian* civilization of Europe. [Britain's and France's] tactics should be and are to hold the line steadily and firmly both on land and at sea until the pressure squirts Hitler and his gang out of their posts in the way you squeeze the pus out of an ulcer.

In public he was just as robust, if more decorous. On March 7, 1940, *The New York Times* published an eloquent, even noble statement of his views. An increasing number of Americans felt, Stimson wrote, that our government "should follow a policy of far-sighted affirmation rather than one of drift and negation"; and, as everyone knew, he was one of their number:

> I believe that our foreign policy cannot with safety be geographically limited to a defense of this hemisphere. . . . On the contrary, I think that if we should stand idly by without protest or action until Britain, France and China are either conquered or forced to make terms with militaristic aggressors, our own hemisphere might become economically so affected and militarily so endangered that it would be neither a safe nor a happy place to live in for a people with American ideals of life.†

The fundamental mistake people were making, Stimson argued, was in failing to see that the Axis nations represented "a complete reversal of the whole trend of European civilization." It was not merely that the attacks on Manchuria and China, Ethiopia, Spain, Austria and Czechoslovakia had shown that this was a system with which the rest of the world could not live at peace:

> Fascism has involved a serious moral deterioration; an increasing and callous disregard of the most formal and explicit international obligations and pledges; extreme brutality towards helpless groups of people; the complete destruction within their jurisdiction of that individual freedom of speech, of thought and

---

*One must note that Stimson used the word "Caucasian," so redolent of the pseudoscience of Houston Stewart Chamberlain and his racialist followers, rather than speaking of the Christian or Judeo-Christian tradition of Europe.

†*The New York Times*, March 7, 1940.

of the person which has been the priceless goal of many centuries of struggle.

Shall we bury our heads in the sands of isolationism and timidly await the time when our security shall be lessened and perhaps destroyed by the growing success of lawlessness around us? Or shall we use our present strength and security from attack to throw our weight into the vacillating scales in favor of law and order and freedom?*

After the event, such language may seem unremarkable, the statement of what have since become clichés. But they were not clichés in March 1940. It was not only Stimson's own Republican Party that avoided such blunt statements of the issues. The Democrats did so too. Franklin Roosevelt may have felt, indeed the evidence suggests he did feel, much the same repugnance for European fascism and for its Japanese analogue as did Stimson. But Roosevelt did not believe that he could afford to speak his mind. Stimson, in 1939 and 1940, was the American Churchill. He was articulating the New Deal Democrats' instincts more clearly than their own leaders. Beyond Left and Right, above Republican and Democrat, he was setting forth the lasting values of the American tradition. In Churchill's phrase, this was perhaps Henry Stimson's finest hour.

The summons of Stimson to FDR's War Department did not, of course, come out of the blue. It was, for one thing, an election year, and it has been suggested that Roosevelt was attracted by the idea of embarrassing the Republicans by dramatizing the split between their isolationist and internationalist wings. That hypothesis may be, not too Machiavellian for Roosevelt, since he could be devious enough when he felt the situation demanded it, but too crudely Machiavellian. FDR did not want Stimson as a "low road" ploy to embarrass the Republicans. He wanted him to emphasize the "high road" attractions of a broad national coalition for peace and prosperity, always the best platform on which to run for the presidency.

In practical terms, the President had been worried for some time about his previous Secretary of War, the Kansas isolationist Harry Woodring. In January 1940, when Roosevelt wanted to sell military equipment to Finland, which had been attacked by the Soviet Union, Woodring demurred, and again in the spring, with Britain and France desperate to buy military aircraft in the United States, Woodring op-

*Ibid.

posed the sales. In April, Roosevelt ordered him to go along or resign, and Woodring went along.

The additional embarrassment was that Louis Johnson, Assistant Secretary of War, had set his heart on Woodring's job and thought he had been promised it. By the summer the President wanted not only a Secretary of War who would carry out his policies, but one who could take the department by the scruff of the neck and make it ready for the war he could clearly see coming. And he saw it would be a bonus if the Secretary was a Republican who would be the living symbol of the reality that no recklessly partisan Democratic President was dragging the American people into that war; rather, war itself was approaching on its own feet.

Henry Stimson was not the first Republican he thought of. Some months earlier he had contemplated a reshuffle that would have brought two Republicans into the Cabinet, Frank Knox of Illinois and Alfred Landon of Kansas. It was at this point that two of Henry Stimson's old friends took a hand.

Grenville Clark* was one of a very interesting kind of active citizen: a New York lawyer with wide contacts in the government and in both political parties who was dedicated to the public service but had no interest in holding public office himself. Such men had been active in the "good government" movement that purified New York politics at the turn of the century. They were to be found among the "dollar-a-year-men" who came to Washington to serve in the New Deal. And they were to be the core of the American Establishment in the Cold War years. Although Stimson himself had held public office and a man like Grenville Clark did not care to, their instincts were similar. In a sense, Clark was part of the soil in which Stimson's ideals of public service grew. Part of the legacy that men of Stimson's and Clark's generations handed on to those who took responsibility for U.S. defense and foreign policy after 1945 was the idea that private citizens might properly lobby public officials in the executive branch when they felt strongly that policy needed to be changed. Another part of that legacy was the existence of networks of contacts, many originating in universities and graduate schools such as Yale and the Harvard Law School, but also associated with law firms and investment banks. Such

---

*I have drawn this account of Grenville Clark's role in putting Stimson's name before Roosevelt from HLS, *Diary*, Reel 6, vol. xxix and xxx; *On Active Service*, p. 323; Morison, *Turmoil and Tradition*, pp. 479–82; Frankfurter, *Columbia Oral History Project*, pp. 57 ff. Morison's account is particularly valuable because he interviewed Clark.

people and networks continue to influence both appointments and policies in national security and foreign policy to a perhaps surprising extent in a federal democracy as large as the United States, all the more so given its strong populist and antielitist tradition. Whether one finds that circumstance admirable or offensive, it was Harvard contacts that brought Henry Stimson back to the War Department at the age of seventy-two.

Clark's particular concern, since before the First World War, had been with military training. He had been one of the moving spirits of the Plattsburg camps that trained officers to supplement the tiny corps of regulars before the United States entered World War I. No predictable partisan, he had organized lawyers against Roosevelt's plan to pack the Supreme Court with amenable justices in 1936. Now he was convinced that the country would need universal, compulsory military training. He talked to the new chief of staff, General George C. Marshall, who told him that the Army had its doubts about the idea, and to the Democratic majority leader in the Senate, Senator James Byrnes, who said there was not a "Chinaman's chance" that a universal-training bill would pass the Congress. Clark became convinced that the only way to make the plan succeed, which he thought vital for national survival, was to persuade the President to hire a Secretary of War who could "push it through."

Clark talked to his Harvard Law School classmate, Stimson's ubiquitous friend Supreme Court Justice Felix Frankfurter,* and together they considered several names, including that of William J. ("Wild Bill") Donovan, later wartime head of the Office of Strategic Services, forerunner of the CIA. Stimson would be far better, they thought. The only snags were his age and his health. The answer, they thought, would be to propose Stimson, supported by a younger man, Judge Robert Patterson, who had come to Roosevelt's approving notice by writing a letter to Secretary Woodring volunteering to resign his judgeship and serve the country in any capacity, even as a private, because he considered the emergency so grave. On June 3 Frankfurter went to see the President, who found the idea appealing but worried about Stimson's health. Clark then asked Stimson if he was interested. Stimson said he might be but posed certain conditions, among them that he would not be expected to get involved in domestic politics, and

---

*Frankfurter said of him in 1953 that he was "a fellow whom I now respect as I respect few people in this country . . . one of those deep but slow minds." Felix Frankfurter, *Columbia Oral History Project*, p. 57.

that he would be allowed to work for universal military service. The conditions were perfectly acceptable to the President, but he still had doubts about Stimson's health. In the end, against all etiquette, Clark went to see Stimson's family doctor, who, greatly shocked, nevertheless confirmed that there was nothing whatever wrong with his patient—unless it were that he was frustrated, what with the protracted Blaustein case and his impotence to do anything about the international situation. The lawyer told the Supreme Court Justice, the Justice told the President, and after a nervous week's wait, the President made his fateful phone call and Colonel Stimson, after appropriate hesitations, unsurprisingly accepted. It was, he admitted in his memoirs, in spite of all the dangers ahead and all that needed to be done, a pleasure to be back in charge of the United States Army, which he had known and loved and trusted for thirty years, and this under a chief he admired and with a chief of staff at his side he could work with. "No man," he said looking back, "could have asked more of fortune in a time of national peril."*

The nation was indeed in peril. But what made the times even more dangerous was that the danger was not obvious to the great majority of the American people. Long protected by the oceans and by the historic dominance of the Royal Navy from the danger of attack, Americans found it hard to imagine that they could be vulnerable. For the isolationists, who still predominated in the Congress, and for the man in the street, the danger of war took the only form it had taken in anyone's lifetime: the danger that American soldiers would be sent overseas to pull the chestnuts of one group of Europeans out of the fire; and for that there was no enthusiasm whatever.

Stimson and his friends saw matters differently. They believed that Britain, France and the smaller democracies of Europe deserved to be supported, and that it would be dishonorable for the United States not to do all it could to help them against the dictators, fascist or Communist. But they also believed that if the dictators swept away the barriers to world conquest that the British and French empires constituted, it would be America's turn to be attacked next. And in military terms the United States was pathetically weak, weaker in immediately available forces than either Britain or France.

Stimson was given an opportunity to expound his ideas at his confirmation hearings in the Senate Military Affairs Committee, when

On Active Service, p. 331.

he was given a rough ride, especially by Senator Robert Taft, son of the first President in whose Cabinet he had served. "As I understand you," said Taft, by way of venomous example, "you are in favor of joining in the war just as soon as you figure the British have no longer a chance."

Stimson kept his temper and held his own, but it was an unpleasant experience to have his fitness for office so aggressively challenged by the leaders of the party he had belonged to all his life, indeed by the son of the President he had served loyally. Some of the edge to the questioning, though, may have been lent by frustration. For one thing, the isolationists knew they did not have the votes to block Stimson's confirmation, which passed the Senate on July 9 by fifty-six votes to twenty-eight. For another, as they contemplated the Nazi *Blitzkrieg,* some of them began to wonder in their inner hearts whether they had been wrong and Henry Stimson had been right all along.

It is hard for us to appreciate the full magnitude of the task Stimson faced as he arrived in Washington and moved back into Woodley, the home he had bought in 1929 and never sold even though it stood empty most of the time. For one thing, it requires us to erase almost every assumption we have made about the power and purposes of the United States for the past half-century.

The United States in 1940 was not the dominant economic and military superpower it was to become. *Potentially,* it was no doubt the most powerful nation in the world, but the potentiality was largely unfulfilled. It was deficient in manpower and materiel. It had no allies, it was disunited and it had no political will to make war. Even its gigantic industrial strength was desperately underutilized. Steel production, one of the most important measures of the ability to wage war with the weapons of the 1940s, is an excellent example; in 1938 the United States produced 26.4 million tons of steel against Germany's 20.7 million, the Soviet Union's 16.5 million and Japan's 6.0 million. But where Germany, Russia and Japan were all working at full capacity, and indeed in the case of the Soviet Union were adding new capacity at a breathless pace, the U.S. was operating at only one-third of full capacity.*

*The source of these comparative figures is Hillmann, "Comparative Strength of the Great Powers," in Arnold Toynbee (ed.), *The World in March 1939,* p. 443 and footnote. I owe these

The United States had a large, well-equipped navy, smaller than that of Great Britain but with fewer tasks to cope with than the Royal Navy. It had fairly efficient, medium-sized air forces attached to both army and navy. And it had a regular army of only 140,000 men, far smaller than that of any other great power, which had only begun to adopt modern tactics and modern equipment. True, the American economy had been the biggest in the world since it passed that of Great Britain in the 1870s. Alone of the great powers, the United States had been virtually unscathed and indeed in certain respects strengthened by World War I, which shattered Russia, destroyed Austria-Hungary, ruined Germany, crippled France and cost even Britain dear in lives, money and economic strength. By the eve of the crash of 1929 the U.S. had advanced so far ahead of any competitor that it seemed to be moving into a new era. Aldous Huxley irreverently suggested that events should be dated "in the year of our Ford." In the 1920s American industry pioneered the substitution of electricity for steam power, mechanization of production techniques, and the application of "scientific" management. A single statistic illustrates how far the United States had outstripped even the most advanced of its competitors. In 1929, the last year before the Depression, more than 4.5 million automobiles and trucks were manufactured in the United States, as against 211,000 in France, 182,000 in Britain and 117,000 in Germany. In other machinery of the time, including agricultural equipment, machine tools, radio and domestic appliances, the U.S. had a comparable lead.

By the time Stimson was sworn in as Secretary of War in July 1940, however, this industrial strength seemed less impressive than it had a decade earlier. For one thing, the controlled economies of the dictatorships had leaped forward. Where in 1938 U.S. manufacturing production stood at 143 per cent of its 1913 level, that of Germany stood at 149 per cent of its prewar level, this after falling to only 59 per cent in 1920. Japan's manufacturing production stood at 552 per cent of its 1913 level, while under Stalin's ruthless whip the Soviet Union, where production had actually fallen to less than 13 per cent of its prewar level after the Revolution and the Civil War, had by 1938 reached an impressive 857 per cent.

The United States, having enjoyed unparalleled prosperity in the 1920s, had been far more grievously affected than its European rivals

figures, however, and others in the succeeding paragraphs, as well as some interpretative ideas, to Paul Kennedy, *The Rise and Fall of the Great Powers*, New York, 1988, pp. 275–343.

by the Depression, and indeed it experienced, as they did not, a second wave of depression in 1937. The consequence of these cyclical depressions was that while the *potential* of U.S. industry was enormous, it was far from being realized. Again, a single comparison illuminates the state of affairs Stimson faced, while at the same time reminding us how different the realities of power were then from those to which later generations became accustomed. The comparison is of the aircraft production of the major powers in 1939*:

U.S.S.R.	10,382
Germany	8,295
Britain	7,940
Japan	4,467
France	3,163
U.S.A.	2,195

Henry Stimson, therefore, found himself with four urgent and gigantic tasks to perform. He had to convert the vast manpower of the United States into modern fighting forces. He had to do what he could to facilitate the application of the very large spare capacity of American industry to making the weapons, munitions and everything else required, first by Britain, desperate to arm after the fall of France and the losses at Dunkerque, then by the nascent American forces. He had to do what he could to put the United States into a posture for self-defense, which included improving the alliances with Britain and with Canada. Perhaps most important of all, he had to do what he could to help the President in the great task of teaching and leadership that would be needed if the American people were to understand in time what needed to be done.

Stimson's success in these four tasks—even without the part he played in the strategy and diplomacy of the grand coalition, let alone his contribution to the development of the atomic bomb—would entitle him to the title the French gave to Napoleon's Minister of War, Lazare Carnot: the "Organizer of Victory."

*R. J. Overy, *The Air War, 1939–45*, New York, 1980. A handwritten note preserved among Stimson War Department papers gives the intelligence estimates for the air strength of the Powers. It makes the United States, as of July 1940, equally the weakest with France: Germany has 2,000 combat aircraft; Italy, 2,000; Britain and Japan, 1,700 each; Soviet Union, unknown but total military aircraft 3,400; France and the United States, 1,500 each.

Three roughly scrawled benchmarks give the measure of his achievement. When Stimson became Secretary of War, the U.S. Army stood nineteenth in the world in numbers, ahead of Bulgaria but behind Portugal! It mustered 174,000 men, with its divisions sometimes as much as 50 per cent below strength and scattered in posts all over the United States. When he retired five years later 15,145,000 people had served in the armed forces, of whom 10,420,000 had been in the Army, and its current strength was about 8,500,000.*

In terms of materiel, the best measure is given by a German historian. In 1940, German armaments production was worth $6 billion (in constant 1944 dollars), British production, $3.5 billion, and U.S. production, an estimated $1.5 billion. By 1943, Germany had managed to more than double its arms production to $13.8 billion; Britain had more than trebled production, to $11.1 billion; and U.S. production, in three years, had risen from $1.5 billion to $37.5 billion, or by a factor of 25!†

In those figures alone can be read the explanation for the third and last benchmark, which is best expressed in the simplest possible terms. In 1940 the United States was one of eight Great Powers, stronger than some in certain categories of armaments or economic resources, weaker than others in other respects. Five years later, she stood alone.

Of course this leap was not Stimson's personal achievement. It was not as if he sat at the top of a rigidly structured machine with absolute power over war production or the armed services. The United States never worked like that, and least of all in the presidency of Franklin D. Roosevelt. Authority over the armed services was divided between the Army and the Navy, the latter having its own air forces and its own army in the shape of the Naval Air Service and the Marines Corps. Even within the War Department, authority was divided among the Secretary, the chief of staff, and the President himself, who was, when he chose to be, Commander-in-Chief. Procurement, from March 1942 on, was the province of the Army Supply Services, under Under Secretary Patterson and General Brehon Somervell. And of course pol-

---

*See Eric Larrabee, *Commander-in-Chief*, p. 114. Altogether 216,000 women served in the United States armed forces, though unlike women in the Soviet and British forces they were not allowed to engage in combat. S. E. Morison and H. S. Commager, *The Growth of the American Republic*, vol. ii, p. 673.

†R. Wagenfuehr, *Die Deutsche Industrie im Kriege 1939–45*, Berlin 1963, quoted in Kennedy, *The Rise and Fall of the Great Powers*, p. 355 and note p. 595.

icy, procurement, funding and administration were all subject from
time to time to the financial and investigative powers of the two houses
of Congress. Sales to France, before the collapse of May 1940 a major
purchaser of U.S. military aircraft and other materiel, and thereafter to
Britain, had come under the authority of the enthusiastic Henry Morgenthau, at the Treasury, by default of the War Department under
Woodring. As to responsibility for the supreme task of converting the
economy to a war footing, that was divided among dozens of what
New Deal Washington called "alphabet soup" agencies; such was
Roosevelt's way.

Franklin Roosevelt was proud of his prerogatives as Commander-
in-Chief. He was, the official historian of the U.S. Army has written,
"the real and not merely a nominal Commander in Chief. Every President has possessed the Constitutional authority which that title indi-
cates, but few Presidents have shared Mr. Roosevelt's willingness to
exercise it in fact and in detail and with such determination."* In July
1939, almost a year before Stimson took office, the President quietly
ordered the Joint Army-Navy Board, predecessor of the Joint Chiefs
of Staff, out of the armed-services departments and transferred them
to his own executive office. Thereafter senior military officers reported
directly to him, and Stimson could be, and from time to time was,
pushed aside and cut out of the circuit of authority. He was not invited
to all or even most of the key conferences at which alliance strategy
was hammered out with the British and was not even on the circula-
tion list for Joint Chiefs of Staff papers. This bureaucratic isolation,
moreover, did not diminish as time went on. It became greater.

So far from being a "czar" or "supremo," therefore, Stimson
achieved his great effect on preparation for war, and on its conduct
when it came, in spite of bureaucratic handcuffs that would have driven
many men less imperious than he into angry resignation. Why did he
put up with the anomalous and in some respects even humiliating
position Roosevelt put him in? Partly, no doubt, because he passion-
ately believed that winning the war came first, and that the dignity or
convenience of even the highest official must be subordinated to that
supreme end. Partly, too, because if a great American war machine was
to be created in record time almost from scratch, there was going to
be plenty of work for everyone, President and Secretary and chief of
staff too.

*Mark S. Watson, *Chief of Staff: Pre-war Plans and Preparations,* pp. 5–6.

It was Stimson's greatest administrative success, he himself wrote, that he kept his desk free for those problems which, by their importance or peculiarity, only he could undertake. "Where there is mutual confidence," he wrote, "there can be decentralization, and where there is initiative, decentralization will produce programs and policies and results which no higher commander need expect to find in his biography."

The twenty-two volumes of Stimson's wartime diary are a sustained and detailed gloss on that sentence. They paint a *pointilliste* picture, built up of hundreds of colorful details, of a master craftsman of the art of government at work. Now he intervenes to help an energetic official overcome an obstructive one. Now he puts tactful pressure on the President himself, now cheers him up with a ringing phrase when even Roosevelt's spirits seem to be flagging. He was, after all, one of the few men, and perhaps the only man, in Roosevelt's official family who was at once his senior, his old acquaintance, his social equal and arguably his superior in experience of government. At other times he saw an opportunity to help the President in Congress, sometimes sallying forth to Capitol Hill, all colors flying, to testify on behalf of the President's policy, sometimes quietly approaching a congressman or senator to supply him with the fact or the argument he needed to clear a bill the administration wanted from committee. He had as close a contact with the British as Secretary of State Cordell Hull. The journalist Philip Kerr, who was one of the most successful British ambassadors in Washington until he died in late 1940, took the trouble to call frequently at Woodley to keep Stimson on his side, as he could usually, but not always. At the same time Stimson made it his business to give a hand to William M. Knudsen, the former head of General Motors who was laboring in 1940 to transform military requirements into operating production lines but was held back by the unwieldy character of the National Defense Advisory Commission, which he headed and on which Stimson and five others sat. Stimson could see that war production ought to be run by one man. He could also understand the President's fears that, if it were, that man would trespass on the functions of the War and Navy departments. Stimson played a leading part in the compromise that substituted for the NDAC the Office of Production Management, with Knudsen in charge, the former union leader Sidney Hillman as his deputy, and Stimson (and Navy Secretary Frank Knox) as members of his board. The real reason, however, why Stimson could make the complex system work though

many would have found it intolerable was because of his human relationships with the two men whose roles squeezed that of the Secretary
of War: the President and the chief of staff.

Stimson's age and standing as a distinguished former Secretary of
State gave him cards to play with the President and therefore also with
the President's men. Powerful members of the White House circle like
Harold Ickes and Harry Hopkins treated him with more respect than
White House staff usually show to even powerful Cabinet secretaries.

Stimson's personal relationship with the President was a complex
one. The two men shared many fundamental values. They were robust
and unashamed patriots. They were both New Yorkers, they had both
been to Harvard (Stimson, of course, only to the Law School). They
had networks of friends in common, and they shared many of the
assumptions of the privileged class in which they had both been
brought up. And they had both admired and to some extent modeled
themselves on Theodore Roosevelt.

They had both been brought up in the code of the Victorian
gentleman. Each interpreted that code in very different ways, however.
Stimson's private life was above reproach and his marriage exemplary,
whereas Roosevelt had a serious affair with Lucy Mercer and may have
been involved with other women, and his marriage was to a considerable extent a façade kept up for political reasons.* What was in any
case far more relevant to the working relationship between President
and Secretary of War was that Roosevelt's was consummately the political temperament, whereas Stimson's was not: he had failed in his
only foray into elective politics in part because he could never quite
conceal his contempt for what politicians had to do. Stimson's honesty
was something more than an absence of dishonesty. It was the deepest
instinct of his being. He was enough of an advocate and man of the
world to know how to control his temper, to bide his time, to speak
only a part of his inner mind. But when great questions of state, of
policy, of war and peace were at stake, Stimson's way was to say what
he believed, directly, bluntly and as often as he felt was necessary to
win his point. He disliked, almost distrusted, FDR's deviousness, his
ability to present one side of his thinking to one interlocutor and a
different face of it to another, though never descending to outright
deception. And he was infuriated by Roosevelt's caution and by his

*See Joseph P. Lash, *Eleanor and Franklin*, New York, 1971.

ability to give the impression, over and over again, that he had been persuaded by argument and his mind was made up, only to slip away and wait until he had weighed new evidence or until events had helped to take his decision another way.

For all that, Stimson admired his third President. He also had a profound respect for his office.

Neither respect for the office nor admiration for the man, however, stopped Stimson from taking liberties that few if any other men in Washington would have taken. Once, when it seemed to him that his Commander-in-Chief was talking nonsense about foreign policy, at intolerable length on the telephone, he simply hung up on the President of the United States. Near the end of the war, when Roosevelt tried to persuade Stimson that he had not accepted the Morgenthau Plan for reducing Germany to an agrarian economy after the victory, Stimson, who had seen the papers and knew what Roosevelt had signed, wagged his finger and said, in the scolding tone one might adopt toward a fibbing child, "Mr. President, I don't like you to dissemble with me!"*

The other relationship that made Stimson's position as Secretary of War, if anomalous, nevertheless tolerable, was that with his chief of staff, George Catlett Marshall. One simple fact sums it up: the office of the chief of staff was next to that of the Secretary of War and the door was always open.

Stimson first met Marshall at the Staff College in Langres in France during World War I, and he was so impressed that when he was sent as Governor General to the Philippines he tried unsuccessfully to persuade Marshall to come with him as a military aide. Marshall and Stimson, Eric Larrabee has written, "were cut of similar cloth," and together they "gave a singleness of purpose to the uneasy mix of civil and military rarely seen before or since." If Stimson's achievement as Secretary of War owed much to the quality of the chief of staff, Marshall's almost legendary reputation may also owe a great deal to the fact that no other chief of staff in Washington has been so unselfishly and ably protected on his vulnerable political flank as Marshall was by Stimson.

The difficulties of the relationship should not be underestimated. Indeed, Stimson and Marshall disagreed on an issue so fundamental

*Morison, *Turmoil and Tradition*, p. 609, apparently based on a conversation with John J. McCloy.

that it could easily have led to irreconcilable hostility: Stimson believed that, at least where "strategic national defense" was at issue, the Secretary of War was the President's chief adviser, and recommendations from the chief of staff should come to him for discussion before being passed by him to the President; Marshall, on the other hand, insisted, courteously but stubbornly, not only that the chief of staff must have direct access to the President but that the President must have direct access to the chief of staff as well. In practice, Marshall was vindicated, because Roosevelt saw himself as Commander-in-Chief and meant to have direct access to his chief of staff—so that was that. But Stimson was upset by the haphazard way in which Roosevelt ignored the formalities of government, and while he accepted the accomplished fact with his usual realism, he also fought his theoretical corner with great determination. Only the reciprocal esteem between Secretary and general prevented the difference of opinion from degenerating into bitterness. Marshall would say to Stimson that it was all right for the Secretary of War to represent the views of the Army when the Secretary was Stimson, but what about other Secretaries whom the Army could not implicitly trust? Stimson found an uncharacteristically dramatic way of answering this point by turning it around, and that surely did not come easily to his reticent temperament. On the evening of the last day of the war in Europe, Mrs. Marshall found her husband unusually silent, even for him. With some difficulty she got out of him what had happened that afternoon at the office. Stimson had invited Marshall into his office and ushered him into an empty chair in the middle of a half-circle of generals and high civilian officials. "I want to acknowledge my great personal debt to you," Stimson then said. "I have never seen a task of such great magnitude performed by one man. It is rare in late life to make new friends; at my age it is a slow process but there is no one for whom I have such deep respect and I think greater affection. I have seen a great many soldiers in my lifetime, and you, sir, are the finest soldier I have ever known."*

Some of Stimson's greatest contributions to winning the war were made before the United States entered it.† The most urgent task

---

*Katherine T. Marshall, *Together: Annals of an Army Wife*, pp. 250–51.
†A useful, if uncritical, account of Stimson's work in his first two years at the War Department is contained in a Yale thesis by his wife's niece's husband, David L. Daggett, *The Emergency Officer: Henry L. Stimson as Secretary of War*.

in the summer of 1940 was to provide the armed forces with men. That meant a draft, or selective service, or universal military training: in any case, it required conscription in peacetime, something which had been regarded in the United States as un-American since the Revolution.

Stimson was convinced that the draft would be needed and that no time was to be lost. He had already made speeches to this effect, and he had made his right to go on speaking for it a condition of agreeing to be Secretary of War. But though Roosevelt accepted that condition, he was not sure that the country was ready for the draft. No politician running for re-election in November 1940 was keen to put himself on the record by voting for the draft bill.

After the fall of France, the country's mood began to change fast, and Stimson did his best to help it change. Within his first few weeks in office, Stimson moved swiftly with Marshall to avoid friction between Grenville Clark's approach, which was to train as many officers as possible at Plattsburg-style camps, and that of the Senate Military Affairs Committee, which favored a broad draft with no privileged officer commissions. Tactfully Stimson kept his old friend Grenny Clark at arm's length, and on July 31 he gave powerful testimony to the committee about the need for men. But perhaps his most important service in this whole area was the bold way he worked on the President. On August 1, for example, he wrote in his diary: "the President has taken no very striking lead in regard to the Selective Service law and that is reflected in the Congress." The very next day he pressed the President to do more in Cabinet for the bill on Capitol Hill, and he was soon back at it again in the same forum. On August 22, when FDR was due to give a press conference, Stimson sent him a memo explaining why various amendments to the bill could not be accepted, and he was rewarded with what he called FDR's "first vigorous stand on Selective Service." The country was moving, and so was Congress. Roosevelt moved with them, and Stimson was pushing for all he was worth.*

On September 14 Congress passed the draft bill, and the President signed it. On October 16, 1940, sixteen million American men registered for the draft. Roosevelt might call the draft bill no more than the "age-old American custom of the muster," but it was a decisive turning point in American history, one that made possible the late twentieth-century commitment to opposing first fascism and then

---

*For Stimson's role in the campaign for the draft, see Robert Dallek, *Franklin Roosevelt and American Foreign Policy, 1932–45,* especially p. 248.

Communism by military force. It fulfilled long-held convictions of Stimson's, and he was both relieved and delighted. But he was characteristically afraid that, the moment the obvious danger had passed, his countrymen would not live up to his own vigilant sense of struggle. In August, when the news from the Battle of Britain was at long last good, he wrote in his diary that he hoped that

> just as soon as people get out of their panic and their fear, they [would not] let up on the work of preparedness.
> It is the old case of the people saying to Noah:
>
>> Oh, get along now,
>> With your darned old scow,
>> It ain't going to rain much anyhow.*

So in the same dramatic weeks, while the Royal Air Force and the Luftwaffe were shooting each other down over Kent and Sussex, Henry Stimson was doing all he could to "prod production." He even made the suggestion to Knudsen, almost sacrilegious to a former chief executive of General Motors, that the American automobile industry might consider giving up its annual model changes in order to release machine-tool capacity for armaments production. (Nothing came of that!)

After the fall of France, Stimson had written in his diary, in early August, "The only pillar of defense is the indomitable spirit of the British. Upon that psychological feature hangs about the only defense there is." On the other hand, Stimson was a realist, accustomed to weigh evidence, and the evidence about Britain's prospects was none too bright. On July 24, for example, "some reports . . . of our people" were "quite depressing." Meanwhile FDR had given to the Treasury the task of coordinating the increasing and clamorous British and French requests for war materiel of every kind. Stimson was in favor of doing all that could be done; for example, he saw no difficulty about giving British ordnance factories the secrets of an improved new American bombsight; conversely, he realized there was much U.S. industry could learn from British experience of the combat use of aircraft and tanks.

In early September Stimson was given responsibility for the U.S. response to British purchases, now being requested on a staggering

*HLS, *Diary,* August 22, 1940.

scale. Pro-British as he was, Stimson was concerned about the effects of this buying on the prospects for U.S. rearmament. "The British have by their contracts," he wrote on September 10, "occupied the capacity of so much of the industry of this country that they seriously limit the amount of our own preparations and it is of the utmost importance that the matter be regularized."

It was in late July that Stimson had first become aware of the most significant of all British requests for help. The Australian minister in Washington, Richard Casey, called to say that "the great thing that Great Britain needed now was destroyers and that 50 or 100 more destroyers might . . . make the difference between defeat or victory."* Only five weeks earlier Stimson had been preaching in his national radio speech that the United States must rely on the shield of the British navy. Now suddenly there came the disconcerting thought, for a man of his generation: perhaps that shield was not sure.

On May 15, when Winston Churchill became Prime Minister—and also First Lord of the Admiralty (that is, navy minister)—he immediately appreciated the danger. Britain depended on importing oil, food and munitions from North and South America, Australasia and the Middle East, all of which must pass through the narrow seas of the western approaches to British ports. British power, in turn, could be projected to the Middle and Far East only through those same waters. Now, abruptly, the equation of war had changed. German U-boats† had proved deadly enough at attacking merchant ships in World War I. In 1940 the whole coastline of Western Europe, more than 2,000 miles from the Pyrenees to the North Cape of Norway, was under German control. To make matters worse, Italy, which joined in the war on Germany's side on June 10, had a fleet of more than 100 modern submarines, substantially more than the Germans. One of the very first things Churchill did as Prime Minister was to fire off a letter to Roosevelt asking for "the loan of 40 or 50 of your older destroyers to bridge the gap between what we have now and the large new construction we put in hand at the beginning of the war. This time next year we shall have plenty but if Italy comes in against us with another hundred submarines we shall be strained to breaking point."‡

For the next two and a half months, in personal letters and cables

*HLS, *Diary,* July 28, 1940.
†*Unterseebooten,* or submarines.
‡Winston Churchill, *The Second World War,* Vol. ii, *Their Finest Hour,* p. 23.

and through his talented ambassador in Washington, Philip Kerr, Lord Lothian, Churchill hammered away with all his persuasive arts about the destroyers. On the last day of July, with his incomparable gift for conveying his conviction that he spoke on behalf of the whole history of the human race, he ventured so far as to say that "the whole fate of the war may easily be decided by this minor and easily remediable factor. . . . Mr. President, with great respect I must tell you now, in the long history of the world, this is the thing to do now."*

Roosevelt would have been pleased to send to Britain fifty out of the two hundred or so World War I "four-stacker" destroyers that were lying in mothballs in East Coast navy yards, but the thing was not so simple. An old statute made it illegal to transfer naval ships to a belligerent, and in early June Congress had passed a new law prohibiting the transfer of any material of any kind to foreign powers unless either the Army chief of staff or the chief of naval operations certified that it was surplus to requirements. How could Admiral Harold Stark do that, when the retired destroyers might be needed for the defense of the United States, all the more so if Britain collapsed and the Germans acquired the British fleet?

The problem was not only legal but political. Congress would not pass laws permitting the destroyers to go to Britain unless the isolationists and the doubters on Capitol Hill could be persuaded that the transfer of the destroyers was part of a deal that was good for the United States. Roosevelt conveyed through Lord Lothian the suggestion that the destroyers might be traded for British bases in Bermuda and the Caribbean.† On August 6 Lothian cabled Churchill that Roosevelt wanted something else, in addition: a declaration that, if Britain fell, the Royal Navy would not be surrendered to the Germans but would be transferred to the United States or Canada.

Churchill was not unhappy about the destroyers-for-bases swap in itself, though he tried to insist that it was not "in the nature of a contract, bargain or sale." Finally he was persuaded that the destroyers would not be available except as a *quid pro quo,* and on September 5 he announced the deal to the House of Commons. But he was very reluctant to go along with Roosevelt's request that he promise in ad-

*Ibid., p. 356.
†There is an excellent brief account of the "destroyers for bases" deal in Robert Dallek, *Franklin Roosevelt and American Foreign Policy: 1933–45.* See also *On Active Service,* pp. 355–59; HLS, *Diary,* vol. xxx.

vance to send the fleet across the Atlantic if Britain fell. As he cabled to the President on August 15, "We intend to fight it out here to the end. . . . please bear in mind the disastrous effect from our point of view, and perhaps also from yours, of allowing any impression to grow that we regard the conquest of the British Isles as any other than an impossible contingency."

The most he would agree to was a prearranged exchange of cables on August 27 and 31, in which the President asked whether it was true that, in the event that the waters surrounding the British Isles should become untenable, the British fleet would in no event be surrendered but would be sent overseas for the defense of other parts of the Empire. Churchill accepted that this certainly represented his settled policy, but growled a characteristic defiance: "these hypothetical contingencies seem more likely to concern the German Fleet, or what is left of it, than our own."*

Stimson believed that the British fleet was America's first line of defense until American rearmament was completed, and that to keep it going until British-built tonnage could be launched in 1941 was a bargain. He also more or less consciously shared Teddy Roosevelt's conviction that it was the destiny of the United States to replace Great Britain as the world's leading power, but in the meantime the two Anglo-Saxon nations should act together to save the world from tyranny. So although the destroyers-for-bases deal was not his direct responsibility, he did all he could indirectly to help make it come about.

Specifically, he helped to untangle the legal constraints on the President. After a meeting with the President, Knox, Morgenthau and Sumner Welles, Under Secretary of State, on August 13, he called his old lieutenant Justice Frankfurter, and was given the assurance that the old statute prohibiting sale of naval vessels did not apply because it "was related to filibustering," and not to legal operations. At a Cabinet meeting on August 16 Stimson was pleased to note that "the Attorney General has grasped the point that congressional consent is not necessary." At this crisis in Britain's affairs, these two Anglophiles were not going to let a law aimed at antebellum adventurers stand in the way of helping Britain. Nor had anything in Stimson's long experience—from the affair of General Ainsworth by way of the Versailles Treaty and the foreign policy of the Hoover administration to his own

*Winston S. Churchill, *The Second World War*, vol. ii, *Their Finest Hour*, p. 367.

recent confirmation hearings—imbued him with any very high regard
for Congress's prerogatives in foreign affairs. (Even before the 1940
election, Stimson could not resist a dig at his congressional opponents.
"At last they have got what they have been talking about—isolation.
The U.S. is isolated except for one great power, and that is the British
Commonwealth.")

For Stimson, indeed, the destroyers-for-bases deal was a key moment. Following a meeting with the Canadian premier immediately
after it had gone through, he recalled a remark of Benjamin Franklin's
during the Constitutional Convention in 1787. He had been staring for
days, he said, at the sun carved on George Washington's chair, and
wondering "whether it was a rising or a setting sun." Finally, said
Franklin, after listening to the convention's debates, "I have come to
the conclusion that it is a rising sun." Stimson said he felt the same
way about the President's meeting with Mackenzie King, the Canadian
premier, and about the destroyer deal. "It was very possibly the turning point in the tide of the war."* When it was suggested, however,
that the U.S. might do better to hand the destroyers to Canada rather
than to Britain, Stimson's reaction was characteristic. That, he rumbled contemptuously, would be a "discreditable subterfuge."†

The fifty overage four-stackers, badly needed as they were, were
only the beginning of Britain's requirements from American factories.
Stimson helped to smooth over difficulties that arose because Britain
had also ordered, and the United States had forgotten to send in the
same package with the destroyers, five Flying Fortresses out of only a
few dozen in the country, rifle ammunition and other items. Even
before the November election was over, the British were asking for
2,000 aircraft a month by 1941 and the weapons, ammunition and
equipment to outfit ten divisions. The orders meant returning prosperity for American industry, but how was Britain going to pay for
them? For, as Ambassador Lord Lothian announced cheerfully to a
group of reporters on November 23, "Well, boys, Britain's broke; it's
your money we want."‡

Britain had entered the war with $4.5 billion in gold and dollar
reserves and since then had managed to increase that hoard by another
$2 billion by selling South African gold, Scotch whiskey and other

*HLS, *Diary*, August 17, 1940.
†*Ibid.*, August 21, 1940.
‡Robert Dallek, *Franklin Roosevelt and American Foreign Policy, 1932–45*, p. 252.

luxury goods in the United States. British citizens had also been compelled to sell large holdings of American stocks and bonds to the British government, to be reimbursed in pounds sterling, not dollars. But all this was not enough. When the war began in earnest in May 1940 and Churchill became Prime Minister, he decided it would be "false economy and misdirected prudence" to worry about what would happen when the dollars ran out. "We followed a simpler plan," he wrote in his memoirs, "namely, to order everything we possibly could and to leave future financial problems in the lap of the Eternal Gods."*

In mid-November, Lord Lothian was staying with the Prime Minister at Ditchley Park, the Oxfordshire mansion belonging to Ronald Tree and his wife, Marietta; there Lothian made Churchill focus on the dollar problem, which was "grim indeed." The result was a letter, "one of the most important I ever wrote," that Churchill sent on December 8 and Roosevelt pondered, reading it and rereading it alone in his deck chair in the sunshine on the deck of the cruiser U.S.S. *Tuscaloosa*. Churchill asked for the guns, the shells, the tanks and ships but above all the aircraft to defeat Germany. "Give us the tools," he told the House of Commons, "and we'll finish the job." "I believe you will agree," he now wrote to Roosevelt with the superb assurance of desperation, "that it would be wrong in principle and mutually disadvantageous in effect if at the height of this struggle Great Britain were to be divested of all saleable assets, so that after the victory was won with our blood, civilization saved, and the time gained for the United States to be fully armed against all eventualities, we should be stripped to the bone." This was not an appeal for aid, Churchill ended, but "a statement of the minimum action necessary to achieve our common purpose."†

From this letter, as Churchill himself put it, there sprang "a wonderful decision," which he later called "the most unsordid action in the history of any nation."‡ The decision was Lend-Lease, which President Roosevelt explained to the American people in his historic press conference on December 17, the day after he returned from his Caribbean vacation. He used the homely and now famous illustration of the garden hose which you lend to your neighbor when his house is on fire. Unsordid it was. But Lend-Lease was not purely altruistic. As

*Churchill, *The Second World War*, vol. ii, p. 492.
†*Ibid.*, pp. 490, 501.
‡*Ibid.*, p. 503, quoting an earlier speech in the House of Commons.

Stimson had been telling the President on every occasion for the nine months since he returned to government, the British had to be supported because they were the only means of defense the United States had to provide itself with the precious time to rearm. Now, at long last, American opinion was gradually moving in the direction of agreeing with that estimate.

On September 16, 1940, the Secretary of War sent a note to General Edwin ("Pa") Watson, begging off from the long train trip to attend the funeral of Speaker of the House William B. Bankhead in Jasper, Alabama.* "Please catalogue me," Stimson wrote to General Watson, "as an 'emergency' Cabinet officer for purposes of National Defense only. . . . I am pretty nearly at the limit of my strength. Remember I am 73 years old Saturday."

Almost five years later Henry Stimson was still meeting his daily responsibilities as Secretary of War in the greatest war the United States had ever fought. Of course he was not at war in the sense that Churchill was in his underground dugout under the Admiralty in London, or as was a theater commander like Eisenhower in Europe after the Normandy landings, or like MacArthur from Corregidor to Australia and back up the island chains of the Pacific. Stimson was never under fire, not even on his visits to Europe, and in Washington he was never awakened by an air-raid siren. His wartime life-style† was the austere yet luxurious one of a wealthy elderly gentleman. He lived in the sober splendors of Woodley, a large eighteenth-century mansion standing on a rise above its own wooded grounds, only minutes by car from the old State, War and Navy building, next to the White House, where Stimson worked until 1943, and from the Pentagon, where he worked thereafter. Throughout the war, he spent the weekends at Highhold as often as he could, and the weekends ran from Friday to Monday and occasionally from Friday to Tuesday morning.

It was sensible of him to get a lot of rest, for his health was

*The trip had one very significant consequence. On the way home, Under Secretary of State Sumner Welles, a close friend of the President and Mrs. Roosevelt, a man whose portentous self-importance covered raging insecurities, started "throwing back one whiskey after the other." He retired to his sleeping car and started ringing the bell for the sleeping-car attendants (male and black), to whom he made indecent proposals. The incident led ultimately to Welles's disgrace and to some ugly infighting in Roosevelt's inner circle. Ted Morgan, *FDR*, pp. 678–79.
†What follows is based on the *Diary*, vols. xxx–li.

indifferent and he tired easily. From time to time he had to take a few days off, in winter hunting quail at the Oakland Club in St. Stephen's, South Carolina, in summer riding and fishing at the St. Hubert's Club in the Adirondacks. He still suffered from insomnia. There is no hint in the diaries, though, that the responsibilities of wartime made sleep any harder to find than the Blaustein case had done. If anything, Stimson's health seems to have been better than before. Power often rejuvenates old men. And Stimson not only took good care of himself; he was well looked after by Mabel, and repaid her somewhat stern devotion by a chivalrous passion that was as fervent after almost fifty years of marriage as ever. "Riding with Mabel," the seventy-four-year-old Secretary confided to his diary in 1942, "is the best refreshment to my soul."

There are larks and owls, said Harvey Bundy, and Colonel Stimson was a lark. Bundy, who worked closely with Stimson both in Hoover's State Department and in the Roosevelt administration, was in a position to know. "He got up about 5 or 6 in the morning, dictated his diary, and was armed for bear by 8." Conversely, Bundy said, "he never wanted to tackle a really tough problem after four o'clock in the afternoon," and in fact Stimson's diary is full of complaints that Bundy or Jack McCloy or another aide had insisted on talking business after dinner.

The Secretary's passion was still for sports and games. Once in a while he mentions listening to a concert of classical music on the radio *Ford Hour* or reading a book. But almost every afternoon he returned to Woodley early enough for a ride with Mabel, a swim or a round of golf at Chevy Chase, or—with great regularity—a game of deck tennis with some of his officials or young relatives before dinner. He made some concessions to advancing years. For example, he changed his hard-mouthed, tough horses for a gentle-gaited Tennessee walking horse. And as the war went on he began to play lawn bowls more and more often instead of the more strenuous deck tennis.

As far as possible the Stimsons avoided official entertaining, and they stayed away from the hard-drinking evenings of the President's inner circle. Sometimes one or more of his favorite officials with their wives—the Harvey Bundys or the Robert Lovetts or the McCloys—would come to dinner, and an old friend like Alfred Loomis or one or another of Mrs. Stimson's nieces and her husband would visit. But the Stimsons were happiest dining alone, under a cedar tree in summer or by the fire in winter. In the summer of 1942, the summer of Midway and Stalingrad and El Alamein, the Secretary noted how sweet was the song of the wood thrush, though he couldn't be sure whether it lived in the maple or the copper beech. In this genteel arcadia, in the style of a wealthy retired lawyer, frail but healthy and mentally vigorous in the evening of his days, Henry Lewis Stimson presided over the greatest, most lethal and fastest-moving war machine the world had yet seen.

One of the secrets of his ability to function so well in his late seventies lay in the quality of the people he surrounded himself with.* On the military side, of course, General Marshall's presence as chief of staff owed nothing to Stimson; we have seen how well the two men worked together. Another key figure, whom Stimson appreciated and entrusted with the crucial task of supplying the army, was General Brehon Somervell, a strong-willed and energetic officer who reminded Stimson of Leonard Wood. He relied a good deal, too, on the advice of another old friend, General Frank McCoy, in such matters as appointments in the abruptly expanded army.

The Japanese attack at Pearl Harbor on December 7, 1941, was a tactical but scarcely a strategic surprise. A week earlier, on November 25, at a meeting with Cordell Hull, Frank Knox, General Marshall and Admiral Stark, the President had warned, "We are likely to be attacked, perhaps next Monday." The Japanese, Roosevelt reminded the meeting, were "notorious for making an attack without warning." The question was, Roosevelt said with remarkable frankness, "how we should maneuver them into the position of firing the first shot without too much danger to ourselves."

On Sunday, December 7, "we were all wondering where the blow will strike." Stimson worked at the office in the morning, then went home for lunch at Woodley. At about two o'clock, while he was still at table, the phone rang. It was the President, calling in "a rather excited voice."

Colonel Stimson confirmed that he had been following Japanese movements in the Gulf of Siam.

---

*For the following description of Stimson's "official family" in the War Department I have relied on the Stimson *Diary*, vols. xxxvii–l; *On Active Service*, especially pp. 340–44; Walter Isaacson and Evan Thomas, *The Wise Men*, especially pp. 179–209; Columbia Oral History Project, interviews with Harvey H. Bundy and John J. McCloy; author's interviews with McGeorge Bundy, William P. Bundy, and David Ginzburg.

"Oh, no," said Roosevelt. "I don't mean that. They are attacking Hawaii. They are now bombing Hawaii."

Stimson's first reaction was relief. The indecision was over. Now "the crisis would come in a way which would unite all our people. This country united has practically nothing to fear," he wrote, "while the apathy and diversions stirred up by unpatriotic men have been hitherto very discouraging."*

The reins with which Stimson guided the affairs of his department—as it coped first with the task of growth from the tiny peacetime force to an army of 8.5 million, and then with the conduct of operations on a titanic scale from North Africa, the British Isles and Europe to the Pacific—comprised a tiny inner group of civilian appointees. Most of them were graduates of Yale and the Harvard Law School like their boss. They were knit together by a thousand ties of education, family and friendship; but their first loyalty was to a certain ideal of how Americans ought to behave, and then to Colonel Stimson because, in spite of his temper and his other foibles, which they openly teased him about, they saw him as an incarnation of that ideal.

Judge Robert Patterson, the First Assistant Secretary (promoted to Under Secretary before the end of 1941), had been *Harvard Law Review* editor in his day. He came to the War Department as part of a package, so to speak, with Secretary Stimson, a package negotiated with the President by Felix Frankfurter and Grenville Clark. Patterson relieved Stimson of direct responsibility for the giant task of procurement for the army. The chief trouble Stimson had with him was that Patterson, who had fought in World War I, was forever trying to get back into the army and go himself to fight as an infantry officer. He was, as Stimson put it in his memoirs, a man who liked a fight, "and although he was perhaps not always perfect in his choice of a battleground, his instinct in the choice of enemies was unerring."

In September 1940 Stimson noted laconically in his diary that he was "getting McCloy down because of his work on Black Tom." It had fallen to Stimson, in his years as Hoover's Secretary of State, to try to persuade McCloy to drop a lawsuit he was bringing, as counsel for Bethlehem Steel, against the international Mixed Claims Commission, an action arising out of a 1916 explosion at the U.S. munitions plant at Black Tom, near Jersey City. It took McCloy ten years to

*HLS, *Diary*, December 7, 1941.

prove that German agents had been responsible, and in the process he delved deep into the undergrowth of international espionage. McCloy had ignored Stimson's request, amassed a formidable quantity of evidence, and won his case; Stimson did not hold McCloy's uncooperativeness against him. One day in September 1939 McCloy and his wife were at the St. Hubert's Club at Ausable when he was hailed by a gentleman staying at a nearby cabin. "Jack McCloy!" he boomed, "I'm Henry Stimson!"

John J. McCloy was not born into the sort of circle where former Secretaries of State call you by your nickname at exclusive private hunting clubs. His father was a claims officer with an insurance company in Philadelphia who died young, and McCloy's mother worked as a home nurse, masseuse and hairdresser to send her son to good local private schools. After he got a scholarship to Amherst, she also encouraged him to knock on the doors of great estates in Maine and in the Adirondacks, offering his services as a tutor and tennis coach. That was how he first met the Rockefellers, whose personal lawyer he was eventually to become. McCloy went to Grenville Clark's camp at Plattsburg and served in the artillery in France in the First World War before going to the Harvard Law School and from there, drawn by his lifelong ambition to match himself against the best, to Wall Street, where he eventually became a partner in the Cravath firm. "The friendships and associations I made," McCloy recalled later, "and the work habits I developed, were of lasting value."

One of the friendships was with a young investment banker named Robert Abercrombie Lovett.* Lovett's father, Judge R. S. Lovett, quit school at fifteen and went to work as a railroad clerk in rural Texas before going to law school and becoming, first, a partner in Baker and Botts, the leading law firm in Houston,† and later the chief lawyer to E. H. Harriman, creator of the Union Pacific Railroad. Judge Lovett's son, Robert A. Lovett, grew up as the friend of Averell Harriman, the railroad magnate's son, and after Yale he went to work for Brown Brothers, which subsequently merged with the Harriman family's investment bank. Tall, with an irrepressible sense of humor and a lifelong streak of hypochondria, Bob Lovett became a figure of note not only on Wall Street but in New York café society. Among the friends who

---

*See Isaacson and Thomas, *The Wise Men, passim.*
†And the family firm of James A. Baker III, Secretary of the Treasury under President Reagan and Secretary of State under President Bush.

visited his spacious apartment on East Eighty-third Street were Archibald MacLeish, Robert Sherwood, Robert Benchley, Lillian Hellman and Dorothy Parker.* He played hard, but he also worked. He joined his friend Harriman on the board of the Union Pacific, and was heavily involved in loans to European industry, particularly to Germany. After serving as a star Navy pilot in World War I, Lovett became fascinated by aviation. Before Congress prohibited railroads from investing in airlines, he tried to persuade his father that the Union Pacific should take to the air. He learned to fly his own plane.

Lovett spent much of the 1920s and 1930s in Europe, doing business for Brown Brothers Harriman and keeping his eyes wide open. In the summer of 1940, he was in Milan listening to German officers at the bar of his hotel bragging about what they would do to England. When he got home to New York, he took a call from Averell Harriman in Washington. After listening to the latest news from Europe, Harriman asked his old friend if he would come to Washington to work for Frank Knox. Lovett was not happy about Knox's position. "The public utterances of Colonel Knox and Mr. Stimson seem to me to be an invitation to war." America needed time, Lovett thought. He was willing to work to get the country armed and mentally prepared for war, but he could not "give undeviating loyalty" to people like Knox and Stimson. Instead, he set off on a tour, ostensibly of the Union Pacific but actually of the country's aircraft-manufacturing facilities. He was unimpressed by what he saw, and wrote a report in which he argued that the United States would never get the production it needed from the aircraft industry with its traditions of craft work and small orders. Instead, he argued, production should be entrusted to the automobile industry, with its familiarity with mass-production techniques.

So far Lovett was a private citizen, a well-informed one, but with no standing or access from which to argue this case. He was, however, a Wall Street investment banker with unrivaled contacts. One of these was with a neighbor in Locust Valley on Long Island, James V. Forrestal. Previously the president of the investment bank Dillon Read, Forrestal had gone to Washington to be Frank Knox's Under Secretary at the Navy Department. Lovett showed his report to Forrestal. For-

*Lovett was also a friend of William Faulkner, and told him the story of World War I flyers and coastal boat patrols which Faulkner used in a short story, "Turnabout"; Howard Hawks subsequently turned the story into the movie *Dawn Patrol,* with Errol Flynn.

restal showed it to Stimson. And Stimson hired Lovett there and then. Within a few weeks, in November 1940, he had been made Assistant Secretary of War with responsibility for the United States Army Air Corps.

During the international economic crisis of 1931 and the fight for the Hoover debt moratorium, Stimson had worked closely with George Harrison, then president of the New York Federal Reserve Bank. Harrison came from Stimson's approved stable: he was a member of Skull and Bones at Yale, a graduate of the Harvard Law School, and had been secretary to Stimson's old friend Justice Oliver Wendell Holmes. His term over at the Fed, Harrison became president of the New York Life Insurance Company. When the war began, Stimson asked him to come to Washington to help him as a special assistant and gave him responsibility for the heaviest burden of all: atomic energy.

The man Stimson relied on most closely of all over the full range of his own job, however, was Harvey Hollister Bundy, who had been his Assistant Secretary of State in 1931–33 but was designated only as a special assistant to the Secretary of War in 1941. Bundy was a Middle Western-er. His grandfather was a Republican congressman from upstate New York, but his father practiced law in Grand Rapids, Michigan. There was Yankee descent there, however. When Harvey Bundy married a lady who was related to Cabots and Lowells, Putnams and Lawrences, they soon discovered they had an ancestor in common—in 1750!

After Yale, Bundy started life as a teacher at St. Mark's School and then decided to go to law school. It was, as he recalled later, "sort of automatic to think of law school as the Harvard law school." He enjoyed the "violent mental competition" there and became, like Harrison, a law secretary to Justice Holmes, known to Bundy's wife, Kay, as "Cousin Wendell." He was living at the very center of an American aristocracy. Before he married Katharine Putnam, Bundy lived with Lord Eustace Percy of the British embassy and Felix Frankfurter in the famous "House of Truth," a bachelor establishment where it was not at all unusual for Franklin Roosevelt, Louis Brandeis or Walter Lippmann to drop by for tea.

Bundy practiced law in Boston with Hale and Dorr and then with his father-in-law's firm, Putnam, Putnam and Bell. He specialized in wills and trusts and sat on the board of the Boston Personal Property Trust with no less an emblem of all that was ancient and solid in Boston than Charles Francis Adams. Bundy enjoyed corporate practice, too. It meant, he explained much later, "sitting with" bankers and businessmen, "greasing the wheels of this industrial enterprise system." Almost everyone he ran into, he mentioned in an aside, was a Harvard Law School graduate.

Harvey Bundy knew Colonel Stimson slightly through his Yale friend Allen Klots, Stimson's law partner and special assistant. In 1931 he was practicing law in Boston, with no thought of going into government, when Joseph Cotton died and Stimson wanted a new special assistant. He took Bundy partly because as a cautious Republican bond and trust lawyer he would be reassuring to President Hoover.* This prudent Yankee sometimes infuriated Stimson, who called him—affectionately!—"a lily-livered coward."* But he made himself invaluable with his tact, his shrewdness, and his quiet capacity for work. After 1933 he went back to Boston, moving to Choate, Hall and Stewart, which was scarcely a different world, and playing a leading part in the Foreign Policy Association. When Stimson first asked him to come to Washington, he refused. He felt he needed to practice law to support his large family. But when Stimson called again, saying that he wanted a personal assistant "to stay with me all the time," he felt he couldn't refuse. He was soon installed in the office next to the Secretary's, on the other side from General Marshall. For the rest of Stimson's time in the War Department, he relied more on this cautious Bostonian trust lawyer than on any other man on his staff and came to have a higher opinion of him than of anyone except General Marshall himself.

Stimson, Bundy, Lovett, Harrison were all members of Skull and Bones.† Only McCloy and Patterson of the inner circle were not. Stimson, Bundy, Harrison, McCloy and Patterson were all graduates of the Harvard Law School; only Lovett was not. Stimson, Harrison, Lovett, McCloy, and Patterson were all prominent on Wall Street; only Bundy was not, and he practiced law on State Street, the nearest thing to Wall Street in Boston. All six men were Republicans. The plain fact is that, during a war for democracy conducted by a Democratic President—which was also, more than any previous foreign war in American history, a democratic war in the sense that millions of men from every corner of American life fought it together—the War Department was directed by a tiny clique of wealthy Republicans, and one that was

*H. H. Bundy, *Columbia Oral History Project*, p. 135. Bundy had worked for Hoover during World War I.
†See H. H. Bundy, *Columbia Oral History Project*, *passim*.

almost as narrowly based, in social and educational terms, as a traditional British Tory Cabinet. It was certainly far narrower than Churchill's wartime Cabinet.* For this striking class composition, Henry
Stimson was very much responsible. As Harvey Bundy put it, "he told
the President about it, but he had carte blanche from FDR, so we had
the most united team in the War Department you've ever seen"—the
most united, and the most dominated by alumni of Yale and the Harvard Law School.

Because together they presided over triumphant victory in Europe
and in the Pacific, the men who served under Stimson in the War
Department had in the postwar years an aura about them. Lovett and
McCloy, in particular, went on to great proconsular careers: Lovett as
Under Secretary of State and Secretary of Defense (President Kennedy
offered him the choice of the three top jobs in his Cabinet in 1961,
State, Treasury or Defense; Lovett turned them down, but suggested
the three men—Dean· Rusk, Douglas Dillon and Robert S. McNa-
mara—who got them); McCloy as U.S. High Commissioner in West
Germany, president of the World Bank, chairman of the Chase Bank,
and chairman of the Council on Foreign Relations. The line of continuity from Henry Stimson's War Department in World War II to the
men who directed American policy in the Cold War was unbroken.

One of the issues that gave Stimson a good deal of trouble as
Secretary of War was what he called the "insoluble problem of the
black man in this country." Stimson's attitude, like that of many educated northerners of his generation, was strangely compacted of theoretical idealism, defeatist "realism" and unacknowledged prejudice,
as three entries in his diary suggest.† In January 1942, he returned from
a brief vacation at a (totally segregated) hunting camp in South Carolina to be confronted with "my colored aide," Judge Hastie, who
wanted to discuss "the grievances of his race." Some of them, Stimson

---

*Churchill's war Cabinet had only five members. His coalition Cabinet, a larger body, included
Lord Beaverbrook, a self-made entrepreneur from Nova Scotia; Ernest Bevin, a longshoreman,
born illegitimate; Clement Attlee, a middle-class social worker from East London; Fred Wool-
ton, a department-store executive from Liverpool; and John Reith, the Scots engineer who
created the BBC. While the Roosevelt administration as a whole cast its net wider than the War
Department, the class, almost caste character of Stimson's entourage is very striking.
†For January 13, 17 and 24, 1942. These entries are taken almost at random from many other
similar comments recorded by Stimson in his *Diary*.

wrote in his diary, "were well founded and probably remediable, and as to those Patterson and I promised to do our best. Others were more trivial and some were of the impossible class to solve which represents the hopeless side of the insoluble problem of the black race in this country." A few days later, he returned to the problem in his diary. "The race problem," he wrote, "is making trouble for us. We are suffering from the persistent legacy of the original crime of slavery. . . . I am insisting, however, that we shall create colored divisions and use them." These would be useful in West Africa, he pointed out, where both the British and the French had used black troops. Black men, the Secretary believed, with no physiological basis whatever, found the climate there less wearing than white men.

The induction of black soldiers into the army in large numbers presented the War Department with a range of different problems. One was simply that the army had always been essentially a segregated institution, and one, moreover, in which a disproportionately high number of both officers and noncommissioned officers were white Southerners, most of them with the then still largely unreconstructed attitudes of their section. Many army posts and camps were in the South, and Stimson was irritated to learn that black soldiers were expected to ride in the back of the bus there, and furious to discover that it proved impossible to bring to justice Mississippi state troopers who had murdered a black military policeman.*

Attitudes were complex and not necessarily what they would be today. For example, black leaders complained that black soldiers were only grouped in small black units. They demanded the formation of black divisions, in effect consolidating military segregation; and Stimson, going along with their demand, was in effect furthering segregation in the army. He favored special training for black officers, though not for what could be called enlightened reasons: "I am very skeptical about the possible efficiency of such officers, but, as it has been determined that we shall have them, I propose that we shall educate them to the highest possible standards and make the best we can of them."

A week later his ambivalence and unrecognized prejudice were even more frankly revealed in the diary. Stimson learned through Harvey Bundy that Archibald MacLeish, who had left his own Boston Brahmin law firm to become a poet, was planning to make a speech

---

*On Active Service, p. 462; HLS, Diary, July 1943.

to a black audience in New York about the problems blacks were encountering in the army. Stimson summoned MacLeish and, according to the diary, braced him sharply.

> I told him how I had been brought up in an abolitionist family; my father fought in the Civil War, and all my instincts were in favor of justice for the Negro. But (!) I pointed out how the original crime of our forefathers had produced a problem which was almost incapable of solution. . . . I told him of my experience and study of the incompetency of colored troops except under white officers. . . . what these foolish leaders of the colored race are seeking is at the bottom social equality, and I pointed out the basic impossibility of race mixture by marriage.

MacLeish sat through this outburst in silence, but even Stimson was not sure that he had been converted. "I am quite certain," he muttered to his diary, "he has been put up to this by Mrs. Roosevelt's intrusive and impulsive folly."*

Stimson held all the prejudices of his class and generation about blacks. To his credit, however, he allowed his prejudices to be dented to some extent by observation. He showed General Somervell pictures taken by *Life* magazine photographers of the Detroit riot of 1943, pointing out that the photographs "in every case show the victim was a negro and was being beaten and assaulted by white men."

Stimson was impressed by the "progress" made by black military units under white officers. When he encountered an outstanding black officer such as Colonel (later General) Benjamin O. Davis, Sr., he found him "the direct refutation of the belief that all colored officers were incompetent," and added, grudgingly but yet with good will, that Davis was exceptional, but "in the development of more such exceptions lay the hope of the Negro people."

Diary, January 24, 1942. See also the revealing remarks in the *Diary* about his preference for his black aide Truman K. Gibson over his predecessor: "[Gibson] was a brave man who withstood the pressures of his race, to which Judge Hastie . . . had yielded." HLS, *Diary,* vol. lii, p. 150, December 11, 1945. Again, on June 24, 1943, he commented on a report by Louis E. Lowenstein on the Detroit race riot: "one of the reasons why this tension has arisen [has been] the deliberate effort . . . on the part of certain radical leaders of the colored race to use the war for obtaining the ends which they were seeking [including] race equality and interracial marriages [and] complete inter-mixing in the Army." The view is purely segregationist and bears little relation to the ascertained facts about the Detroit riot. See *e.g., Report of the National Advisory Commission on Civil Disorders* ("The Kerner Report"), and A. M. Lee and N. D. Humphrey, *Race Riot,* pp. 130, 140.

Only a few days after the painful interview with MacLeish, Stimson first confided to his diary his worries about what he called another "very difficult problem": the presence in the United States of 126,000 Japanese-Americans—or rather the determination of the United States Army, prompted by some of the most powerful politicians on the West Coast, to evacuate and intern them. With one or two honorable exceptions, the treatment of the Nisei reflects little credit on any of those involved, from President Roosevelt down. Although there were extenuating circumstances, it is one of the least creditable episodes in Stimson's career. John McCloy, the man he entrusted with dealing with the problem on his behalf, behaved as if he had an almost complete blind spot where civil liberties were concerned. Stimson himself, though fully aware of a potential conflict between national security and civil liberties, uncritically accepted unsupported allegations of disloyalty where Japanese aliens or citizens were concerned; and it is impossible to escape the conclusion that he did so in part because he shared the essentially racist assumptions of those pressing for evacuation.*

In the 1860s, 1870s and 1880s, there was virulent hostility in California to Chinese immigrants, but little or no feeling against the much smaller number of Japanese, who were sometimes referred to as "honorary Caucasians." But in 1892 the Irish immigrant Denis Kearney turned his anti-Oriental campaign against "another breed of Asiatic slave"; the Oriental Exclusion League, founded in 1905, was one of several organizations that campaigned against Japanese immigration. In 1908, in the so-called "Gentleman's Agreement," the Japanese government agreed to cut off virtually all new immigration, and in 1906 there were demands to send Japanese children to segregated Chinese schools on the ground that they were "crowding" white schools, although there were only ninety-three Japanese students in seventy-two Californian schools.

After World War I the clamor against the Japanese, led by V. S. McClatchy of the (now liberal) *Sacramento Bee,* became feverish. "Japanese boys," the *Los Angeles Times* reported in 1920, "are taught to look on American girls with a view to future sex relations. . . . the proposed

---

*See Peter Irons, *Justice at War: The Story of the Japanese-American Internment Cases,* p. 7. I have relied throughout my account of the Nisei on this fine study, which draws on the voluminous testimony given at the 1981 hearings of the congressional Commission of Inquiry. See also Morton Grodzins, *Americans Betrayed,* 1949; and Eugene V. Rostow, *Harper Magazine,* September 1945; HLS, *Diary,* February 3, 10, 11, and July 7, 1942.

assimilation of the two races is unthinkable. It is morally indefensible and biologically impossible.* American womanhood is too sacred to be subjected to such degeneracy.'' In 1922 the Supreme Court of the United States, in the *Ozawa* case, denied citizenship to a well-educated, Christian and highly assimilated Japanese on the sole ground that he was ''clearly of a race which is not Caucasian.'' And in 1924 Japanese immigration was ended by the Immigration Restriction Act.

By December 1941 there were about 126,000 people of Japanese descent in the United States, 112,000 of them on the West Coast and 92,000 of those in California. Long before Pearl Harbor the G-2 intelligence arm of the United States Army, the Office of Naval Intelligence and the FBI had alerted themselves to the dangers of sabotage and espionage by Japanese-Americans in and around army camps, naval bases, aircraft plants and other defense installations. With FBI help, Lieutenant Kenneth D. Ringle of ONI broke into the Japanese consulate in Los Angeles and found evidence that a Japanese naval officer, Itaru Tachibana, was a secret agent masquerading as a student. All three agencies maintained, and issued statements confirming, that the Japanese espionage ring on the West Coast had been broken by December 7, 1941. However, they had compiled lists of Japanese who were suspect. In the first two months after Pearl Harbor, 2,192 Japanese whose names were on these ''ABC lists'' were arrested.

From the beginning, as might be expected in the atmosphere of outrage that succeeded the Japanese sneak attack, there were rumors of sabotage at Pearl Harbor, but these were denied on the highest authority. Stimson stated on March 30, ''The War Department has received no information of sabotage committed by Japanese during the attack on Pearl Harbor,'' and Attorney General Francis Biddle† wrote on April 20, 1942, that ''Mr. John Edgar Hoover has informed me

---

*If the last were the case, it is not clear why the *Times* was getting so excited.

†Francis Biddle was descended from a family that had been wealthy and distinguished in Philadelphia since colonial times. Educated at Groton, Harvard College and the Harvard Law School, he practiced corporation law in Philadelphia before having a political conversion from his family's Republican faith to the ideals of the New Deal. In 1934 he became chairman of the National Labor Relations Board. In 1939, after returning to practice law in Philadelphia, he was briefly a federal district judge, then Solicitor General of the United States. After Robert Jackson was appointed to the Supreme Court, Biddle was named Attorney General in 1941. Stimson disliked him, perhaps because of his part in the Nisei affair. In 1945 he wrote in his diary of Biddle, ''That little man is such a small little man and so anxious for publicity that he is trying to make an enormous show out of this performance—the trial of two miserable spies.'' *Diary*, vol. 50, January 5, 1945. The reference was to the trial of two German spies.

that there was no sabotage committed there" on, before or since December 7.

With the danger of Japanese sabotage or Japanese raids in mind, Stimson designated the eight Western states as a "theater of operations" to some extent under military control on December 11. Nevertheless, there were at first appeals for calm. The *Los Angeles Times* published an editorial two days after Pearl Harbor under the headline "Let's Not Get Rattled," and Attorney General Biddle said he was "determined to avoid mass internment and the persecution of aliens that had characterized World War I." He also promised that "at no time will the government engage in wholesale condemnation of any alien group."

In the New Year, James Rowe, a strongly liberal former White House official now working as an assistant attorney general for Biddle in the Justice Department, flew out to California to talk to Lieutenant General John L. DeWitt, commanding the Western Defense Command, with headquarters in the historic Presidio, next to the Golden Gate Bridge in San Francisco. DeWitt wanted to bar enemy aliens from the areas around certain coastal defense installations and also to conduct mass raids on Japanese-Americans to confiscate any arms or short-wave radios they might have. Rowe left for Washington under the impression that he had made DeWitt understand that the Justice Department did not want mass raids and that, whatever might be permissible with enemy aliens, it was illegal to evacuate American citizens merely because of their ethnic descent.

But it is plain that General DeWitt, his friend General Allen W. Gullion (provost marshal general, or head of the army's legal division) and Gullion's assiduous assistant, Colonel Karl Bendetsen, were convinced that all Japanese-Americans, alien or citizen, were untrustworthy. Indeed on January 4, 1942, DeWitt told Rowe so in as many words. Of the native-born Japanese he said he had "no confidence in their loyalty whatsoever"; Rowe missed this plain warning.

DeWitt and Gullion, who had become friends in 1912, had served for a lifetime in a racially segregated army in which hostility to Orientals was common, not to say rife. DeWitt had formally expressed a preference for "a white regiment," though the same might have been true of many other officers. Indeed DeWitt's record was superficially that of the very kind of officer Stimson admired: a Princeton graduate, he had volunteered for the Cuban expedition in 1896, then switched to the regular army; he fought in France in 1917, and then served many years in the Philippines. Bendetsen, a Stanford graduate from Washington State, was, as the course of events revealed, both ambitious and, at least where the Japanese were concerned, openly racist.

DeWitt had at least this reason for concern about the possibility of Japanese espionage and sabotage: there really were Japanese submarines off the West Coast between December 17 and December 23, 1941, which engaged seven or eight ships and sank two tankers. He was convinced—though no evidence was ever produced—that they were being fed information by Japanese residents on shore with short-wave radios. It was, again, entirely rational to be concerned with protecting naval bases or Boeing, Lockheed or Douglas aircraft plants; but quite irrational to see a Japanese farmer as a danger merely because he lived close to a "railroad, highway . . . power line . . . [or] telephone transmission line."*

The first thunderclap of the storm over the California Japanese came from a Republican congressman from Los Angeles, Leland Ford, who wrote letters to both Stimson and Biddle on January 16, 1942, demanding that "all Japanese, whether citizens or not, be placed in inland concentration camps." Biddle replied, as one might expect, that the Japanese who were American citizens could not be interned "unless the writ of *habeas corpus* is suspended." Stimson however, in a letter drafted for his signature by Colonel Bendetsen,† wrote back that the War Department was prepared to provide internment facilities, and that the congressman and his colleagues ought to lobby the Justice Department, which several congressman proceeded to do.

By mid-January officials in both Washington and California were being hit by a veritable blizzard of anti-Japanese hysteria. Organizations like the American Legion, the Kiwanis, and the Native Sons of the Golden West orchestrated letter-writing campaigns. Columnists such as Harry McLemore in the Hearst-owned *San Francisco Examiner* demanded forced evacuation of all Japanese, citizens or not. Vigilantes attacked Japanese in several parts of California; altogether, seven Japanese were killed in apparent vigilante attacks between Pearl Harbor and mid-February 1942.‡

---

*This particular list of potential targets of sabotage was suggested, after discussion with General DeWitt, by—of all people—Earl Warren, then attorney general of California and subsequently Chief Justice of the United States Supreme Court.
†Irons, *Justice at War,* p. 38.
‡Grodzins, *Americans Betrayed,* p. 138.

Although the anger directed at the Japanese was no doubt inflamed by the publication of a report, by Supreme Court Justice Owen Roberts, looking into the attack on Pearl Harbor, the anti-Japanese feeling had deeper roots, economic and political as well as racial and national. Vegetable growers and their organizations, for example, joined in the campaign for removing Japanese truck farmers from their highly competitive enterprises. Austin Anson, of the Salinas Vegetable Grower-Shipper Association, was asked by a journalist about his group's motives: "We're charged with wanting to get rid of the Japanese for selfish reasons," he replied, and then went on, "We do. It's a question of whether the white man lives on the Pacific coast or the brown man."

California politicians bowed before the storm. Three major figures, in particular, lobbied General DeWitt in favor of forcible evacuation of citizens as well as aliens. On January 27 DeWitt saw the Governor of California, Cuthbert Olson. That same day Los Angeles County fired all its Japanese-American employees. Two days later DeWitt saw the state attorney general, Earl Warren. At a later meeting, with Warren present, after Los Angeles mayor Fletcher Bowron had set forth his views in no uncertain terms, General DeWitt told Thomas C. Clark, a Justice Department emissary who was highly sympathetic to the General's anti-Japanese instincts, that he was "not going to be a second General Scott." (The reference presumably was to General Winfield Scott, "Old Fuss and Feathers," who after conquering Mexico City was ordered by President Polk in 1848 to appear before a commission of inquiry and, in Robert E. Lee's words, "turned out like an old horse to die." He survived to play an honorable part in the Civil War, but memories in the old regular army were long.)

If the military were being stiffened by politicians like these in their demand that the Japanese be evacuated, they also did their best to increase the pressure on Washington. On February 12 Walter Lippmann, of all people, wrote a column calling for the evacuation of Japanese aliens and citizens after visiting General DeWitt and being shown the order Bendetsen had drafted for him.

The tragedy of the Nisei was that their fate depended on a struggle between the Department of Justice, upholding the civil liberties guaranteed in the Constitution, and the War Department, upholding the dictates of supposed military necessity. What was even more sharply their tragedy was that the Justice Department upheld their rights with far less certainty or tenacity than the War Department held the belief that they could not be trusted.

On February 3, General Gullion told Stimson and McCloy that he had evidence* that there was regular communication between Japanese spies and Japanese submarines and added his belief that the Nisei were more dangerous than their "unnaturalized" parents. Stimson made his opposition to mass evacuation clear; but when McCloy telephoned the Presidio to report this to DeWitt, the general said, "Out here, Mr. Secretary, a Jap's a Jap."

The Justice Department's position was clouded, first, by an opinion written by three famous liberals, Benjamin V. Cohen, Oscar Cox and Joseph L. Rauh, which advised the Attorney General that "in times of national peril any reasonable doubt must be resolved in favor of action to preserve the national safety." And Clark, Biddle's man on the West Coast, had gone over to the other side. On February 2 he met DeWitt and Governor Olson to plan an outrageous scheme whereby Japanese were to be evacuated from the "combat zone" (that is, coastal California) to work as farm laborers inland. The scheme was supposed to be voluntary, a proposition McCloy demolished laconically on the phone by saying, "The bad ones . . . will not volunteer, will they?" Worst of all, Biddle was overcome by deference toward the military in general and the Secretary of War in particular.

On February 11, Stimson discussed the matter with McCloy and decided to ask President Roosevelt himself to decide the issue. He asked the President for an appointment, in itself an indication of the seriousness with which he took the matter, and was told FDR was "far too busy." Stimson and McCloy, with the help of General Mark Clark, who was working in the Secretary's office at the time, hastily prepared a memo for a telephone conversation with the President. Was the President willing to authorize us to move citizens as well as aliens? If so, should they be moved from the entire West Coast, only from major coastal cities, or from a restricted list of areas around, for example, major aircraft plants? Roosevelt, whose sympathy for persons of Japanese descent may not have been strengthened by the fall of Singapore the previous day, seems to have told Stimson to do whatever he thought right—something Stimson was not usually reluctant to do. McCloy telephoned Bendetsen at the Presidio to say, "We have *carte blanche,*" then added, "Be as reasonable as you can."

---

*Stimson wrote in his diary that Gullion "*thinks* he has evidence" (my italics). Not only were there were no spies; by February there were no submarines either.

How Bendetsen interpreted this was all too clear from the order he drafted. It proposed the evacuation of 101,000 people, and it did so on nakedly racist grounds. "Racial affinities," Bendetsen wrote, "are not severed by migration." In the second and even the third generation "the racial strains are undiluted." "We have 112,000 potential enemies," he added. That "final recommendation"—there is an unpleasant echo there of the "final solution"—was signed by DeWitt on February 13. On February 17 Bendetsen arrived in Washington for a meeting with Stimson and McCloy. In the meantime Lippmann and Westbrook Pegler ("to hell with *habeas corpus"*) were keeping up the journalistic pressure for evacuation. Stimson overrode Mark Clark's objection that shepherding a hundred thousand Japanese men, women and children out of their homes in coastal California was a waste of troops who should be fighting Japanese soldiers in the Pacific.

The final scene came in a meeting at Attorney General Biddle's home on the evening of February 17. It was a walkover. James Rowe and Edward Ennis of the Justice Department kept arguing up to and indeed after the final decision. But Biddle, who—unknown to his men—had spoken to Stimson on the telephone before the meeting, caved in. His position was that he did not believe it was right or possible in time of war to stop the army doing what it needed to do on a matter it considered, as a professional judgment, to be one of military necessity. But that position seems to have owed much to the deference he felt for Stimson. Much later, in a 1962 memoir, Biddle tried to turn that issue on its head by saying, "If Stimson had stood firm, had insisted as apparently he suspected, that this wholesale evacuation was needless, the President would have followed his advice." This may be true. But by deferring to Stimson, instead of doing his best to persuade him that the case for evacuation based on "military necessity" was a bogus one, Biddle made it certain that the evacuation would take place.

Stimson was aware of the constitutional difficulty of evacuation, and brooded about the legal issues it raised. "If we base our evacuations upon the ground of removing enemy aliens," he wrote in his diary on February 3, "it will not get rid of the Nisei, who are second-generation naturalized Japanese [actually U.S.-born, not naturalized] and as I said the more dangerous ones." (He had apparently been persuaded of this highly dubious proposition by General Gullion.) "If on the other hand we evacuate everybody including citizens, we must base it so far as I can see upon solely the protection of specific plants. We cannot discriminate among our citizens on the ground of racial origin." Stimson was a good enough lawyer, in other words, to understand the constitutional principle involved; he was enough of a lawyer to see the constitutional principle as a difficulty to be got round, not as an imperative to be vindicated. In any case, he seemed unaware of the human dimension.

The evacuations took place. The Nisei suffered in their pride, their persons and their property. More than 100,000 of them were forcibly evacuated with only the possessions they could carry to "relocation centers" in the interior of the West, from California to Arkansas. They sold their farms at distress prices; the Federal Reserve has calculated that their losses may have come to $400 million. On the scale of suffering endured by twentieth-century internees, from British South Africa to the Gulag, from Nazi prisons to Palestinian refugee camps, their sufferings were perhaps not severe, but the camps were miserable places; what their inhabitants remember most often is the dust and sandstorms that tore through them. Many of their inmates were not freed until 1946; the average Japanese-American spent 900 days in the camps.

Long after the war, four of the internees brought suit. The Supreme Court eventually found that their evacuation was within the President's emergency powers, but most authorities now condemn both the Court's arguments and the original decision. Lawrence M. Friedman, for example, a leading historian of American law, has said that "these decisions, shot through with racism and hysteria, are a blot on the Court's reputation." The constitutional scholar Edwin S. Corwin has said (surely with some exaggeration, when one thinks, for example, of the Supreme Court's decision in *Plessy* v. *Ferguson*, legalizing segregation) that the evacuations constitute "the most drastic invasion of the rights of citizens of the United States by their own government that has thus far occurred in the history of our nation."*

Stimson's close friend and loyal protégé John McCloy never accepted that view. Two Justice Department lawyers, Edward Ennis and John R. Burling, came to suspect that General DeWitt's contention that there was evidence of Japanese espionage was simply false. In one of the Supreme Court cases they inserted into the government's brief a footnote recording that there was "contrariety of evidence" on this point. According to the most detailed study, "McCloy intervened with

*Friedman, *History of American Law*, p. 672; Corwin's comment is quoted in Morison and Commager, *Growth of the American Republic*, vol. ii, p. 788.

Solicitor-General Fahy to remove this from the brief.''* McCloy remained unrepentant, even defiant, to the last. He courageously appeared, at the age of eighty-six, at the 1981 congressional commission hearings on the internments, and was repeatedly hissed by an audience that contained many Nisei. McCloy maintained that what he called the "deconcentration" of the Japanese had resulted in their living in "a healthier environment." It was an insolent thing for a man whose experience of camps was that of the St. Hubert's Club in the Adirondacks to tell men and women who had suffered in harsh conditions. To a Japanese-American member of the commission, Judge William Marutani of Philadelphia, McCloy shouted that internment was "by way of retribution" for Pearl Harbor, though he subsequently tried to retract the word "retribution." He even tried to argue that if there was a "raid" on South Florida the government would be justified in forcibly removing all persons there of Cuban descent.

McCloy's outbursts should not be too harshly judged. He was faced with what he must have regarded as a kangaroo court. As James Rowe has suggested, his attitude may have been motivated by the wish to "try to protect his boss, Henry Stimson, who was indeed a great man." And so he was, but in this matter, perhaps, less so than in any other major test that had come his way. For if we ask *why* Stimson, so scrupulous in most legal matters, was so careless of the rights of American citizens simply because they were of Japanese descent, one must listen to his own words, written in the calm and privacy of his diary on February 27, 1942, after the crucial decision was taken:

> The second generation Japanese can only be evacuated as part of a total evacuation, giving access to areas only by permits, or by frankly trying to put them out on the ground that their racial characteristics are such that we cannot understand or trust even citizen Japanese. This latter is the fact but I'm afraid it will make an awful hole in our constitutional system.

Just what was the Secretary of War, an eminent lawyer of not quite fifty years' standing, saying in that passage? "It is the fact," he was arguing, "that we cannot understand or trust even citizen Japanese" because of their "racial characteristics." Such a proposition, he understood, makes "quite a hole" in the constitutional philosophy

---

Korematsu v. *United States*. See Irons, *Justice at War*.

that underlies the Bill of Rights and the Fourteenth Amendment. But he accepted the need to evacuate these citizens anyway. *Salus populi, suprema lex;* the people's safety is the supreme law. Stimson was experienced enough to know that these Japanese fishermen and truck farmers were not a danger to the people's safety. His own intelligence people conceded that.* It is hard not to believe that, as one critic put it, "his own susceptibility to racial stereotypes helped to tip the balance."† Stimson never clearly dissented much from the frank belief in racial inferiority proclaimed by his closest friends, men like Elihu Root and Leonard Wood.

There is something else. Stimson was also vulnerable to the seductions of that style of statesmanship which is not "sicklied o'er with the pale cast of thought." His conception of the role of the executive in constitutional law was robust, to say the least: it could verge on the scarcely disguised expression of the ancient and profoundly un-American code of statecraft that is summed up in the phrase *raison d'état:* the state has its own reasons. It is always dangerously close to the proposition that the state *is* its own reason.

Henry Stimson's part in the forcible evacuation of the Nisei, one of the few grave stains on the conduct of the United States in World War II, may be indefensible. It was also understandable in the climate of panic and paranoia that succeeded Pearl Harbor. Stimson himself was acutely fearful of a Japanese descent on the Panama Canal, which he considered would have been an even more devastating target for surprise attack than Pearl Harbor. For the first time since the War of 1812, Pearl Harbor had suggested that the territory of the continental United States itself might be vulnerable. Add to that the horror many Americans felt at the atrocities already committed by the Japanese in many places, including Shanghai and Nanking, and it was not surprising that pressures mounted from the military and the general public alike to remove the Japanese, whether or not they were citizens.

Stimson's agreement to the evacuation was also altogether of a piece with his overall strategic perception and the advice he gave to two Presidents, from before Pearl Harbor until the debate over the use of the atomic bomb. The temperamentally robust Stimson was un-

---

*Colonel Kendall J. Fielder, assistant chief of staff for military intelligence, in charge of military intelligence in Hawaii, stated that there were no known acts of sabotage, espionage or fifth-column activities by the Japanese in Hawaii.
†Irons, *Justice at War*, p. 363.

apologetic about the use of force in what he considered to be a good cause. As a hunter, he never rested until he had killed "some poor damned animal or another." As a lawyer, his method was to arm himself with as much preparation as he could achieve, and go gnawing away at the central issue of the case until the other side collapsed. And as a strategist he argued consistently for the single-minded and ruthless pursuit of the central objective: "the easiest way to the center of our chief enemy's heart," as he put it in a 1942 memorandum to the President. The first issue to be decided was which front, the Atlantic or the Pacific, should have the highest priority. This was no automatic or easy decision. The deepest instinct of what had for twenty years been the overwhelming majority of American public opinion, and was still as late as 1941 a very substantial isolationist block, was that the United States must never again be dragged into involvement in Europe. Most isolationists had never had any objection, on the other hand, to the United States's using military force in defense of the Philippines or of its interests anywhere in the Orient or Latin America.

On November 12, 1940, as soon as the election was out of the way, Admiral Stark, chief of naval operations, sent to Navy Secretary Frank Knox what became known as the "Plan Dog" memorandum, because its chief recommendation was contained in paragraph D for Dog.* It has been called "the most important document in the development of World War II strategy" and "the corner-stone of American politico-military thought." It recommended a holding defense in the Pacific and a strong offensive in Europe, and it recognized that to that end the U.S. would need to cooperate closely with Britain and to send large naval, air and land forces to Europe. This, it should be remembered, was more than a year before Pearl Harbor. The Army-Navy Joint Board began to prepare a basic war plan on the basis of this strategic appreciation. Written mainly by Captain (later Admiral) Richmond Kelly Turner and Colonel (later General) Joseph T. McNarney, it accepted that "the issues in the Orient will be largely decided in Europe" and that the United States would have to launch "a major offensive in the Atlantic." On January 16, 1941, Stimson, Knox, Cordell Hull, Admiral Stark and General Marshall met the President at the White House to discuss this paper. Stimson was all in favor, and so was the consensus of the others present. To their surprise, the Pres-

*Larrabee, *Commander-in-Chief,* pp. 48–49; Louis Morton, *Strategy and Command: The First Two Years,* Office of the Chief of Military History, Department of the Army, p. 81.

ident did not agree. According to Marshall's notes of the meeting, Roosevelt said that the United States was not ready; "our military course must be very conservative until our strength had developed." It is possible, of course, that Roosevelt, with his incomparable antennae for the mood of the American people, really meant that the country was not politically ready. At any rate, he was not yet ready to commit the country to a military offensive against a Europe united, except for Britain, under Hitler.

Nevertheless on September 11, 1941, *before* Pearl Harbor, Stimson and Frank Knox carried over to the White House a new war plan, called the Joint Board Estimate of Over-all Production Requirements. It had been written by Albert C. Wedemeyer, a bright staff colonel who had studied in Germany, and the economist Robert R. Nathan, and was signed by General Marshall and Admiral Stark. Once again the basic prescription was for making victory in Europe the first priority, and that was now accepted.*

In late August 1941—after taking time off a tour of inspection in the West to visit St. Mary's Lake, in Glacier National Park, close to Chief Mountain, the place of warrior dreams—Stimson set to work to produce "a strategic plan for the means necessary to produce a successful termination of the war against Hitler." It was, he noted in his diary, "a plan which I have long had in mind," and it was given the confident, not to say hubristic, code name Victory Parade.

Stimson was not alone in advocating "Europe first" as a strategic priority, but he believed in it with passionate intensity. As early as October 1941, when the mercurial William C. Bullitt had proposed to Frank Knox the idea of a diversionary invasion in northwest Africa, Stimson took time to explain why this would be "a diversion from our true line of action." (He only wavered from this strategy once, and then only for tactical reasons; or rather, he never wavered but once found it advantageous to pretend that he had. In July 1942, when a telegram arrived from London which suggested that the British were reconsidering their commitment to a cross-Channel invasion, Stimson and Marshall agreed to threaten that "as the British won't go through with what they have agreed to, we will turn our backs on them and take up the war with Japan." That—whatever George Marshall may have meant—Stimson saw this as a purely tactical threat is proved by

*Ironically enough, General Wedemeyer was to become, after World War II, one of the pillars of the China Lobby.

another diary entry, a couple of days later: "I hope the threat to the British will work."*

Stimson fought for the principle of strategic concentration from the beginning. He fought for it in Washington, and when he saw Winston Churchill in England, he fought for it in London. Most crucially, he fought for it in the mind of Franklin Roosevelt.

There is among Stimson's papers a curious piece of evidence about his own strategic thinking. It takes the form of scribbled notes for a talk to his fellow members of the golf club at Yeaman's Hall, South Carolina, where he went in early 1945 for a few days' relaxation and winter sunshine:

> 1. HLS & FDR
>
> 1940
>
> Isolationists
> 2. Period of <u>defense</u> and <u>nightmare.</u>
> Draft law.
> Shortages, men, equipment.
> Destroyers-bases deal.
> Lend-Lease
> 3. <u>1941</u>
> <u>Luck</u>
> Nazi vs. Russia
> Pearl Harbor
> 4. Main strategy
> Hold in Pacific
> <u>Fight</u> Hitler <u>First</u> REASONS
>
> Issue of National Viewpoints US vs. UK

If that does not "say it all," it certainly gives a graphic picture of how clearly Stimson saw the grand outlines of strategy.

Throughout the war Stimson intervened forcibly whenever he thought U.S. or Allied policy was drifting out of the right course. One example is his role in promoting new tactics to win the Battle of the Atlantic against Nazi submarines. He took a personal interest in Robert Watson-Watt, the Scots scientist who invented radar, and he was one of the first people in Washington to understand its practical implica-

*Diary, July 12, 1942.

tions. In the spring of 1942 he argued on the basis of research he had
sponsored that radar made it possible for aircraft not just to find submarines but to kill them; and the next spring he took on the redoubt-
able Admiral Ernest J. King by insisting that if the Navy was not willing
to take on antisubmarine warfare, the Army Air Corps would do it for
them. This was no trivial issue. Not only the survival of Britain, but
the possibility of shipping American armies and their equipment to
Europe depended on getting the upper hand in the submarine war,
and Stimson's contribution played a major part in the eventual defeat
of the U-boats.

In August 1944 and again in the spring of 1945 he successfully
fought the plan,* dreamed up by Henry Morgenthau and seriously
considered by the President, for punishing Germany by transforming
it into a deindustrialized, agrarian nation. Even before the North Africa landing, Stimson had insisted that Roosevelt confront the problems of organizing government in liberated territories, and had insisted
that the War Department was the right agency for carrying that job
out. For Stimson, the quasicolonial experience of his friends Elihu
Root, Leonard Wood, Frank McCoy and George W. Goethals in Cuba,
the Philippines and Puerto Rico was something to be proud of and to
imitate.

In early September 1944 Stimson knew full well that there was a
bitter division within the administration between those who, while
intending to be firm in eradicating Nazism, saw the best hope for the
future of Europe in building a prosperous new Germany, and those,
led by Henry Morgenthau, Secretary of the Treasury, who wanted to
destroy forever Germany's capacity to make war by dismantling the
vast coal, iron and steel industries of the Saar and Ruhr basins, second
only to the Great Lakes section of the United States in terms of heavy
industrial production. Stimson and McCloy had a "pleasant" dinner
with Morgenthau and his deputy, Harry Dexter White. But Stimson
found the Treasury Secretary "not unnaturally"—that is, apparently,
because he was Jewish—"very bitter." To Stimson's surprise, first Secretary of State Hull, then the President himself seemed to be leaning
toward Morgenthau's proposal. On September 13 Stimson learned that
Morgenthau had been summoned to the conference between Roosevelt and Churchill at Quebec. Three days later, he heard that Churchill
had been converted to the Morgenthau Plan by the argument that

---

*On Active Service, pp. 568–91. See also Diary, vols. xlviii–l, passim.

eliminating German competition would open up new markets for British heavy industry. That day the President and the Prime Minister initialed a memorandum of agreement "for eliminating the war-making industries in the Ruhr and the Saar . . . looking forward to converting Germany into a country primarily agricultural and pastoral in character."

Stimson was horrified. Such a plan would be not only foolish but in breach of the Atlantic Charter, which committed both the United States and Britain to allow "all States, great and small, victor or vanquished," access to trade and raw materials. With drafting help from McCloy, Stimson sat down to write a great state paper, although he knew it would annoy the President, who, he noted, "dislikes opposition when he has made up his mind." The Morgenthau Plan, he argued, would involve a "chaotic upheaval" and would doubtless "cause tremendous suffering." It would be attributed to "mere vengeance" and "shortsighted cupidity." It would be "an open confession of the bankruptcy of hope for a reasonable economic and political settlement of the causes of war." Stimson and McCloy took the high ground. There is no question that the older man was influenced by the tragic experience of watching the legacy of the First World War inexorably drag Europe toward the second.

Shortly after he received this powerful pleading, the President telephoned his Secretary of War at Highhold. He sounded defensive, perhaps because the press were already loudly denouncing the Morgenthau Plan. He didn't mean to make Germany a purely agricultural country, he said, no doubt tailoring his argument to Stimson's known loyalties; he merely wanted to help Britain recover markets from Germany after the war. Stimson ignored the argument, and the two men agreed to meet. They lunched together at the White House on October 3. When Roosevelt tried to say he had never meant to turn Germany into an agrarian state, Stimson reproved him, even wagged his finger at him, as we have seen, and reminded him that he had signed a paper using the words "primarily agricultural and pastoral." Roosevelt backed off, and Stimson pressed home the moral advantage. Throughout the war his leadership had been on a high moral plane, Stimson reminded his President, and now in the postwar settlement "you must not poison this position."* It was, by any standard, frank speaking. But FDR was prepared to take it from Stimson, and nothing more was heard of the Morgenthau Plan.

Important as these and other contributions Stimson made were to shaping U.S. policy, they were not so vital for him as the central question of how to fight and win the war. There were in fact two grand strategic issues, but to Stimson they were one. The first was whether to attack Germany first or Japan. Stimson was for dealing with Germany first, not only because it was threatening Britain and also Russia, but because his deepest fear was that if Germany once triumphed in Europe, knocking out either Britain or Russia and then turning her combined forces on the other, the United States could find itself confronted with a savage and implacable enemy with the resources to carry the war to the United States. In spite of temporary worries about the security of the Panama Canal and the West Coast after Pearl Harbor, Stimson—rightly or wrongly—never feared Japan so much. The war in the Atlantic *versus* the war in the Pacific was in essence an argument between Americans. Indeed, to some extent it was an argument between those whose sympathies lay with the now discredited isolationists and those like Stimson whose sympathies had lain with Britain.

The second large strategic debate was essentially between the Americans and the British, and there Stimson, with Marshall in total agreement, was heart and soul in opposition to Winston Churchill. The quarrel consumed infinite quantities of energy and words throughout 1942 and 1943. It took different forms, focused on successive issues. In essence it was between those who wanted to go bald-headed for Germany as soon as possible and by the most direct route, and those, like Churchill, who wanted to fence rather than bludgeon, and delay the frontal assault until Germany had been weakened by diversionary attacks in the Mediterranean.

The argument first came up at the time of the Arcadia Conference between Roosevelt and Churchill in January 1942. Churchill was infatuated with the idea of stabbing away at what he called the "soft underbelly" of Nazi Europe. There were many reasons for this. For one thing, Britain had never been a land power. Like the United States, but unlike her continental rivals, Britain had never maintained a large standing army. In the wars against Spain, against Louis XIV and against Napoleon, Britain had avoided direct confrontation on land until the opposing land power had been economically weakened by naval blockade and distracted and bled by gadfly attacks anywhere but where his main forces were assembled. Churchill was much influenced by history; indeed, more than most men, he lived in history. He was the biographer as well as the descendant of one of the great British captains, John, Duke of Marlborough, the strategist of the alliance against Louis XIV's design for French domination of Europe. He had also commanded a battalion in the trenches on the Western Front, and he was determined that slaughter of the kind that had bled Britain and the other European nations white in World War I must never be allowed to happen again. As First Lord of the Admiralty he had tried at the time—with disastrous effect—to turn the Germans' strategic flank with his Gallipoli campaign in 1915. Lastly, Churchill was an imperialist. He "had not become his Majesty's first minister in order to preside over the liquidation of the British empire," he said, even though most people in British public life had long known that the Empire in its old form could not, and many said should not, be preserved. He wanted Britain to control the Mediterranean as the route to India and the East and as the lifeline to Britain's supplies of oil in Iraq and Iran. And as the war went on he became more and more anxious to preserve some influence in Greece and the Balkans to prevent Eastern Europe from falling wholly under Stalin's control.

The Americans, including Roosevelt, Stimson and Marshall, had little sympathy for Churchill's arguments. Indeed, they tended to caricature them. His adherence to the traditional strategy of the sea power against the land power they saw as timidity. His determination to avoid the slaughter of the Western Front they interpreted as weakness, even cowardice. His concern with Britain's strategic interests in the Mediterranean and Eastern Europe they brushed aside with statements that they were determined not to fight for Britain's empire. (Stimson was so sure he was right and the British were wrong about strategy that he put the disagreement down to their "decadence." "I have come to the conclusion," Stimson wrote in his diary in April 1944, infuriated ostensibly by some passing disagreement with the British about the purchasing of uranium for the atomic bomb but in reality, it seems, by the underlying strategic argument, "that if this war is to be won, it's got to be won by the full strength of the virile, initiative-loving, inventive Americans, and that the British really are showing decadence—a magnificent people, but they have lost their initiative.")

The Americans' strategic memory was of a war won by Grant's massive concentration on the direct axis to the enemy's capital. (It was as if they had forgotten the role played by Sherman's giant encirclement.) Their consciousness was of massive and growing resources of men and munitions. Their intention was to impose American strength not only on the United States's enemies, but also on her friends. For they saw themselves—even those like Stimson who were in their late seventies—as young and fresh and the British as old and tired. Quite often they said so. Yet Churchill was not perhaps as wrong as they thought he was. He was certainly right that the forces for an invasion of France in overwhelming strength could not have been assembled in 1943, even if there had been no diversion of troops, ships and aircraft to Tunisia, Sicily, Italy, Greece and the Aegean. He may also have been right to want to acquire as much influence for the West in Eastern Europe as possible.

So Churchill persuaded Roosevelt to go along with his plans for an Anglo-American invasion, code-named TORCH, of French North Africa. Stimson argued for concentrating American forces. On April 1 General Marshall sent a memorandum to the White House arguing against delaying the cross-channel invasion, code-named first ROUND-HAMMER, then OVERLORD. That day Stimson and Harry Hopkins "held the laboring oar" in a discussion at the White House, and Marshall and Hopkins were sent to London, where with great difficulty they induced Churchill to agree to an invasion of France in 1943.

Roosevelt vacillated. In May and June 1942 first Churchill, then Admiral Lord Louis Mountbatten talked up the North African expedition. On June 19 Stimson sent a strong letter to Roosevelt and three days later attended what he called "a very unhappy meeting" with Churchill and the President. This time Roosevelt sent Admiral King with Marshall to London, and on July 23 they reported that the British "definitely refused to go on" with a second front in France in 1943.

Stimson went straight to the White House. In a memo to the President he said British policies were "the result of a fatigued and defeatist government which had lost its initiative, blocking the help of a young and vigorous nation whose strength had not yet been tapped by either war." There spoke the authentic voice of Teddy Roosevelt. "Defeatist," after all, was not a word that was used about Winston Churchill every day.

For the next year, Stimson continued to play the watchdog, growling in a threatening manner whenever he suspected the British of wavering from their commitment to a cross-channel invasion in 1943 and attributing the worst motives to Churchill's successive plans for small-scale operations to weaken the Germans in the Mediterranean.

His campaign reached a climax in the summer of 1943, when the old big-game hunter bearded the British lion in his den. He matched his arguments and his will with the seductively persuasive, formidably determined British Prime Minister. And he won.

July 6 was Henry and Mabel Stimson's golden wedding anniversary. The next day they celebrated with a pleasant dinner at which Harvey Bundy read a highly flattering, rather ingeniously versified poem he had composed for the occasion. And the day after that the seventy-six-year-old Secretary set out for London, flying by way of Gander (Newfoundland), Iceland and Scotland. On July 12, at a small private dinner party at Number Ten, Downing Street, Stimson "outlined the political danger" of a delay in the invasion. Anthony Eden, Churchill's deputy and foreign minister, "painted a rosy picture of the possibilities of stimulating trouble in the Balkans and Greece." Stimson's suspicions were thoroughly aroused.

The climax came on July 22, in a conference with Churchill at Number Ten. Afterward, in a secret report to the President, Stimson observed that though "we differed with extreme frankness" Churchill was "extremely kind," and he hoped that their working relationships would be improved by the exchanges. Stimson certainly pulled no punches. If the British drew the United States into Mediterranean adventures, he said, "we would be subjected to campaign arguments to the effect that we were being made to fight for interests which were really those of the British Empire." He did not want American troops bogged down in fighting all the way up the long boot of the Italian peninsula. The American people did not hate the Italian people, Stimson said; they "took them rather as a joke." It had only been "by an intellectual effort that they had been convinced that Germany was their most dangerous enemy and should be disposed of before Japan." If the United States became entangled with Greece, the Balkans or the Middle East, the President's "prestige" would be seriously damaged.

Churchill made psychological mistakes in his handling of Stimson. He dwelled on the "superlative fighting qualities" of the Germans in Sicily and pictured the Channel "full of the corpses of defeated allies." This was the wrong tack to take with the bellicose Secretary. "This stirred me up," Stimson admitted to Roosevelt, "and for a few minutes we had it hammer and tongs."*

---

*Stimson's report is to be found in his *Papers,* Reel 127, p. 525, as well as at the appropriate date (July 1943) in the *Diary.*

Stimson directly charged Churchill with not being in favor of the invasion and declared that the things he was saying came like a blow in the eye. Churchill, no doubt not a little stirred up himself at Stimson's tone (interestingly, he does not report the conversation in his memoirs) replied that "if we start anything we will go through with it with the utmost effort."

Stimson flew from London to Marrakech for a brief rest and then to Carthage, where he saw General Eisenhower, commanding the army that had just taken Sicily. With his usual tact, Eisenhower agreed that he would be against moving troops into the south of France or the Balkans after the Italian campaign in enough strength to weaken ROUNDHAMMER; he did not come out flatly against all operations in Italy, and indeed Churchill's argument was about to be strengthened, at least temporarily, by the fall of Mussolini and the collapse of Italy as an Axis partner, brought about by those very operations Stimson opposed so strongly. From Africa he hurried back to Washington by way of London on purpose to reach there before Churchill could get to see Roosevelt.

On August 9 the Stimsons had a pleasant, quiet evening with the Bundys, and the Secretary retired to bed early. It was, however, the hottest night he ever recalled in Washington, and he slept wretchedly. In the morning he got up and dictated immediately after breakfast, with some effort, a paper for the President:

> We cannot now rationally hope to be able to cross the Channel and come to the grips with our German enemy under a British commander. His Prime Minister and his Chief of the Imperial Staff are frankly at variance with such a proposal. The shadows of Passchendaele and Dunkerque still hang too heavily over these leaders of his government. Though they have rendered lip service to this operation, their hearts are not in it.

After a few more contemptuous phrases about British strategy—"a series of attritions . . . pinprick warfare," the thoroughly aroused Colonel Stimson moved to his conclusion: ROUNDHAMMER must go ahead. And furthermore, it must have an American commander. The British had offered that more than a year earlier. The time had come to hold them to their offer. And the American must be Marshall.

He carefully signed this paper before showing it to Marshall, who, as Stimson expected, demurred from the proposal in so far as he was concerned. He transacted certain other business with Harvey Bundy. And then at one o'clock he went over to the White House. Roosevelt read his paper with interest, nodding his approval point by point. At the end he told Stimson that he had "announced the conclusions he had just come to himself," and he asked Stimson to sit in on his next meeting with the Joint Chiefs. At that meeting, as Stimson put it in his diary that night, "the President went the whole hog on ROUNDHAMMER. He wanted to make sure that the United States had more men in Britain than the British were committing to ROUNDHAMMER. It then became evident what his purpose was and he announced it. He said he wanted an American commander."

Two days later Churchill met Roosevelt at Quebec, and agreed to the invasion plan at last. And Churchill announced that, although he had offered the supreme command to Alan Brooke, he now wanted it to go to Marshall.

In retrospect, Stimson thought that conclusion might have been his greatest contribution to grand strategy. The day of Roosevelt's funeral, April 14, 1945, he wrote his own assessment of FDR's performance as a strategist—and of his own contribution.

> On the whole he has been a superb war President—far more so than any other President of our history. . . . He has pushed for decisions of sound strategy. . . . The most notable instance was when he accepted the views of our staff in regard to the final blow at Germany across the Channel and when he accepted my advice on my return from Europe in July 1943 that he should insist on having American command of the Normandy invasion. That was a great decision. . . . Events have shown that we were right.

Stimson may have overplayed his hand as far as Roosevelt was concerned. Certainly his influence on strategic matters declined. Already in November 1942 the irrepressibly tactless Bill Bullitt had crashed into Stimson's office and irritated him by asking how it felt to be a "mere housekeeper of the War Department now that the President had taken over all relations with the military men." Stimson was right to be annoyed, for at that time his greatest service was still to come. As the war went on, however, it is true that Roosevelt became with increasing relish his own commander-in-chief in practice as well as in constitutional theory.

That was, however, in large part because he came to find himself in harmony with the military chiefs, especially with Marshall, about how the war should be fought. And Stimson's forceful and courageous advocacy played the decisive part in bringing Roosevelt to see that the way he wanted to win the war, the American way, it could be said, was the way George Marshall and Henry Stimson had been proposing to him, not the elaborate way of fencing with quickness of foot and wrist which was Winston Churchill's instinct.

Churchill did not give in, however, and Stimson did not cease to be infuriated by his tenacity. In October 1943 Churchill mounted an operation against the Dodecanese, the Italian-held Greek islands near the coast of Turkey, in the hope of bringing Turkey into the war on the Allied side. The Germans threw half their air force from Italy into the battle, and the British were forced to withdraw. Churchill asked for American help, and the Joint Chiefs said no. There was a bitter fight in which the President backed his chiefs of staff. Churchill was told there must be no more diversionary campaigns.

"Jerusalem! This makes me angry," Stimson wrote in his diary a few days later when he learned that the British Prime Minister had slyly forwarded to Stalin a negative report from the British commander, Alexander, about the prospects of the Italian campaign. "This shows how determined Churchill is to knife OVERLORD." It was "what I would call dirty baseball on the part of Churchill."*

There were to be many more rows before the Anglo-American armada crossed the Channel in June 1944, but now it was too late to knife OVERLORD. And the man who, in the rarefied high politics of the grand coalition, had saved OVERLORD, and in the process knifed any number of Winston Churchill's schemes for strategic judo, was Henry Stimson. No doubt his victory owed much to the steadily growing preponderance of American manpower and production. But Stimson also won because he remained true to a perception of elemental simplicity. In July 1942 he "met head-on" with Roosevelt on the same issue, although, like two elderly gentlemen with good manners, "we did it in a semi-humorous way to keep from letting it get too serious, he offering to bet me on his point of view."

---

*While bitterly, perhaps sometimes unfairly, critical of Churchill's strategic diversions, Stimson remained a convinced Anglophile. One evening with Felix Frankfurter in 1942, the talk turned to the prevalence of Anglophobia in political Washington. "My best lesson in confidence in Great Britain," said Stimson, was "my experience with the 51st Division" in World War I.

Stimson could not have been more serious. The United States was seeking to establish a prompt offensive to destroy Hitler's power in Europe. The British, "while professing the same purpose," were equally if not more insistent on preserving their empire in the Middle East." Stimson was desperately worried that if the strength of the Allies was dissipated on this or other unworthy causes, it would mean disaster. Yet he was not cast down. "My faith," he wrote in his diary, "rests upon my belief that there is a Power in the universe that makes for righteousness and that Power cannot allow such a clear issue of right and wrong to go the wrong way."

He did not, however, propose to rely on faith alone without works. He lobbied tirelessly for his conception of the way the war could be won: by a direct assault on the citadel of Nazism. To convert Franklin Roosevelt to his belief, and to hold him firm in it under all the distractions and diversions and the pressures brought upon him by Churchill and many others, was Stimson's great contribution to victory in Europe. It is time to turn now to the even more decisive contribution he made to victory in Asia.

VII

The Least Abhorrent Choice

> The face of war is the face of death. . . . The decision to use the atomic bomb was a decision that brought death to over a hundred thousand Japanese. No explanation can change that fact and I do not wish to gloss it over. But this deliberate, premeditated destruction was our least abhorrent choice.
>
> Henry L. Stimson, *Harper's*, February 1947

> The historic fact remains, and must be judged in the after-time, that the decision whether or not to use the atomic bomb to compel the surrender of Japan was never even an issue.
>
> Sir Winston Churchill, *Triumph and Tragedy*, p. 553

The victory in Europe, for which Henry Stimson had worked so hard for five long years, came on May 8, 1945. Hitler had shot himself in the ruins of Berlin a week earlier, on April 30. The German army, which had conquered Europe from the North Cape to the Pyrenees and in defeat had fought with murderous professionalism from Libya and the Caucasus to the streets of Berlin, had surrendered at last.

The next day, May 9, Secretary of War Stimson received in his office at the Pentagon a delegation of senators and congressmen led by Senator Alben Barkley of Kentucky. The legislators had just returned from Europe, where they had visited three concentration camps, Buchenwald, Dachau and Nordhausen. Several of them freely admitted that before leaving they had been skeptical of reports of Nazi atrocities, dismissing them as exaggerated or even as figments of Allied propaganda. The horrors they had seen had shocked these practical, healthy-minded politicians to the soul. "They were unanimously of the opinion," Stimson wrote drily in his diary, "that the so-called atrocities had represented a deliberate and concerted attempt by the government of Germany to eliminate by murder, starvation and other methods of death large numbers of Russians, Poles, Jews and other classes of people."

That meeting began at eleven o'clock. Slightly more than an hour earlier there had taken place in the same room the first conference of the Interim Committee charged by the Secretary, with the formal approval of President Truman, with deciding various matters arising out of the impending use of the mysterious weapon, then approaching readiness, but still known by its cover name, S-1.*

There is a striking, if superficial, irony in the fact that the end of what many people in the democracies saw as the worst danger ever to threaten the fabric of civilization should have overlapped so closely with a decisive moment in the development of what may yet turn out to be an even greater threat.

The coincidence is worth dwelling on, though, for another reason. The atomic bomb was in a significant sense a monument to the terror and hatred Hitler inspired. It was not until the last weeks of the war in Europe—not, in fact, until the War Department's secret Alsos† teams found the last unaccounted-for tons of Belgian Congo uranium ore and a powerful American army corps shouldered its way across the front of the French army to seize the German nuclear physicists who had been evacuated to the little Black Forest town of Hechingen—that

---

*HLS, *Diary*, May 9, 1945. In this chapter I have drawn extensively on the *Diary*, vols. xli–lii. References to "S-1," infrequent and oblique in the early volumes, come thick and fast in vols. li and lii. The atomic-energy project was known in the United States sometimes as "S-1," for Section 1 of the Office of Scientific and Defense Research, also as the Manhattan Project, because in 1942 it was assigned to the Manhattan Engineer District of the Army Corps of Engineers, under Major General Leslie R. Groves. In the British government, it went under the code name "Tube Alloys." For its history I have relied principally on Richard G. Hewlett and Oscar E. Anderson, Jr., *The New World*; Richard Rhodes, *The Making of the Atomic Bomb*; Henry DeWolf Smyth, *Atomic Energy for Military Purposes*; Leslie R. Groves, *Now It Can Be Told*; Len Giovanitti and Fred Freed, *The Decision to Drop the Bomb*; Robert Junck, *Brighter Than a Thousand Suns*; I also owe a great debt to McGeorge Bundy for allowing me to read before publication chapters I and II of his magisterial history *Danger and Survival: Choices About the Bomb in the First Fifty Years*.

†A near-pun on the name of General Groves, commanding the Manhattan Engineer District; *alsos* is the Greek for "grove." Groves, *Now It Can Be Told*, pp. 191, 236.

it became certain that there would be no German atomic bomb. Until then, everyone involved in building the atomic bomb in the West assumed that they were in a deadly race against a rival team working for Hitler, and that he would not hesitate to use an atomic weapon the moment he possessed one. Moreover, many of the European scientists who persuaded Churchill and Roosevelt to explore the possibility of building an atomic bomb were themselves Jewish. They believed the bomb was a weapon whose use would be justified by Nazi barbarism, first as a desperate measure to save the lives of millions of European Jews and, if that failed, to avenge them. Without Hitler, it is hard to believe that even the crimes of the Japanese army in China, the Philippines and elsewhere would have evoked the anger that spurred on Anglo-American determination to build a bomb; and although as early as April 1941 the Japanese Imperial army air force authorized research toward the development of an atomic bomb,* there was no fear of such a Japanese weapon in the United States.

Nazi Germany collapsed just before the American atomic bomb was ready for use. But the decision to drop two bombs on Japan cannot be understood except in this anti-Nazi context. Not that the rulers of imperial Japan were innocent or squeamish, as their behavior both toward civilian populations in the countries they invaded and toward their prisoners of war proved. But as late as November 1944, when American army intelligence officers entering Strasbourg found definite evidence that Hitler had been told in early 1942 of the scientific possibility of building a nuclear weapon, it was thought that the Germans were close to success in that enterprise. And in December General Eisenhower's chief of staff, General Walter Bedell Smith, told the President's science adviser, Dr. Vannevar Bush, that he thought the reason why the Germans were resisting so fiercely was because they were close to successfully developing an atomic weapon. Bush doubted they had reached the production stage but thought they might well have made the essential breakthroughs in research.

There was no specific decision to drop the atomic bomb on Japan for the simple reason that it was always assumed that, once the bomb had been developed, it would be used. It was taken for granted that, however many times more powerful the new weapon might be than even the largest bombs using TNT or other conventional high explo-

*Rhodes, *Making of the Atomic Bomb,* p. 346

sives, the atomic device was just that: a new weapon of war. President Truman said it in so many words: "Let there be no mistake about it. I regarded the bomb as a military weapon and never had any doubt that it should be used."*

It was seen as a weapon legitimately available for the armory of the power that had had the vision, skill and resources to produce it. Scientists working on S-1 were aware that nuclear radiation might be dangerous. There is no indication in the record, however, of anyone ever making the point that a weapon whose radiation would contaminate a large area for a very long time was in some way qualitatively different from one that relied only on blast and fire to kill human beings more or less instantly.

The hard truth is that standards of conduct had fallen precipitously since September 1, 1939, when President Roosevelt appealed to the belligerents not to perpetrate "the ruthless bombing from the air of civilians in unfortified centers of population. If resort is had to this form of inhuman barbarism during the period of the tragic conflagration with which the world is now confronted," Roosevelt went on, "hundreds of thousands of innocent human beings who have no responsibility for, and who are not even remotely participating in, the hostilities which have now broken out, will lose their lives."† Great Britain agreed immediately, Germany two weeks later.

Even before the war in Europe began, the Japanese indiscriminately bombed civilians in Shanghai and elsewhere from 1931 on. German and Italian dive bombers killed civilians in Spain, and the Royal Air Force bombed "rebel" tribal villages in Iraq and Afghanistan. In 1940 the Luftwaffe bombed unprotected cities like Rotterdam, where 1,000 people were killed in a single night in 1940. Many more were killed in London in the night raids of 1941.

The scale of civilian casualties in those raids was dwarfed, however, by the Anglo-American reprisals in Germany. It was the British and the Americans, not the Germans, who first consciously articulated the idea that cities were to be bombed not as military targets where civilians might be killed incidentally, but in order to destroy the enemy's morale and will to fight. When Sir Arthur ("Bomber") Harris took over the Royal Air Force's Bomber Command in February 1942, he

---

*Harry S Truman, *Year of Decision*, p. 419.
†*Public Papers of the Presidents: Franklin Delano Roosevelt*, September 1, 1939. See also McGeorge Bundy, *Danger and Survival*, p. 63.

issued an order stating that "the primary objective of your operations should now be focused on the morale of the enemy civil population."* More than 40,000 civilians were killed in the Hamburg firestorm caused by British and some American bombers in July 1943. The most lethal air raid in history, at least before Hiroshima,† was the Dresden raid of February 13–14, 1945, ordered by Churchill and carried out by British and American bombers, in which 135,000 people are known to have been killed.

Churchill and Roosevelt both began to claim more and more explicitly that deliberate bombing of civilians was justified because the effect on their morale would "shorten the war" and "save lives." By 1945, the sheer scale of the frightfulness inflicted by the Nazis in Europe and in Russia and by the Japanese in China had hardened military hearts and relaxed military consciences. With few exceptions, commanders and their staffs found it easy to rationalize terror bombing with the argument that to destroy such wickedness the infliction of any number of civilian casualties was justified.

Although no one raid inflicted quite so many casualties as the Dresden raid, the climax of this ruthless infliction of civilian casualties in the name of destroying the enemy's war industry or, more nakedly, of breaking his will to fight, came in the Tokyo fire raids of the spring of 1945, in one of which—led by the future third-party vice-presidential candidate General Curtis LeMay, on March 9–10, 1945—83,000 people were killed. Indeed, one of the strangest ironies of the story of the atomic bomb is that, only weeks before ordering the dropping of the weapons which killed more than 100,000 people in each of the two raids on Hiroshima and Nagasaki, Stimson indignantly reprimanded his air commander, General H. H. ("Hap") Arnold, for the severity of the civilian casualties the Army Air Corps had caused in Tokyo.

A more humdrum psychological and political factor was involved. By the spring of 1945, the United States government had invested the

---

*Rhodes, *The Making of the Atomic Bomb,* p. 470.

†Richard Rhodes (without, however, giving a source), reports deaths at Hiroshima as 145,000 up to the end of 1945 and 200,000 within five years. At Nagasaki, he states, 70,000 died by the end of 1945 and 140,000 altogether. Lower estimates are to be found; for example, official Japanese statistics quoted in Giovanitti and Freed, *The Decision to Drop the Bomb,* say that 71,379 were killed at Hiroshima. The U.S. Strategic Bombing Survey estimated the dead at between 70,000 and 80,000. Many find such computations obscene. It is, however, relevant to moral judgments of the bombing of Hiroshima and Nagasaki that comparable or even larger numbers of civilians had recently been killed by Allied bombing in Dresden, Tokyo and elsewhere.

then-gigantic sum of $2 billion in the Manhattan Engineer District, the equivalent of tens of billions of dollars in current money. Gifted scientists had been working night and day, great companies driving on their people to extraordinary efforts, all justified by the imperative need to arm the United States with this new weapon. Once the atomic sword had been forged, it was almost unthinkable in the context of those years of effort that it would not be drawn.

Roosevelt, Churchill, General Marshall—all assumed that once the bomb was there, it would be used; and so too (with a few qualified exceptions, to be noted) did virtually everyone else who had anything to do with either making or dropping it, including Stimson. Indeed the atomic bomb seems to have been seen as a lesser evil in comparison with an invasion by United States ground forces of the Japanese home islands; and that not only from an American point of view, which was logical enough, since the War Department estimated that the invasion might cost half a million American casualties, but from the Japanese point of view too. That certainly would seem to be the only explanation of Stimson's remarks to the Committee of Three* on June 26, 1945:

> I took up at once the subject of trying to get Japan to surrender by giving her a warning after she had been sufficiently pounded, possibly with S-1. This is a matter about which I feel very strongly and feel that the country will not be satisfied unless every effort is made to shorten the war.†

The passage clearly suggests that, at least at the moment, Stimson thought not only that the highest priority ought to be to limit American casualties, but also that being "pounded" with atomic bombs was, for the Japanese themselves, a lesser evil than invasion.

Although from time to time, those with a voice in the consideration of policy, including Stimson, did acknowledge the possibility that the bomb need not be dropped, such occasions were grace notes to the main theme, which was that as soon as the bomb was there, it would be used. Yet that was not the end of the matter. A dozen important questions had to be decided. On what targets should the

---

*The Secretary of War, Secretary of the Navy James V. Forrestal, and Acting Secretary of State Joseph C. Grew, who was standing in for Secretary of State Edward R. Stettinius, then away at the conference in San Francisco where the United Nations was to be born.
†HLS, *Diary*, June 26, 1945.

bomb be dropped? On cities, and if so on which cities? How should
the attack be announced to the world? Should the bomb be used without warning? What kind of warning could safely and effectively be
given? Should the scientific and technological secrets of its construction
be revealed, domestically and internationally, and if so to whom, in
what manner, and in return for what, if any, reciprocal guarantees?
Those were only some of the immediate questions that had to be decided about S-1 once it became plain, in the spring of 1945, that—as
Stimson wrote in his diary on April 11, the day before President Roosevelt's death—"success is 99% assured."

Tricky questions of timing had to be considered. Even before Hitler's power for evil had been finally removed from Europe, the threat
of Stalin had become palpable. American policy-makers therefore had
to weigh a whole set of interlocking calculations. Was Soviet entry into
the war against Japan to be desired? Or was it to be avoided because
of the price Stalin would exact for it? Everyone agreed that an American invasion of the home islands was to be avoided at all costs. The
Japanese had fought with desperate tenacity on Okinawa. They could
be counted on to do so even more on Kyushu and Honshu, and American casualties would be correspondingly heavy. Worst of all, these
questions demanded to be decided before anyone knew for dead cold
certain that the bomb would work.

In the meantime, how should the United States go about governing prostrate Germany? How best to sow the seeds of a democratic
future there? How to address the Soviet Union's new military power
in Europe and Asia? How could the Japanese be persuaded to surrender? Plainly Asia and the world would not be safe until Japanese militarism had been tamed forever. But what about the Emperor? Was he
one of the war criminals or one of their victims? Should he be swept
from the throne, perhaps executed? Or used to help persuade his people to accept defeat and to set out upon another road?

On all these questions there was no one in the United States government with more influence than Henry Stimson. For on April 12,
less than a month before the end of the war in Europe, yet before
attention in Washington had focused sharply on the issues of the war
in the Pacific, let alone on the shape of the postwar world, Franklin
Roosevelt died. His successor might be brave and determined to do
right; but his knowledge of world politics was sketchy at best. The
understudy was pitchforked into the leading role at a time when world

politics were shifting faster and more unpredictably than perhaps at any previous time in history.

"Boys," President Truman said to the reporters who crowded round him on his first day in office, "if you ever pray, pray for me now. I don't know whether you fellows ever had a load of hay fall on you, but when they told me yesterday what had happened, I felt like the moon, the stars and all the planets had fallen on me."*

That was on April 13. President Truman had not yet even been let into the secret of the atomic bomb. On two occasions, as chairman of the Senate Committee to Investigate the National Defense Program, Truman had come close to stumbling on the truth.† In June 1943, he had been easily foiled by Stimson in a telephone conversation. But in March 1944, when Truman wanted to send investigators into the vast plants at Oak Ridge, Tennessee, and Hanford, Washington, where materials for the bomb were being produced, Secretary Stimson warned him off, courteously but firmly. "Senator," Stimson had said, as Truman remembered it, "I can't tell you what it is, but it is the greatest project in the history of the world. It is most top secret. Many of the people who are actually engaged in that work have no idea what it is, and we who do would appreciate your not going into those plants."

"I'll take you at your word," Truman replied, and called off his dogs.‡

So it was not until April 12, 1945, that Truman first heard of the atomic bomb, from Stimson, and not until almost two weeks later that he was fully briefed, again by Stimson.§

Since 1942 Stimson had been one of no more than half a dozen men with knowledge and authority over the whole breathtaking scope of the atomic-bomb project. As it approached fruition, he and General Marshall were the only two who knew all the secrets, were privy to all the considerations of grand strategy, and were trusted by all concerned—by the army engineers, the top scientists and top industrialists, and by two Presidents. They were really the only two who were steadily focused on all the interlocking problems: the need to finish with Japan, the threat of Stalin, the potential and the dangers of the bomb. Others had thought deeply, some of them perhaps more deeply than

---

*Harry S Truman, *Memoirs:* vol. i, *Year of Decision*, p. 19.
†See Martin J. Sherwin, *A World Destroyed*, p. 150.
‡Truman, *Year of Decision*, pp. 10–11.
§*Ibid.*, p. 419; HLS, *Diary*, April 13, 23, 24, 25, 1945.

Stimson, about the political and moral problems raised by atomic energy. But Stimson followed all the questions from the standpoint of a man with the authority not only to raise issues, but to resolve them.

The one thing Stimson did not decide was whether or not the bomb should be dropped, since that was never in serious doubt. He did sanction every crucial stage in the process that led to the bombing. Once the uranium bomb had devastated Hiroshima on August 6, 1945, Stimson could have decided to spare Nagasaki. He did not. He did decide to save Kyoto. The ease with which he made that decision stick makes it clear that, if he had decided to save Nagasaki, he could have done so.

More than anyone else in the American government except Franklin Roosevelt, Stimson encompassed in his thinking not only *how* first Germany, then Japan could be defeated, but *why* it was imperative that they must be beaten, and what sort of world could be built on the ruins they left behind them. Roosevelt, for all the maddening jumps of his grasshopper mind, for all his political ploys and endless playing off of one personality against another, *had* tried to comprehend the problems of world crisis in all its moral and historical dimensions. And now, just when decisions could wait no longer, Roosevelt was gone. Truman had the nerve to take responsibility but neither the knowledge nor the philosophic breadth to comprehend exactly what he had to take responsibility for. To Stimson there fell the two crucial questions presented by nuclear energy: how it was to be used in war, and how it was to be controlled in peace. The first is the subject of this chapter, and the second of Chapter VIII.

Stimson has been rightly praised for the breadth of vision and the integrity with which he addressed these great questions, yet he was not infallible. In the spring of 1945, he was seventy-eight years old and tired, and he had frightening symptoms of heart disease. His wife was not well, and he had recently lost his sister, his law partner and several of his oldest friends. From time to time, he became confused and lost some of the threads in a puzzle that was baffling in its complexity. He made mistakes, and for some of them the world has paid dearly. Yet for all his failings, he played the board like a grand master. Let us go back over some of the opening moves that set up the game.

Just before Christmas 1938, the Austrian nuclear physicist Lise Meitner, exiled by the Nazi racial laws from Germany to a small town on the west coast of Sweden, learned in a letter from her colleague at the Kaiser Wilhelm Institut in Berlin-Dahlem, the chemist Otto Hahn, that he and his collaborator, Fritz Strassmann, had succeeded in splitting the nucleus of an atom of uranium. On Christmas Eve, the sixty-year-old nuclear physicist went cross-country skiing with her nephew, the physicist Otto Frisch, who was visiting her from his own exile in Copenhagen. "That's impossible," said Frisch when she passed on the news from Berlin. But she knew it was true, or rather, as she wrote to Hahn, "we have experienced so many surprises in nuclear physics that one cannot say about anything 'it is impossible.' "* As a chemist, Hahn had succeeded in fractionating uranium and producing barium, many places below it in the periodic table. In Sweden, sitting on a log in the snow, Meitner remembered a lecture she had heard Albert Einstein give at a conference in Salzburg twenty-nine years before about how much energy would be released if an atomic nucleus could be split. She had the formulae for the calculation in her head, and there and then in the snow she did the sum. It fitted.

Lise Meitner was a brilliant physicist, but she was not the only one. Ever since the New Zealander Ernest Rutherford, working in Manchester, England, first discovered the structure of the atom before World War I, nuclear physics was the most exciting of all the branches of science. All over Europe and the United States, some of the best minds in the world, chemists and mathematicians as well as physicists, burned with the passion to unlock the secrets and the power of the atom.

In the 1930s, in spite of the calamity of Nazi persecution, science still aspired to be international. Scientists belonged to an international confraternity. Over bottles of wine and in personal letters, as well as in lectures and in the proceedings of scientific journals, they kept one another abreast of their theories and their discoveries. Before Hitler came to power, the great German centers of scientific study, especially Berlin and Goettingen, attracted students from all over the world. The Dane Niels Bohr and the Russian Peter Kapitza studied with Rutherford in Manchester, then in Cambridge. Americans like young Robert Oppenheimer, Karl Compton or Norbert Wiener were as much at home in Goettingen as in New York or Chicago, and the English ex-naval officer Pat Blackett, the Anglo-Swiss Paul Dirac, and the Italian Enrico Fermi were just as much at home there too.

*Lise Meitner to Otto Hahn, December 21, 1938, quoted in Rhodes, *The Making of the Atomic Bomb*, p. 253.

The world of nuclear physics, like the nucleus it studied, was tightly packed and highly energetic. Everyone in the field knew as a matter of course what problems everyone else was trying to solve and heard without much delay when they had succeeded. There was never any chance that Otto Hahn's discovery could be kept secret. As a matter of fact Irène and Frédéric Joliot-Curie had all but anticipated the same discovery in their lab in Paris. Within weeks Niels Bohr had taken the news to New York, where he had been invited to Columbia. Fermi was at work on atomic fission with his colleague Emilio Segrè in Rome. So were Rutherford's star pupil, James Chadwick, the discoverer of the neutron, and a dozen other first-rate scientists in Britain.

In the United States there were more competent physicists than ever before. After Hitler's persecutions began in earnest, Jewish scientists had been leaving Germany in numbers. More than a hundred of them were physicists. A few found refuge in Scandinavia and more, like Otto Frisch and Rudolf Peierls, in England. But the only country where there were enough universities with enough money to find jobs for more than a fraction of the highly trained physicists now in need of them was the United States.

Not that American physics depended on the refugees to be able to share in the excitement. Until the late 1920s, it is true, American physics had been somewhat sleepy and old-fashioned; but that had begun to change even before the refugees arrived from Europe. At Columbia, Princeton, Berkeley and Chicago, to name only some of the best-known centers, a brilliant generation of native American scientists was there to greet the wave of European physicists who came to the United States in the late 1930s.

So in January 1939, when Niels Bohr arrived in New York on his way to lecture at the fifth Washington Conference on Theoretical Physics and to spend a few months at the Institute for Advanced Study in Princeton, he was met at the pier by Enrico Fermi, who had newly moved from Rome to Columbia. Within days American physicists all over the country had heard the news of Hahn's discovery and knew that Bohr had a telegram from Frisch confirming it by laboratory experiment. The very issue of the *Physical Review* that carried Bohr's account of the European breakthroughs also published reports of corroborating experiments by physicists at Berkeley, Johns Hopkins, and the Carnegie Institute.

In January 1940 the *Review of Modern Physics* published a twenty-nine-page review article by Louis A. Turner, of Princeton, citing almost one hundred articles on nuclear fission in the twelve months since Hahn and Strassmann's discovery—that was the measure of the interest that had been aroused. There was a fever of theoretical speculation. Not everyone, to be sure, jumped to conclusions as fast as Turner, who by May was asking colleagues for advice on whether an article he had written for the *Physical Review,* boldly entitled "Atomic Energy from U238," was too dangerous for publication. At that same moment, two young physicists at Berkeley, Edwin McMillan and Philip Abelson, discovered element 93, neptunium, as a result of the fission of uranium. Every competent physicist in Europe and America was aware that nuclear fission implied, sooner or later, a new source of energy which might be controlled to generate power . . . or unleashed in an atomic bomb.

Niels Bohr in Copenhagen and James Chadwick in Cambridge, England, were among the many scientists who were concerned from the start about the moral and political consequences of this new source of power. Chadwick started taking sleeping pills the day he realized that a nuclear bomb was possible and took them every night for the next twenty-eight years. Among the first to feel that something must be done to prevent the Nazis from having a monopoly of the new weapon were three young Hungarian refugee physicists: Eugene Wigner, Edward Teller and Leo Szilard.

In the summer of 1939, spurred both by physicists' excitement about the prospects for fission, and also by the inevitability of war in central Europe, the three determined to find a way of interesting the United States government. They were soon sidetracked by the thought that it was vital to prevent Germany's obtaining the only known large supplies of high-grade uranium ore, which came from the Katanga mines in the southern Belgian Congo. One of them remembered that Albert Einstein, doyen of refugee physicists, was a friend of the Queen of the Belgians. The great man was then spending the summer in Peconic, on the tip of Long Island, and one July day Wigner and Szilard drove out to see him and enlist his help in this matter, and on the more general issue of nuclear fission. Secure in his Olympian reputation and preoccupied with the ambition to persuade the world of his unified field theory, Einstein had not paid much attention to the implications of fission. When Szilard, over soda water and open sandwiches, pointed out the probability of a chain reaction, the great man observed

modestly, *"Daran habe ich gar nicht gedacht* ("I never thought of
that!"). The conspirators soon realized they would have to inform the
U.S. government of their thoughts, and through an acquaintance they
were introduced to the man who was to make the approach in the
most effective possible way.

This was Dr. Alexander Sachs, a Russian-born economist then
working on Wall Street with the Lehman Corporation. He had written
speeches for Roosevelt in the 1932 campaign, and remained his friend
and adviser. On October 11, 1939, Sachs was ushered into the Oval
Office by General Edwin Watson (universally known as "Pa"), bearing
the umpteenth draft of a letter, or memorandum, hammered out by
Einstein, Szilard and Wigner—but signed only by Einstein—together
with his, Sachs', own covering letter. Sachs found two ordnance officers, one from the army and one from the navy, with the President.

After warming up Roosevelt with a little joke about how Napoleon refused to see Robert Fulton, inventor of the steamship, who was
offering to take his army across the Straits of Dover even if there was
no wind, Sachs read out the letters. It was always best to get to busy
men through their ears, he told his friends; they were all punch-drunk
with printer's ink.

Sachs' own letter stressed the need for government funding. Both
letters stressed the simple fact that work on nuclear fission by Fermi
and Szilard in America and by Joliot-Curie in France made a chain
reaction inevitable, and that a chain reaction made it possible, though
not certain, that a bomb far more powerful than anything then in
existence could be made. The Einstein letter pointed out the need to
secure Belgian uranium ore, proposed that someone (the job description made it sound like someone remarkably similar to Leo Szilard!)
should be put in charge of liaison between the government and the
scientists, and ended by reporting ominously that the Germans had
just banned sales of uranium from the Joachimsthal mines in Czechoslovakia, the only source in Europe.

We now know that, as a result of a paper on the nuclear fission
of uranium published by the French physicists Frédéric Joliot, Hans
von Halban and Lew Kowarski in the April issue of the British scientific journal *Nature,* one German physicist alerted the Reich Ministry of Education and another wrote to the War Ministry that the
latest developments would probably make possible an explosive many
orders of magnitude more powerful than existing bombs and observ-

ing that "that country which makes use of it has an unsurpassable advantage over the others." One or both of these moves had their effect: uranium sales were banned, a secret conference was held in Berlin, and a research program was initiated on the advice of Hans Geiger, inventor of the Geiger counter. This activity did not, however, lead to a German atomic bomb. The precise reasons why Germany's brilliant physicists and engineers did not succeed in building a bomb remain obscure. By 1942 they understood theoretically how to build a plutonium bomb, but they lacked engineering experience and were limited by the fact that the only cyclotron in Europe was that controlled by Joliot (secretly a Resistance leader) in Paris. In early 1942, at lunch in a private room at Horcher's restaurant in Berlin, General Fromm, commanding the home army, told Albert Speer, the highly intelligent architect turned Nazi munitions minister, that the only hope of winning the war was to develop a weapon, which certain German scientists were on the track of, that could annihilate whole cities. Speer drew Hitler's attention to the need to support basic research on the project, and as a result responsibility for it was transferred from an ineffectual party hack to Field Marshal Hermann Goering, head of the Luftwaffe. Yet later in 1942, when Werner Heisenberg and other top-flight German physicists invited the most powerful Nazi leaders to a conference in the hope of interesting them in the atomic bomb and other scientific possibilities, the Nazi bigwigs stayed away. At a second meeting in June 1942, Heisenberg stressed the military potential of atomic energy. Speer questioned him in private later, and Heisenberg was more evasive, giving Speer "the impression that the atom bomb could no longer have any bearing on the course of the war." After the war Heisenberg hinted at what was perhaps the truth, that because his mistrust of the Nazis ultimately overcame his loyalty to Germany he deliberately underplayed the possibility of building an atom bomb. And Speer adds an enlightening touch of great verisimilitude. Hitler had been impressed by the conviction of Philipp Lenart, the Nobel laureate for physics in 1920, that nuclear physics, like relativity, was "Jewish physics." A text published in 1935 by L. W. Helwig, *Die Deutsche Physik,* stated that relativity and nuclear physics were "outgrowths" which "the German *Volk* must shun as racially incompatible." Speer believed that this view helps to explain why the Nazi ministry of education was loath to fund nuclear physics! It is also remarkably corroborative of the old

Latin tag that "Whom God wishes to destroy, he first takes his mind away."*

Franklin Delano Roosevelt's mind was not wholly free from prejudices of various kinds, but he was not mad. He was also unusually quick on the uptake. As his Jewish friend Sachs finished reading his letter in the summer of 1939, FDR said, "Alex, what you are after is to see that the Nazis don't blow us up." Then he called in "Pa" Watson and pronounced winged words that would fly a long, long way. "This needs action," he said.†

The action President Roosevelt took after he saw Alex Sachs was to hand consideration of uranium fission over to a uranium committee run by Dr. Lyman J. Briggs, the elderly and cautious director of the Bureau of Standards, the nation's official physics laboratory. Although small grants were from time to time parceled out to Fermi and Szilard at Columbia and to other researchers, essentially nothing happened between the fall of 1939 and the summer of 1941. The United States was still at peace. A few European refugees might get themselves worked up about the danger of Hitler's getting his hands on a super-weapon, and some solid citizens of the scientific community seemed to think that nuclear fission might be an important thing one day. But there was little urgency, no sense that finding out whether a nuclear weapon could be built, let alone building one, might be a matter of life and death for the United States. As late as March 1941 James Bryant Conant, president of Harvard University and an organic chemist with an international reputation, who happened to be in England, learned of the possibility of a nuclear bomb for the first time from Winston Churchill's friend the Oxford physicist F. A. Lindemann (after 1956 Lord Cherwell), over lunch at his London club. Several months later, with the Atlantic submarine war reaching its crescendo and 160 German divisions launched against the Soviet Union in Operation BARBAROSSA, the physicist Arthur Compton concluded soberly that "the government's responsible representatives were . . . very close to dropping fission studies from the war program."

---

*Rhodes, *Making of the Atomic Bomb, passim,* especially pp. 401–5. Albert Speer, *Inside the Third Reich,* pp. 225–29.

†I have followed the official historians, Hewlett and Anderson, *New World.* Their sources, listed at p. 669, include (slightly differing) accounts by Szilard and Wigner, the original Einstein letter of August 2, 1939, and the memorandum and covering letter Sachs took with him on October 11, 1939, all in the FDR Papers at Hyde Park; and two accounts by Sachs, one in a manuscript now in the archives of the Manhattan Engineer District in the National Archives; and one in a personal letter to Hewlett and Anderson.

That there was a war program for scientific research at all was largely the work of a small group of scientists, mostly New Englanders and New Yorkers, who were the opposite numbers in the scientific Establishment of Henry Stimson and those others in the political sphere who believed that the United States must be awakened to the danger of the war. Conant was one of these. So was Stimson's first cousin Alfred Loomis, the multimillionaire investment banker turned physicist who conducted experiments in his privately funded laboratory at Tuxedo Park, New York. By far the most important was a sharp-eyed, sharp-minded electrical engineer of old Yankee stock (both of his grandfathers had been sea captains) named Vannevar Bush. Bush had been dean of engineering, then vice president of the Massachusetts Institute of Technology. A self-described Tory, Bush was something of a throwback to an earlier New England generation, an inventor who had worked on submarine detection and automatic telephones. He was also a master of organizational politics, a shrewd, worldly man who had a knack for getting what he wanted. In 1939 he moved from MIT to become president of the Carnegie Institution in Washington so as to put himself at the center of preparations for the war he could see coming. In short order he became chairman of the National Advisory Committee for Aeronautics, and in the summer of 1940, before Henry Stimson had come to Washington, Bush talked Harry L. Hopkins, the ultimate insider in the Roosevelt White House, into letting him propose to the President a National Defense Research Council (NDRC) to coordinate all scientific research for the war effort—with himself, naturally, as chairman, reporting, not through the War Department, but direct to the President. On June 12, Bush recorded with satisfaction, he got his ten minutes in the Oval Office, put in his idea in four paragraphs on a single sheet of paper, and got his "OK-FDR."

Bush might be effectiveness and energy personified in comparison with Lyman J. Briggs. But it was a full year before anything began to happen in terms of government support for a program of nuclear research oriented toward weapons.

The impetus, when it arrived, came from Britain. In the spring of 1940, Otto Frisch and Rudolf Peierls, refugees at the University of Birmingham, wrote a memorandum concluding that the critical mass for a chain reaction in fast-neutron fission of uranium-235 was very much less than anyone had imagined—perhaps no bigger than a golf ball, given the weight of uranium. They then further calculated that a pound of reasonably pure uranium-235 might be separated from uranium-238 in a matter of weeks. "At that point," Frisch wrote in his memoirs, "we stared at each other and realized that an atomic bomb might after all be possible."* Frisch and Peierls were conscious from the start that what they were contemplating was a weapon of terrifying mass destruction. "The answer," Frisch wrote nearly forty years later, "was very simple. We were at war, and the idea was reasonably obvious; very probably some German scientists had had the same idea and were working on it." We know now that they had, and they were.

The crackpot idea of these two young refugees reached Sir Henry Tizard, the Oxford chemist who was in charge of all British wartime scientific research. Tizard set up a committee under George Thomson, son of the great J. J. Thomson. As a code name, Thomson called it the "Maud" Committee. (This was a typical sly British joke. Lise Meitner had sent a cable to a British friend with a message to another friend named Maud Ray in Kent. Thomson's physicist friend John Cockcroft insisted that "Maud Ray Kent" was an—imperfect—anagram for "radium taken." Thomson didn't know about that, but thought Maud would make a splendid name for his committee, and no doubt derived professorial amusement from the thought of Abwehr cryptanalysts puzzling over what words it could be an acronym for.)

By July 1941 the Maud Committee had a draft report. What it said was that "it will be possible to make an effective uranium bomb which, containing some 25 lb of active material, would be equivalent as regards destructive effect to 1,800 tons of TNT and would also release large quantities of radioactive substances." The Maud Committee calculated that to build a plant capable of making three such bombs a month would cost the "very large expenditure" of £5 million (then about $20 million). The first bombs could be ready, the report added, by the end of 1943. It ended with three recommendations: that a uranium bomb was practicable and would lead to decisive results in the war; that the work should be given the highest priority; and that "the present collaboration with America should be continued and extended especially in the region of experimental work."†

At a final meeting, at the rooms of the Royal Society in Burlington

---

*O. R. Frisch, *What Little I Remember*, 1979, p. 126; see also Rudolf Peierls' memoir *Bird of Passage*, 1985.
†Rhodes, *The Making of the Atomic Bomb*, p. 369.

House, an American who happened to be in London studying rocket technology, Charles Lauritsen of the California Institute of Technology, was present as a guest. He reported the gist of the draft report to Bush. It is ironic that the decisive part in persuading the American scientific community that a uranium bomb could be built was a report that—while correct in its essentials—was so wildly overoptimistic. Bush, however, a staunch Anglophile, was converted. In July he talked to Vice President Henry Wallace, the only scientist in the Cabinet, and put it to him that the government ought to invest a serious amount of money in uranium fission. And on October 9, 1941, Bush found himself at the White House, this time for a conference with the Vice President and the President.

The chief topic on the agenda was the Maud Report. (Its gist had been known in Washington since July; in October the final report, officially transmitted by Thomson, reached Bush. In the meantime the National Academy of Sciences reported favorably, and two leading American physicists, George Pegram and Harold Urey, visited England specifically to learn about British progress in bomb research.) Roosevelt was impressed, and Bush left with his approval, not to build an atomic bomb, but to spend what was necessary to find out if an atomic bomb could be built.

Two points are worth noticing about this historic meeting. The first is that the decision to build not only a bomb but the vast secret bureaucracy that would be required to create it, was taken by the President alone. The Congress was neither consulted nor informed, the judiciary was irrelevant, and the Cabinet was left in ignorance. If the historic balance of the governing branches separated under the Constitution was tilted by the imperatives of world war and global power, this was one of the decisive moments. Not until much later, and then imperfectly, was Congress able to recapture its authority to watch over this greatest single source of American military and political strength. Until after Hiroshima, leadership was firmly in the executive branch.

The second point is that the U.S. nuclear program went forward from the start in a radically different way from the British program out of which it had, so to speak, evolved. In Britain, policy was decided by the scientists. The questions of high policy—could a bomb be built? ought it to be built?—were referred to a committee of scientists for decision. In the United States neither Roosevelt nor Bush nor Stimson was willing to entrust the scientists with policy. Their role was to decide technical questions; policy was to be reserved for the President and his advisers and servants in the executive branch. That, as we shall see, very much included the Secretary of War.

The first mention of the atomic bomb project in Colonel Stimson's diary comes on November 6, 1941, just one month before Pearl Harbor. "Vannevar Bush came in to convey to me an extremely secret statement from the Scientific Research and Development Office." And then he added: "a most terrible thing."

At the meeting on October 9, the President signified that he wanted policy to be put in the hands of what came to be called the Top Policy Group. The members were to be Vice President Wallace, Vannevar Bush, James Conant, General Marshall, and Henry Stimson. A month later, Bush initiated Stimson into the grim mysteries of atomic energy. In the meantime Bush was energetically leading a review of alternative approaches to the building of a nuclear weapon by some of the most brilliant scientists in the country, men like Ernest O. Lawrence, Harold Urey, Glenn Seaborg, Arthur Compton, Robert S. Mulliken and, significantly, chemical engineers, masters of a technology in which, because of its oil industry, the United States was uniquely rich. Physicists at the University of California at Berkeley, using the university's powerful cyclotron, had already demonstrated the possibility of an alternative type of bomb, using the ninety-fourth element, later called plutonium, instead of uranium-235 as the fissile element.

Only weeks before Pearl Harbor, Vannevar Bush was given the green light to take the research effort out of the hands of the old uranium committee and push forward at high speed under a new section, S-1, of the Office of Scientific Research and Development. Bush explained the new arrangements to NDRC on November 28, and Conant explained them to the old S-1 section on December 6—the day before Pearl Harbor.

On December 16 the Top Policy Group met at the Capitol, with Wallace, Bush and Stimson present, as well as Harold Smith, the long-serving head of the Bureau of the Budget. Bush's reorganization was approved, and the group authorized him to press ahead, not only with the fundamental physics but also with pilot engineering plants costing some $5 million. The order of magnitude of expenditure had gone about halfway from the $6,000 originally granted to Fermi and Szilard for uranium research to the $2 billion it eventually cost to carry the Manhattan District Project through to a successful conclusion.*

As Bush systematically moved aside those older and more cautious men who were unable to grasp his own sense of the urgency of the project, replacing them with younger, more dynamic men like Lawrence and Compton, there was a new sense of optimism. At a meeting at Columbia in early 1942, Compton even laid down a confident timetable:

> By July 1, 1942, to determine whether a chain reaction was
>   possible.
> By January 1943, to achieve the first chain reaction.
> By January 1944, to extract the first element 94 from uranium.
> By January 1945, to have a bomb.

Compton, like everyone else, had underestimated the time, the money, the effort, the sheer technological ingenuity, the morale, and the organizational coherence that would be needed to move from theory by way of pilot plants to full-scale production in what would turn out to be some of the biggest and most complex engineering installations ever built. But soon it became plain that the time had come to hand over the construction and engineering work, as Bush had foreseen from the start it would eventually have to be handed over, to the Army Corps of Engineers, working with private corporate contractors as well as with the university labs at Columbia, Chicago and Berkeley.

Even so, almost another year was lost in indecision, suspicion and misunderstanding between the civilian scientists and the military bureaucracy until, in September 1942, this time with the Secretary of War covering him with his personal authority, Bush found the organizational setup and the people who were going to get the job done. There were difficulties in giving S-1 the priority it needed to pry scarce materials and sought-after personnel from America's war production machine, which in 1942 was just beginning to shift up into top gear. There were delays in getting the army to purchase the Clinton, Tennessee, site for the giant electromagnetic and gaseous-diffusion plants that were to separate the fissile U-235 from U-238. By late August 1942, the official historians of atomic energy in the United States record, "the S-1 ex-

*Hewlett and Anderson, *New World*, pp. 21, 724.

ecutive committee realized that if some action were not taken soon, the atomic bomb would never be a weapon in the present war."*

At the organizational level, the problem was solved by putting both the Army Corps of Engineers officers and the civilian scientists firmly under the control of a new military committee. Bush forged a highly effective working relationship with his fellow-Yankee Harvey Bundy, and together they were able to devise a bureaucratic solution that enabled the job to be done. Bush's idea was to create in effect a "board of directors" with both military and civilian members supervising a new "chief executive."

The new chief executive was an army colonel, a West Point graduate with long experience in the Canal Zone, named Leslie R. Groves. Groves was a large, bluff, somewhat insensitive man with the heavy-handed manner of the career army, but he was also imbued with its dedication and discipline. His last assignment had been to build the Pentagon, a job in which his weekly budget was bigger than the whole of that for S-1 at that time. His dearest ambition was to command troops on active service abroad. When General Somervell, now head of the army's services of supply, met him in a Capitol Hill corridor and told him Stimson had chosen him for "a very important assignment" in Washington, he was not pleased.

"I don't want to stay in Washington."

"If you do the job right," said General Somervell carefully, "it will win the war."

General Wilhelm D. Styer, Somervell's chief of staff, made it sound even simpler: "You just have to take the rough designs, put them into final shape, build some plants and organize an operating force and your job will be finished and the war will be over."†

So far as can be learned, nobody used the analogy, but if the new committee corresponded to a corporate board of directors, and Groves‡ was chief executive, then Colonel Stimson for the next two years was chairman of the board. In Hollywood terms, he was neither the director—that was Groves; nor the producer, which was Bush's role. He was the executive producer. Stimson's function, which he fulfilled with

*Hewlett and Anderson, *New World*, p. 79.
†Quoted in Leslie R. Groves, *Now It Can Be Told*, pp 3–4.
‡Groves was promoted to brigadier general on September 23, six days after his appointment as head of the Manhattan Engineering District, as the atomic bomb project was called by the army.

great skill, was to move in only when the men running the project were at loggerheads, or when they needed protection from the outside. On September 8, 1943, his position was given more formal status: his name was written into a previously drafted agreement on nuclear cooperation with the British as chairman of the Policy Committee. Stimson took Roosevelt and Churchill, who was then visiting the White House, to one side and pointed out that the job would give him "a great deal of routine work which I could not possibly do in addition to my present labors." Both the President and the Prime Minister were so eager to keep him as chairman that they arranged for him to stay on with General Styer as his deputy "to take care of the routine work."*

Stimson kept firm control on relations between S-1 and its ultimate sponsor, the President of the United States, though Vannevar Bush and James Conant, using their positions within the executive office, could also get access to the President on certain occasions. Stimson had the final choice of key personnel, from General Groves on down.

In 1944 Stimson worked hard at the complex negotiations about uranium between the United States; Britain; Canada; the Belgian government-in-exile in London; the Union Minière du Haut Katanga, whose Shinkolobwe mine was the largest and purest source of uranium ore in the world; and the Union Minière's chief executive, who was in New York. On August 25, he got a free hand from the President to negotiate a quick, short-term contract to obtain uranium from the Congo; it did not give the American and British governments all they had hoped for, but did make sure of an initial 1,720 tons of ore.

One of Stimson's most important tasks was to run interference for S-1 on Capitol Hill. At first President Roosevelt assured Bush that he would have access to funds that would keep research going without requiring congressional appropriations. At the Capitol meeting in December 1941, Harold Smith of the Budget Bureau gave similar assurances. But as the gigantic construction operations got under way in Tennessee and, for a plutonium plant, at Hanford, Washington, the monthly expenditures of the Manhattan District, running at less than $100,000 in September and October 1942, reached $50 million a month in the fall of 1943, $68 million in January 1944, $93 million in April and

*HLS, *Diary,* September 8, 1943.

peaked at $111 million a month in August 1944.* Expenditure on such a scale had to be squared with Congress somehow, not only as a matter of constitutional propriety, but in order to avert the destructive political firestorm that would otherwise erupt once the truth became widely known.

On at least two occasions Stimson blocked requests from Senator Truman's special committee investigating the national defense program, and on each occasion Truman instantly accepted Stimson's assurances that the huge plants in Tennessee and Washington must be kept secret for reasons of national security. On June 17, 1943, Truman telephoned about an installation in the Hanford complex. The following conversation is recorded in the Secretary of War's telephone transcripts:

> STIMSON: Now that's a matter which I know all about personally, and I am one of a group of two or three men in the whole world who know about it.
> TRUMAN: I see.
> STIMSON: It's part of a very important secret development.
> TRUMAN: Well, all right then—
> STIMSON: And I—
> TRUMAN: I herewith see the situation, Mr. Secretary, and you won't have to say another word to me. Whenever you say that to me, that's all I want to hear.†

The exchange reveals a good deal about the willingness of Congress, in wartime, to soften its normally suspicious attitude toward the executive branch. It also suggests why, in an executive branch where senators and congressmen were habitually treated as if their patriotism was suspect, President Truman was to be swiftly accepted as "one of us."

On February 14, 1944, however, Stimson recorded in his diary that at least $600 million more would be needed for the Manhattan District. With Bush, General Styer, Groves and Bundy, he decided to "take Congress into our confidence." The curtain was opened only a chink, however. Four days later, with Bush and General Marshall, Stimson went to the office of Speaker of the House Sam Rayburn,

*See the very interesting financial summaries in Hewlett and Anderson, *New World*, pp. 723–24.
†HLS, *Papers*, Reel 127, p. 441, June 17, 1943.

where they also found House Democratic Leader John W. McCormack and his opposite number, the Republican Joe Martin. Stimson gave a brief outline of the history of the project, Marshall stressed its vital military importance, and Bush explained the scientific details. The persuasion must have been overwhelming. Indeed, with a patriot like Rayburn, at that moment in the war, little persuasion was needed:

> The whole meeting went off satisfactorily and the three gentlemen whom we met professed themselves to be completely satisfied that we were right and should have the money which we asked. We discussed with them the best ways of doing it and they agreed to take the matter of breaking the way for us with the members of the Appropriations Committee into their own hands.*

On June 9 General Somervell came in with a "bombshell," as Stimson called it. The S-1 appropriations had duly passed the House, and now the Secretary would have to repeat his bravura performance with the Senate. But the Senate proved as patriotic, or compliant, as the House: the very next day Stimson saw Senator Barkley, of Kentucky, the Democratic majority leader, Senator Wallace H. White, Jr., Republican of Maine, the minority leader, and Senator J. W. E. Thomas of Oklahoma, chairman of the Appropriations Committee's subcommittee for military affairs. He told them, misleadingly if not actually untruthfully, "We had saved out of our appropriations for past years a surplus unused of an amount more than necessary to cover the amount we are asking." He added, with perfect truth, that his purpose was to prevent public discussion. And he explained that the Germans started working on an atomic bomb six months ahead of the United States, and it was "a race as to which one would finish first." Not surprisingly, the Senators were as good as gold.

Another of Stimson's responsibilities as "chairman of the board" was dealing with the British, who caused rather more trouble than Congress. One difficulty was that the British had started on nuclear-weapons research before the United States, and independently, so that they had entered into obligations whose security implications horrified Stimson. As early as December 1942, he was telling the President that the British had an agreement with the Soviet Union dating back to

*HLS, *Diary,* February 18, 1944.

September of that year to exchange information about all new weapons. Unable to send troops to help the embattled Russians, and not yet in a position to make diversionary attacks, Churchill was keen to do all he could to help Stalin beat the Germans. Still, Roosevelt shared Stimson's concern.

A far more serious row blew up at the end of 1944, when France was liberated from German occupation and the handful of French physicists who had come to Canada or to the United States to work on the atomic bomb became impatient to go home. The Americans were adamant that they must not be allowed to go, not least because it would be impossible to stop them from talking to Frédéric Joliot, who had not only spent the war in France, allowing the Germans to use the cyclotron in his lab at the Collège de France, but had announced his membership in the French Communist Party! Joliot had in fact been a courageous member of the Resistance, who played a dangerous game with the Germans to save his lab and slow down German research if he could. But Stimson and Groves were horrified. There was also the delicate matter of agreements between the British government and two of the French scientists, Hans von Halban and Lew Kowarski,* in respect of an exchange of patents relating to nuclear research.

Sir John Anderson, the sternly upright Scots bureaucrat who was wartime Chancellor of the Exchequer and also in charge of British participation in "Tube Alloys," insisted that Britain must honor these agreements and argued in a memo that the United States could not treat French scientists as prisoners. Groves, unaware of pre-existing British commitments to the Frenchmen, was deeply suspicious, and Stimson exploded with fury at a December 30 meeting in the White House, accusing Anderson of "hoodwinking poor old John" Winant, the U.S. ambassador in London. FDR, who shared Churchill's feeling that the heaviest cross he had to bear was the Cross of Lorraine (badge of the Free French), was furious too. Stimson accused Anderson—a dry administrator more at home with tax problems than with "riding in triumph through Persepolis"—of being dominated by "the imperial instinct."

Like many men with a well-advertised reputation for good judgment, Stimson was prone to these occasional misreadings of character.

---

*Both men were refugees, Halban from Austria, Kowarski from Russia, who had worked with Frédéric Joliot-Curie in Paris.

We have seen how he admired Somoza and thought General Sandino could be left out of account in the Nicaraguan future. But perhaps his most spectacular misjudgment was of General de Gaulle. In June 1944, as Free French troops clashed with Anglo-American units over who should administer a liberated area on the French-Italian frontier, Stimson told Roosevelt he thought De Gaulle was virtually stabbing American troops in the back. De Gaulle was, he wrote angrily in his diary, "a man of egocentric and unreliable nature and cannot be relied to be steadfast and to place the welfare of his country before himself."* Egocentric the General certainly was, and Stimson was entitled to dislike his style or policies, but few men have been more steadfast than De Gaulle through the changes and chances of their generation. Even his critics agree that when in the opening paragraph of his memoirs he wrote that all his life he had set before himself "a certain idea" of how France could be great and dedicated himself to the service of that ideal, he was telling the plain truth. It is strange how limited was Stimson's ability to recognize in others, including Churchill and De Gaulle, the counterpart of his own passionate patriotism.

In the end, though, Stimson's common sense triumphed over his irritation with the British and the French. Although he remained adamant that the United States would make no commitments to the French scientists in respect of their patents, it was he who found a solution acceptable to the British, if less so to the French.

The external relations of S-1 were the Secretary of War's province. That included keeping a weather eye on the Soviet Union. As early as September 1943 Stimson noted in his diary that there was a "scare about S-1": the CIO was trying to unionize the lab at Berkeley, "and they are already getting information about vital secrets and sending them to Russia." On December 13, 1944, he warned the President that the Russians were still spying at Berkeley. It is not clear what Stimson's source was for this information, or allegation. It may have been the FBI. Or it may have been General John DeWitt, army commander on the West Coast, who warned FBI Director J. Edgar Hoover (who passed the word on to FDR) of the "obviously sinister designs" of Harry Bridges, the West Coast longshoremen's leader, who was a Communist. On the face of it, it is most unlikely that "the CIO" was giving atomic secrets to Russia. Although many employers and con-

*HLS, *Diary,* June 12, 1944.

servatives, not to mention leaders of the rival American Federation of Labor, believed the Congress of Industrial Organizations was virtually dominated by Communists, the true position was that the Communist Party, and Communist union leaders such as Harry Bridges, were involved in a constant battle for influence within the CIO with strong anti-Communists such as John L. Lewis and Walter Reuther, as well as with the CIO's more ambiguous and vacillating president Philip Murray. It is, of course, conceivable that individual Communist union members were passing secrets to Russia this early, but I have found no corroborative evidence.*

Closer to home, Stimson also intervened to stop a Justice Department antitrust action against the DuPont company, a major contractor at both Oak Ridge and Hanford. Stimson had missed the point when it first came up in a Cabinet meeting. Alerted by Bundy, he rushed a letter to the President saying how "disastrous it would be from the standpoint of our hurried manufacture to distract these key people who are handling our most secret and important project with an anti-trust suit."†

Most important of all, the chairman of the board's duties, of course, are to look ahead and decide, with the appropriate advice if necessary, what policy ought to be. By the fall of 1944, after the battle of Leyte Gulf, in which the imperial Japanese navy was destroyed as a battle-worthy force—this was, perhaps, the greatest naval battle in history—and with Stalin's army battering at the eastern gates of the Reich and Eisenhower's armies threatening the Rhine, policy-makers in Washington could at last look forward with confidence to victory, first in Europe, then over Japan. They began to focus on a cluster of linked problems: the future of Germany; the defeat of Japan; dealing with the Soviet Union as a great power ensconced not only in the heart of Europe but also possibly in the Far East; and the prospect that the United States would face that new world possessed of a superweapon. They began to ask themselves how that weapon should be used. Beyond that they also debated whether it should be kept as a secret of American (and perhaps to some degree British) power, or whether its secrets should be shared under some form of international control. Bush and Conant, especially, began to raise searching questions about the postwar arrangements for domestic and international control.

*See Harvey A. Levenstein, *Communism, Anticommunism and the CIO*, Greenwood Press, 1981.
†HLS, *Diary*, May 22, 1944.

• • •

In June 1944, Colonel Stimson recorded proudly in his diary, his cousin Alfred Loomis told him at dinner that Vannevar Bush, a quarter of a century Stimson's junior, had said "the most forward-looking man in either the Army or the Navy . . . was a man 75 years old* who had been trained as a lawyer." The fact is, though, that Bush and his friend Jim Conant were generally quicker than Stimson to identify the great issues that would have to be resolved, and while they held the Secretary of War in affection and respect, they sometimes wished they had a younger man to deal with.

One problem that focused their minds on the future of atomic energy was that presented by the proposed cutbacks in jobs at the Chicago Metallurgical Laboratory. On December 2, 1942, the uranium "pile" built by Enrico Fermi in a squash court at the University of Chicago's Stagg Field football stadium had "gone critical"; that is, it had demonstrated the possibility of a controlled nuclear chain reaction. Thereafter, in early 1943, scientists began to move from Chicago (as also from Princeton) to Los Alamos, New Mexico, to continue the work of building the bomb. Although the prospect of a 75 per cent cutback in employment did not arrive until early 1945, for more than a year Chicago scientists had been among those aware that the postwar future of nuclear research was in danger.

The scientists, frightened of losing their jobs, were naturally unhappy. And in their unhappiness they began to raise all sorts of questions about the future. Who should control nuclear energy? The government? The universities? Big corporations? The scientists themselves? Some international organization? Those of them who were refugees from Nazi Europe could see their interest in building a nuclear bomb ebbing with their fear of Hitler, and they tended to be far less interested in dropping bombs on the Japanese. It was only human nature that, with the fading of the nightmare, their moral scruples about building the most frightful weapon the world had ever seen became stronger.

This ferment of questioning led to the setting up of two committees in the fall of 1944. One, chaired by an industrialist named Zay Jeffries, and including Enrico Fermi, James Franck and Robert S. Mul-

*He was in fact 76.

liken, looked at postwar problems from a more liberal standpoint. The other, led by Richard C. Tolman, the Caltech physicist who had persuaded Albert Einstein to emigrate to the United States, took a more pessimistic view, and the members concluded that postwar planning would be dominated by the quest for military superiority, and that the government would need to spend money on research into U-235, on the production of Pu-239 and U-233, on weapons development and on the use of nuclear technology for naval propulsion.*

A number of threads came together in mid-September 1944, when Winston Churchill, after meeting the President at Quebec, traveled south to spend a couple of nights with him at his family estate at Hyde Park, where both men initialed an agreement of the greatest importance for nuclear policy. Churchill had been infuriated to be lobbied by Niels Bohr, the great Danish physicist who was also a pacifist, about the need for internationalizing nuclear science. (Unknown to Churchill and, until much later, to Stimson, Bohr had also approached Justice Felix Frankfurter and tried to use him to transmit these internationalist ideas to the President.) Churchill, whose commitment to secrecy was much stronger than his knowledge of the way the international scientific community thought and worked, threatened to have Bohr shot as a spy. The Hyde Park agreement flatly rejected Bohr's internationalist approach and proposed instead that, once a bomb was available, "it might *after mature consideration* be used against the Japanese, *who should be warned* that this bombardment will be repeated until they surrender" (my italics).†

The passage suggests two extremely interesting thoughts: that as late as September 1944 neither FDR nor Winston Churchill took it *entirely* for granted that the bomb would be used; and that they were thinking in terms of giving the Japanese a warning, though admittedly the language suggests that this warning would be given *after*, not before, first using the atomic weapon.

Finally the President and Churchill added their initials to a promise that "full cooperation between the United States and the British government in developing Tube Alloys for military and commercial purposes should continue after the defeat of Japan unless and until terminated by joint agreement."

The Hyde Park agreement caused a good deal of trouble, and not

*Hewlett & Anderson, *New World*, p. 325.
†*Ibid.*, p. 327.

only because the American copy of it seems to have disappeared. For one thing, Congress was never informed of it. When, after the war, Congress started writing atomic-energy legislation in such a way as to forbid interchange of atomic secrets with foreign powers, there were those in Britain* who believed the U.S. had gone back on an agreement made with the President. Moreover, neither Vannevar Bush nor James Conant knew what had been agreed to at Quebec and Hyde Park. A series of accidents and misunderstandings with damaging consequences ensued.

There was throughout a disagreement between the scientists and the military about how long the so-called "secrets" of the atomic bomb could be kept. Scientists understood that little in the basic physics of atomic fission was not well known to leading scientists in half a dozen countries. The United States, especially as long as the war lasted and Europe was under Nazi rule, had a vast advantage in terms of engineering skills and production facilities, but that advantage would not last long. While the soldiers believed the United States would preserve its nuclear monopoly for twenty years, if not forever, the scientists thought in terms of five years, or even less.

Because he did not think the technology of bomb manufacture could be kept secret for long, Vannevar Bush favored making a virtue of necessity and handing over control of atomic energy to an international agency associated with the Allied nations, that would emerge after the war as some kind of United Nations. The Soviet Union, Bush was well aware, would be a leading member of such an agency. Because he wanted atomic energy and the power to build an atomic bomb put under international control, he opposed exclusive nuclear sharing between the United States and Britain. Logically, an exclusive relationship with Britain was incompatible with internationalism. Politically, it would prejudice relations with the Soviet Union. Psychologically, it would feed Stalin's paranoia. Shut out from a secret Anglo-American partnership, other nations would be driven to join an arms race. And the first other nation with the scientific competence and the resources to build its own bomb would be the Soviet Union.

---

*And in the United States. One of them was Dean Acheson, who wrote in his memoirs, *Present at the Creation*, p. 164, "It was to disturb me for some years to come, for with the knowledge came the belief that a Government, having made an agreement from which it gained immeasurably, was not keeping its word and performing its obligations." See Margaret Gowing, *Independence and Deterrence: Britain and Atomic Energy 1945–52*, Vol. i, *Policy-Making*, pp. 95–123.

On September 19, the day after the Hyde Park agreement, Bush and Conant wrote Roosevelt a letter stressing the need for releasing basic scientific information internationally and at the same time for strengthening U.S. law to control atomic power. At the same time they pointed out the need for a treaty to regulate nuclear relationships with Britain and also with Canada, where substantial research efforts were taking place.

Three days later Bush saw the President at the White House. He did not, unfortunately, see him alone. Admiral Leahy, the President's chief military aide, was also there, and so was Churchill's close personal scientific adviser F. A. Lindemann, and their presence prevented Bush from speaking his mind freely. The President told Bush about Bohr's approach through Felix Frankfurter, and seemed to share Churchill's view that it had been highly improper, if not actually treasonable. Roosevelt declared that there should be complete U.S.–British interchange of nuclear information after victory. Bush didn't agree, but he felt he couldn't say so. He wanted interchange with the Soviet Union, as well as with Britain and Canada, but he felt he couldn't say that either.

The incident was an appalling example of the havoc that could result from Roosevelt's informal, almost chaotic way of running his government. Stimson inveighed against it constantly in his diary. But there was no changing FDR now. For one thing, Bush, the President's own top science adviser, who had little enough of the President's time anyway, was put in a position where he could not give and explain his clear advice on a major issue of postwar policy. That was bad enough. Worse, Roosevelt also asked whether the bombs should actually be used or should be test-exploded, in the U.S. or elsewhere, as a threat to the Japanese. Bush replied that the question ought to be seriously discussed, but a final decision would have to be postponed until a weapon had been successfully tested. You couldn't make a threat until you really had a weapon in your hand. Roosevelt agreed, and the question was put aside. It is hard to avoid a suspicion that, if Bush had been able to talk more frankly without the presence of F. A. Lindemann, who was after all a senior official of a foreign government, he could have thrashed out the issue whether the bomb should be used or merely threatened in advance of a successful test. As it was, Roosevelt died before the test. The all-important question that Roosevelt and Churchill had left open at Hyde Park and on which FDR still seems to have had an open mind, became closed.

Bush was seriously concerned about how his meeting had turned out. He consulted his friend Harvey Bundy, who arranged for him to see Stimson on September 25. Stimson was sympathetic and noted in shocked terms in his diary that the President had been discussing this problem without talking to any of his top American advisers. Stimson's suspicions of Churchill had been inflamed in the previous year by the controversy over OVERLORD, and he had no high opinion of Cherwell, whom he had described in his diary only a few days earlier as "an old fool . . . a pseudo-scientist for whose attainments no one has much respect."*

Stimson's inclination was to be sympathetic to Bush, therefore, not because he had any great liking for a policy of international control of atomic power, but because he was annoyed by the British and did not see why they should take advantage of the vast investment the United States had made in the Manhattan Project for their own strategic or commercial advantage after the war. When Bush explained that he was afraid that Roosevelt was planning postwar cooperation with the United Kingdom and argued that this would be dangerous because it would lead Russia to make an extraordinary secret effort to build a bomb, Stimson seemed to agree, but sounded pessimistic about getting Roosevelt's attention for long enough to make the case.

Something about the way Stimson addressed himself to the problem brought home to Bush that this man was seventy-seven years old. Whatever difficulties the President might have in finding time for some of the most important questions in the world, his Secretary of War, too, had neither the time nor the energy to address himself to the future control of atomic power. So Bush volunteered to draft a statement for Stimson to carry over to the White House.

In the event, he and Conant drafted two papers, a brief case for international control, and a longer argument going into more detail. In both they argued that it was foolish to rely on secrecy. They recommended a demonstration of the bomb's explosive force over either United States or Japanese territory, before it was used in earnest. And they favored a free exchange of scientific and technical information by an agency set up under the aegis of whatever international association of nations came out of the war.

About a month later, to illustrate his point, Bush sent Secretary Stimson a paper suggesting how the international approach was equally

*HLS, *Diary,* September 15.

valid for chemical and biological weaponry, and taking biological weapons as an example of how it might be done. Forty-five years later, effective international control of chemical and bacteriological warfare remains a pious aspiration, largely because of the climate of suspicion that Bush correctly predicted would come into existence in default of effective internationalization of atomic weapons.

Things moved slowly. Not until December 8, 1944, did Bush and Conant confer with Bundy and McCloy. They decided to recommend the appointment of an advisory committee to address all sorts of issues arising out of the impending perfection of the bomb. Chief among these were whether it should be used without a demonstration and whether information should be made internationally available. The next day Bundy put this suggestion to the Secretary, and on December 13 Stimson saw Bush again. Again, Bush was frustrated. Stimson agreed that the time had come to let the State Department in on the secret, but he was not sure that the time was ripe for an advisory committee.

Stimson kept pressing for an appointment to raise all these issues with the President. Finally, at eleven o'clock on Saturday morning, December 30, General Watson telephoned to say that the President would see him in an hour, for half an hour. Even the most powerful figures in the Roosevelt administration got used to the fact that the President was both so genuinely overwhelmed with work and also so chaotic that they had to make the very best of unexpected, inconvenient opportunities to see the great man. Only in these circumstances did the Secretary of War get his chance to press Bush's twin case for an advisory committee and for international control of atomic energy. For whatever reason, however, Stimson did not use his time with FDR for that purpose. Instead, he first brought up the question of the French scientists, what he saw as their divided loyalties, and the annoying fact that the British had honored their prior obligations to them without consulting the United States. This was, to be fair to Stimson, more than a run-of-the-mill security issue or a typical inter-Allied spat. For both Roosevelt and Stimson were convinced that allowing crucial information about the atom bomb to get into the hands of the French government might also mean giving it to the Russians. It is not quite clear why they made this assumption. It may be that they extrapolated from Joliot's Communist Party membership and concluded that he would hand any information in his possession to the Russians, which might or might not have been true. At the same time they seem to have been impressed by the fact that Joliot and several other French physicists were (because of the centralization of French research) nominally French civil servants. Roosevelt and Stimson were in addition deeply suspicious of General de Gaulle. Perhaps they thought the General, not Joliot, would make sure the Russians knew all the French could tell them. Whatever the exact train of reasoning, Roosevelt was fascinated by this issue. He was particularly concerned with whether Churchill knew about the French scientists. Stimson and Groves, who had come with him to see the President, thought not; they blamed Sir John Anderson and his "imperial instinct."

In what was left of his time, Stimson showed the President a report that Groves had prepared for General Marshall on the probable availability of nuclear weapons. Two types of weapon were in production. One was a "gun-type," in which the critical mass of uranium-235 would be assembled by firing one subcritical lump through a gun with a cordite charge into another subcritical quantity; together they would add up to the critical amount, and a chain reaction would follow. One such bomb, Groves estimated, should be ready by August 1, 1945, and a second by the end of the year. Work was also being done on an implosion bomb: shaped segments of plutonium would be "imploded," or blown inward, to produce the critical mass. One comparatively small implosion bomb would be available in late July and others, progressively rising in size, as 1945 went on. Groves proposed that plans should go ahead for an operation against Japan using the gun weapon first and the implosion bomb as soon as it was ready. The President agreed. But Stimson's half-hour was now more than up: when he asked for another appointment, the President told him to come back the next day at noon.

When Stimson arrived, the President was still in bed. The conversation turned to the coming conference with Churchill and Stalin at Yalta. Stimson took up some of his time by repeating his near-obsession about Churchill's intention of dispersing his forces because he wanted to protect the British Empire. Even if Stimson had originally been right, and Churchill wrong, about that, it does not seem to have crossed Stimson's mind that Churchill himself was on the way out; in less than six months Churchill was to be voted out of office, in large measure precisely because most of the British people did not share his desire to protect the British Empire.

The talk turned to Stalin, who was showing increasing signs of intransigence over Poland and other issues. In fact, only the previous day Roosevelt had written to complain about Stalin's recognition of the puppet Polish government the Russians had formed at Lublin, in southeast Poland, rather than the legitimate successor of the prewar democratic government, which had subsisted in London throughout the war.

So the Secretary of War took advantage of the opportunity to pass on the warnings he had received from Ambassador Averell Harriman in Moscow and from the U.S. military attaché there, General John R. Deane, about how difficult they had both found the Russians. He pressed an argument he had been developing about how the Russians should not be let in on the secrets of the atom bomb yet and should not be let in without paying their membership dues:

> I told him of my views as to the future of S-1 in connection with Russia; that I knew they were spying on our work but had not yet gotten any real knowledge of it and that, while I was troubled about the possible effect of keeping from them even now that work, I believed that it was essential not to take them into our confidence until we were sure to get a real *quid pro quo* from our frankness. I said I had no illusions as to the possibility of keeping permanently such a secret but that I did not think it was yet time to share it with the Russians. He said he *thought* he agreed with me. [My italics: vintage FDR!]*

It is pleasant to imagine these two vastly experienced men, one perhaps the most gifted political and strategic genius his country has produced,† the other the epitome of the grave, worldly-wise counselor, sitting and chatting in a relaxed way appropriate to such old

*HLS, *Diary,* December 31, 1944.
†Eric Larrabee, in his interesting book *Commander-in-Chief,* has argued the case for Roosevelt's retaining the reins of strategy in his own hands. See also the remark by the historian Maurice Matloff: "All too often the historian who has struggled through mountains of paper finds the trail disappearing, at the crucial point of decision-making, somewhere in the direction of the White House"; quoted by Forrest C. Pogue in "The Wartime Chiefs of Staff and the President," a paper delivered at the Military History Symposium, *Soldiers and Statesmen,* held at the Air Force Academy, published in Washington, D.C., 1973, pp. 69–70. "The basic outline," concludes Larrabee, after paying due tribute to the role and achievements of Marshall, Admiral King, Stimson and others, "was the President's, and for all the delight he took in playing it by ear, what is most remarkable about his strategies is their consistency." Larrabee, *Commander-in-Chief,* p. 16.

comrades-in-arms in the presidential bedroom about high politics and the future of the world. The fact of the matter is, however, that, in two meetings on consecutive days, Stimson brought up neither of the two points he had encouraged Bush to believe were the purpose of his appointments with the President: creating an advisory committee to plan the circumstances surrounding the use of the bomb, and the question of its future internationalization.

Did Stimson simply forget to bring these issues up? That seems unlikely. Or did he not fully understand what Bush was proposing? While he entertained a vague sympathy for the idea of international control at some future time, for him instinctively national interest came first. The perception that Niels Bohr was attempting to propagate—that atomic weapons represented a quantum jump into a world where it would be simply too dangerous to rely on the ultimate arbitrament of the nation-state—was beyond him. Not that it was an idea his intellect was incapable of grasping: Stimson's brain was still in very good working order, and as Bush had noticed, for a man in his late seventies he was unusually flexible. Still, for the time being, he rejected the idea that was obvious both to a self-styled American Tory like Bush and to Niels Bohr: that this new weapon was too dangerous to be left to the monopoly of a nation-state, so dangerous that unless it were internationalized every nation-state would want to acquire it.

Whatever his precise evaluation of these unfamiliar arguments, the Secretary of War preferred to use his time with the President to air other pet ideas. So an opportunity for the Secretary to talk through whether and how the bomb should be used against Japan with his old friend and Commander in Chief was wasted.

For the next three months, Stimson's mind was preoccupied with other matters. When he turned to S-1, as he did from time to time, it was often to pursue his implacable conviction that at all costs the French must be kept out of the secret. His diary shows this took up a disproportionate share of the limited time he could spare for atomic issues. He spent January 19, 1945, the day before inauguration day, preparing with Groves and Bundy for a meeting with the British on S-1, and noted in his diary, "The main thing that I was insistent on was that there should be no commitment of any kind on the part of the United States to the French." The meeting itself was almost entirely taken up with the row over what answer Sir John Anderson should give to Joliot. As we have seen, Stimson moved swiftly to smooth relations with the British, but also to make sure that the French were not given an inch.

Vannevar Bush was naturally disappointed that Stimson had not gone to bat for him with the President as he had hoped.* But he was a patient and wily operator. On February 15, when he got his day in court with Stimson, he showed him a draft letter to Roosevelt proposing that the Charter of the United Nations, whose founding conference in San Francisco had just been announced from Yalta, should contain a provision for a scientific office to exchange information about technological developments with potential military applications.

Stimson understood very well what Bush was about. Bush, he noted, "hopes in this way to prevent secret plans for secret weapons."† The objective was bound to seem less than self-evident to a man who was approaching the triumphant fruition of a four-year covert project to build the secret weapon of all time. Stimson confined himself to observing that the time was not quite ripe for a general pooling of ideas. He suggested to Bush that it might be wise to start with one sort of scientific research, then, if that worked, broaden the application of the international principle. Bush dusted off his idea for internationalizing information about bacteriological warfare. "Stimson is a very wise man," Bush wrote to his partner Conant, and added significantly, "I only wish he had more of the vigor of youth."

Certainly things continued to move slowly. On one matter, Bush had been belatedly successful in his lobbying. He wanted decisions on a whole range of practical matters. Should the Chicago Metallurgical Lab be kept going? What was the future for the Hanford plutonium factory? What announcement should be made once a bomb had been successfully tested? Behind these bureaucratic questions there lurked great strategic ones. Did the United States mean to go on making atomic bombs after the war? Did it mean to keep the methods of doing so secret? Under what authority would atomic policy be set in the United States? Would atomic power be retained as a secret asset of the United States, or shared with potential rivals and enemies?

*Letter from Vannevar Bush to James B. Conant, January 2, 1945, cited by Hewlett and Anderson, *New World*, p. 335. Drs. Hewlett and Anderson discovered a "sealed safe containing the correspondence of Vannevar Bush and James B. Conant from 1940 to 1945," on which their first volume of the official *History of the United States Atomic Energy Commission: The New World 1939–46* is largely based. These papers are held by the Atomic Energy Commission at its Germantown, Maryland, headquarters.
†HLS, *Diary*, February 15, 1945.

Patiently, Bush had tried through Bundy to get Stimson to commit himself, or—if he did not want to take these decisions himself—to set up a committee that would advise the Secretary of War: a committee, no doubt, on which Vannevar Bush would be not only represented but influential. On February 13 Bush learned from Bundy that the Secretary had accepted the idea of a committee in principle, though he had done nothing to make it happen. Stimson was not only old, tired, and overworked, but also involved in a strategic battle about manpower. He thought it complacent of the United States to stop recruiting and training new levies, and he feared that the army did not have a big enough strategic reserve. It turned out that he was right.

On December 16, 1944, General Sir Bernard Montgomery, commanding the Twenty-first Army Group in Belgium, told his troops that "the enemy . . . cannot stage major offensive operations." General Omar N. Bradley, commanding the Twelfth Army Group, agreed. That same day, however, spearheaded by assault troops riding U.S.-made jeeps and dressed in U.S. army uniforms, the German Army Group B, under Hitler's young, Eastern Front–hardened generals like Walther Model, Hasso von Manteuffel and Sepp Dietrich, launched the Reich's last forlorn gamble. On the opening day the U.S. army sustained what the official history describes as "the most serious reverse suffered by American arms" in Europe in World War II.* Fighting ferociously in fog and snow, the German troops, said their Commander-in-Chief, Field Marshal von Rundstedt, "really believed victory was possible, unlike the higher commanders, who knew the facts"† about how outnumbered they were and how short of fuel, ammunition and reserves. In spite of everything, they nearly broke through.

Colonel Stimson was enough of a soldier to know that the German offensive of 1944 was no insignificant blip on the Allied progress toward victory. With the armies still locked in the forest on the Belgian-German frontier, and with George Marshall in the office next to his

---

*H. M. Cole, *The European Theater of Operations: The Lorraine Campaign,* Washington, D.C., U.S. Department of the Army, Historical Division, 1950, quoted in B. H. Liddell Hart, *History of the Second World War,* p. 653.

†*Ibid.* p. 647. After the war, Captain Liddell Hart interviewed Field Marshal von Rundstedt and a number of other captured German generals.

hard at work planning the forces that would be needed for a successful invasion of Japan, Stimson went to the Senate Military Affairs Committee on February 6 and testified on behalf of the Bailey-May limited service bill. "We are *now* at the *very crisis* of the war," he wrote in his notes.*

Although by Christmas the German offensive had been held, it was not until March 7, 1945, that the tanks of the U.S. Third Army, under Colonel Stimson's friend and favorite general George S. Patton, broke through in the Eifel, the extension in Germany of the rolling, wooded hills of the Ardennes, and began to sweep unimpeded toward the Rhine.

On February 7 Stimson had his first "long chat" with Marshall about plans for the coming campaign against Japan. It was "a new problem" for him, but one to which he had no difficulty in applying his strategic philosophy of concentration. The United States should no more be diverted by Chiang Kai-shek into fighting on the Chinese mainland than it should be drawn by Winston Churchill into Mediterranean adventures. Colonel Stimson favored a carefully prepared invasion of the Japanese home islands in overwhelming force, and the staff eventually settled on November 1 as D-Day for this last great campaign of the war.

For all these reasons it was not until the first week in March that Stimson gave his full attention to the problems of the atomic bomb. On March 8, indeed, he commented in his diary, "This matter is now taking up a good deal of my time and even then I am not doing it justice. It is approaching the ripening time and matters are getting very interesting and serious."

He was getting old, and so was Mabel. On March 9 she "toppled over unconscious at her end of the table and gave me the fright of my life." It turned out there was nothing to be alarmed about: Mrs. Stimson had been suffering from no more than a heavy cold. Still, it was an intimation of mortality, like the death of Stimson's beloved sister Candace and his partner and friend Bronson Winthrop, both of whom died in the first six months of 1944. On March 4, the Colonel and Mrs. Stimson had gone for a walk together from Woodley around Washington Cathedral, a gentle uphill climb of a mile or so, then a gentle mile back downhill. The old gentleman found "the long pull

*HLS, *Diary,* February 6, 1945.

up the hill around the cathedral harder than ever before," and wrote sadly in his diary: "I am overweight and overage."

Next day Harvey Bundy came in, and they had "a most thorough and searching talk" about S-1:

> We are up against some very big decisions. The time is approaching when we can no longer avoid them, and when events may force us into the public on the subject. Our thoughts went right down to the bottom of human nature, morals and government, and it is by far the most searching and important thing that I have had to do since I have been here in the office of Secretary of War because it touches matters which are deeper even than the principles of present government.*

According to Bundy, their talk swept over a wide range of issues raised by the existence of a bomb capable of destroying a city and its whole population. Those issues specifically included both domestic and international control. Stimson had now fastened on the moral issues involved. How fine it would be, he mused aloud, if the international control agency could be run by someone like Phillips Brooks,† who could use the fear of the bomb to touch men's souls and bring about a spiritual revival on Christian principles. More pessimistically, the old warrior reflected on the evil emotions unleashed by war and on how unprepared the world was to cope with this new and terrible power. At the end of this conversation, when Bundy had gone, Stimson walked through into General Marshall's office and although the chief of staff was about ready to go home, engaged him, too, in these philosophical and strategic speculations.

On March 15 Stimson went to the White House, after a morning spent in careful preparation, for what was to be his last talk with FDR about S-1. Now he was passing on the message Vannevar Bush had been dinning into him for months:

> I outlined to him the future of it and when it was ready. I went over with him the two schools of thought that exist in respect of future control after the war . . . one of them being the secret closed-in control of the project by those who control it now, and the other being international control based upon freedom

*Diary, March 5, 1945.
†1835–93. Episcopal clergyman and bishop of Massachusetts 1891–93. Famous preacher.

both of science and of access. I told him those things must be
settled before the first projectile is used and that he must be
ready with a statement to come out to the people on it just as
soon as that is done. He agreed to that.*

The talk, the Colonel noted, was "on the whole . . . successful."
Perhaps. But it still left questions of the profoundest importance un-
resolved. In the six months since Hyde Park, in fact, nothing had been
decided except the most important thing of all. At Hyde Park, Winston Churchill and Franklin Roosevelt had left it that the bomb might
perhaps be used, "after mature consideration," on the people of Japan. As March gave way to April and the countdown at Los Alamos
continued ticking, there had been some talk, some thought, but nothing that could seriously be dignified as structured consideration, and
certainly no clear decision whether or how an atomic bomb would be
used.

Early in April Secretary Stimson was scheduled to visit the vast
complex of plants that the Army Corps of Engineers had built in the
slanting Appalachian valleys around Clinton, Tennessee. For one reason and another the trip had been postponed, so it was not until April
10 that he set out with a small party to visit the whole cluster of
installations. He was enthusiastic about what he saw. "Spent a long
afternoon," he wrote in his diary, "going over the most wonderful
and unique operation that probably has ever existed anywhere in the
world. . . . Although every prophesy thus far has been fulfilled by the
development and we can see that success is 99% assured, yet only by
the first actual war trial of the weapon can the actual certainty be
fixed."
    When he got back to Washington he found a message from the
President's secretary, Grace Tully, summoning him to the White House
as soon as possible. He had an immediate foreboding of the reason,
and "my fears were well-founded. Word had just come of the death
of the President at Warm Springs from a cerebral haemorrhage."† Roosevelt had collapsed while he was having his portrait painted by the
society painter "Mopsy" Shoumatoff: Lucy Mercer Rutherfurd, the

*Diary, March 15, 1945.
†Diary, April 12, 1945.

woman Roosevelt had wanted to marry so long before, was with him when he died.*

Roosevelt's death transformed the nature of Stimson's responsibility for the atomic bomb. As the makers of the 1964 *NBC White Paper* "The Decision to Drop the Bomb" put it, "Only Stimson was informed on all the facets of the atomic project: the progress of its development, the plans to use the bomb, the arguments over how to use it. . . . Only Stimson was personally and professionally involved in all its aspects: political, scientific, fiscal, military and moral."†

The new President knew next to nothing about the Manhattan Project. As we have seen, when in the course of his investigation into the war effort he came near the subject, Senator Truman had been happy to accept Secretary Stimson's word that the matter was something he had neither the need nor the right to inquire into. Now, on his first day in office, it was from Stimson that he first learned the nature of this vast secret enterprise.

It had been from Mrs. Roosevelt that Harry S. Truman had learned that he was President of the United States, at about 5:25 P.M. on April 12, 1945. She put her arm around his shoulders to break the shock. Within twenty minutes or so the Chief Justice arrived to swear him in. At nine minutes past seven, the ceremony was performed. President Truman spoke briefly to the Cabinet, assuring its members that he intended to carry on both President Roosevelt's domestic and his international policies for the time being. The Cabinet members rose and quietly left the room, all except for Secretary Stimson, who asked to speak to the President about "an urgent matter." He said he wanted Truman to know about an immense project for developing a new explosive of "almost unbelievable destructive power." But at that stage he said little more. Truman was puzzled, for this was the first he had heard about the bare existence of the bomb project. He gleaned a little more from a talk to James Byrnes‡ the next day and was subsequently given a scientific briefing by Bush. But it was not until April 25 that Stimson briefed the President in detail.

That first day, Friday, April 13, Stimson met Truman again at the

---

*Ted Morgan, *FDR*, p. 763.
†Giovanitti and Freed, *The Decision to Drop the Bomb*, p. 24.
‡Byrnes was a former Senator from South Carolina, Supreme Court Justice, and potential vice-presidential candidate in 1944. An old friend as well as rival of Truman's, Byrnes became Secretary of State on June 30, 1945.

White House together with General Marshall, Admirals King and Leahy and James V. Forrestal, the new Secretary of the Navy. The judgment Stimson recorded was friendly but patronizing:

> He made the impression of a man who is willing and able to learn and to do his best but who was necessarily laboring with the terrific handicap of coming into such an office where the threads of information were so multitudinous that only long previous familiarity could allow him to control them. On the whole my impression was favorable although, as General Marshall said in the car coming back with me, "We shall not know what he is really like until the pressure begins to be felt."*

In the circumstances, it was going to fall to the man who had "long previous familiarity" to take the decisions about S-1 that could not now be much longer delayed. So on April 23 the Secretary of War suggested to the President that they talk; he then spent the rest of the day rereading a memorandum from General Groves on S-1 and composing, with the help of Harvey Bundy, an "analytical picture" of his own "of what the prospects of S-1 are and the problems which it presents to this country."

At noon on April 25 Stimson went to the White House, where he met General Groves, who had been spirited in through the underground passage from the Executive Office Building so as not to give any clue to the lurking press as to the subject of the meeting. Groves gave the President an account of the manufacturing operation, but the main function of the meeting was to discuss Stimson's memo.

Within four months, Stimson began, "we shall in all probability have completed the most terrible weapon ever known in human history, one bomb of which could destroy a whole city." Although development had been shared with the United Kingdom, "the U.S. is at present in the position of controlling the resources with which to construct and use it and no other nation could be in this position for some years." On the other hand, he went on, it was practically certain that the United States would not maintain its monopoly of the bomb indefinitely. Much of the process of producing the weapon was widely known among scientists, and in time it was "extremely probable" that smaller nations would be able to build a bomb and

*HLS, *Diary,* April 13, 1945.

perhaps one day use it "suddenly and effectively with devastating power."

Stimson therefore turned to the problem of international control. In its present state of moral, as contrasted with technical, development, the world would be at the mercy of such a weapon. It would be unrealistic even to think of a world peace organization without considering the power of the new weapon, and the question of sharing its secrets with other nations was "a primary question of our foreign relations." If the problem could be solved, "the peace of the world and our civilization can be saved."*

These were the fruits of Stimson's long conversations with Bundy, Bush, Groves and Marshall and of his own private communings. He had thought deeply about the implications of the bomb for international relations. He had not seriously addressed the question whether or not the bomb should be used. Indeed, it is clear that the two former World War I artillery officers both took it for granted that if the bomb were available before the end of the war, then it would be used. They were not alone. The introspective, ethically sensitive Robert Oppenheimer said the same long afterward: "The decision was implicit in the project. I don't know whether it could have been stopped."† Although in a later magazine article about the bomb, Stimson implied that he had set up what became known as the Interim Committee to advise, among other things, on whether the bomb should be dropped on Japan or not, this in fact is not what he wanted its advice on; the issue was listed neither in the description he gave to President Truman of his purpose in appointing the committee Bush had pushed for, nor in the formal letters of appointment to it he wrote as Secretary, nor in his interventions defining the committee's task at the two meetings where he was in the chair, on May 9 and May 31.

What concerned Stimson was not whether but how the bomb should be dropped, and how this action should be presented to the world. Now, at long last, Stimson approved the names of the committee members who were to advise him on all these matters. On May 2 he pleased the President by suggesting the name of Jimmy Byrnes—whom everyone knew Truman planned to appoint as his Secretary of State in the near future—as the President's personal representative on the Interim Committee. On May 8, after a meeting of the Committee

---

*HLS, *Diary*, April 25, text at p. 70.
†Giovanitti and Freed, *op. cit.*, p. 328.

of Three, he "shooed everyone out" except Secretary of the Navy Forrestal and Acting Secretary of State Joseph C. Grew, and told them about the Interim Committee. Will Clayton of State was already a member, and Stimson asked Forrestal if he would send Ralph Bard, his Under Secretary, to represent him. So the members were: Henry Stimson; George L. Harrison; James F. Byrnes; Ralph Bard, Under Secretary of the Navy; William L. Clayton, Assistant Secretary of State; Dr. Vannevar Bush, director of the Office of Scientific Research and Development; Dr. Karl T. Compton, OSRD and president of M.I.T.; Dr. James B. Conant, chairman of the National Defense Research Committee and president of Harvard University.

The atomic bomb had been developed as a weapon largely because it was feared that Germany would soon possess one. The fear that thought inspired was only increased by everything that was learned about the ruthlessness of German behavior. The first conference of the Interim Committee, though, as we have seen, took place on the day after Nazi Germany surrendered. If the bomb was to be used now, it would have to be used against the Japanese.

The decisive meeting took place three weeks later, on May 31. The committee gathered in the Pentagon at ten in the morning. Present, in addition to the members, were Generals Marshall and Groves; two Stimson special assistants, Harvey Bundy and Arthur W. Page (an old friend hired by Stimson—as Page put it later—to listen to him talk about the atom*); and the four members of a Scientific Advisory Panel, Ernest O. Lawrence, Enrico Fermi, Arthur Compton and Robert Oppenheimer.

Stimson opened the meeting by defining what he wanted the committee and the four scientists to discuss.† He expressed the hope that the project would not be considered "simply in terms of military weapons, but as a new relationship of man to the universe." He went further. "The project might even mean the doom of civilization or it might mean the perfection of civilization; that it might be a Frankenstein‡ which would eat us up or it might be a project by which the

---

*Morison, *Turmoil and Tradition,* p. 618.
†My account of the Interim Committee's meeting is derived from the minutes published in Barton J. Bernstein, *The Atomic Bomb: The Crucial Issues,* and previously declassified in "Notes of the Interim Committee Meeting . . . 31 May 1945," in the Manhattan Engineering District Papers, National Archives, Washington, D.C.; the official history of the Atomic Energy Commission, vol. i, *New World,* by Hewlett and Anderson, pp. 356–61; HLS, *Diary,* May 31; Rhodes, *Making of the Atomic Bomb,* pp. 642–51; James F. Byrnes, *Speaking Frankly,* p. 261.
‡*Sic:* Stimson was making an error which many others have made, before and since. Franken-

peace of the world might be helped in becoming more secure." He
suggested that he hoped to have five areas discussed during the course
of the meeting: future military weapons; future international competition; future research; future control; future developments, "particularly non-military."*

The scientists then gave the committee a technical briefing.
Compton guessed it would take any competitor six years to catch up
with the United States. Conant said the United States could build a
thermonuclear, or "super," bomb in three years. Lawrence spoke up
for an expanded program to make sure the United States stayed ahead.
Oppenheimer, backed by Fermi and Compton, argued for a broader
program of fundamental research. One after another the scientists came
out for internationalizing atomic research under international inspection. The secrets of nature, they knew, could not be hidden, and
scientists would have an interest in making international inspection
work. The laymen, especially General Marshall, were not so sure about
that.

At this point, Colonel Stimson had to excuse himself for a private
and official duty: he was due at the White House with Mabel to award
a posthumous Medal of Merit to his friend and fellow-Republican in
the Roosevelt administration, Frank Knox, who had died a year earlier.

While he was away the talk turned to the subject of how to deal
with the Soviet Union about atomic energy. General Marshall gave it
as his opinion that many of the charges made against the Soviet Union
were unfounded. What seemed like an uncooperative attitude was really the result of the Soviet obsession with security. He believed that
a combination of like-minded powers could force the Russians to behave. Certainly there was no danger of their disclosing atomic information to the Japanese. In fact, Marshall asked, why not invite two
Russian observers to witness the forthcoming atomic test?

Now the President's personal representative made a decisive intervention. Jimmy Byrnes had come up the hard way, starting as a
stenographer in South Carolina before becoming lawyer, congressman,
senator, Supreme Court justice and "assistant president." In his experience of life, you got nothing for nothing, and you certainly did
not do any favors to Communists unless you had lost all your wits. If
the United States gave information to the Russians, said Byrnes with

stein, in Mary Wollstonecraft Shelley's 1818 novel, is, of course, the name of the inventor, not
the monster.
*HLS, *Diary,* May 31, 1945.

all the confidence of his experience and all the authority of a man who
was known to be the future Secretary of State, he feared that Stalin
would ask to be brought into the partnership. The existing cooperation with Britain made this all the more likely. Bush pointed out that
even the British did not have blueprints for the bomb-production
plants. Byrnes swept him aside. He expressed the view, which according to the minutes was "generally agreed by all those present" that
the best plan would be to push ahead as fast as possible with both
production and research to make sure the United States stayed ahead,
and to share nothing with the Russians, while doing whatever was
possible to improve political relations with them in other ways.

The Secretary of War returned to the discussion just before lunch.
"I found them still in the course of the argument—still hard at work
at it and I plunged in and at one-twenty we went up to luncheon and
continued the talk up there so I didn't get away until three-thirty—a
pretty full day."* The old gentleman was enjoying himself. The scientists were a fine bunch of Americans—Stimson was particularly impressed by Oppenheimer, even if he was the only one without a Nobel
Prize; and he hoped he and Marshall had come across as statesmen,
not as mere military men hell-bent on winning the war.

Still, at lunch Byrnes asked Lawrence about an idea he had thrown
out in the course of the morning: that it might be possible to give the
Japanese an impressive but harmless demonstration of the bomb's
power before using it in a way that would cause heavy casualties. For
perhaps ten minutes at lunch this idea was discussed, but the discussion occurred while the committee members were sitting at two separate tables in the Pentagon dining room, Byrnes at the head of one,
Stimson at the other.

Something of the dynamics of like-mindedness, familiar to anyone
who has attended a conference or seminar, especially where secret material is under discussion, seems to have pervaded this unofficial chat.
Oppenheimer remembered afterward with admiration that Stimson had
discoursed on the "appalling lack of conscience and compassion that
the war had brought about [and] the complacency, the indifference,
and the silence with which we greeted the mass bombings in Europe
and, above all, in Japan," an ironic remark in view of the nature of
the decision that was being taken, and of the way it was being taken.

The response to Byrnes's question about a relatively nonlethal

*Diary, May 31, 1945.

demonstration was unenthusiastic. One speaker after another presented objections. Would the Japanese government be influenced by "an enormous nuclear firecracker detonated at a great height doing little damage?" asked Oppenheimer, and answered himself, "Your answer is as good as mine. I don't know." Two years later Byrnes recalled that the lunching committee members

> feared that, if the Japanese were told that the bomb would be used on a given locality, they might bring our boys who were prisoners of war to that area. Also, the experts had warned us that the static test which was to take place in New Mexico, even if successful, would not be conclusive proof that a bomb would explode when dropped from an airplane. If we were to warn the Japanese of the new highly destructive weapon in the hope of impressing them and the bomb then failed to explode, certainly we would have given aid and comfort to the Japanese militarists.*

Someone else questioned whether the bomb would do any more damage than General LeMay's recent fire raids. That irritated Oppenheimer, who reminded the committee that the bomb, having a fireball that they estimated would rise twenty thousand feet into the sky with a blinding light, not only would be visually terrifying, but would produce neutron radiation for a radius of at least two-thirds of a mile. Later that afternoon Oppenheimer reported a Los Alamos estimate that the bomb would kill some twenty thousand people. Although both the radius of radiation effects and the number of likely casualties were serious underestimates, the Interim Committee knew well enough what was at stake.

It becomes evident, indeed, that these men were determined to shoot down the case for a nonlethal demonstration of the bomb. Each argument produced against such a trial could in turn be easily demolished. Prisoners of war? But how would the Japanese know where to take them? The danger of a fizzle? But that would apply at least as much to an attack on a city. And so on. The idea that the bomb was there to be used had gathered so much momentum that it was not questioned, however serious the moral compunction with which the alternative was discussed.

In the closing stages of the discussion, according to one partici-

*James F. Byrnes, *Speaking Frankly,* p. 261.

pant, Stimson brought up his insistence that the ancient Japanese city of Kyoto, which he and Mabel had visited with such pleasure in 1926 and 1929, must not be bombed. He proclaimed, too, that "the objective was military damage . . . not civilian lives."* Yet when he came to sum up what he took to be the sense of the discussion, here is how the minutes record what he said:

> The Secretary expressed the conclusion, on which there was general agreement, that we could not give the Japanese any warning; that we could not concentrate on a civilian area; but that we should seek to make a profound psychological impression on as many of the inhabitants as possible. At the suggestion of Dr. Conant the Secretary agreed that the most desirable target would be a vital war plant employing a large number of workers and closely surrounded by workers' houses.†

In the brief interval before they were incinerated, or the longer and more painful interval before they died of radiation sickness, such a course of action could certainly be relied on to produce a very profound psychological impression.

So that was it. Someone suggested several atomic strikes at once. Oppenheimer thought this would be "feasible," but Groves did not, for severely practical reasons: "(1) We would lose the advantage of gaining additional knowledge concerning the weapon at each successive bombing; (2) such a program would require a rush job on the part of those assembling the bombs and might, therefore, be ineffective; (3) the effect would not be sufficiently distinct from our regular Air Force bombings."‡

At half past three Secretary Stimson went home, well satisfied with the day's work. The Interim Committee stayed on to discuss the problems of the Chicago group, where the employees at the Metallurgical and Argonne labs now faced unemployment and where the scientists were discontented.

The next day's meeting of the Interim Committee, this time with four industrialists instead of the four scientists, was something of an anticlimax. The main question explored was: How long would it take other countries to catch up? The industrialists assumed the Secretary

*Arthur H. Compton, *Atomic Quest*, p. 237.
†Barton J. Bernstein (ed.), *The Atomic Bomb: The Crucial Issues*, p. 24.
‡*Ibid.*, p. 25.

of War meant the Soviet Union. Their replies varied, but they came closer to the three- to four-year lag estimated by Bush and Conant than to the twenty years' lead that Groves thought the United States possessed. The point was made that if the Russians could get hold of German scientists and engineers, their task might be speeded up considerably.

Two side issues suggest the contradictions in Stimson's attitude to the moral questions raised by the atomic bomb. On May 30, General Groves had been in the Secretary of War's office in the Pentagon when Stimson suddenly asked whether the targets had been chosen yet. Groves said he hoped to take the list over to General Marshall in the morning. Stimson demanded to see it and would take no evasion. ''I have all day and I know how fast your office works. Here's a phone on this desk. You pick it up and you call your office and have them bring that report over.''*

Of course Groves, like any good soldier, was terrified of going outside the chain of command and letting the Secretary see the report before the chief of staff did. Stimson cut him off sharply. ''This is one time I'm going to be the final deciding authority. Nobody's going to tell me what to do on this. On this matter I'm to be the kingpin and you might just as well get that report over here.''

While they waited for the report Stimson asked which targets Groves was planning to bomb. Groves said Kyoto was the first choice.

''I don't want Kyoto bombed,'' said Stimson, and when the report arrived he walked to the door and summoned General Marshall and repeated: ''I don't like it. I don't like the use of Kyoto.''

After the war there were reports that Kyoto, the ancient capital of Japan and a city with a religious and artistic heritage for the Japanese comparable to those of Athens or Rome for Western civilization, had been saved by the intervention of Langdon Warner, an expert in oriental art at the Fogg Museum at Harvard University, who had spent many years in Japan. Warner's wife was a Roosevelt, and it was speculated that he had somehow used this connection to save Kyoto. Warner's family, however, denied this, and a more curious explanation eventually surfaced. What persuaded the Secretary to dig in to spare Kyoto was the chance visit of a cousin, Henry Loomis, who had dined with the Stimsons at Woodley only a few months before. Young

---

*Giovanitti and Freed, *The Decision to Drop the Bomb,* pp. 40–41. The material comes from an interview tape-recorded with General Groves in 1964.

Loomis had taken courses at Harvard on Chinese and Japanese history and culture with John K. Fairbank and Edwin O. Reischauer. It was his innocent enthusiasm for the glories of Japanese art in general and of Kyoto in particular that stuck in the Secretary of War's mind.*

On June 1, another dimension of the confusion in the old gentleman's mind surfaced. "I had in General [H. H.] Arnold and told him . . . of my promise from Lovett that there would be only precision bombing in Japan and that the press yesterday had indicated a bombing of Tokyo that was very far from that." Arnold squirmed and said it was hard to destroy Japan's war output without hitting more civilians than would be the case in Europe. With the examples of Hamburg and Dresden in mind, the comparison was not particularly persuasive. But in truth Stimson's position was strangely inconsistent for such a normally rational man. Here he was reprimanding the commander of his air force for straying from a policy of precision bombing that had in fact been abandoned long before. As far back as October 1943 intelligence reports by the Army Air Corps under his command concluded that incendiary raids would be more effective against Japanese cities; the largely spurious justification was advanced that Japanese manufacturing was dispersed in the workers' homes. In March, General LeMay, under orders to launch "maximum effort incendiary strikes," had destroyed 267,000 buildings in Tokyo, killing 83,000 people, and had also fire-bombed Osaka, Nagoya and Kobe. In May, General Groves's target committee had been officially informed by a colonel from the Twentieth Air Force that it was "systematically bombing out the following cities with the prime purpose in mind of not leaving one stone lying on another: Tokyo, Yokohama, Nagoya, Osaka, Kyoto, Kobe, Yawata, and Nagasaki."†

That scarcely sounds like precision bombing. In fact the irony is

---

*See Melville B. Millar, unpublished memorandum, "How Kyoto Was Saved," in the Yale University library archives. The identity of the Stimsons' dinner guest is given in a curious paper, written in both English and Japanese, and preserved in the Library of Congress, by Otis Gray, long the head of the Amherst House in Kyoto: *Notes on Mr. Stimson's Pet City: The Sparing of Kyoto, 1945.* Gray established that "Mr. and Mrs. H. L. Stimson" paid Y30 (then worth $15) to occupy Room 18 in the Mikayo Hotel on October 2 and returned on October 30 through November 4, during which they were registered in Room 56, while Room 57 was occupied by "Miss Stimson," presumably a traveling companion. Apparently when Loomis came to dinner and the subject of Kyoto came up, Colonel Stimson went to his bookshelves and produced a book of photographs of Kyoto, perhaps acquired on the spot in either 1926 or 1929.

†Rhodes, *Making of the Atomic Bomb,* pp. 626–27, quoting Manhattan Engineer District records, 5D; Giovanitti and Freed, *The Decision to Drop the Bomb,* pp. 34–36.

that cities had to be protected from General LeMay's fire-bombing only to be left sufficiently undamaged to demonstrate the potential of atomic weapons. And yet here was Stimson—in the same breath, so to speak—with which he deplored departures from a precision-bombing policy that had long been a pious memory, agreeing with Conant's proposal that the ideal target for an atomic bomb would be "a vital war plant . . . closely surrounded with workers' houses."

If Stimson was morally perplexed and intellectually confused, Jimmy Byrnes had no such qualms. At the very moment when the Secretary of War was ineffectually reprimanding Arnold for the fire raids, the future Secretary of State was moving ahead. "Mr. Byrnes recommended," say the minutes of the June 1 Interim Committee meeting, "and the Committee agreed, that the Secretary of War should be advised that . . . the present view of the Committee was that the bomb should be used against Japan as soon as possible; that it be used on a war plant surrounded by workers' homes; and that it be used without prior warning."* Byrnes saw the President immediately. Truman said "with reluctance he could think of no alternative." It was five days before Stimson followed, noting that Byrnes seemed pleased with what he had done.

That essentially was an end of it. But the scientists were troubled. James Franck, Leo Szilard and Niels Bohr were among those who attempted during the spring of 1945 to persuade policy-makers, including Byrnes (in Szilard's case), Henry A. Wallace† (in Franck's) and Stimson (in the case of Bohr) to think twice before they actually used the bomb on a human population. In early July a poll of 150 scientists at the Metallurgical Lab in Chicago found that only 15 per cent favored using atomic bombs in whatever way was most likely to bring about Japanese surrender; 46 per cent wanted a military demonstration over

---

*Minutes in Rhodes, *Making of the Atomic Bomb*, p. 650. To summarize for the sake of clarity, the Interim Committee met with the Scientific Advisory Panel on May 31. The minutes record that Stimson "expressed the conclusion, on which there was general agreement, that we could not give the Japanese any warning; that we could not concentrate on a civilian area; but that we should seek to make a profound impression on as many of the inhabitants as possible. At the suggestion of Dr. Conant the Secretary [Stimson] agreed that the most desirable target would be a vital war plant employing a large number of workers and closely surrounded by workers' houses." The next day, June 1, when the Interim Committee met the industrialists' panel, Stimson was absent, and it was Byrnes's summary that was sent to the President, in the words recorded by the Committee's secretary, Gordon Arneson, and quoted above.

†Wallace, former Secretary of Agriculture and Vice President, 1941–45, was at this time Secretary of Commerce.

Japan; 26 per cent voted for a demonstration before Japanese observers in the United States as a warning; 11 per cent wanted a warning, but no use; 2 per cent thought the whole project should be returned to the secrecy in which it had been born.

On June 18 Harvey Bundy sent his chief a note asking if he wanted to see Bohr. In firm letters the Secretary minuted simply: "No."

The truth is that by June, after the crucial Interim Committee meeting, Stimson felt that the question of whether the bomb would be used had been decided. He was focusing instead on two other issues: the deteriorating relationship with the Soviet Union, which must come to a head at the summit meeting already planned; and how best to bring the war against Japan to a close, if possible without incurring the casualties, estimated at half a million men,* that would be the cost of an opposed invasion. The atomic bomb played a part in his calculations, but it was only one factor out of many.

When Stimson saw Truman on June 6 to transmit the Interim Committee's recommendations, he expressed concern at the prospect of the President's meeting Stalin before he could know whether the bomb worked or not. Truman had thought of that, and he reassured his Secretary of War that the meeting had been put back to July 15 "on purpose to give us more time." Stimson pointed out that even that might not be time enough, but the timetable lay in the lap of the gods, and in the hands of Oppenheimer's racing technicians at Los Alamos.

The conundrum of Japanese surrender was more complex. By June, the War Department was committed to an invasion plan, timed to start with a landing on Kyushu on November 1, 1945. The Army Air Corps was raining fire on Japan's cities, and the Navy would soon be in a position to add its share of death from carrier-borne aircraft

---

*Some recent scholars have cast doubt on the magnitude of these casualty estimates. In an article in the London weekly *The Listener,* for example, published on August 10, 1989, after this chapter was written, Gar Alperovitz cites the research and conclusions of the Stanford historian Barton J. Bernstein, who, he says, "has demonstrated that the Joint War Plans committee . . . concluded that about 40,000 Americans would die if an assault were launched on both the island of Kyushu and, thereafter the main Japanese home island. . . . On 18 June 1945, U.S. Army Chief of Staff General Marshall informed President Truman that casualties for the Kyushu operation were not expected significantly to exceed 31,000 (including dead, wounded and missing)." However, the Japanese army still had 5 million men under arms, 2 million of them in the home islands, and the ferocity of the Japanese defense elsewhere, for example at Iwo Jima, undoubtedly impressed Stimson and others with the scale of the casualties the army he had helped to raise must expect if the atomic bomb were not used.

and coastal shelling. Even so, there were doubts whether the Japanese would surrender. The military had been impressed by the fanatical stubbornness with which small Japanese units and even individual soldiers, brainwashed about the horrible fate the Americans would deal them if they surrendered but also obsessed with the code of *bushido* honor, had allowed themselves to be winkled out with flamethrowers rather than raise their hands in surrender. Although the Army's estimate for casualties in the Kyushu landing was only 31,000, both Stimson and other American policy-makers, including both President Truman and Byrnes, were thinking ahead to the American casualties of the march to Tokyo, which—rightly or wrongly—they estimated variously at 500,000 to one million.

On the other hand, the Japanese government had been putting out feelers about surrender since April at least. If he knew that, however, Stimson discounted the sincerity of the Japanese interest in peace. Only three factors might prevent a bloody ground campaign, he believed: the atomic bomb; a Russian declaration of war; and a proclamation that the policy of unconditional surrender would be modified to the extent of allowing the Japanese to keep their Emperor, or at least their imperial dynasty.

With Stettinius tied up in San Francisco, the acting Secretary of State was no less than Joe Grew, the aristocratic Bostonian who had been ambassador in Tokyo for ten years.*

For a long time, Grew later wrote Stimson in 1947, "I had held the belief, based on my intimate experience with Japanese thinking and psychology over an extended period, that the surrender of the Japanese would be highly unlikely, regardless of military defeat, in the absence of a public undertaking by the President that surrender would not mean the elimination of the present dynasty if the Japanese people desired its retention." Later, though not at the time, Grew was frank about his desire to avoid dropping the atomic bomb, both because, while angrily critical of Japanese militarism, he had great affection for the Japanese people and because he feared that dropping the bomb would drive Japan into the Soviet camp.

On May 28, Grew gave President Truman a memorandum to this effect. Truman said he agreed with it, but asked Grew to check with

*For his role in the Japanese surrender, see Joseph C. Grew, *Turbulent Era*, vol. ii, pp. 1421–42; letter from Joseph C. Grew to Henry L. Stimson, Grew Papers, Houghton Library, Harvard University, published in Bernstein, *The Atomic Bomb: The Critical Issues*, pp. 30–32.

Stimson. The next day Grew met at the Pentagon with Stimson, General Marshall, John McCloy and a fair-sized crowd of other people—including Roosevelt's former speechwriter Judge Sam Rosenman; the former broadcaster Elmer Davis, director of the Office of War Information; and another State Department representative—several of whom were not in the know about S-1. Stimson knew that to discuss it was impossible under these circumstances, and the subject was dropped. At the Potsdam Conference, S-1 was to be raised again, but then it was too late. And even if there had been the faintest hope that allowing the Japanese to keep their Emperor might still have persuaded them to surrender, that was dissipated by the foolish response of Prime Minister Suzuki Kantaro. Although he had been, in Grew's words, "surrender-minded" even before May, he apparently did not regard the language used in the United States proclamation from Potsdam as a clear enough guarantee about the future of the dynasty, and he therefore rejected it.

If the carrot proved ineffective in persuading the Japanese to surrender, what of the stick? Would the news that the Soviet Union was entering the war against them have been a last straw that broke the back of Japanese resistance? Revisionist historians* have argued that President Truman's (and Stimson's) motive for dropping the atomic bomb was the need at all costs to defeat Japan without Soviet help, in order to forestall Stalin's inevitable demand for a share of power in the Far East comparable to the share in Eastern Europe that he had demanded at Yalta and helped himself to thereafter. But the imputation is too crude. It is true that, though until April 1945 the Americans wanted Soviet help against Japan, once they could count on the atomic bomb they wanted to keep Stalin from coming in at the last minute and demanding more than a latecomer's share of the political spoils.† But Stimson saw the puzzle not as a matter of using a Soviet declaration of war against Japan or an American proclamation of clemency for the Emperor to head off the need to drop an atomic bomb, but the other way around: the atomic bomb itself would be dropped as a warning of American resolution and a portent of the utter destruction the Japanese could expect if they did not surrender before the final assault was launched.

*For example, Gar Alperovitz, *Atomic Diplomacy,* revised edition, pp. 139–74.
†Alperovitz points out that what was urgently to be prevented was not a Soviet demand for a share in the occupation of Japan, but Soviet domination of Manchuria. *Atomic Diplomacy,* pp. 160–61.

On June 26, for example, after a meeting of the Committee of Three, Stimson noted that he "took up . . . the subject of trying to get Japan to surrender by giving her a warning after she had been sufficiently pounded, possibly with S-1."* It was, he added, a matter on which he felt strongly and felt, too, that "the country could not be satisfied unless every effort is made to shorten the war."

This motif recurs in the statements of many of those who helped to shape policy.† At a press conference President Truman said,

> The question was whether we wanted to save our people and Japanese as well and win the war, or whether we wanted to take a chance on winning the war without killing all our young men. Well, I'd say you question any young man who was over there and see what he thinks about it and he won't use polite language.‡

The syntax is muddled, but the thought is plain enough. Jimmy Byrnes said exactly the same with even greater clarity:

> There was no dissent from anybody in government who knew of the intention of the government to use that bomb. . . . Any weapon that would bring an end to the war and save a million casualties among American boys was justified and we were talking about people who hadn't hesitated at Pearl Harbor to make a sneak attack destroying not only ships but the lives of many American sailors. It was our duty to bring the war to an end at the earliest possible moment.

General Marshall made the point that precisely because the bomb was so shocking, it would allow the Japanese to surrender without losing face. According to David Lilienthal,§ Marshall argued that the bomb, by shortening the war, made it unnecessary to exterminate the Japanese. Vannevar Bush said he had no doubt about the desirability of using the bomb, because "it would end the war and . . . save very many American lives." Conant did not see how, as technical advisers,

*HLS, *Diary*, June 26, 1945.
†See the very interesting anthology of comments about whether or not dropping the bomb was justified in an appendix to Giovanitti and Freed, *The Decision to Drop the Bomb*, pp. 320–35.
‡President Truman, press conference, quoted—Giovanitti and Freed, *op. cit.*, p. 320.
§David Lilienthal, chairman of the Tennessee Valley Authority, co-author of the Acheson–Lilienthal report of atomic energy, first chairman of the United States Atomic Energy Commission and adviser to the Shah of Iran.

the Interim Committee could have advised against using the weapon "which, if used, would shorten the war."

Others were not so sure. General Eisenhower recorded in his memoirs that he had expressed the hope that the bomb would never be used, "because I disliked seeing the United States take the lead in introducing into war something as horrible and destructive." Admiral Leahy, the senior American military officer at the time, no blushing violet but a tough old sailor, said that the bomb was "of no material assistance" because the Japanese were already defeated and ready to surrender. "My own feeling," he wrote in his memoirs, "was that in being the first to use it we had adopted the ethical standards common to barbarians in the dark ages." And one member of the Interim Committee, Under Secretary of the Navy Bard, said in an interview for NBC that "with the proper kind of warning the Japanese would have made peace and we wouldn't have had to drop the bomb."

As for Stimson, he was troubled enough to compose a long article for *Harper's* magazine on the subject, published early in 1947, and he also gave his view to McGeorge Bundy, his collaborator on his autobiography, *On Active Service in Peace and War*, published later in the same year. Stimson was conscious of the weight of the moral burden he took upon his soul, but he was willing to bear it. The error made by critics after the war, he thought, was in assuming that policy ought to have been influenced by a choice either to use the bomb or not to use it. But the dominant fact in 1945, he believed, was war, and the dominant objective was therefore victory. If victory could be speeded by using the bomb, it should be used. If victory must be delayed in order to use the bomb, it should *not* be used. . . . No effort was made and none seriously considered to achieve Japanese surrender merely in order not to have to use the bomb. Surrender was a goal sufficient in itself, wholly transcending the use or nonuse of the bomb. And as it turned out, the use of the bomb in accelerating surrender, Stimson argued, may have saved many more lives than it cost.

In his *Harper's* argument Stimson justified his decision to recommend the use of the bomb to President Truman in more personal terms. The Japanese still had five million men under arms in 1945, he pointed out, and as long as the Japanese government refused to surrender, their unbeaten armies had the strength to cost us a million more. In order to end the war in the shortest possible time, Stimson believed, the Emperor must be used as the instrument to command his people to stop fighting. The bomb furnished him with a compelling reason to do so.

> My chief purpose was to end the war in victory with the least possible cost in the lives of the men in the armies which I had helped to raise. In the light of the alternatives which, on a fair estimate, were open to us, I believe that no man, in our position and subject to our responsibilities, holding in his hands a weapon of such possibilities for accomplishing this purpose and saving those lives, could have failed to use it and afterwards looked his countrymen in the face.

Yet he conceded that to use the atomic bomb against cities populated mainly by civilians was to assume a terrible responsibility. Stimson added two closing paragraphs to his article:

> As I read over what I have written, I am aware that much of it, in this year of peace, may have a harsh and unfeeling sound. It would perhaps be possible to say the same things and say them more gently. But I do not think it would be wise. . . . The face of war is the face of death; death is an inevitable part of every order that a wartime leader gives. The decision to use the atomic bomb was a decision that brought death to over a hundred thousand Japanese. No explanation can change that fact and I do not wish to gloss it over. But this deliberate, premeditated destruction was our least abhorrent choice. The destruction of Hiroshima and Nagasaki put an end to the Japanese war. It stopped the fire raids, and the strangling blockade; it ended the ghastly specter of a clash of great land armies.
>
> In this last great action of the Second World War we were given final proof that war is death. War in the twentieth century has grown steadily more barbarous, more destructive, more debased in all its aspects. Now with the release of atomic energy, man's ability to destroy himself is very nearly complete. The bombs dropped on Hiroshima and Nagasaki ended a war. They also made it wholly clear that we must never have another war.*

In the very weeks when he was focusing his attention on the issues raised by the atomic bomb, Stimson recorded in his diary the pleasure he had gotten from an evening at Woodley with McCloy talking about

*HLS, "The Decision to Use the Atomic Bomb," *Harper's,* February 1947.

bear hunts. John McCloy knew Stimson as well as anyone. Many years later he was asked when his chief took the decision that the bomb must be used.* He replied that he thought Stimson took it a long time before the bomb was ready, and on his knees. If so, we may take it that the Colonel addressed his prayers to a warrior God, just but stern, in his own image.

Harry Truman did not at first intend to take his Secretary of War with him to meet Stalin and Churchill at Potsdam. On July 2, when Stimson brought some papers over to the White House bearing on the question whether it was worth trying to "warn Japan into surrender," he taxed Truman directly with this, and asked whether the trouble was his own health.

"Yes," the President answered, "that's just it."

The President's reliance on Jimmy Byrnes, and Byrnes's reluctance to be second-guessed by a former Secretary of State, may have had just as much to do with the decision, however. In any case, at Byrnes's swearing-in ceremony the next day, Stimson talked Truman into sending both him and McCloy to Europe; he might be tired, but he did not want to be left out when the great decisions were being taken.

The next day, at a meeting of the Combined Policy Committee, Britain gave her formal consent to the use of the atomic bomb, as was required under the Hyde Park and earlier agreements. Roger Makins (now Lord Sherfield), joint secretary of the committee, pointed out in an interview that just as American forces were poised to invade Japan, British forces were poised to invade Malaya at the end of August in an operation that would have involved heavy casualties. In any case, his principals, the British ambassador in Washington, Lord Halifax, and General Sir Henry ("Jumbo") Maitland-Wilson, had no qualms whatever about signing.

Two days later Stimson left Pier 3 in Brooklyn on the U.S.S. *Brazil*. One of his more fascinating fellow-passengers was a young woman named Louise de Mont-Reynaud, known as the Black Panther of the French Resistance. In her and others' congenial company the voyage slipped away pleasantly, and Stimson traveled comfortably by way of Gibraltar, Nice and Marseilles to Berlin, where he flew into Gatow

*By Elting E. Morison. See *Turmoil and Tradition*, p. 619.

Airport at 3:50 in the afternoon of July 15, just in time to greet the President and his new Secretary of State, who were sharing a villa. Stimson was assigned by the Russians, who were running the conference, to a luxurious home in the former Berlin film colony at Babelsberg, on Lake Griebnitz, in the wooded western fringes of shattered Berlin.

He had scarcely time to unpack when he learned that Stalin, who was late in arriving, was putting on heavy pressure for concessions in Manchuria. The Americans were divided. Some thought they needed the Russians to tie up a million or so Japanese troops in Manchuria. Others, including those in the know about S-1, were not sure that Stalin's time had not passed.

Stimson's position at the Potsdam Conference was somewhat anomalous. He was the nominal civilian superior of the conquering soldiers who were everywhere to be seen. He was not a member of the conference and did not attend meetings in the paneled room at the Cecilienhof. Yet he met and talked to all the high plenipotentiaries, including Churchill and his deputy Clement Attlee (who became Prime Minister as a result of a general election held during the conference) and, after the conference was over, Stalin.

What made the Secretary of War, even outside the conference room, in one sense the most important man there was the news he brought. For on July 16 it was to Stimson that a first message came from George Harrison announcing the successful test of an atomic device at Alamogordo in the New Mexico desert:

> Operated on this morning. Diagnosis not yet complete but results seem satisfactory and already exceed expectations. Local press release necessary as interest extends great distance. Dr. Groves pleased. He returns tomorrow. I will keep you posted.*

Stimson turned to Harvey Bundy, who had carried more of this burden than anyone. "Well," he said, "I have been responsible for spending two billion dollars on this atomic venture. Now that it is successful I shall not be sent to prison in Fort Leavenworth."†

Stimson took the news to the house the President shared with Byrnes. "I feel fine," the President said, and told one of those jokes

*Hewlett and Anderson, *The New World*, p. 383.
†Harvey Bundy, "Remembered Words," *Atlantic Monthly*, March 1957.

the boys enjoyed so much back in the old days in Kansas City, about a girl who said she would drown herself if she found she was pregnant. "It has taken a great load off my mind!" said the President.*

The next morning Stimson tried to persuade Byrnes that the successful test only strengthened the case he had made on July 2 and argued again in a memo he, Bundy and McCloy had drafted in favor of warning the Japanese. Byrnes did not agree.

Stimson lunched with Churchill and Attlee. Contrary to much myth and many apocryphal anecdotes, Churchill and Attlee had a friendly relationship, founded on mutual respect acquired over the five years of war, even if Attlee's milk-and-water socialism and Churchill's richly imperial conservatism did not mix well.† After a wide-ranging talk Churchill walked Stimson to the gate, and Stimson told him the news from Alamogordo. Churchill was delighted, but insistent that Stalin must not be told. Stimson argued with him then and there by the villa gate.

The arguments about whether, and how, to warn the Japanese, whether to tell them they could keep their Emperor, and whether to let them know that the Soviet Union was about to attack them, went on and on. Then, on Wednesday morning, July 18, Stimson had another cryptic report from Harrison:

> Doctor has just returned most enthusiastic and confident that the little boy is as husky as his big brother. The light in his eyes discernible from here to Highhold and I could have heard his screams from here to my farm.‡

The bomb was not just a reality. It was far more successful than anyone could have hoped or imagined. Harrison was saying that the plutonium implosion bomb was as powerful as the gun-type uranium weapon; that it could be seen at a distance of 250 miles and heard 50 miles away. In the heat of the debate about whether the Japanese should be warned or not, however, not to mention the other preoccupations of the Potsdam Conference, no one seems to have focused

---

*Unpublished diary of Joseph Davies, in the Library of Congress, July 16, 1945, cited in Yergin, *Shattered Peace,* p. 115.

†At lunch on the following day, when it was plain that Attlee's Labour Party had beaten him in the election, Clementine Churchill told her husband, to comfort him, that his defeat might well be a blessing in disguise. "At the moment," he replied, "it seems quite effectively disguised."

‡Hewlett and Anderson, *op.cit.,* p. 386.

on the question whether it would really be necessary to drop *both* these terrible weapons on Japanese civilians.

At 11:30 on Saturday morning, July 21, a special courier arrived delivering General Groves's personal report on the test held at Alamogordo. It was overwhelming. The device had gone off with the force of 15,000–20,000 tons of TNT and with the brightness of several suns, vaporizing the steel tower to which it had been attached. But what counted, Groves insisted, was the test of battle. Stimson took the letter to Marshall, then read it to the President and Byrnes. Truman was ecstatic, so much so that he was moved to say how pleased he was that Stimson had come to Potsdam. Stimson hurried on to inform Churchill, but the Prime Minister only had time to glance at the letter from Groves before he was due in the next plenary session. The next day, when Stimson briefed him in full, Churchill said that he had noticed at the previous day's meeting of the Big Three that "Truman had been much fortified by something that had happened and that he stood up to the Russian in a most emphatic and decisive manner."*

Atomic diplomacy had been born.

By agreement, Truman took advantage of an opportunity to give Stalin a veiled warning about the bomb. He told Stalin that the United States had a new weapon of unusual destructive force. Stalin showed no great concern and replied mildly that he hoped the United States would make good use of it. Churchill, who was standing five yards away, said later that the bland way in which Stalin received the news, and his lack of interest in following up and finding out more, convinced him that "at that date Stalin had no special knowledge of the vast process of research on which the United States and Britain had been engaged for so long."† Others have concluded otherwise, and seen in Stalin's calm the proof that his espionage had already told him the essentials of the truth.

Stimson received two further messages from Harrison. One asked once again whether Kyoto could not be reinstated as the priority target, as the military planners wished. Stimson was firm, and Truman backed him up. The other message reported that the uranium bomb would be ready by August and that operational plans were moving so fast that Washington would need to know of any change of plan by July 25.

*HLS, *Diary,* July 21, 1945.
†W. S. Churchill, *The Second World War,* vol. vi, *Triumph and Tragedy,* p. 580.

July 24, 1945, has been called "perhaps the most momentous" day "in his long career" for Stimson.* At 9:20 A.M. he saw the President in the yellow stuccoed house, Number 2 Kaiserstrasse in Babelsberg, that the press called the Little White House. He was able to report to his Commander-in-Chief that General Marshall believed there was now no reason to seek Russian help against Japan. He briefed him on the new, advanced dates Harrison had sent for the atomic-bomb operations. The President brought up the matter of the warning. Stimson "then spoke of the importance which I attached to the reassurance of the Japanese on the continuance of their dynasty." He felt it was important to insert this concession into the formal warning. That "might be just the thing that would make or mar their acceptance."

While Truman half-briefed Stalin on the existence of the bomb, Stimson had to concern himself with operational arrangements. A draft directive for General Carl ("Tooey") Spaatz, whose 509th Composite Group was gathering at Tinian Island in preparation to receive the bombs, was cabled to Potsdam and Stimson OK'd it.

> To General Carl Spaatz, CG, USASTAF:
>
> 1. The 509 Composite Group, 20th Air Force will deliver its first special bomb as soon as weather will permit visual bombing after about 3 August 1945 on one of the targets: Hiroshima, Kokura, Niigata and Nagasaki. . . .
>
> 2. Additional bombs will be delivered on the above targets as soon as made ready. . . .
>
> 3. Dissemination of any and all information concerning the use of the weapon against Japan is reserved to the Secretary of War and the President of the United States. . . .
>
> 4. The foregoing directive is issued to you by direction and with the approval of the Secretary of War and of the Chief of Staff, USA.

Strangely, although President Truman in his memoirs stated correctly that "the final decision of where and when to use the atomic bomb was up to me," there is no evidence that he authorized or even saw this order, though he does say that he "instructed Stimson that the order would stand unless I notified him that the Japanese reply to our ultimatum was acceptable."†

*Hewlett and Anderson, *New World*, p. 392.
†Truman, *Memoirs*, vol. i, *Year of Decision*, pp. 419, 421.

It was not. On July 29 (Potsdam time) Radio Tokyo announced that the Japanese would fight on. Yet in fact there was evidence that the Japanese wanted to end the war. On the same day that Radio Tokyo carried Prime Minister Suzuki's statement that he would *mok-usatsu** the Western warning, Stalin announced that he had received a new proposal from Japan, regarding a proposed mission of Prince Ko-noye, who had special instructions from the Emperor to convey his desire to avoid further bloodshed. Stalin said there was nothing new in this except that it was more definite, and therefore his own answer would be a more definite no. Truman thanked Stalin, and that was that.

By then, Stimson had flown home to New York. On August 4 he received information that the first atomic operation had been postponed from Friday to Saturday, then again from Saturday to Sunday. That day "Mabel and I went over to call on the Riggs at Port Washington," Stimson recorded in his diary and added laconically, "we had a very pleasant afternoon."

At two seconds after 8:16 in the morning of August 6, Japan time, the uranium bomb, Little Boy, exploded over Hiroshima. One of the crew of the *Enola Gay,* the B-29 that dropped it, Robert Lewis, kept a journal. "If I live a hundred years," he wrote, "I'll never get these few minutes out of my mind."

At half a mile from the epicenter, where the temperature was 5,400 degrees Fahrenheit, the light of the bomb's flash was three thousand times stronger than sunlight.†

Birds disintegrated in midair.

It was much the same with people on the ground. Their bodies were peeled like grapes. Their skin hung from them like rags. Men without feet walked on their ankles. They scorched, they burst, they screamed, they died.

Those who survived for a while fell ill with strange and agonizing diseases. Perhaps 70,000 died, perhaps 100,000, perhaps 140,000.

President Truman was told the news when he was still on board the cruiser *Augusta* bringing him home from Potsdam. He telephoned

---

*There is controversy about the exact meaning of this word. Truman interpreted it to mean "to ignore" or "to regard as unworthy of notice"; it has been suggested by Alperovitz that it should rather be translated "to withhold comment at this time." Alperovitz, *Atomic Diplomacy,* p. 233. But see also Hewlett and Anderson, *New World,* who translate the word to mean "ignore," as does the offical record in *Foreign Relations of the United States: The Conference of Berlin,* vol. ii, p. 1293.

†Rhodes, *The Making of the Atomic Bomb,* p. 711.

Jimmy Byrnes on board the same ship to give him the news, then said to a group of sailors, "This is the greatest thing in history." And so perhaps it was.*

Mr. Stimson, true to training and character, was less emotional. "It was a rainy day," he wrote in his diary for August 6, "and I didn't miss much by my occupation on the telephone." There were ten calls, beginning with one from Marshall at 7:45 A.M., imparting the news.

He flew to Washington. But when he got there, "the immediate plunge into work set me back again and this morning I had a rather sharp little attack at five o'clock in the morning which worried me."† Stimson had been in the doctors' hands because of a heart condition for some weeks, and now he learned that he had had a heart attack. There is no reason to suppose that it was triggered by excitement, still less by compunction caused by what had been done on his orders to the people of Hiroshima. He is clear in his diary that it was the "plunge into work" that brought on the attack.

Once the doctors had given him a check-up, the attack was not alarming enough to stop the Colonel's going into his office. He saw Harvey Bundy and Harrison at the Pentagon and recorded happily that "the publicity of the new atomic bomb . . . seems to be terrific." He and his staff had devoted some thought to arranging that.‡

Stimson then saw the President, and showed him a report and the first photographs of the devastation at Hiroshima. Truman, with his instinctive decency, said something about the "terrible responsibility" such destruction placed on all of them. Stimson brought with him three papers about the postwar treatment of Japan, and especially commended one by an Air Corps colonel, deForest Van Slyck, which urged generosity in the effort to help Japan rebuild her shattered economy and her lost democracy. The President said that he had already urged General MacArthur to proceed along these lines. Stimson contributed a homely metaphor. "When you punish your dog," he said, "you don't keep souring him all day after the punishment is over."§

*Truman, *Memoirs*, vol. i, *Year of Decision*, p. 421.
†*Diary*, August 8, 1945.
‡As far back as March 1944, Harold D. Smyth, chairman of the physics department at Princeton, had been assigned to write a master report, "A General Account of the Development of Methods of Using Atomic Energy for Military Purposes under the Auspices of the U.S. Government." The Smyth Report was published, with Stimson's approval, on August 9 and long extracts carried in the newspapers on August 12. News-release policy was carefully discussed by the Interim Committee on a number of occasions. Hewlett and Anderson, *New World*, pp. 368, 406-7.
§*Diary*, August 8, 1945.

The punishment for the Japanese, however, was not yet over. Shortly after eleven o'clock on the morning of August 9 (Washington time), the implosion plutonium bomb exploded over Nagasaki.

The B-29, *Bock's Car,* had been given as its primary mission the Kokura arsenal. When they were overhead, though, the crew found it obscured by ground haze, and the Japanese were sending up fighters after the B-29 and its escorts. So they turned south and dropped the bomb, Fat Man, through a hole in the cloud cover several miles from the original target. The configuration of the ground confined the effects of the explosion, and fewer were killed than at Hiroshima: only some 70,000 by the end of 1945 and 140,000 altogether when radiation had finished its agonizing work.

The Hiroshima bomb had destroyed communications with Tokyo, so that it was not until August 7 that the Japanese leadership knew that the city had been destroyed by a single bomb. That day they renewed their diplomatic pleas for peace through Moscow. On August 8 the Japanese ambassador in Moscow, Sato Naotaki, called on the Soviet foreign minister, Vyacheslav Molotov, to ask the Russians to mediate. Instead, Molotov announced, the Soviet Union had accepted an Allied invitation to adhere to the Potsdam Declaration and declare war on Japan.

Now, at last, those in Tokyo who wanted peace came into the open. Prime Minister Suzuki, after meeting with the Emperor, decided that Japan would accept the Potsdam terms, with their ambiguous guarantee on the future of the imperial dynasty. There were rumors that an atomic bomb might be dropped on Tokyo in three days' time. Even then, the military members of the Supreme Council wanted to hold out for conditions that would avoid an Allied occupation of their homeland. Not even the news of the Nagasaki bombing ended the debate. It was not until almost midnight that the inner Cabinet met the Emperor in his bomb shelter. Only then did Suzuki, in a preplanned breach of precedent, ask the Emperor to indicate his wishes. Only then did Hirohito say that the war must be brought to an end.

Early that morning a message was conveyed to Washington by way of the neutral capitals of Sweden and Switzerland that the Japanese accepted the Potsdam terms provided they did not prejudice the status of the Emperor as sovereign. This message reached Stimson by telephone from the Pentagon just as he was about to leave for the holiday his exhausted body cried out for and his doctors warned him he must take.

On August 9, the Secretary of War took a personal decision of great moment. Years before, he had asked Harvey Bundy, the totally trustworthy man, to tell him if he was getting too old for his job. Now at last, Stimson's greatest task brought to a triumphant if terrible conclusion, and the end of the war evidently only days away, Bundy had the courage to give him the message. On August 8 the Secretary of War told the President that he would be leaving the Department for good in a short time, and he made plans to go away at last for a long rest.

The next day he noted, if anything more laconically than three days earlier, that a second bomb had been dropped, on Nagasaki. "These two heavy blows," he wrote in his diary, "have fallen in quick succession upon the Japanese, and there will be quite a little space before we intend to drop another. During that time I hope something may be done to negotiate surrender."

"Today was momentous," Stimson wrote in his diary for Friday, August 10. Mabel and he were "all packed up" and the car was waiting to take them to the airport. They were all ready to fly to New York and thence, by way of Highhold, for a good long rest at the St. Hubert's Club in the Adirondacks. Then "word came from Colonel McCarthy at the Department that the Japanese had made an offer of surrender." It was another two days before they got away.

The President called in Stimson, Byrnes, Admiral Leahy and Forrestal. Stimson had argued consistently for a commitment to allow the Japanese to keep their Emperor, not because—with the memory of Manchuria in his mind—he had any special sympathy for him, but because only the Emperor could persuade the Japanese to surrender and therefore save American lives. Leahy agreed. Byrnes did not: he saw the Japanese approach as evidence of their weakness; peace terms must be unconditional surrender. Forrestal suggested a sort of compromise: let the United States say it was willing to accept, then define the terms in such a way that they expressed the intent of the Potsdam Declaration. Truman asked Byrnes to draft a reply in that sense, and the Cabinet accepted a somewhat legalistic formulation whereby the Emperor's authority would be subject to the supreme commander appointed by the Allied powers—in point of fact, to General Douglas MacArthur. On the morning of August 11, after consultation with Britain, China and the Soviet Union, this text was sent to Tokyo. There the military members of the Supreme Council still argued against acceptance. Hirohito overruled them, and the war was over.

The world sighed with profound relief. After more than a third of a century, off and on, in the public service, Colonel Stimson, too, could think of coming home from the wars. There was, however, one last task to which he meant to address himself.

In bearing his great share of the burden of responsibility for opening the atomic age, Henry Stimson had not shirked. He had behaved with his usual caution and sagacity. Yet he did not seem to grasp, before the bombs fell on Hiroshima and Nagasaki, the full and awful dimension of the decision to use them. He refused to accept the argument, raised by Roosevelt, hinted at by Bush, and openly proclaimed by some of the scientists, that the atomic bomb could not be considered as just another weapon. That, he insisted, fully understanding the moral weight implied by his position, was exactly what it was.

Should one accuse Stimson of a lack of historical imagination, of a hard, even self-righteous approach? It is certainly strange that his diary betrays so little self-questioning as the countdown went by and the destroyer of cities moved inexorably toward its grim fulfillment. Perhaps by then Stimson was too ill, too tired to care. More likely a lifetime of self-discipline had taught him not to wring his hands or beat his breast over events that could no longer be averted. Even the most heroic self-control, even the most saintly sense of sin might not completely suppress the entirely human thought that he, Henry Lewis Stimson, had presided over this culminating achievement of his country's powers of intellect, organization and determination and so had plucked for himself no mean share of the glory of the great victory. Even with 200,000 Japanese dead and many thousands more about to die as a result of his counsel and decisions, such would be the way of the world.

The extraordinary thing is that, in the moment of national victory, and at the point of utter personal exhaustion, Stimson did have second thoughts. Because those thoughts, about the ethics and the politics of the postwar settlement, sprang from all he had learned in forty years of dealing with the world, from Wall Street to Potsdam by way of Manchuria and the Argonne and because they were to be woven into the fabric of the Stimson tradition of American leadership, they deserve a chapter of their own.

VIII

A Fair and Tempting Challenge

> If there was one thing which Stimson understood above all else, it was the importance of moral leadership.
>
> Henry A. Wallace, *New Republic,* February 17, 1947

> The chief lesson I have learned in a long life is that the only way you can make a man trustworthy is to trust him; and the surest way to make him untrustworthy is to distrust him and show your distrust.
>
> Henry L. Stimson, memorandum to President Truman, September 11, 1945

> Mankind must put an end to war—or war will put an end to mankind.
>
> President John F. Kennedy, address to the United Nations General Assembly, September 25, 1961

The decision to drop the atomic bomb on Japan and the problem of the subsequent control of atomic weapons, which swiftly dissolved into the larger question of relations between the United States and the Soviet Union, were analytically two quite separate issues, but psychologically, for Henry Stimson, they were two facets of a single moral and intellectual conundrum: how to adjust the policy of the United States to the monstrous new power and responsibilities conferred by possession of the atomic bomb.

As we have seen, for almost a year before Hiroshima and Nagasaki, Vannevar Bush and James Conant had been urging Stimson to focus on the postwar control of the bomb. That issue, as they quickly understood, subdivided into domestic and international questions. Under what legal and administrative regime was nuclear energy, whether for military or for peaceful purposes, to be researched, produced, sold and regulated in the United States? Stimson was to have only an insignificant part in that debate. How was it to be controlled and regulated internationally? This was the last subject to which he applied his intellect, his experience and his accumulated political and bureaucratic capital. On April 25, 1945, in the memorandum he sent to President Truman less than two weeks after the latter had taken office, Stimson laid out his understanding of the ambivalence of nuclear power itself. "Modern civilization might be completely destroyed," he warned the President. At the same time, if the problem of the weapon's proper use could only be solved, "the peace of the world and our civilization can be saved."* American leadership in the development of the bomb, he added, "has placed a certain moral responsibility on us which we cannot shirk." Stimson's whole response to this responsibility reflected not only the ambivalence of the message of the weapon itself, at once a Promethean achievement of the human intellect and a sinister harbinger of the reign of death, but also the division he had carried within himself all his life, between a Puritan's hope and the prudence of a man of the world.

Henry Stimson was a conservative Republican. He had never been tempted for a moment by the vaguely pro-Soviet sentiment evinced, for example, by Eleanor Roosevelt† or Henry A. Wallace. Still, like even well-informed Americans, he knew little of the hideous reality of Stalin's purges and persecutions. And like even conservative Americans, he hoped that the wartime alliance with "Uncle Joe" would lead to the democratization of the Soviet Union after the war.

---

*Memorandum discussed with President Truman, HLS, *Diary*, April 25, 1945.
†Mrs. Roosevelt was no Communist, and attempts by conservatives to suggest that she was were either paranoia or propaganda. But in the period of the Popular Front strategy, when Communists sought alliance with liberals, the fact that Communists supported so many of the causes dear to her heart softened her criticism of the Soviet Union. In a private letter, for example, on August 28, 1939, a few days after the forming of the Nazi-Soviet pact, she wrote, "I have always felt that, in theory, Communism was closer to Democracy than Nazism. In spite of the realization that Stalin was a dictator and that Russia was going through the same kind of thing that all revolutions seem to have to go through, still one had the hope that in the future the theory of Communism would make a world in which Democracy and Communism might live together." Eleanor Roosevelt to Anna Louise Strong, August 28, 1939, in Joseph P. Lash, *Eleanor and Franklin*, p. 598.

It was Averell Harriman, U.S. ambassador in Moscow from 1943 to 1946, who first made Stimson think about the nature of Soviet society and the difficulties it implied for relations with the Soviet Union after the war. In October 1944, after sitting in on a meeting between Stalin and Churchill, Harriman came to see Stimson at the Pentagon. "As I listened," Stimson wrote in his diary, "to his account [of] the way the Russians are trying to dominate the countries which they are 'liberating' and the use which they are making of the secret police, my mind was cleared up a good deal."*

"It very evidently is a problem," he wrote, "upon the proper solution of which the success of our relations with Russia ultimately will depend." There could be no freedom in countries with a secret police. And he added, perhaps echoing some horror story or other that Harriman had told him, that there was nothing to choose between the Gestapo and the OGPU.†

Then, however, he launched into a train of thought that suggests how far he still was from understanding the depths of Stalin's iniquity and the reality of the tyranny in which he had shackled all the Russias. "Stalin recently promised his people a constitution with a bill of rights like our own."‡ Stimson was no doubt referring to the new constitutions for the constituent republics of the Soviet Union, introduced later in 1944. The so-called "Stalin constitution" had gone into force in 1936, at the very height of the Stalin terror. Its nominal chief author was none other than A. A. Vyshinsky, a hardened tool of Stalin, and chief prosecutor at the scandalously rigged Moscow Trials. Formally, it contained guarantees of civil rights, but in reality it was a cynical sham behind which the state committed mass atrocities with impunity.

*HLS, *Diary,* October 23, 1944.
†Stimson was out of date in his nomenclature. What is now called the KGB, for Committee for State Security *(Komitet Gosudarstvennoy Bezopastnosti)* started out shortly after the Revolution in December 1917 as the *Cheka* (from the Russian pronunciation of CK, initials standing for Extraordinary Commission); in 1922 the Cheka was abolished and replaced by the GPU, a division of the NKVD (People's Commissariat of Internal Affairs); in 1923 the GPU became the OGPU, or Unified State Political Directorate. After it had dispossessed and collectivized the peasants, in an operation in which at least 3.5 million and perhaps more than 5 million people died, the OGPU was reconstituted as the chief directorate for state security in the NKVD again. The infamous G. G. Yagoda, N. I. Yezhov and L. P. Beria were all heads of the NKVD, which was what the organization was generally called at the time Stimson wrote. In 1946 it became the MVD (Ministry for Internal Affairs), and the KGB was not formed until 1954, after Stalin's death. See John Barron, *KGB,* Appendix A, pp. 338–42, and for background, Robert Conquest (ed.), *The Soviet Police System.*
‡*Diary,* October 23, 1944.

Stalin was never slow to assure Western visitors, when it suited him, that reforms were on the way. There was, of course, never any chance of any worthwhile reform as long as he was alive, and it was more than thirty years after his death before any significant progress in the direction of civil liberties in the sense in which they are understood in the West was achieved by Mikhail Gorbachev.

Stimson was convinced, however, that the United States could use its political and military strength and its moral credit to force Stalin to turn this shabby fraud into a palladium of rights for the Soviet people. "It seems to me," he wrote, "that our success in getting him to carry out this promised reform, which will necessarily mean the abolition of the secret police, lies at the foundation of our success."* Harriman warned Stimson that he did not understand what he was saying, though he seems to have done so too politely to register on Stimson's naively optimistic mood. Harriman did say that "it will be practically impossible to get the Russians to do it for themselves just at the present," but he went on—or so Stimson understood him—that "we ought certainly to prevent them from introducing [secret police] into the countries which they are now invading," particularly Hungary.

At this point Colonel Stimson went off into a wholly unrealistic speculation about how the Hungarians, not being "Slavic," would not "willingly accept" the OGPU. The Hungarians are indeed not Slavic. (For what it is worth, they are Magyars, descendants of Turko-Ugrian peoples, among the most ferocious who ever invaded Europe.) The notion that whether or not one nation suffers under a cruel secret police or not depends on its ethnic composition was, even in 1944, an untenable survival of nineteenth-century ethnocentric history. As for the notion that there was any question of Hungary, or any other country, accepting the apparatus of Soviet state terror "willingly," it reveals all too sadly how out of touch with East European reality Stimson was in 1944—though no doubt few of his colleagues in the Roosevelt administration knew what they were talking about on the subject of Eastern Europe any more than Stimson did.

To be fair, these were private musings. In his official work Stimson was more cautious. And he had always preserved the ability to learn. He kept in touch with Harriman and with General John Deane, U.S.

Diary, October 23, 1944.

military attaché in Moscow, when they visited Washington for consultations. By the last day of 1944, on the occasion when he visited
President Roosevelt at his bedside, if not before, he had made the
connection between his conception of the incompatibility between a
free society and a police state, and the atomic bomb.*

Throughout the spring of 1945 Stimson was made aware of the
new Soviet intransigence. On January 23 he dictated a paper on the
probable shape of the postwar world at the request of Secretary of State
Stettinius, in which he drew attention to the "clash of fundamental
ideas" with Russia. In March there was trouble with Stalin over Allied
prisoners of war and a "bombshell" from Molotov about separate
Allied negotiations for a surrender of the German armies in Italy. The
Red Army was demanding the handing-over of Ukrainian and Cossack
Soviet citizens who had gone over to the German side, and Allied
commanders were troubled by the thought that they were sending
these men to virtually certain death.

By late April "Stettinius has gotten into a jam with Molotov . . .
the subject is Poland";† Stalin insisted on recognizing the "Lublin
Poles" of his own puppet government, not the "London Poles" of
the government in exile. In fact, the Soviet Union was ignoring the
Yalta agreements and moving to consolidate its hold over every country of Eastern Europe. Poland, Rumania, Bulgaria—each was a pressing
issue between the Soviet Union and the United States. At the same
time an ominous confrontation was impending with Marshal Tito, the
victorious Yugoslav partisan leader, over the major port of Trieste and
the Istrian Peninsula between Italy and Yugoslavia; and behind Tito
in those days stood Stalin.

At first Stimson was inclined to think Harriman and General
Deane were prejudiced by the personal irritations of living in Moscow
and experiencing Soviet pressure tactics. He applauded General Marshall as a "brave man and a wise man" when at a White House meeting on April 23 he "like me, was troubled and urged caution."

But it was Harriman more than anyone in the spring of 1945 who
influenced Stimson into taking a strongly anti-Soviet position. On
May 10, with Bundy and McCloy, Stimson lunched with the ambassador,
back from Moscow for consultations. Harriman gave a gloomy report.

*See above, pp. 307–9.
†HLS, *Diary*, April 23, 1945.

"He didn't think there was any chance of getting the seeds of liberalism into Russia."* Yet, Harriman said, Stalin was afraid of, "or at least respects," American power. He would ride roughshod over his neighbors in Europe, but he would not destroy the agreement on postwar cooperation reached at Dumbarton Oaks in Washington the previous September, nor would he break openly with the United States.

A few days later Stimson dined on board the presidential yacht *Sequoia* as Secretary Forrestal's guest to meet the British foreign secretary, Anthony Eden. The spirit of Theodore Roosevelt, speaking softly and carrying a big stick, moved in his old friend.

> I told him [Stimson noted in his diary that night] that the time now and the method now to deal with Russia was to keep our mouths shut and let our actions speak for words. . . . We have got to regain the lead and perhaps do it in a pretty rough and realistic way. They have rather taken it away from us because we have talked too much and been too lavish with our beneficences to them. I told him this was a place where we really held all the cards. I called it a royal straight flush and we mustn't be a fool about how we play it. They can't get along without our help and industries and we have coming into action a weapon which will be unique.†

But it was Harriman, once again, who seems to have inspired Stimson to write the document which represented the high-water mark of his willingness to argue that, with the biggest stick ever given to human beings to wield on their shoulder, the Americans should now use it to force Russia to change her internal system.

On the evening of the day Stimson arrived at Babelsberg for the Potsdam Conference, Harriman came around for a visit with the veteran diplomat Robert Murphy. He was "much worked up," Stimson found, though the focus of his fears of Soviet expansionism had shifted from Europe to the Far East. Stimson passed his concerns on, no doubt as Harriman had intended, in a memo for President Truman. Four days later, in the late afternoon of July 19, he sat down with McCloy and Bundy for a "long and interesting discussion on our relations with

---

Diary, May 10, 1945.
†*Ibid.,* May 14–15, 1945.

Russia; what the cause[s] of the constant differences between our countries are; and how to avoid them.''

As a result Stimson dictated a memo that ''boiled down to the
possibility of getting the Russians to see that the real basis of the evil
was the absence of freedom of speech in their regime, and the iron-
bound rule of the OGPU.'' (Stimson had experienced trivial examples
of that iron-bound rule himself, because the American delegation in
Babelsberg was housed in an enclave within the greater enclave of
Russian-controlled Berlin, where the Russian officials and troops were
openly highhanded, even with senior U.S. officials such as the Secretary of War.) At the same time Stimson knew the problem was complicated by the messianic aspects of Soviet Communism. ''They are
crusaders for their system and suspicious of everybody outside trying
to interfere with it.'' Yet there could be no compromise with a regime
that denied freedom and relied on the ''iron hand of the secret police.''* This was the question of the hour, Stimson understood. And
he understood, too, how the imminent birth of the Atomic Age would
bring it into focus.

The next day the Secretary—with plenty of time for reflection,
since he was excluded, apparently at the instigation of Byrnes, from
the formal sessions in the Cecilienhof—showed his paper to Harriman.
It wound up saying that the Russians must have a bill of rights. Harriman agreed with the analysis, but he was ''pessimistic as to the
chances of getting Russia to change her system.'' The next day, however, Stimson took his paper around to the Little White House and
left it with the President. It was in no sense an official paper, he
stressed, it might not even contain the Secretary's matured opinions,
but he was ''pretty sure the reasoning was correct.''

''Reflections on the Basic Problems Which Confront Us''† had as
its central focus, Stimson told McGeorge Bundy later,‡ ''the Russian
police state, and only secondly the atomic bomb.'' With each conference and each passing month it became clearer that the great basic
problem of the future was the stability of relations between the Western democracies and Russia. The problem arose from the fundamental
differences between a nation ''of free thought, free speech, free elec-

*Diary, July 19, 1945.
†Foreign Relations of the United States, 1945, Potsdam, vol. ii, pp. 1155–57.
‡On Active Service, p. 639.

tions, in fact, a really free people [and] a nation* which is not basically free but is systematically controlled from above by secret police and in which free speech is not permitted." In such an autocratic system policy could not be permanent, since it was tied up with the life of one man, and when he died or was removed, his successor might have an entirely different policy. Every effort at organizing a world composed of two such radically different systems was subject to frustration.

What, then, Stimson asked, could we do to move Russia in the direction of freedom? Private diplomacy, explaining the reasons for distrust, encouraging open discussion, setting conditions for aid or concessions the Russians might ask for: these might help. But in the beginning they could only chip away at the corners of Stalin's tyranny.

Stimson's conclusions, if more optimistic than was warranted by the realities of Russia in 1945, were not euphoric. His logic led him to advocate using the atomic bomb, not indeed by dropping it, but by offering to share it, as one of the few effective levers with which the United States could affect the situation in Russia. His concluding paragraph of the memorandum is worth quoting at length:

> The foregoing has a vital bearing upon the control of the vast and revolutionary discovery of X [atomic energy] which is now confronting us. . . . [The Interim Committee] has called for an international organization. . . . After careful reflection I am of the belief that *no* world organization containing as one of its dominant members a nation whose people are not possessed of free speech, but whose governmental action is controlled by the autocratic machinery of a secret political police, can give effective control of this new agency with its devastating possibilities.
>
> I therefore believe that before we share our new discovery with Russia we should consider carefully whether we can do so under any system of control until Russia puts into effective action the proposed constitution which I have mentioned. If this is a necessary condition, we must go slowly in any disclosures or agreeing to any Russian participation whatsoever and constantly

*Stimson, in this hour before the birth of the Western Alliance, unconsciously revealed an ambiguity that has dogged attitudes in the United States to its allies ever since. He spoke of "Western democracies," but in the same breath he switched to speak of "a nation." On April 23, 1945, he wrote in his diary, "I know very well from my own experience . . . that there are no nations in the world except the US and the UK which have a real idea of what an independent free ballot is. I learned that in Nicaragua and in South America."

explore how our headstart in X and the Russian desire to participate can be used to bring us nearer to the removal of the basic
difficulties which I have mentioned.

When at Potsdam on July 21, Stimson handed the President General Groves's long and powerful report on the Trinity test at Alamogordo. "The President was tremendously pepped up by it," Stimson
wrote in his diary, "and spoke of it again and again when I saw him.
He said it gave him an entirely new sense of confidence."* Churchill,
too, noticed that after reading Groves's report Truman was "a changed
man. He told the Russians just where they got on and off and generally
bossed the whole meeting." Ambassador Harriman "commented on
the increasing cheerfulness evidently caused by the news."

Byrnes, one of the few outsiders to have early knowledge of the
bomb project,† experienced the same heady sense that the atomic
bomb could be used, if not to *force* the Russians to do as we wanted,
at least as the pistol in a gambler's pocket is used, to keep the other
players from cheating.

It was arranged at Potsdam that the foreign ministers of the United
States, Britain, France and the Soviet Union should meet in London
in the fall of 1945; in August, Stimson was told that Byrnes wanted to
go to the London conference with "the implied threat of the bomb
in his pocket."‡ By September 4, however, Henry Stimson had
changed his mind and no longer agreed with Byrnes about that.

He had flown back from Potsdam on July 25. He was at Highhold
when the bomb was dropped on Hiroshima on August 6, and early
on the morning of August 8 he had the minor heart attack that led to
his decision that day to resign. On August 10, after the second bomb
had been dropped on Nagasaki, the news was telephoned through

*Diary, July 21, 1945.
†In his memoirs he says that he did not remember when President Roosevelt told him the
secret, but he believed it was in the summer of 1943. It is not clear whether Roosevelt singled
him out to receive the secret as director of the Office of War Mobilization, or as an influential
Democrat with powerful contacts from the Supreme Court to the Senate lobbies.
‡Stimson got the same impression from Byrnes on September 4. They were both right. At a
reception in the House of Lords in London during the foreign ministers' conference Byrnes
asked Molotov when he would finish sightseeing so that they could "get down to business."
Molotov asked Byrnes if he had an atomic bomb in his pocket. "You don't know Southerners,"
Byrnes answered. "We carry our artillery in our hip pocket. If you don't quit stalling and let
us get down to work, I'm going to pull an atomic bomb out of my pocket and let you have
it." Molotov laughed. See the diary of Walter Brown, September 13, 1945, quoted in Yergin,
Shattered Peace, p. 123.

from the Pentagon that the Japanese had surrendered. It was not until Monday, August 13, that the Stimsons got away for the rest the doctors had ordered, at the St. Hubert's Club.

Colonel Stimson was a few days away from being seventy-eight years old, he had had at least one heart attack, and he was mortally tired. At first the doctors kept him on a very strict regimen, forbidding him his usual round of exercise. For two weeks he made shaky progress. But the club was psychologically comforting. The Stimsons were among old friends, and were cheered when they first appeared in the dining room. (The club was arranged with separate cabins for guests, who shared central facilities, including the restaurant and a hall where the Secretary of War and his wife gave thanks for victory over Japan in a nondenominational service.) Gradually his strength began to return. By the third week he was able to row Mabel on the lake three times for short periods.

Frail as he was, the Secretary of War was still on duty. The hunting club's telephone log records several calls a day from the Pentagon on matters of greater or lesser moment. One concerned a lost rug. Others were on more momentous subjects. Harvey Bundy called about a number of matters, including the troublesome Pearl Harbor investigation. (On August 24 President Truman was to release reports by both the Army and the Navy on responsibility for the disaster; this led to a congressional joint committee of investigation which held hearings from November 1945 to May 1946.) It was McCloy, however, who was helping the Secretary on his chief project, and twice McCloy flew up to Ausable to confer with him in person.

The Stimsons' retreat in Ausable was, as he put it in his diary, "a most pleasant and delightful stay among old friends."* One day they drove over to visit with Judge Augustus Hand in nearby Elizabethtown, where the Hand family had lived for five generations. This conversation also, as we shall see, had a critical influence on Stimson's thinking.

On September 3 the Secretary was well enough to return to Washington. The next day he went to a Cabinet lunch at the White House dominated by the President and his Secretary of State reminiscing about old times in the Senate. Afterward he had a long, friendly but disturbing talk with Byrnes:

*Diary, September 7, 1945. On that day Stimson dictated an account of his stay at Ausable, which was from August 12 to September 3, 1945.

I took up the question I had been working on with McCloy up at St. Hubert's, namely how to handle Russia with the big bomb. I found Byrnes was very much against any attempt to co-operate with Stalin. His mind is full of the problems with the coming meeting of the foreign ministers and he looks to having the presence of the bomb in his pocket, so to speak, as a great weapon to get through the thing he has.*

The next day the Secretary of War had a fifteen-minute appointment with the President, but he realized that matters had arisen that would take longer than that to resolve. He asked for a longer appointment to hammer out the differences between his newly evolved position and that of Byrnes. He added that he thought that while there were risks both to his plan and to Byrnes's, "in my method there was less danger than in his and also that we would be on the right path towards . . . establishment of an international world, whereas on his we would be on the wrong path in that respect and tending to revert to power politics."†

What were the differences between the Secretary of State and the Secretary of War, and how had they arisen?

Not quite twenty years after the war in Europe ended, an American graduate student at King's College, Cambridge, in England, Gar Alperovitz, was working on a doctoral dissertation on political economy when he found himself puzzled by the "abrupt stops and starts" in U.S. diplomacy between April and September 1945. His curiosity led him to the investigation whose results he published in a book called *Atomic Diplomacy.*‡

In bare outline, Alperovitz's theory was, and is, that President Truman never shared President Roosevelt's belief that it was going to be possible to "get along" with the Russians. In part, this was because

---

*Diary, September 4, 1945.
†Ibid., September 5, 1945.
‡Gar Alperovitz, Atomic Diplomacy. Hiroshima and Potsdam. The Use of the Atomic Bomb and the American Confrontation with Soviet Power (1965), reissued with a new introduction by the author (1985). A critical view is to be found in: Robert James Maddox, The New Left and the Origins of the Cold War (1973). While he has unearthed mistakes and perhaps also biases in Alperovitz, his critique would be more persuasive if it were less violent. See also: Barton J. Bernstein (ed.), The Atomic Bomb: The Critical Issues (1976), which includes the important essay by Gregg F. Herken, "Atomic Diplomacy Revised and Revisited"; P. M. S. Blackett, Atomic Weapons and East-West Relations (1956); Gregg F. Herken, The Winning Weapon: The Atomic Bomb in the Cold War, 1945–1950; R. L. Messer, The End of an Alliance: James F. Byrnes, Roosevelt, Truman and the Origins of the Cold War (1982), a Byrnes-eye view; Martin J. Sherwin, A World Destroyed (1975); Daniel Yergin, Shattered Peace: The Origins of the Cold War and of the National Security State (1977).

Truman had always been strongly anti-Communist; in part, because Soviet behavior, over Poland especially, was getting more and more flagrant. As early as April 23 Truman spoke sharply to Molotov about the Soviet failure to carry out the agreements reached between Stalin, Churchill and Roosevelt at Yalta in February.

"I have never been talked to like that in my life," said Molotov.

"Carry out your agreements," said Truman, "and you won't get talked to like that."*

American policy-makers, in Alperovitz's view, decided that it was time for an immediate showdown with the Soviet Union, relying on American economic strength, before U.S. forces in the European Theater were demobilized. And Stimson persuaded Truman single-handed, between April 25 and the first week in May, to adopt instead the strategy of a "delayed showdown"; delayed, that is, until the United States would be in possession of a proven atomic bomb that would transform the power relationship with the Soviet Union. One consequence of Stimson's persuasion, said Alperovitz, was Truman's postponement of his planned meeting with Stalin until a date that gave a reasonable prospect that a bomb would by then have been satisfactorily tested.

Alperovitz suggested that fear of Soviet ambitions in both Europe and the Far East influenced the decision to drop the bomb on Hiroshima, and that the knowledge that the bomb worked was the decisive factor in setting strategies for dealing with the Soviet Union after August 6. Potsdam, he said, was dominated by the atom bomb. The Americans dawdled until they heard the news from Alamogordo, and then wanted to hurry off and use the bomb before Stalin could move in Manchuria. Truman and Byrnes, confident in the power the bomb would give them, ignored the need for a quick settlement with Stalin before (in Churchill's phrase) "the armies of democracy melted away." Instead, American diplomacy took the offensive, under the illusion shared by Truman and Byrnes that the atomic bomb—as Byrnes put it to Truman—"might well put us in a position to dictate our terms,"† or, as Truman himself put it more crudely, "I'll have a hammer on those boys."

This is not the place for yet another critique of the "atomic di-

*Truman, *Memoirs,* vol i, *Year of Decision,* p. 82. Given that he had worked for Stalin for years, Molotov may be presumed to have been exaggerating.
†*Ibid.,* p. 87. The reference to a "hammer" is in Jonathan Daniels, *Man of Independence,* p. 266. To "have a hammer on" someone is a strange phrase; is it possible that the President was thinking, not of hitting the Russians, but of getting a hammer lock on them, as in wrestling? In either case, it is a combat metaphor.

plomacy" thesis or of its numerous detractors. My own reading of the sources, and especially of Stimson's diaries, does not support the idea that Stimson, having in his possession, like Adam's knowledge of good and evil, the perilous secret of the bomb, talked Truman into adopting anything so specific or conscious as a "delayed showdown strategy." That overestimates the clarity of Stimson's perception of a situation that was extremely intricate in itself and complicated still further by uncertainties, especially the uncertainty whether the bomb would in the end actually work. Cautious to a fault, Stimson insisted that that could not be assumed, even though he was "ninety-nine per cent" sure it would.

Secondly, Alperovitz misses the distinction, indeed eventually the flat opposition, between Byrnes's approach and Stimson's.

It is true that Stimson did counsel the President to wait to discuss the outstanding issues with Stalin until he knew whether the atomic bomb worked or not. It is also true that up to the Potsdam Conference and perhaps until the moment when the two bombs were actually exploded, Stimson did incline to believe that they were a "master card," a "royal straight flush." It came naturally to him as a lawyer to advise his client to wait until he knew with certainty the quality of the evidence he could produce before he tried to use it to pressure his adversary to seek a settlement.

The point is, though, that he changed his mind.

On July 25 he left Potsdam still apparently cockahoop about how the atomic bomb would help the United States win its diplomatic objectives. On September 5 he set out to persuade President Truman that Byrnes's intention to use the bomb to make the Russians more manageable* was dangerous, and that he had a better way to propose.

What is far from clear is *why* he changed his mind.

It is foolish to be categorical about such things, but I believe that the circumstances and atmosphere of the St. Hubert's Club played their part. For five years Colonel Stimson had been in the trenches, as it were, and under fire. Now, abruptly, he had been sent back from the firing zone for rest and recuperation. He was surrounded by old friends in an atmosphere of idealism and high-mindedness. (The members at Ausable included a number of leading New York clergy as well as the headmaster of Andover and several other leading boarding

---

*HLS, *Diary*, September 5, 1945.

schools and the headmistress of the Chapin School in New York.) In his diary, dictated after he returned to Washington, he summarized what he had said in a talk, in effect a little sermon, to his "dear friends" at Ausable:

> We have been compelled to invent and unleash forces of terrific destructiveness. Unless we now develop methods of international life, backed by the spirit of tolerance and kindliness, *viz.* the spirit of Christianity, sufficient to make international life permanent and kindly and war impossible, we will with another war end our civilization.

There was perhaps something else. In his heart attack, Stimson had had a warning: it was time to think about his immortal soul. His response to the use of the bombs on Hiroshima and Nagasaki was notably unemotional, even callous, yet there are indications that he was indeed troubled by the moral issues raised by the use of atomic bombs.* This sense of moral unease was something a man cast in Stimson's mold would not choose to express in public, but it would have made him skeptical of, even fastidious about, the President's and Byrnes's confidence that the bomb could be used to threaten the Soviet government into compliance.

Stimson had been thinking about the implications of atomic energy and atomic bombs much longer than either the President or the Secretary of State. Just as he arrived before them at the idea that the bomb could be played as a diplomatic "master card," so too he was one of the first to think through that argument and conclude that it would not work. It is significant, I believe, that the only other person to come to that conclusion as early and as clearly as Stimson was one of the few who had carried responsibility for the bomb even longer than he had: Vannevar Bush, who warned Truman in that same September that the "gun on our hip" might not be effective because

---

*In a press statement issued on August 9, ironically the very day of what most people regard as the unnecessary bombing of Nagasaki, he said: "The world has changed and it is time for sober thought. . . . any satisfaction we may feel must be overshadowed by deeper emotions. The result of the bomb is so terrific that the responsibility of its possession and use must weigh heavily on our minds and on our hearts." In *On Active Service* and in his February 1947 article in *Harper's* he justified the decision to drop the bombs on the grounds that they shortened the war, yet he obviously felt a further need for justification. To repeat the words with which he closed the *Harper's* piece, "The bombs dropped on Hiroshima and Nagasaki ended a war. They also made it wholly clear that we must never have another war."

"there is no powder in the gun, for it could not be drawn, and this is certainly known."* Stimson was also aware that the United States would not have a monopoly of nuclear weapons for long, and that the world had moved into an era when civilization itself was at risk.

The evidence is not overabundant, but I believe it is probable that there was an ethical, perhaps even religious, foundation for Stimson's change of mind. More prominent in the way he argued his new case, however, was a logical point of the kind a successful advocate would instinctively rely on, and the nature of the argument, in turn, pointed to an alternative policy. The logic was simply that if the United States kept the "secrets" of the bomb to itself and sought to use this monopoly in order to compel Soviet compliance, the strategy was bound to fail, and the world would become a more dangerous place; the Soviet Union, denied access to American know-how, would be obliged, given its ideology and Stalin's psychopathology, to build its own bomb. This would end only in an arms race and what would soon be called a Cold War.

In early September, Stimson did not yet see this in such simple terms. But he was clear about the two essential points: Byrnes's gun-slinging was dangerous; and the key to a safe international future lay in entrusting control of atomic energy, gradually and under appropriate safeguards, to an international organization set up for the purpose.

That was the brief he gave himself. For the last time the old advocate sat down, with the help of his protégé McCloy, to prepare his case. Over the weekend of September 8–9 he drafted some thoughts at Highhold, and on Monday September 10 labored on it with McCloy "to complete the work that he and I did up at Ausable." His old friend from the U.S. Attorney's office, Goldthwaite Dorr, now working as a special assistant in the War Department, was excited by his boss's ideas and contributed a highly idealistic memorandum for McCloy. Stimson was not wholly pleased by the enthusiasm his thinking was generating. The trouble was, it had been "tinkered over" by people in the Department and Stimson, ever the craftsman, wanted "something snappy for an ending."†

On Tuesday, September 11, he sent the memo over to the White

---

*Quoted in Yergin, *Shattered Peace,* p. 123, citing a quotation in an unpublished Ph.D. thesis by Gregg Herken, Princeton University, 1973.
†HLS, *Diary,* September 10, 1945.

House with a covering letter in which he acknowledged that he had changed his attitude.*

> Dear Mr. President,
>
> In handing you today my memorandum about our relations with Russia in respect to the atomic bomb, I am not unmindful of the fact that when in Potsdam I talked with you about the question whether we could be safe in sharing the atomic bomb with Russia while she was still a police state. . . .
>
> I still recognize the difficulty and am still convinced of the ultimate importance of a change in Russian attitude toward individual liberty but I have come to the conclusion that it would not be possible to use our possession of the atomic bomb as a direct lever to produce the change. I have become convinced that any demand by us for an internal change in Russia as a condition of sharing the atomic weapon would be so resented that it would make the objective we have in view less probable.

As we shall see, it was uncharacteristically incautious of Stimson to use, twice in that short covering letter, phrases about "sharing" the atomic bomb with Russia. In the crucial showdown between his policy of international cooperation and the Byrnes approach, that phrase was to be a hostage to fortune.

Still, what Stimson proposed *did* go pretty far in the direction of proposing to share the bomb with Stalin. Britain, he pointed out, was in effect already a partner. So "unless the Soviets are voluntarily invited into the partnership on a basis of co-operation and trust," he wrote, "we are going to maintain the Anglo-Saxon bloc over against the Soviet." That would lead to "a secret armament race of a rather desperate character." Indeed there was reason to believe that race had already begun.

"If we feel," Stimson went on, "as I assume we must, that civilization demands that some day we shall arrive at a satisfactory international arrangement respecting the control of this new force, the question then is how long we can afford to enjoy our momentary superiority." It mattered less whether Russia got the necessary secrets of production in four years or in twenty than that they should be peace-loving partners when they did get it.

*Both memo and covering letter are published in full in *On Active Service*, pp. 642–46.

Our relations with Russia, he went on, "virtually dominated" by the question of the bomb, might be "irretrievably embittered" if we continue to negotiate with them "having this weapon rather ostentatiously on our hip." Then he recited one of his favorite axioms, the one he had first used in speaking of his relations with Manuel Quezon in the Philippines so long before: "The chief lesson I have learned in a long life is that the only way you can make a man trustworthy is to trust him; and the surest way to make him untrustworthy is to distrust him and show your distrust."

Stimson proceeded to make an argument that contradicted the fundamental assumption that had guided the decision to use the bomb, the assumption that it was, however powerful and terrible, just another weapon of war. Now he said the bomb was *not* "merely another though more devastating military weapon," but the first step in a new control by man over the forces of nature "too revolutionary and dangerous to fit old concepts." Indeed, he said, it was the climax in a race between man's growing power of destruction on the one hand and his self-control and group control, "his moral power," on the other.

Stimson proposed that the United States should, after discussion with Britain, offer to enter into an arrangement with the Russians to control and limit the use of the atomic bomb as an instrument of war and to encourage the development of atomic power for peaceful purposes. He emphasized (and later italicized this passage when he quoted it in his memoirs as being "the most important point of all") how important it would be to make this offer "as a proposal of the United States—backed by Great Britain but peculiarly the proposal of the United States. Action of any international group of nations . . . would not, in my opinion, be taken seriously by the Soviets."

At three o'clock the next day he took a carbon copy of his memo to the White House. Besides discussing Russia and the bomb, Stimson used his time to put in a plea for retaining military service, and for the union of the War and Navy departments into a Department of Defense, something that had been under discussion for years and was finally to be achieved by the National Security Act of 1947.

He followed his usual practice and left the original of the atomic-arms memo with Truman, keeping the carbon on his knee as an *aide mémoire*. As he went through his argument, Truman seemed to agree with it, and as he finished he said that we must take Russia into our confidence. Once again, Stimson told the story of his experience with the Filipinos, and the President seemed interested.

Stimson was busy winding up his affairs at the Pentagon, writing citations for the generals and the civilians who had borne the heat and the burden of five years of war and arranging for Distinguished Service Medals to be awarded to his inner group of helpers—Bundy, McCloy, Lovett and the rest. He sold his ideas about how to deal with Russia to his designated successor, Judge Patterson, who like a good soldier had agreed to stay on at the Pentagon (though he had set his heart on going on to the Supreme Court, which Truman had previously promised him). Stimson also handed on his torch to a man who would be his successor in a more important sense: Dean Acheson, now emerging as a strong Under Secretary of State under Byrnes, whom he would succeed in 1949: "I called up Dean Acheson himself and told him of my talk with the President and of his attitude and he asked me whether I could send him a copy of the paper which I had given the President yesterday. Acheson is evidently strongly on our side on the treatment of Russia."*

At a Cabinet lunch on Tuesday, September 18, the President said he wanted to devote the Cabinet meeting on Friday, September 21, to a full-dress debate on Stimson's proposal, and he asked the Secretary of War to be there. Stimson had hoped to get away before that. September 21 was his last day in office; it was also his seventy-eighth birthday. But he said, of course, he would be there, "if I could walk on my two feet."

When Friday morning came, there were rites of passage to be performed. The Secretary of War went to his Department. He signed a few letters. He was presented with a silver tray by his civilian aides. He had a last talk with General Marshall, whom he had called "the finest soldier I have ever known," and he had known some fine ones. At half-past twelve he went to lunch in the General Officers' Mess and was presented with an enormous birthday cake. At the White House, the President presented him with the Distinguished Service Medal for "service exceptional in the history of the nation." And then he went in to bat—as he had so often before with such an impressively high average—for his proposal.

Truman asked Stimson to lead off, and he did so with a sense of urgency, speaking *ex tempore* this time. Acheson, as acting Secretary of State, followed. Cool and tough behind his elegant manner, Acheson was beginning to take responsibility for nuclear matters. (He had at-

---

*HLS, *Diary,* September 12, 1945.

tended a meeting to discuss domestic legislation to control atomic energy that very morning.) In his memoirs, written in the late 1960s, Acheson took the line that Stimson's memo was misunderstood, partly because the covering letter referred to "sharing the atomic bomb with Russia." It was really, Acheson maintained, addressed to the "much narrower question of how to approach discussion with the Russians on the questions raised by our development of the bomb." Acheson also tried to give the impression in his memoirs that he never took Stimson's proposal very seriously, only going along with it "partly out of deference and respect for Colonel Stimson" and partly because he agreed with the approach of getting a policy agreed with Britain and Russia before putting it to the United Nations. But it seems probable that Acheson was influenced, consciously or not, by hindsight when he came to write that account. Perhaps he was also at pains to dispose of any suspicion that in 1945 he had been in any way "soft" on policy toward Russia. The long torment to which he was subjected by the followers of Senator McCarthy* may have made him unwilling to recall his true attitude at the time. If so, there could hardly be a more striking illustration of the way McCarthy, Jenner and their kind shifted the center of gravity of discussion about how to deal with the Soviet Union by intimidating those who wanted to try a little openness. On the other hand, it may be that Acheson really did think in 1945, as he argued in 1968, that "it seems most unlikely that even if given complete control of method and means, Colonel Stimson could have persuaded Stalin to have foregone a Soviet nuclear-armament system." That may be true. But at the time Stimson believed that Acheson favored his proposal.

One cannot, however, disagree with Acheson's judgment in his memoirs that at the momentous September 21, 1945, Cabinet meeting "the discussion was unworthy of the subject." Acheson thought that this was because "no one had had a chance to prepare for its complexities." Secretary of the Treasury Fred Vinson, Attorney General Tom Clark, and Clinton Anderson, Secretary of the Interior, all op-

*Senator Joseph R. McCarthy, Republican of Wisconsin, made a speech in Wheeling, West Virginia, on February 9, 1950, asserting that there were numerous Communists in the State Department and other government agencies. This set off an uproar in which Acheson, in particular, was a prime target. Senator William Jenner, Republican of Indiana, for example, said in September 1950 that "this government of ours [has been turned into] a military dictatorship, run by a Communist-appeasing, Communist-protecting betrayer of America, Secretary of State Dean Acheson." See Acheson, *Present at the Creation*, pp. 362–65.

posed Stimson's proposal simply because they did not like the idea of "sharing the bomb." Henry Wallace, Secretary of Commerce, was in favor, but in a way that probably hurt Stimson more than it helped. Wallace "soared into abstractions," Acheson wrote to his daughter, "trailing clouds of aphorisms as he went." James Forrestal, Secretary of the Navy—even more disgusted by Wallace, who was, he wrote in his diary, "completely, everlastingly and wholeheartedly in favour of giving it to the Russians"*—spoke strongly against. The bomb, he suggested, was "the property of the American people," who had invested two billion dollars of public money in it. The Russians might cease to be allies, he suggested, just as the Japanese had been allies in one war and enemies in another. (Half the men in the room probably thought of the Russians as enemies already, come to that.) Forrestal also argued that the Russians were "essentially Oriental in their thinking," whatever that meant, a remark which drew Wallace into a learned digression, appropriate to the former publisher of *Wallace's Farmer,* on the difference between agrarian and stock-rearing peoples.

Who won? The editor of Forrestal's diaries believed that the September 21 Cabinet "laid the foundations on which were erected, in turn, the Lilienthal-Acheson report, the Baruch plan and the United Nations . . . program" for the international control of atomic energy.† To Acheson, the discussion was inconclusive, but "distorted accounts of it to the effect that the President was contemplating sharing the bomb were leaked to the press, putting the Congress into an uproar."

The truth is that Stimson's last Cabinet meeting marked neither a decision to adopt Byrnes's strategy and confront the Soviet Union, gun more or less ostentatiously on hip, still less an unequivocal commitment to share nuclear knowledge with the Soviet Union. It was, however, a fork in the road. From it, one track led on to the various attempts to arrange international control of atomic weapons. One milestone on its course was the Truman message to Congress less than two weeks later on October 3 which, as Acheson put it, "put the President squarely behind the Stimson approach to international control." A second was the Lilienthal-Acheson Report of spring 1946, which boldly "set up a plan under which no nation would make atomic

---

*Quoted from Forrestal's diary by its editor, Walter Millis, in his introduction. Millis (ed.), *The Forrestal Diaries.*
†*Ibid.*

bombs or the materials for them" and provided for "a monopoly of
. . . dangerous activities by an international Authority."* A third was
the Baruch Plan—"We are here to make a choice between the quick
and the dead"†—in June that same year. Ultimately it led to the "Atoms for Peace" initiative of the Eisenhower administration. That road,
so broad and inviting when viewed from the fork, became sandier and
more overgrown until it dwindled to a path along which no man or
woman with political ambitions would tread. The idea, launched by
Stimson in September 1945, of international control of atomic missile
warheads petered out. It was not until the acquisition by both the
United States and the Soviet Union of intercontinental missile *delivery
systems*—in other words, not until after the Cuban missile crisis of 1962,‡
that a new cycle of interest in arms control began.

The alternative route, along which Jimmy Byrnes set out so confidently, may have looked less promising. At first it seemed rough and
dangerous. Byrnes himself was to learn how hard it was to intimidate
the Soviet Union, especially when few of its leaders, men hardened by
revolution, purges and the terrors of dealing with both Hitler and
Stalin at the same time, believed that his impressive weapon was for
use, and not just for show.

The whole climate of international relations darkened as a result
of the Americans' interpretation of a speech Stalin gave on February 9,
1946. The story is well known. Stalin's speech was bombastic, full
of recitation of the might of the Red Army, of its heroic deeds in the
Great Patriotic War just concluded, and of scathing denunciations of
capitalism. It contained, however, no hint of an overt threat to Western Europe. H. Freeman Matthews, director of the Office of European
Affairs in the State Department, asked his chief for Eastern Europe,
Elbridge Durbrow, to "goose" George Kennan, a Soviet expert in the
embassy in Moscow, into sending an "interpretive analysis" of what
Stalin had said. Kennan, who had been overworked and ill, responded
with what has come to be known as his "long telegram." "At the

---

*Acheson, *Present at the Creation*, p. 153.
†See McGeorge Bundy, *Danger and Survival*, p. 165. The phrase comes from a speech made by
Bernard M. Baruch at Hunter College on June 14, 1946. According to Bundy, the speech was
written by Herbert Bayard Swope.
‡It was set off by Soviet leader Nikita S. Khrushchev's attempt to neutralize a temporary U.S.
monopoly of intercontinental delivery systems by installing missiles (and some aircraft) in Cuba
which could reach targets in much of the United States. See, in a vast literature, James G. Blight
and David A. Welch, *On the Brink*.

bottom of Kremlin's neurotic view of world affairs," Kennan wrote, "is traditional and instinctive Russian sense of insecurity. . . . We have here a political force committed fanatically to the belief that with US there can be no permanent *modus vivendi,* that it is desirable and necessary that the internal harmony of our society be disrupted, our traditional way of life destroyed, the international authority of our state be broken if Soviet power is to be secure." Kennan himself later came to regard the telegram with "horrified amusement." "Much of it reads," he said later, "like one of those primers put out by alarmed congressional committees or by the Daughters of the American Revolution, designed to arouse the citizenry to the dangers of Communist conspiracy."*

Policy-makers in the United States responded enthusiastically. They overreacted to Kennan's telegram as much as Kennan had overreacted to Stalin's speech. And public opinion overreacted to the messages given out by government officials. Copies of Kennan's telegram were carefully leaked to the press and widely published. Forrestal made it required reading for naval officers. First the policy elite in Washington, then the nation, settled grimly into a sullen struggle against a Soviet Union perceived as prowling around, like the hosts of Midian, unsleepingly on the alert for the slightest chink in the armor of the West through which it could inject its deadly poisons.

It was the message of the "long telegram" that Soviet power must at all costs and hazards be contained. Again, Kennan later maintained that he had been thinking of political, not military, containment. But by then it was too late. The United States was committed to the Cold War, and it would be many years before anyone in Washington could have suggested what Stimson proposed at his last Cabinet meeting without being suspected of dementia.†

---

*The texts of Stalin's speech of February 9 and of Kennan's telegram are usefully printed side by side in Joseph M. Siracusa, *The American Diplomatic Revolution: A Documentary History of the Cold War 1941–47.* Kennan's remarks are quoted from his *Memoirs,* vol. i, pp. 292–94. See also, among many other treatments, Daniel Yergin, *Shattered Peace,* pp. 167–71.

†Interestingly, Kennan himself, at the time, rejected Stimson's proposal, though he did not mention Stimson by name. In a dispatch dated just nine days after Stimson's last Cabinet meeting, he wrote that it was his "profound conviction that to reveal to the Soviet government any knowledge which might be vital to the defense of the United States, without adequate guarantees for the control of its use in the Soviet Union, would constitute a frivolous neglect of the vital interests of the people." He could not remember what evoked this dispatch, he wrote in his memoirs, but "probably I had picked up some reflections of the view, then entertained by at least some people in Washington, that we should place at Moscow's disposal, as a

Before long the Soviet Union had acquired its own atomic weapons, thereby fulfilling Stimson's, and falsifying Groves's, guess as to how long the American monopoly would last.

Stimson himself came to have doubts about his own proposal. He realized he had been too hopeful about the way Stalin would respond to trust. Stalin, after all, was not Manuel Quezon. "What if Stalin and his lieutenants were . . . no different from Hitler? What if the police state were no transitional revolutionary device but a fixed and inevitable accompaniment of nationalistic aggression? Would trust and candor by themselves break down or even modify the menace to the world in such a case?"* Such were the questions, he told McGeorge Bundy as they worked together on his memoirs in 1947, that preoccupied him for the first two years of his retirement. Later, he came to believe that the right course might be a synthesis between his two memoranda of July 25 and September 11, 1945.

It was in any case plain enough that the sense of the Cabinet, and no doubt the sense of the nation, was against giving away to an "ally" as unreliable as the Soviet Union the ultimate symbol of American technological prowess, the ultimate guaranty of American security. The case Stimson was making not only rested on an optimistic and overgenerous estimate of how Stalin was likely to react, but was too difficult to grasp for men who had little knowledge of either Soviet policy, international relations or atomic bombs. The Cabinet members were too polite to say so. But if the proposal to share atomic secrets had come from anyone but Colonel Stimson, a byword for sagacity since most of them had been in college, they would have said he had lost his judgment.

It was time to go. The peace of the world was out of his keeping now, and the peace of Highhold beckoned like a newly made-up bed at the end of a long day. He shook hands with the President and the Cabinet and hurried to the Pentagon, where he found Mabel and his aide, Colonel Kyle, waiting. Together they set out for National Airport, where there was a last surprise, a last tribute. Every general officer in Washington was there. Together with the Colonel's own boys from the War Department—Bundy, Lovett, McCloy and the rest—they had been waiting in two long lines for more than an hour. He shook their

pledge of our good faith, complete information on the new weapon and the methods of its production." That was exactly Stimson's view.
*On Active Service, p. 646.

hands too. The guns boomed out a nineteen-gun salute. The band played "Happy Birthday" and "Auld Lang Syne." Henry and Mabel Stimson walked up the stairway and into the plane and went home.*

In an article in *Foreign Affairs,* published on his eightieth birthday in 1947, Stimson presented his last reflections on the great question he had wrestled with in Potsdam and in Washington, at Highhold and at Ausable during that last summer in government: What course should the United States set in the doubly dangerous new world of atomic weapons and ideological rivalry?

In it, he reproved both those who were naïvely disposed to trust Stalin and those who hankered after preventive war. He acknowledged his disappointment in the way the Soviet Union had behaved between 1945 and 1947. He might have acknowledged, though he did not, that he himself had been one of those who had not fully understood how profoundly the ideals of the Russian Revolution had been flawed from the outset by the idea of the dictatorship of the proletariat and had been perverted by the evil genius of Stalin. If he had ever had illusions about the Soviet state, they had evaporated. "Before we can make friends with the Russians," he insisted, "their leaders will have to be convinced that they have nothing to gain, and everything to lose, from acting on the assumption that American society is dying."† Equally, the old man went on, to advocate a preventive war—as some conservative circles in the United States were then beginning to do—not only rested on "cynical incomprehension" of the political realities in the rest of the world, but betrayed "a totally wrong assessment of the basic attitudes and motives of the American people."

And so Stimson, in his last public utterance on those great questions with which he had lived so intimately for so long, came to what was for him an utterly predictable conclusion. "There is," he said, "a middle course."

That was his almost unvarying instinct, and it was to be that of his admirers and successors. In this case it was to halt Soviet expansionism while making clear that "we are not ourselves expansionist." The way to walk this middle road, Stimson said, was "to help threat-

On Active Service, pp. 668–69.
†HLS, "The Challenge to Americans," *Foreign Affairs,* October 1947. See also *On Active Service,* pp. 648–49.

ened people to help themselves." It was a remarkably concise summary of what had already become the policy of the Truman administration, largely at the prompting of the man who was in many respects Stimson's intellectual heir, Dean Acheson. It was also a prescient statement of the instincts of what came to be known—not without a flick of derision—as the American foreign-policy Establishment. As he stepped from the public stage after, as one historian put it, giving "the equivalent of at least two full careers to the service of his country,"* he did his best to hand on to a new generation the tradition he had inherited from Theodore Roosevelt and Elihu Root.

That tradition, unashamedly nationalist but at the same time ideologically centrist, has been in eclipse since the crisis of the Vietnam War. It is, however, very largely Henry Stimson's legacy. I have been concerned to illustrate here its double aspect. The temptations and dangers of atomic power, as they presented themselves to Stimson in the Wagnerian months that saw the twilight of the Third Reich, the downfall of imperial Japan and the barbarous irruption of Stalin's Russia into Central Europe, reflected two sides of his head. The tough side was capable of deciding that the atomic bomb must be used to shorten the war and of taking responsibility for the terrible cost of that decision in human suffering. The generous and optimistic side of his nature insisted that the death-dealing power of atomic fission must be controlled, and understood that international control was impossible unless the United States were wise enough, under appropriate safeguards and over an acceptable timetable, to give away its monopoly.

Perhaps the greatest of the services Henry Stimson performed for his country echoed the Roman proverb that if you want peace you must prepare for war. He was always ready for war, but his purpose was peace. It was this psychological ambivalence that made him change the advice he gave to President Truman, but the change also mirrored a deeper ambivalence in American civilization about the justification of force. A great share in the decisions that defined the policy of the United States for a generation or more fell to a man who was, like his ancestors, both a hunter and a Puritan. If at the end the Puritan wrestled with the hunter and prevailed, the contradictions were not clearly resolved. And in the meantime the fateful precedent of Hiroshima had been set.

---

*Walter Millis, editor of *The Forrestal Diaries,* p. 6.

IX

The Guardian

He who at every age, as boy and youth and in mature life, has come out of the trial victorious and pure, shall be appointed a ruler and guardian of the State; he shall be honoured in life and death. . . . And perhaps the word "guardian" in the fullest sense ought to be applied to this higher class only who preserve us against foreign enemies.

Plato (trans. Jowett), *The Republic*, Book III

Like many men who have worked to the brink of exhaustion, Henry Stimson was almost killed by retirement. He took to his bed to rest his heart. A month later, he suffered a massive coronary occlusion and lay in bed almost unable to move until Christmas. In the spring he had recovered sufficiently to work on his autobiography, *On Active Service in Peace and War*, with McGeorge Bundy, the son of his old friend and helper. At the end of the eighteen months, he was suffering too badly from arthritis to want to travel as he had planned, or even to visit the apartment he had rented on Fifth Avenue at Seventieth Street. First riding became too painful, a sad thing for a man who loved horses as he did. For a time he managed skeet shooting with a light gun from a wheelchair. Up until the very last day of his life he did a little fishing, from the chair, with a friend. On October 20, 1950, he started to go for a drive, felt ill, was carried up to bed, and died. His wife was with him at the end, and held his hand.

During those last, sad years, when he was in a good deal of pain, Stimson continued to take pleasure in his house and farm and in his friends. With his usual courage and self-discipline, he also managed to take care of some remaining items of business. In his memoirs, in the *Harper's* article, in the *Foreign Affairs* article published on his eightieth birthday, and in his very last article in *The New York Times* in March 1950, his concern was to leave behind a clear political testament, not only to justify himself, but to pass on to those who cared to listen the lessons he had learned. In the memoirs, of course, he covered every significant episode of his public life. In the *Harper's* article he sought to respond to criticism of the decision to drop the atomic bombs on Japan. In the *Foreign Affairs* piece, he was, as he put it himself, trying to reach a synthesis between the thesis of his July 25 memorandum—that possession of the atomic bomb should be used to put pressure on the Soviet Union to allow greater internal freedom—and the antithesis contained in his September 11 paper. The *New York Times* article was a defense of President Truman and Secretary of State Acheson against Senator Joseph McCarthy and what Stimson called "these little men" who attacked their loyalty. What was at stake, he argued, was the effective conduct of foreign policy. What was also at stake, as of course he well understood, was his own political legacy and the tradition in foreign policy he had helped to establish.

Stimson took unusual care concerning what might be written about him and the great causes in which he had served. His papers were left to the Yale University library. As well as the account of his life he had helped McGeorge Bundy to write, he expected that a biography would be written. His trustees, Bundy and Arthur Page, selected Professor Elting E. Morison of the Massachusetts Institute of Technology, a former assistant dean at Harvard who had worked for six years as a consultant in the Defense Department. His work* was financed in part by grants from the Stimson estate. Like the prudent lawyer he was, in fact, Colonel Stimson made provision not only for

*Morison, *Turmoil and Tradition*. p. vii. "This book was written at the suggestion of Arthur W. Page and Mcgeorge Bundy, the trustees of the papers of Henry L. Stimson. The expense of its preparation was defrayed by grants from the Stimson estate and the Carnegie Corporation."

his financial but for his political testament, and his reputation was left safe in friendly hands.

Stimson's achievement, historically speaking, is beyond dispute. His work as U.S. Attorney demonstrated that the public interest could be vindicated even against malefactors of great wealth. In his first term as Secretary of War he courageously vindicated the principle of civilian control and helped to fulfill his patron Elihu Root's work of modernizing the fundamental structure of the military system. By so doing, he made possible the expansion he himself was to preside over in 1940–45. He played important parts in the history of both Nicaragua and the Philippines. As Secretary of State, he labored mightily for disarmament, for economic cooperation, and for common action to preserve world peace. In the disarmament negotiations and in the Manchurian crisis, he was the first American statesman seriously to confront the problem of Japanese ambitions. These are all continuing issues in American foreign policy, as alive today as they were sixty years ago.

In a sense, however, even the most Herculean of these labors were only side shows to the great enterprise of Stimson's life. His great task, at which he worked with others, was to bring the United States from the edge to the center of the world. It is easy to forget how rapidly that transformation was accomplished. In 1867, the year of Stimson's birth, the United States, for all the intellectual polish of New England and the commercial energy of New York, remained a remote, raw land, almost outside the main currents of trade, of power, or of ideas, standing to the metropolitan civilizations of Europe rather as Brazil, say, or China, now stand to the United States, more notable for potential than for achievement. Preoccupied with binding up the wounds of the great Civil War, the nation's attention was fixed on the South and even more on the West. It turned its back on Europe, and busied itself with the discovery of its own territory, its own resources and its own destiny.

Contrast that time with the situation, less than eighty years later, when Henry Stimson left the international stage. Stimson had already been, as the American Secretary of State in the crisis of 1931–33, the arbiter of Europe. In the 1930s, out of power and often almost alone, he had stood up to the tempting appeals of the isolationists and insisted that the United States could never avoid the world's quarrels.

When his prophecy was proved right, he passed triumphantly through the trial of war. At Potsdam, he was the messenger of atomic Armageddon, and he seemed to be the herald of the American century, of a new world that must be dominated by American technology and American power.

When he died in 1950, American world leadership was at its zenith. Every rival power acknowledged the incontestable supremacy of the United States. Under American leadership, the British Empire was being dismantled; defeated Germany and Japan were being remade in what was imagined to be the American image; Western Europe was being united; and Soviet power resisted and constrained. Above all, Stimson symbolized and inspired a certain magnanimity in the way American strength was to be used.

These vast transformations, of course, of their nature could not be the work of any one man. On the other hand, Stimson's role in the growth of the U.S. as a world power was not merely a matter of his life's having coincidentally covered an era when so much changed so swiftly. He was himself one of the chief actors in the process. Of all the men who helped to steer the United States from the real isolation of 1867 or even 1911, through the unsustained commitment of 1917–19 and the delusion of isolationism, to the firm commitment to support the ideology of democracy by global political and military involvement, Colonel Stimson was one of the half-dozen most important and perhaps the most representative. So much so that he left the imprint of his style and his strategic thinking on American foreign policy for almost a generation after his death.

Stimson grew up in the period when the United States was acquiring the strength to be a world power, without yet having acquired the intention to be one. His family tradition and background and his schooling at Andover and Yale made the traditions of an older, isolated Republic live for him, though his family's relative wealth and his education made the world outside America real to him as it scarcely was to many of his contemporaries.

The years of his adolescence and youth were also a time of dramatic economic and intellectual change. The opportunity to accumulate great wealth did not attract him, perhaps because he was already comfortably off and had every reason to suppose he would be even more so. Nor did the ferment of new ideas interest him more than superficially. He grew up in the vortex of the "modern movement" in art and literature, yet there are few, if any, references in the diary to music or the theater, and the only signs of sensitivity to the visual arts lie in at most half a dozen references to visits to museums as breaks from the routine of diplomatic assignments in Europe.*

It is perhaps not surprising that Stimson was apparently untouched by, if indeed he was aware of, writers like Kafka, Proust, Joyce and Freud, all of whom were exploring a new consciousness in his youth and early manhood. What is more surprising is that he displayed almost as little interest in the political and economic literature of Progressivism and the social-reform movement, which had a deep impact on public life at precisely the time he was embarking on a career in politics. He may have read Edward Bellamy and Walter Lippman, Karl Marx and Max Weber, Graham Wallas and Eduard Bernstein—but if he did, their ideas left little residue in his mind, so far as I have been able to discover.† When he did discuss political ideas, as he did rather intensively with Elihu Root in the second decade of the century, it was in the language of the constitutional lawyer, of Blackstone and Madison and Hamilton,‡ not in the language of the political theorist.

He was a reformer with a patrician distaste for the corruption and blatant self-seeking of politics; scarcely a progressive, he was instinctively uncomfortable with electoral politics, unashamedly elitist, personally generous and warm in his dealings within his social circle but cold to the outside world, and—for all that visible signs could show—little moved by social injustice or even by suffering. In the ancient world he would have been called a Stoic. In the twentieth century he was an American Tory.

The ideas that did touch and move him were for the most part old ideas: traditional religious loyalty and practice; the patriotic traditions of the Founding Fathers; old and stirring ideals like "justice, duty, honor, trust."§

He was old-fashioned, too, in his reserve and aloofness. Contem-

---

*Stimson's sister, Candace, collected modern painting by good American artists, and Stimson was pleased when she left him several Winslow Homers, among other canvases.

†*On Active Service,* pp. 56–62. Interestingly the only modern reference in this passage is to Herbert Croly and what Stimson calls his "brilliant" book *The Promise of American Life.* Croly's views on nationalism and defense were broadly in tune with Stimson's.

‡Not, however, that of Jefferson, of whom he once wrote, "I have never thought Mr. Jefferson guilty of originating much of any political ideas."

§These words are singled out by Elting Morison as expressing the core of Stimson's beliefs. Morison, *Turmoil and Tradition,* p. 654.

poraries such as Herbert Hoover and Franklin Roosevelt* might both in their different ways be masters of self-promotion and publicity. Stimson was not above cultivating a few congenial opinion-forming journalists who covered State or War when he was in those offices. But personal publicity was distasteful to him, and self-promotion unthinkable. His antique Roman dignity could easily be mistaken for arrogance by those not admitted to his intimacy.†

He was old-fashioned in more personal ways, too: in his tastes and social style, in his attitude to women, to marriage and to social relations generally, including race relations. While he was rather proud of his freedom from vulgar racial prejudice and liked to point out that his family was abolitionist, it is also true that he showed little sympathy with black aspirations for social equality and tended to dismiss legitimate black protest as self-interested agitation. He took a self-conscious pride in his willingness to mix socially with Filipinos, but in fact saw little of any of them but a few powerful political bosses.‡ And his attitude toward Jews was not dissimilar, if it was more complicated, as was inevitable given the complexity of the Jewish experience in America in his lifetime.

Stimson had one or two genuinely close friends who were Jews; Felix Frankfurter is the most conspicuous. But Frankfurter was not a very "Jewish Jew," at least not in terms of the stereotypes of social anti-Semitism in the New York City of Stimson's youth.§ He was, moreover, a graduate of the Harvard Law School and certified to Stimson as brilliant by Dean James Barr Ames. Stimson was certainly not an anti-Semite in the sense that, for example, his colleague James

---

*Herbert Hoover's mastery of publicity and the trouble he took with public relations are both abundantly documented in George Nash, *The Life of Herbert Hoover,* not least in connection with his work for Belgian relief. See vol. ii, *The Humanitarian* 1914–17, *e.g.,* pp. 36–39. For Franklin Roosevelt's virtuosity in using the media, see especially Samuel and Dorothy Rosenman, *Presidential Style,* pp. 329–35 and *passim.*

†As it was, for example, by Drew Pearson, in *Washington Merry-Go-Round,* in two chapters of shrewd but critical profile.

‡See Frederick S. Marquardt, *Before and After Bataan,* p. 102: "Although the Manila newspapers called Stimson's regime the 'Era of Good Feeling' . . . there was little public acclaim or private friendship for the cool, calculating New York lawyer. . . . He lacked the Latin warmth that is so often required to win the friendship of the Filipinos."

§Frankfurter himself recalled an uncle of his telling him as a boy, "You'll encounter a good deal of anti-semitism in your life, but don't go round sniffing anti-semitism." He defined himself as "not a Jewish professor at the Harvard Law School, but a professor at the Harvard Law School who happens to be a Jew." Harlan B. Phillips (ed.), *Felix Frankfurter Reminisces,* pp. 37, 39.

Forrestal was; delusions of persecution by the Jews were a major part of Forrestal's paranoia.* But Stimson did use expressions that suggest that he was not free from the prevailing prejudices of his class and generation—for example, when he decided to exert his influence to prevent a benefaction going to Columbia University because of "the tremendous Jewish influence." And while one may wholly commend his wisdom in opposing Henry Morgenthau's wartime plan for turning Germany into a "pastoral country" after the war, Stimson's description of it as "semitism gone wild for vengeance" was insensitive, to say the least. Nowhere, so far as I am aware, did Stimson express any strong personal feelings about the sufferings of European Jews.†

Again, Stimson prided himself on his appreciation of Japanese culture, yet there is no sign that this was actually more than a tourist's interest. As it happens, the victims of three of the most ethically debatable actions of his life—the bombings of Hiroshima and Nagasaki and the internment of the Nisei—were all Japanese. It would be too much to assert that Stimson consciously followed a double standard, yet one may well ask whether he would have allowed the atomic bomb to be used on German cities to shorten the war or to save American lives. My own guess, and it can be no more than a guess, is that Stimson would have been willing to use the atomic bomb on Berlin only if he had been convinced that the Germans were close to achieving possession of an atomic weapon themselves. One can confidently assume that the army would never have urged on him, nor would Stimson ever have countenanced, the internment of all American citizens of German descent, say, in Pennsylvania.

Stimson's attitude to ethnic groups other than his own was in a sense only a special case of his attitude toward people generally. His manners were admirable and his behavior correct to the point of stuffiness, though he had a short temper and those who worked for him told many stories, almost always affectionately, about his outbursts. Morison, in a perceptive passage, suggests that men like Lovett, Harvey Bundy and McCloy were old enough and confident enough not to be frightened by Stimson's temper: they "airily brushed aside the

*Arnold Rogow, *Victim of Duty,* pp. 160–73. Rogow points out that, while Forrestal was undoubtedly a very sick man when he believed he was being pursued by Israeli agents, it is possible that he *was* under Israeli surveillance.
†For Columbia, HLS, *Diary,* March 19, 1931; for Morgenthau, see HLS, *Diary, passim,* especially September 16, 1944.

symptoms and broke through the stiff plating almost into intimacy. So when they sat, at tea, on the sofa at Woodley, earnestly and patiently explaining to a disbelieving Mrs. Stimson all the things that made her husband impossible to work with, he sat there laughing until the tears came into his eyes.''* Symptoms, though, of what?

In the tight circle of men who shared so much with him—New England, New York, the law, Wall Street, the tastes and acquaintance-ships of an American upper class and the common ideals of a great crusade—he could be relaxed, almost warm. What is striking, though, is how unusually exclusive he was socially. He was very fond of Mabel's niece Mrs. David Daggett and of the ebullient and loquacious Kay Bundy, Harvey Bundy's wife, and he enjoyed the social verve of Nancy, Lady Astor. Outside his immediate family and these wives of old friends, he seems to have felt uncomfortable with women.

His friendships with men were largely formed through bonding in socially exclusive male organizations: Andover; Yale College and, within Yale, Skull and Bones; Harvard Law School; the law firm; the War Department; and the band of mainly civilian helpers he gathered round him there in old age. Toward a very few men who were in effect servants, such as John Culleton, the farm manager at Highhold, he seems to have felt real affection; when Culleton died, Stimson wrote, "His death was as a loss in the family."†

To some extent, these traits and characteristics—sexual reticence and inhibition, ethnic prejudice not virulent but tenacious, social ex-clusivity and a strong sense of caste and class—were those of any Amer-ican (or for that matter British or European) gentleman of inherited wealth and old family in his generation. Stimson's code was the aris-tocratic one, in which superiority is taken for granted, but must be paid for in the coinage of duty.

Still, in many respects he clung to what was already an obsolescent code. For good and ill, he was the incarnation of a philosophy of life that was already old-fashioned before he was old. Family, for one thing, meant more for Henry Lewis Stimson than for most men. It is hard to escape an impression that the tenacity with which he clung to con-servative attitudes was associated with a specific sense of loss, that it was a clue to some of the deeper springs of his personality.‡

*Morison, *Turmoil and Tradition*, p. 495.
†HLS, *My Vacations*.
‡The only writer, to my knowledge, to have noticed, or at least to have written about, the

Here, admittedly, we tread gingerly on the cliff-top path of psychohistory. Yet it is likely that we cannot fully understand the public man unless we have some understanding of the private man lurking within. And about the very private Henry Stimson there are questions that, while they cannot be answered with any degree of confidence, must be asked. What was the effect on his personality, for example, of his mother's death when he was eight years old? More to the point, what was the effect of his father's reaction? His father sold the family home, "buried himself like a monk in years of constant grinding work"* and packed Henry and his younger sister off to be looked after by their grandparents and an aunt, seeing the boy only on Sundays and not always then. Morison, who had the advantage of interviewing Mrs. Mabel Stimson as well as other members of the Stimson family, also quotes from one of Stimson's letters a revealing passage about how when he came back to New York after Harvard, he felt a "craving," shared by his father, to break down "this strange horrible barrier of reluctance of manner between us."† He also quotes "a man who knew him well for forty years" as saying that Stimson "labored under an ill-defined impression that his father in some strange way held him accountable for the death of his mother." More than a hundred years later, one can only say, poor boy! True, the grandparents' home was comfortable, protective, warm within the limits of their capacity to provide warmth, and the aunt did her very best to replace both mother and father. But did the apparently psychosomatic symptoms that plagued Stimson—the premature lumbago and rheumatism that could be kept at bay only by riding and other exercise, the insomnia that began when he was thirty-three and tormented him for the rest of his life, the fierce temper—somehow reflect tensions or stresses deriving from some Oedipal resentment of his abandonment by his father? It was unbearable enough that his mother was not there, infinitely worse to feel that in some obscure way he was to blame for her absence. A

Oedipal side of Stimson's personality is Lewis E. Gleeck, Jr., himself extremely conservative, in his book *The American Governors-General and High Commissioners in the Philippines: Proconsuls, Nation-Builders and Politicians.* "Stimson's relationship with his father," Gleeck wrote, "was so strange that the temptation to adopt a Freudian-type explanation of some of his peculiarities is irresistible." The fact that early death was so much commoner in the nineteenth century in itself suggests the wisdom of caution in extrapolating too much from Stimson's childhood. But a "Freudian" interpretation does seem to explain some aspects of Stimson's infinitely dutiful yet oddly cold personality.

*Morison, *Turmoil and Tradition,* p. 22.

†*Ibid.,* p. 52.

distinguished psychiatrist has commented that Stimson's losing his mother "might well have made him retreat from emotional involvements and reinforced his tendency towards austerity, hard work and self-discipline." He adds that it might also contribute to explaining Stimson's relative indifference to the arts, "since the arts stir up these emotions, and this he apparently wanted to avoid at all costs." And he raises the question whether Stimson's personality was obsessional. Obsessionals fear the "wild-beast nature" in themselves and others. "Obsessionals behave as if the beast were straining at the leash. Moreover they are apt to behave as if other people were similarly constituted; as if the world, therefore, was a jungle in which the unseen hosts of Midian are for ever on the prowl."*

From a distance, Stimson appears as that characteristically nineteenth-century object of admiration, the Hero, a monumental figure cast in bronze without traces of human weakness. No doubt it was unthinkable for his biographers to ask, let alone to press, questions that would have seemed in the worst of taste about parents, childhood, sexual emotions, while the formidable figure of Mabel, incarnation of Victorian propriety, was looking over their shoulders. In all the almost 700 pages of *On Active Service* and the 650 pages of Morison's biography, there is only one reference to their subject's sexual life: little more than a single sentence, followed by discreet speculation about the emotional consequences of the Stimsons' childlessness. Morison writes, "They soon discovered that the attack of mumps Stimson had suffered not long before the wedding, and from which he thought he had received no ill effect, prevented them from having children."† The sentence is elegantly crafted to convey, with Victorian reticence, that Stimson was sterile, not impotent. Certainly in the thirteen thousand pages or so of diary which I have examined there is again and again touching evidence of Stimson's tender and chivalrous love for Mabel. Yet there is not the smallest hint of any erotic event or enthusiasm between them. Whatever the nature of the intimate relationship in his marriage, there is no reason to believe that Stimson ever, as the phrase goes, "looked at" another woman in his life. It would not take a very daring or unconventional psychobiographer to guess, as Freudian terminology has it, that powerful springs of libido were sublimated. Show me a human being, it has been said, and I

*Dr. Anthony Storr, personal communication to the writer.
†Morison, *Turmoil and Tradition*, p. 87.

will show you a sense of loss. To understand, however dimly, the nature of the private troubles which Stimson smelted into the precious metal of personal strength is not to diminish admiration for him. The characteristic traits of his personality seem to have derived from some such mysterious alchemy of personal drives into self-discipline, the capacity for work, the comradeship of the hunting band or the club, and a love of the companionship of the chosen few in the service of the public good.

It is only an apparent paradox that this man whose life was lived in a vortex of change was at his emotional and philosophical core deeply, unshakably conservative. Men who have experienced tumultuous change often cling to traditional beliefs and patterns of habit out of a need for security. Conversely, men who are anchored in sure foundations often find it easier to innovate and to change.

Looking back over more than a century, it is possible to mark off distinct stages in the emergence of the United States as *the* global power. At first, few Americans turned their heads from the urgent tasks of personal enrichment and national development to notice the outside world; population, resources, production all multiplied until by the 1890s the United States was already *potentially* the strongest power in the world, before most Americans had even begun to match their country against others.

The second phase of America's emergence as a world power began a few years before the Spanish-American War of 1898, when the United States exerted itself, in a limited way at first, on the world stage. It challenged European powers, for example in the disputes with Britain over Venezuela in 1895 and over European "spheres of interest" in China a few years later. The Marines were sent to a dozen countries, and the United States acquired not only colonial influence, as in the Caribbean or China, but actual colonial possessions, such as Hawaii, Puerto Rico, Cuba (for a time) and the Philippines.

Stimson was not directly involved in these adventures (though he felt ashamed later that he had not volunteered to serve in Cuba), but he fully shared the imperialists' world view and attitudes. He was powerfully moved by the ideal of an American nation dedicated to its own high standards of conduct and to an exceptional destiny. He found he was not alone. Americans have always believed in their exceptional

378

THE COLONEL

destiny among the nations. But in the 1870s and 1880s and 1890s this feeling was perhaps stronger than ever before or since. Stimson's education at Andover and Yale gave him a sense of American history. His taste for adventure and for the West made him feel the bursting energies of national expansion. Both in the rough camps of the West and in Eastern universities and law firms, Stimson was brought in touch with men who believed, like him, that the time had now come when America's role in the world should match her strength and her convictions. Stimson was the disciple of those men: of Elihu Root in his law office, of Leonard Wood in the War Department, above all of Theodore Roosevelt in New York politics.

These men were expansionists who believed it was the right and the duty of America to bring civilization to "backward peoples," to be "dominant" in the Caribbean, in Latin America, in the Pacific.* "It is to the interest of civilization," Roosevelt once wrote, "that the English speaking race should be dominant in South Africa, exactly as it is . . . that the United States . . . should be dominant in the Western Hemisphere."† They were imperialists. And if they were not racists, because they believed that "backward peoples" might in the course of a long and courageous struggle join "civilized" nations on a "higher" plane, they freely expressed brutal contempt for weak and nonindustrial peoples such as the Chinese and those whom Roosevelt publicly called "dagoes."

Though their formal attitude toward British and European imperialism changed, and Stimson came to be at least in theory an opponent of the British Empire, the expansionists of the turn of the century shared many of the attitudes of the "liberal imperialists" in Europe, men like Joseph Chamberlain, Cecil Rhodes and Frederick Lugard, or Marshal Louis Lyautey and his successors in France, who believed that they had a God-given mission to bring to "lesser breeds without the law" the spiritual and material blessings of civilization. Remarkable men worthy of Stimson's or anyone else's admiration Roosevelt and Root might be. Believers in equality or in self-determination for the world's non-European peoples they were not.

Root's belief in white supremacy was more than once pungently expressed, and as we have seen, he acted with none of his usual energy

*See Howard K. Beale, *Theodore Roosevelt and the Rise of America to World Power*, especially pp. 31–63.
†*Ibid.*, p. 46.

when it was a question of stamping out the torture of Filipinos by American soldiers.* In Cuba, Root and Leonard Wood worked together in the shared assumption that Cubans were not yet fit for self-government. "The people here know they are not ready for self-government," said Wood,† and in the Philippines he made it only too plain that he did not believe the Filipinos were ready for self-government. Theodore Roosevelt, too, did not hide his views under a bushel. "I wish to see the United States the dominant power on the Pacific Ocean," he wrote in 1900. "Our people are neither cravens nor weaklings and we face the future high of heart and confident of soul eager to do the great work of a great power." In less exalted language, five years later, he wrote, "some time soon I shall have to spank some little brigand of a South American republic."‡

One should be careful, of course, not to attribute to Stimson every prejudice or opinion of the American imperialists of his youth. But these men were his models, his tutors and his friends. In Nicaragua, in the Philippines, and as Secretary of War for the first time, he followed their example and—with reservations that can be explained by the way the world had changed since the early 1900s—their policies.

The third phase of the process by which the United States moved toward global involvement began with the outbreak of the European civil war in 1914. The importance of World War I for the United States was not only that the U.S. was all but inevitably sucked into the conflict, first as arms supplier, then as banker, and finally as combatant. The United States began the war as one power among many. It ended up in a position to arbitrate the quarrels of Europe and dictate a Wilsonian settlement as unwise as it was well-intentioned. Germany was defeated and on the brink of revolution, Russia overthrown from within. France was bled white of her best blood and Britain impoverished. Only the United States emerged stronger than before.

Stimson was one of those who not only believed that the United States would inevitably be involved, but after early hesitation welcomed that involvement. He played a part, and as a former Secretary of War a leading part, in the movement to ensure that the United States was prepared for war when it came; his experience of battle,

---

*On the whole subject of atrocities in the Filipino war, see Stanley Karnow, *In Our Image*, pp. 177–95. Karnow points out that there were atrocities on both sides.
†Lane, *Armed Progressive*, p. 103. See also Hagedorn, *Leonard Wood*, vol. i, pp. 261–392, *passim*.
‡Beale, *Theodore Roosevelt*, pp. 47, 50.

courageously sought, left intact his conviction that "into such a struggle a man or nation may well go with lofty faith and burning ardor."*

On the very last page of his memoirs he expressed his attitude
to war with characteristic balance and detachment: "I have lived with
the reality of war, and I have praised soldiers; but the hope of honorable faithful peace is a greater thing and I have lived with that too."
He was not a warmonger. But he was in certain respects a militarist.
He admired men like Wood and Roosevelt who thought that war
would be good for the United States. He sought the experience of
war, and to some extent he gloried in it; he loved to be called Colonel
Stimson. He wanted the country prepared for war. He worked hard
in that cause. And when it was ready, he was unashamedly proud
of victory.

In this respect, he was out of line with many, perhaps most of his
contemporaries, both in the United States and abroad. The United
States had not experienced the war so long or so bitterly as the Russians, the Germans, the French or even the British. The revulsion
against it was not perhaps so profound. Certainly American society
was not stirred to the depths by isolationism as Germany and Russia
both were by defeat or Britain and France by the price of victory. Still,
in 1919 the American commitment to shaping a better world in accor-
dance with American ideals was transient. Woodrow Wilson might
arrive in Paris with the hopes of the world with him and "a prestige
and a moral influence throughout the world unequalled in history,"†
and with several hundred eager young experts ready to redraw the
maps and rewrite the history of Europe. But even before he had left
for Paris the American voters had repudiated him by returning Republican majorities to both houses of Congress.

Stimson regarded the train of events that followed as a tragedy
that led inexorably into the deeper tragedy of fascism and war. He did
not lose his faith in the American mission in Asia or Latin America; it
remained his ambition to bind the Philippines to the United States in
a relationship like the "dominion status" of the British Commonwealth, which would give the Filipinos political independence without
depriving them of the advantages of the American connection. But
when he became Secretary of State in 1929, he soon found that his
chief preoccupation had to be the vacuum left at the heart of the

*Quoted without a source in *On Active Service*, p. 90.
†Keynes, *Economic Consequences of the Peace*, p. 34.

international system by the collapse of European leadership. To be sure, a major issue that showed up the inability of the European powers to take bold initiatives for peace was Japanese naval ambition, and another was Japan's aggression in Manchuria. But the political problem was in Europe, and that remained true when the world economic crisis moved to the front of the stage. At a time when many of his countrymen and most of their representatives in Congress thought that peace meant keeping out of other people's quarrels, Stimson saw that the United States neither could nor should stay aloof.

The fourth stage of the process that absorbed the major energies of Stimson's life began shortly before FDR summoned him to Washington in 1940. After the Chamberlain-Hitler meeting at Munich in 1938, as Stimson saw more clearly than most, it was only a matter of time before Britain and France would have to fight Germany and Italy. A majority of Americans then believed that the United States could again keep out of war. Once again, Stimson did not agree with them. He believed, at least from 1939 on, that Hitler and the forces he led sought world domination and that it would be better for the United States to fight him with European allies than alone. The culminating task of his life was to do his utmost first to persuade his countrymen that this was true, and then to provide them with the military strength—manpower, munitions, leadership, sound strategy and finally atomic weapons—to defeat the Axis of Hitler's Germany, Mussolini's Italy, militarized Japan and the vast territories they had overrun. No one American, except Roosevelt, had more to do than Stimson with every part of that great work.

There was, however, a fifth chapter in the story of America's emergence from isolation to global power. From Stimson's point of view it was the largely posthumous fulfillment of the good old cause he had fought for all his life. That was the establishment after World War II of the network of commitments, alliances, forces and bases that enabled the United States to contain Soviet expansion and encircle it with the whole elaborate structure of the Pax Americana.

The work was not begun until after Stimson had retired to Highhold, and it was not finished when he died in 1950. But in his last comprehensive political testament, the *Foreign Affairs* article of 1947, he drew on his interpretation of the past to offer a program for survival in the dangerous future threatened by Soviet ambitions and nuclear weapons.

Americans must now understand that the United States has become, for better or worse, a wholly committed member of the
world community. . . . It is the first condition of effective foreign policy that this nation put away forever any thought that
America can ever be an island to herself.

By a long series of mistakes and failures stretching back over a
span of more than twenty years, we had in 1941 let it become
too late to save ourselves by peaceful methods; in the end we
had to fight. This is not true today. If we act now, with vigor
and understanding, with steadiness and without fear, we can
peacefully safeguard our freedom. . . . How soon this nation
will fully understand the size and nature of its present mission,
I do not dare to say. But I venture to assert that in very large
degree the future of mankind depends on the answer to this
question. And I am confident that if the issues are clearly presented, the American people will give the right answer.

When that article was written, the Truman Doctrine had been
proclaimed (March 12) and the Marshall Plan proposed (June 5).* The
grand strategy of American leadership in the world, which Stimson
had been advocating for forty years and practicing as best he could
since 1929, had become the guiding principle of national policy. For
the next twenty years after his death, American policy was Stimson's
policy, in the sense that it reflected his instincts and insights, it was
carried out to a remarkable extent by his protégés, and it was expressed
often enough in his style.

The years from 1947 to 1968 were the heyday of the American
foreign-policy Establishment.† It was the British journalist Henry Fairlie who first coined the phrase "the Establishment," in an article in
the conservative London weekly *The Spectator,* in 1955. He did not apply
it, as it has loosely come to be used, to mean the upper class, or the
rich, or conservatives. He coined it to describe what he and others at
the time saw as a fact of political life in Britain: the powerful men (and

---

*The immediate context of the Truman Doctrine was the decision by the British government
that it could no longer afford to support Greece and Turkey. On March 12, 1947, President
Truman told a joint session of Congress: "I believe it must be the policy of the United States
to support the peoples who are resisting attempted subjugation by armed minorities or by
outside pressures. I believe that we must assist the peoples to work out their own destinies in
their own way." See text in Joseph Siranson (ed.), *The American Diplomatic Revolution, A Documentary History of the Cold War 1941–47.*
†In the following passage I have drawn on my own 1973 article "The Establishment," *Foreign
Policy,* No. 10, spring 1973.

a few powerful women) who knew one another, or at least knew someone who would know anyone they might need to know; who shared
assumptions so deep that they did not need to be articulated; and who
contrived to wield power, if necessary, outside the nation's constitutional forms or political institutions. They contrived to have the power
to stop things they disapproved of, to promote men they regarded as
reliable and to block the unreliable; in a word, to preserve the essence
of the *status quo*. Fairlie was explicitly not thinking of politicians. At
that time* the editor of *The Times*, the director general of the BBC,
the Archbishop of Canterbury, the top civil servants in Whitehall and
influential investment bankers in the City of London would have been
archetypal members of the Establishment, and not by any means all
members of the Prime Minister's Cabinet could make the same claim.
Nor was membership in the Establishment a matter of party politics.
The true Establishment type prided himself on his ability to get along
with and work things out with right-minded, moderate fellows of either political party.

In 1961 the *New Yorker* political correspondent Richard Rovere
wrote a spoof article, all tricked out with fake learned references, in
the *American Scholar* in which he imported Fairlie's idea and applied it
to the Washington and New York foreign-policy world. It was a joke.
But ever since, the idea that there was an American Establishment and
that it exercised particular influence over foreign affairs has taken root
in earnest. For a time, it was part of the common coin of political
debate.

What was the American Establishment? It might well help to rise
in its ranks in the 1950s and 1960s if you had inherited wealth, or had
family connections with powerful men, or had been given an Ivy
League education. But many representative and influential Establishment figures had none of those advantages, while many a millionaire
alumnus of Harvard or Yale could not hope to be considered an Establishment type. Typically, the Establishment man came from that
class which George Orwell in one of his essays identified as the back-
bone of the British Empire: the "lower upper middle class." The older

*Things have greatly changed in England during the prime ministership of Margaret Thatcher,
who dislikes the Establishment as both too elitist and too centrist. Many of the functionaries
who would have been *ex officio* members of the British Establishment in the 1950s have been
either excluded from influence (*e.g.*, the Archbishop of Canterbury) or replaced by non-
Establishment types (*e.g.*, Charles Wilson as editor of *The Times*, Michael Checkland as director
general of the BBC.)

generation of Establishment leaders—Stimson himself, Dean Acheson, the two Dulleses, Averell Harriman, Robert Lovett, John McCloy—were almost all graduates of elite New England private schools and of Harvard, Yale or Princeton. After World War II the geographical and sociological catchment area widened considerably, if for no other reason than that the GI Bill enabled almost any keen young man of average intelligence to get into a good graduate school where he could study law—the prime avenue to the seats of the Establishment—or international relations. Even so, until the 1970s the proportion even among the younger men with key foreign-policy jobs who were graduates of either Harvard or Yale was strikingly high.

Nevertheless the foreign-policy Establishment in America in its heyday was defined not by class or money but by a history, a policy, an aspiration, an instinct and a technique.

The history stretches back to the beginning of the twentieth century. We have traced much of it in following Henry Stimson's life. Its essence was the flowing together of two traditions, one of American nationalism, indeed imperialism, going back to Theodore Roosevelt, the other idealistic internationalism, going back to Woodrow Wilson and beyond. Both currents flowed through gloomy defiles after the Senate defeated American membership in the League of Nations and so rejected Wilson's plan for peace in 1920. For the next decade, only a handful of Americans, many of them drawn from the international banking community in New York and from its lawyers, men like Elihu Root, Grenville Clark and Henry Stimson, fought against the isolationist orthodoxy.

Those lonely combats constitute the prehistory of the Establishment. World War II brought together the three groups of which it was composed in the years of the Cold War: the internationally minded bankers, lawyers and corporate executives of New York and to a limited degree also of Chicago, Boston, San Francisco and other "internationalist" cities; the government officials, especially in the State Department, Pentagon, and Central Intelligence Agency, in Washington; and the scholars at major graduate schools with centers for the study of international relations or regional studies.

Government service in World War II—in the War Department or other civilian departments for the slightly older men, in the Office of Strategic Services or elite military units for the younger ones—gave a whole generation of ambitious and educated Americans a taste for power, as opposed to business success, and an orientation toward government service which they never lost. When they went back to their law offices or their classrooms, they took with them contacts, attitudes and beliefs they had learned in war service.

The dangerous complexities of military technology, strategic confrontation and global responsibility after World War II reinforced this triple alliance. Each of the great decisions of foreign policy in the Truman years tied the bonds even tighter. Bankers and professors of history took time off to work for the Marshall Plan, for NATO, or on rethinking strategic analysis. A trickle, then later a flood, of academics and lawyers began to go from Boston and New York to Washington to work as consultants on these international ventures. By the late Eisenhower and Kennedy years they had become a recognizable breed, almost a substitute for the higher bureaucracy Washington had never had; a significant subtribe were known as "defense intellectuals."

More important than these bonds of personnel and experience was the fact that the grand strategy of the Truman administration, left almost untouched under Eisenhower and reinforced under Kennedy, *was* the Establishment's policy. Its kernel was the Janus-faced concept of internationalism: double-faced because it not only opposed isolationism but committed the United States to advanced power positions almost everywhere in the world.

To oppose isolationism had been the bedrock of the Establishment's policy during its years in the wilderness and was the bedrock of American policy for twenty postwar years. The war had taught that appeasement was a disaster, because there were wicked men in the world who could be restrained only by force. The lesson was that force might indeed be justified and military power essential. Thirdly, the country shared the Establishment's anti-Communism: the capitalist Right and the social-democratic Left within the liberal coalition of the Truman years could agree on that.

Establishment anti-Communism, however, was essentially for export. Not that the Establishment was enthusiastic about Communism in America; why should it be, when so many of its members had so much to lose? The Establishment differed from the Right merely in thinking the domestic triumph of Communism a most unlikely development. The distinction was an important issue in the McCarthy era, when a conservative, nationalist anti-Communist like Dean Acheson found himself under attack as if he had been a man of the Left.

Establishment people tended to call themselves "liberal internationalists." What that meant was a tendency to advocate restraint, to shrink from crude militarism or overbearing chauvinism, to show sensitivity to the still, small voice of conscience about the use of force. Such liberal tendencies, however, were only relative. The Establishment deprecated chauvinism—but still wanted American wishes respected, and American strength felt, around the world. It advocated restraint, yet was perfectly willing to use military power; felt conscience, but did not allow it to paralyze will into inaction.

The aspiration of the men who defined American policy from 1945 until 1965 was quite simply to the moral and political leadership of the world. Once, five years after President Kennedy's death, his chief speechwriter, Theodore Sorensen, used that very phrase; Americans should aspire, he wrote, to the "moral leadership of the world." Sorensen wrote that in 1968, when the national temper had been temporarily changed by the Vietnam War. The moral leadership of the world had gone out of fashion for a while. But that had been the core of the Establishment's aspiration, as it had been the core of Stimson's idea of how the United States should conduct itself in the world.

Specifically, the American Establishment believed it had been the destiny of the United States to succeed Britain as the military and economic guarantor and moral leader of the world. Not that nineteenth-century Britain *was* the "moral leader of the world." The crimes and follies of British imperialism alone made that an absurd claim, and even if they had not, it would never have been accepted by, for example, the French or the Germans. But American internationalists often spoke as if Britain had once held that position. "Britain had given up its role as the 'balance wheel,'" Townsend Hoopes once put it. "The idea of a single Western coalition holding the balance against the infidel is fundamental to this particular Establishment."* The idea of a vacant heavyweight title, a "power vacuum" into which it was the grim but grand duty of America to insert herself, is indeed fundamental to the Establishment's perception of the world, as it was part of Colonel Stimson's.

Nor was the idea wholly fantasy. Before 1914, the Royal Navy really had policed the seas, as Stimson pointed out in his radio speech immediately before joining Roosevelt's Cabinet. The Bank of England had assured the stability of the global financial system, while from Napoleonic times to World War II Britain had organized and financed coalitions against those dissatisfied powers who threatened to be peace-

*Assistant Secretary of Defense in the Johnson administration and biographer of John Foster Dulles, in a 1973 interview with the author.

breakers. Now the U.S. Navy and the U.S. Strategic Air Command deterred breaches of the peace. The dollar was the world's chief reserve currency. And it was the United States that had acted as the world leader against Communist expansion and was even to venture a little "gunboat diplomacy" from time to time, as in Guatemala in 1954 and in Lebanon four years later.

It was characteristic of the Establishment to take on the burdens of world power with a show of reluctance that concealed a certain avidity. George Ball once penetratingly observed that Europeans entered into colonialism not so much for economic motives as for "the satisfactions of power." It is interesting that he did not catch the echo of his own contemporaries' feelings. The unprecedented economic, military and political power of the United States in the twenty years after 1945 was their birthright. They found it highly satisfying. Imperialists they were not: they found old-style imperialism, with its elephants and its durbars, its gold-trimmed uniforms and plumed hats, more than a little tawdry. And after all they did not need the trimmings. They had the substance of power. What they understood by liberal internationalism allowed for the Bay of Pigs and for Vietnam. Liberal internationalism was liberal imperialism without the brass bands.

The Establishment's instinct was always for the center. "If American politics have a predilection for the center," McGeorge Bundy, once a key Establishment member, has said, "it is a good thing."* All the major undertakings of postwar American foreign policy, he went on, the Marshall Plan, NATO, strategic deterrence and a list of other presumed successes, "turned upon the capacity of the Executive to take and hold the center."

The center is a treacherous concept in politics. To some extent those who want to occupy it are in danger of finding their positions defined for them by what others are saying. But psychologically it is true that men like Acheson, McCloy, and Bundy always saw themselves as men of judicious, pragmatic wisdom, avoiding ideology and steering a prudent middle course between the crude Yahoos of the Right and the impractical sentimentality of the Left.

This centrist posture has often concealed a fear of, even contempt for, public opinion or at least for every discoverable expression of it. In the case of the foreign-policy Establishment, suspicion of public opinion, at least, would be understandable. For the tradition had its

*Quoted by Godfrey Hodgson, "The Establishment," *Foreign Policy,* No. 10, spring 1973.

origins in the resistance to populist leaders of isolationist mass opinion. It is also true that the Establishment's historical opportunity came not in electoral or congressional politics, but in what C. P. Snow called "closed politics." It wielded power in the corridors of the executive branch. It found acceptance of its instincts and policies in the White House, suspicion and blank incomprehension on Capitol Hill. The Establishment rose with the rise of the executive branch at the expense of Congress, and especially with the rise of the White House and the other "national-security" institutions created since 1945: the office of the Secretary of Defense (lineal successor to Colonel Stimson's "shop" at the War Department); the office of the Assistant Secretary of Defense for International Security Affairs (ISA), latter-day inheritor of the functions performed in Stimson's office by John McCloy; and the CIA, spiritual home of so many good Yale men.*

Finally the Establishment developed a characteristic technique, a recognizable *modus operandi*. It worked out of the public eye, and through the executive branch but not through the White House. It is almost part of the definition of a true Establishment man that he has not run for elective office or—if he has run—that he should have lost, like Stimson.

Each of the Establishment characteristics I have listed above will be familiar to the reader who has followed Henry Stimson's path thus far. Its history was his history. The heart of its policy was expressed in every major speech he made and summed up in his political testament. Its aspiration for the United States to replace Britain as the putative moral and political leader of the world was fundamental to his view (and incidentally explains the apparent contradiction between his general Anglophilia and his irritation with specific manifestations of independence in British policy). Its instinct for the strong center was his instinct. And its technique, of working through elites and through the executive branch, not through legislatures and the force of mass public opinion, was his technique, even if he did make himself into an influential publicist and a highly competent lobbyist in Congress.

Henry Stimson was the link that connects the foreign policy of late nineteenth-century American imperialism to the foreign policy of the Truman, Eisenhower and Kennedy eras; the link between Theodore Roosevelt and Dean Acheson. Not perceiving his influence and the importance of his robust assertion of American claims to world leadership among the sources of Cold War policy, many people have

*See the learned and amusing study of Yale men in intelligence, from Nathan Hale on, in Robin W. Winks, *Cloak and Gown*.

imagined that the United States assumed world leadership—as Britain was said to have acquired its empire—in a fit of absentmindedness. Nothing could be further from the truth. After 1945 the United States did not move to assert world leadership accidentally or reluctantly, in mere reaction to Soviet initiatives. It did so because a group of true believers, of whom Henry Stimson was one of the chief spokesmen, kept alive a vigorous tradition of policy. They, and he, had crossed the desert of isolationism and survived. They had provided leadership in the great crisis of World War II. After it, their moment came, and they did not mean to let it slip. Henry Stimson did not invent the idea that it was the destiny of the United States to be the leader of the world. But his life and that idea are inseparable.

The foreign-policy consensus which lasted from 1945 until the 1960s split on the rock of the Vietnam War. Since then the predominant voice has been that of the new conservatives. Henry Stimson was a conservative in most senses of that difficult word, but he would not have had much in common with the right-wing operatives who trooped into Washington to advise Ronald Reagan in 1980. Their interpretation of the history of the century was very different from Stimson's. In important respects they were heirs of the isolationists he fought so vigorously in public and despised so heartily in private. They did not oppose foreign intervention; they approved of it, so long as it was short, cheap and effective. But they did not share Stimson's picture of a world kept peaceful by collective security, guaranteed by American power but striving for international alliances. Their aspiration was not so much to the leadership of the world, moral or otherwise, as to the building of a system that would protect America from the contamination of foreign entanglements and the persistent perversity and troublesome ingratitude of foreigners. Their preferred technique was not that of the quiet chat, the back room, the steady persuasion of opinion-formers. It was to go public and to organize mass populist movements against the urbane manipulators. Above all, their instinct was not for the center but for the extreme. "Extremism in the defense of liberty is no vice," as their first hero, Barry Goldwater, put it in his acceptance speech at the 1964 Republican convention, "moderation in the defense of liberty is no virtue."*

The center to which Stimson was drawn was not inhabited by careful avoiders of risks, splitters of the difference or seekers of weak

*Text reproduced from Goldwater's speaking copy in Theodore H. White, *The Making of the President—1964*, pp. 215–17.

compromise. He was a prudent man but he was also a militant, even bellicose one once his mind was made up. He was, I have said, both a Puritan and a warrior. There were times, I have also suggested, when his judgment was too conventional, his reading of men narrow or faulty. Beware the man with a reputation for good judgment. Still, there have been few international crises since 1945 when it would not have been wise to follow Robert Lovett's advice to McGeorge Bundy during the Cuban missile crisis, and ask what Colonel Stimson would have done.

Few men have ever more fully lived according to Winston Churchill's motto: in peace, vigilance; in war, courage; in defeat, resolution; in victory, magnanimity. It is the code of the aristocrat and the warrior in all societies, and Stimson was an American aristocrat. He saw clearly that the United States would have to fight to be free, and he did not shrink from the personal or political consequences of that perception. He was willing to wage war totally; he had no difficulty either about building, or about dropping, the atomic bomb. In that sense, he can even be seen as having embodied the supreme act of American history, for which the psychology both of Puritanism and of the frontier both prepared him. It is unlikely that anyone else will take that same decision again. Yet in the moment of victory, his response was not glorification, but conscience and self-abnegation. What did he do? He tried his best to put the unleashed demons of nuclear frightfulness back into the bottle. And he argued that the only way to do that would be to trust the Soviet Union with our atomic secrets. Given Stalin, that might have been a foolish gesture, even a dangerous one. It was the gesture of a man in whom life had formed the double personality of Janus, the god of peace and war. It was the supreme expression of the ambivalence of an American leader whose instinct was, in Virgil's phrase, not only to rule, but to impose the habit of peace. Henry Stimson was identified with the dangerous idea that it is America's destiny to lead the world, and the drives that led him to that conviction come from deep in the American past. But, when all else is said, he was one of the great guardians of the Republic, one of those to whom Plato said the fullest honor should be given because he preserved us from our enemies.

Index

Abelson, Philip, 285
Acheson, Dean, 4, 55, 199, 303 *n.*, 359–61, 366, 368, 384–6
Adams, Brooks, 20, 43 *n.*, 130
Adams, Charles Francis, 9, 51, 74, 82, 85, 187, 247
Adams, Henry, 43 *n.*, 130
Aeneid, The, 137
Aguinaldo, Emilio, 50, 134
Ainsworth, Fred C., 76–7
Aldrich, Nelson W., Jr., 41, 42
Alexander, A. V., 188
Alexander, Sir Harold, 272
Allen, Douglas, 99
Alperovitz, Gar, 328 *n.*, 337 *n.*, 352–4
American Oil Company, 215
American Sugar Refining Company, 64–7
Ames, James Barr, 44–6, 61, 372
Anderson, Clinton, 360
Anderson, Sir John, 298
Anson, Austin, 255
Anti-Masonic movement, 36
anti-trust suits, 59, 63–70, 300
Aquino, Corazón, 123
Arcadia Conference (1942), 266
Arnold, H. H., 278, 324, 325
Arthur, Chester A., 56
Astor, Nancy, Lady, 173, 174, 189, 374
Atherton, Ray, 160
Atlantic Charter, 265
atom, first splitting of nucleus of, 282–5
atomic bomb, 274–341
  Anglo-American agreement on, 302–3
  cost of, 293, 295–6

dropping of, 6, 12–13, 18–19, 275–82, 314, 327–31, 337–41, 366
French physicists working on, 298, 306–7, 309–10
Interim Committee on, 13, 317–26, 330
moral consequences of, 285, 313, 323, 355
plans for postwar production of, 320
possibility of warning or demonstration of, 13, 304–6, 320–2, 325–6, 330, 332, 334, 335
"secrets" of, 299, 303–4, 310, 319, 356, 357
testing of, 333–5
Top Policy Group for, 292
atomic power and weapons, international control of, 7, 300, 303–6, 309, 313–14, 317, 319, 342–3, 355–61
Atoms for Peace proposal, 7, 362
Attlee, Clement, 333, 334
Austria
  banking/financial crisis in, 199–200, 202
  German customs union with, 193, 198
  German takeover of, 217

Baker, Newton D., 84, 161
Baker, Sir Samuel, 42
Ball, George, 55, 387
Bancroft, Cecil F. P., 31, 32
Bank for International Settlements, 195
Bankhead, William B., 240
Bard, Ralph, 13, 318, 330
Barkley, Alben, 12, 217, 274, 297
Baruch Plan, 361, 362

A NOTE ABOUT THE AUTHOR

Godfrey Hodgson, formerly Washington correspondent for the London *Observer* (1960–1965)
and editor and writer for the London *Sunday Times*
(1967–1971), is a leading authority on U.S.
politics. He is currently foreign editor
of *The Independent* in London, where he has
hosted a number of news and discussion
programs on Channel 4 TV. He has taught at
Harvard, Yale and other American universities,
and lectures frequently in the United States.
The present book is his sixth.

A NOTE ON THE TYPE

This book was set in ITC Galliard,
a typeface drawn by Matthew Carter for the
Mergenthaler Linotype Company in 1978.
    Carter, one of the foremost type designers
of the twentieth century, studied and worked
with historic hand-cut punches before designing
typefaces for Linotype, film and digital
composition. He based his Galliard design on
sixteenth-century types by Robert Granjon.
Galliard has the classic look of the old Granjon
types, as well as a vibrant, dashing quality
which gives it a contemporary feel.

Composed by Creative Graphics, Inc.,
Allentown, Pennsylvania.
Designed by Anthea Lingeman